Roman *Luxuria*

Roman *Luxuria*

A Literary and Cultural History

FRANCESCA ROMANA BERNO

OXFORD
UNIVERSITY PRESS

OXFORD
UNIVERSITY PRESS

Great Clarendon Street, Oxford, OX2 6DP,
United Kingdom

Oxford University Press is a department of the University of Oxford.
It furthers the University's objective of excellence in research, scholarship,
and education by publishing worldwide. Oxford is a registered trade mark of
Oxford University Press in the UK and in certain other countries

First Edition published in 2023

Published in the United States of America by Oxford University Press
198 Madison Avenue, New York, NY 10016, United States of America

British Library Cataloguing in Publication Data
Data available

Library of Congress Control Number: 2022945695

ISBN 978-0-19-284640-2

DOI: 10.1093/oso/9780192846402.001.0001

Printed and bound in the UK by
CPI Group (UK) Ltd, Croydon, CR0 4YY

To Laura, Claudia, and Livia

Preface and Acknowledgements

This book explores the development of the idea of *luxuria* from the beginning of Latin literature to the first Church Fathers, stressing the concept's key issues and their evolution with respect to social and cultural contexts, literary genres, and philosophical backgrounds. The introductory chapter deals with etymology, semantics, and Greek antecedents; the second chapter presents *luxuria* in a selection of authors from Plautus to Martial; the third and fourth chapters focus on Seneca as a pivotal author on this subject and as personally involved in this vice; and the final chapter identifies the semantic shift from the sphere of 'luxury' to that of 'lust' in Apuleius, hints at the treatment of this passion by some Church Fathers, Tertullian and Augustine, and ends with its personification in Prudentius' *Psychomachia*.

For both theoretical and practical reasons, I shall mainly consider passages in which the term explicitly recurs. From a theoretical point of view, there is no doubt that this word implies a label of immorality, a negative and explicit moral judgement, and it is this judgement I would like to explore, in its particular contexts and historical evolution. Searching for recurrences of *luxuria* means focusing not as much on banquets or luxury dress per se, as on the expression and judgement of these kinds of things as a vice. From a practical point of view, it would be a difficult and potentially endless task to consider every passage somehow related to *luxuria*, and some general accounts of the topic already exist.[1] I have thus chosen to limit my study to the most relevant authors in this regard—and some of them are relevant by dint of *not* using the word—and have ordered them along both chronological and literary lines. Seneca the Younger will occupy a privileged space here: this is due to the attention he pays to this concept in developing philosophically most of its key aspects, and also due to his personal issues with this vice: extremely powerful and wealthy, he was indeed accused of inconsistency, and he had a nuanced attitude towards both wealth and poverty, trying to defend both the idea of being rich (as long as one was not dependent on one's assets) and the ideal of frugality that was so important in Roman culture.

The idea of this book comes from my mentor, Paolo Mantovanelli. He himself wrote a book on the history of a word, *profundus*;[2] more than twenty years ago, during one of our long discussions of Latin semantics, he wondered about the precise meaning of *luxuria*, and the development of the erotic nuances of this

[1] See below, n. 4. [2] Mantovanelli (1981).

word over time. I am trying to answer his questions, and thereby to honour his teachings.

There are many friends and colleagues I would like to thank for their help at various stages, too many for the space available to me, and too dear to be confined in a mere list. I will only mention, with immense gratitude for their precious advices on specific subjects, Enrico Berti, Andrea Cucchiarelli, Rita Degl'Innocenti Pierini, Paolo Falzoni, Stephen Harrison, James Ker, Francesco Lubian, Marco Maiuro, Ermanno Malaspina, Arianna Punzi, Christopher Star, Chiara Torre, and Pietro Vannicelli. I am grateful for both scientific advice and long-distance friendship to Yelena Baraz, Tommaso Gazzarri, and Daniel Markovic. Special thanks for their careful reading of the opening and the conclusion of the book go to Marco Mancini and Sabine Koesters. My former PhD students in Classical Philology, Martina Russo and Ivan Spurio Venarucci, together with Walter Mazzotta, who works at the library of Sapienza dept. of Classics, generously offered me tireless help with the bibliography.

I could not be thankful enough to Filippomaria Pontani, Eleonora Tagliaferro, and Elio Lo Cascio, for spending so much time answering my questions.

This book would have not existed without the support of Alessandro Schiesaro, who was always there for my literary and existential issues.

My family, and in particular my mother and my husband, deserve gratitude not merely for having believed in my project, but, especially, for having endured me during its fulfilment.

Contents

Abbreviations

DELG	Chantraine, P. (1999), *Dictionnaire étymologique de la langue grecque. Histoire des mots* (Paris) (1968[1]).
DELL	Ernout, A. and Meillet, A. (eds.) (2001), *Dictionnaire étymologique de la langue latine* (Paris) (1932[1]).
FGrHist	Jacoby, F. (ed.) (1923–1958), *Fragmenta Historicorum Graecorum*, 15 vols. (Berlin-Leiden).
FRHist	Cornell, T. J. (ed.) (2013), *The Fragments of the Roman Historians*, 3 vols. (Oxford).
HRR	Peter, H. (ed.) (1967), *Historicorum Romanorum Reliquiae*, 2 vols. (Lipsiae) (1906[1]).
OLD	Glare, P. G. W. (ed.) (2016), *Oxford Latin Dictionary* (Oxford) (1982[1]).
ORF[4]	Malcovati, H. (ed.) (1976), *Oratorum Romanorum Fragmenta Liberae Rei Publicae* (Augusta Taurinorum).
RE	Pauly, A. (ed.) (1893–1980), *Realencyclopädie der classischen Altertumswissenschaft*, neue Bearbeitung unter Mitwirkung zahlreicher Fachgenossen, ed. by P. Wissowa, 34 vols., 15 suppl., reg. (Stuttgart).
TLL	(1900–), *Thesaurus linguae Latinae* (Lipsiae/Berlin).

Critical editions of Latin and Greek texts are those established or used by the respective translators.

1
What Does *Luxuria* Mean?

> 'Elle se résigna pourtant; elle serra pieusement dans la commode sa belle toilette et jusqu'à ses souliers de satin, dont la semelle s'était jaunie à la cire glissante du parquet. Son coeur était comme eux: au frottement de la richesse, il s'était placé dessus quelque chose qui ne s'effacerait pas.'
>
> (G. Flaubert, *Madame Bovary*, 1.8)

Luxuria is a difficult word to translate, because it has a nuanced meaning, which moves gradually from an economic to an erotic semantic field; in each of these we find a morally negative connotation, which often appears even in its 'biological' meaning. If we look in the *OLD*, we find the following general definitions: (1) '(of plants) immoderate growth or fruitfulness, rankness, luxuriance, etc.'; (2) 'unruly or wilful behaviour (of persons or animals)'; (3) 'indulgence (esp. excessive) in good living, luxury, extravagance'.[1] The feature common to these definitions is excess, while the fields in which this excess manifests itself vary; this notion of excess is evidenced in its etymology and in its philosophical uses.

This semantic blur is further complicated by a taxonomic problem. From the ancients' point of view, *luxuria* belongs to the passions, i.e. moral vices, because it is grounded in desire (below, 1.1 and 1.2); modern thinking goes in a different direction: while some ancient passions like anger or love are now labelled as emotions,[2] which in turn facilitates their classification and the increasing study of them in recent years,[3] *luxuria* cannot be defined as such. It is therefore excluded from research on the emotions and remains in limbo, and it thus becomes easier, although sometimes reasonably so, to reduce it to its material counterpart, luxury.

[1] Cf. *TLL* VII 1.1919.53–1925.83, *s.v.*

[2] On the theoretical issues raised by this correspondence, see (Konstan 2020). On the definition of immorality in Rome and the polysemic meaning of *luxuria*, see Edwards (1993), 1–9.

[3] See e.g. Morton Braund/Gill (1997); Konstan (2006); Cairns (2019); with attention to the connections with Christian thought, Knuuttila (2004); Boehm/Ferrary/Franchet d'Espèrey (2016). The most studied passions are anger (Harris (2001); Braund/Most (2004); Kalimtzis (2012)), hate (Aubreville (2021), shame (Kaster (2005)), and pride (Baraz (2020)). Special scholarly attention is given to Stoic ethics: cf. below, 1.2.

Roman Luxuria: *A Literary and Cultural History*. Francesca Romana Berno, Oxford University Press.
 DOI: 10.1093/oso/9780192846402.003.0001

In this introductory chapter, I shall tackle the etymological, semantic, and philosophical issues associated with this concept.[4]

1.1 Etymology: Twisted, Luxuriant, Luxurious: In a Word, Excessive

Luxuria is a denominal abstract, derived from *luxus*, plus the derivational morpheme—*uro* with a desiderative connotation, to which the *-ia*/*-ies* ending is added.[5] It follows either the first or the fifth declension, so that the form *luxuria* coexists with *luxuries*: the former appears to be the most ancient, and is indeed attested in Plautus. *Luxuries* is about ten times less frequent (about fifty versus five hundred occurrences); after a quotation of Gaius Gracchus in which it is opposed to what is necessary,[6] we find it twice in Caesar, sometimes in Cicero, and, with a prevalently biological meaning, every now and then after him; it reappears in Apuleius and in the *Historia Augusta*; no one uses this form exclusively, while many authors, e.g. Seneca the Younger, use only *luxuria*. Apart from metrical reasons (in poetic compositions), there may be a stylistic explanation for this coexistence: for example, Caesar employs the fifth declension form when the vice is particularly evident and undermines the character of the person who is accused of it.[7]

As for the original substantive, *luxus*, it is ambiguous in that it may refer either to excess in any form, especially luxury (so the basic meaning of *luxuria* would be 'desire for excess' or 'desire for luxury'), or to luxation, a dislocation due to a traumatic misplacing of a joint. This second meaning may derive from the first, in the sense of an excess leading the joint the wrong way.[8] It would then mean 'desire for going out of track.' This is indeed the interpretation of Isidore of Seville (*Orig.* 10.L 160):[9]

> Luxuriosus, quasi solutus in voluptates, unde et membra loco mota luxa dicuntur.
>
> Voluptuous (*luxuriosus*), as if dissolute (*solutus*) with pleasure (*voluptas*); whence also limbs moved from their places are called *luxus* ('dislocated').
>
> (Trans. Barney/Lewis/Beach/Berghof 2006)

[4] Some general bibliography: Citroni Marchetti (1991); Edwards (1993); Dalby (2000); Romano (2003); Wallace-Hadrill (2008), 315–55; Baltrusch (2009); Gorman/Gorman (2014), esp. 329–44; with special attention to economic issues, Berry (1994); Aßkamp/Brouwer/Christiansen/Kenzler/Wamser (2008); White (2014); Weeber (2015); Pérez González (2021); with special attention to food, Gowers (1996); Fellmeth (2001), 102–15.

[5] Below, n. 8; on *-ia*/*-ies*, see Piwowarczyk (2016), esp. 108–9.

[6] *ORF*[4] 48.51 = Gell. 9.14.17: *non est ea luxuries, quae necessario parentur vitae causa.*

[7] Below, 2.2.2.

[8] *DELL*, 374; de Vaan (2008), 356. *TLL* VII 1.1934.83–4, *s.v. luxus*, indicates two separate meanings, with the word intended in an ethical sense is considered as a derivative from *luxuria* via apocope.

[9] Cf. *Diff. Verb.* 326 A. (= 72 C.), where Isidore distinguishes *luxuriosus* from *prodigus*: *luxuriosus, quasi solutus in voluptates, unde et membra loco mota luxa dicuntur. Prodigus autem sumptuosus, qui omnia porro agit, et quasi proicit.* As for joint luxations, Plin. *NH* 17.267 *luxata membra.*

In both senses, the idea of excess is evident, and further stressed by the combination with desire; since ancient morality is grounded in the idea of right and virtue as something measured, and of wrong and vice as excess,[10] a negative moral judgement is implied in both uses of *luxuria* for persons. A supplementary idea, that of softness, is frequently mentioned in association. In my opinion, this is due not so much to etymology as to the association of ideas: the association of right/virtue/measure often goes together, in the Romans' *Weltanschauung*, with that which is hard and strong, given the fact that their ideal man was a hardened farmer and soldier, sober and used to labour:[11] this ideal affected their representation of the wise man, too. The intertwined ideas of wrong/vice/excess are therefore, correspondingly, linked with softness and tenderness (and also femininity and weakness). In this archetypical dichotomy, *luxuria* falls within the negative pole and thereby acquires the additional meaning of softening, and is charged with weakening the toughness of soldiers. Furthermore, its connection with leisure (*otium*), which originally indicated the time free from service in the army, when soldiers profited from licentiousness and the absence of rules, also supports its opposition to active military life.[12] The perfect example in this regard is Hannibal's so-called 'Capuan laziness', the Carthaginian army's winter rest at Capua right after the enormous victory at Cannae in 216 BCE, after which Hannibal never managed any further gains.[13]

Luxuria has some derivatives, such as the adjective *luxuriosus*, most frequently applied to persons, and the verb *luxurio/luxurior*, pre-eminently referring to the development and growth of beings.[14] There are several Greek words which are translated with *luxuria*, and they specify the various semantic nuances of the term: *tryphe*, 'delicacy', is frequent in historiography, and derives from *thruptein*, 'to crumble, to weaken';[15] *asotia*, 'prodigality', comes from *asotos*, 'the one who destroys', opposed to *sos*, 'safe';[16] *lagneia*, 'licentiousness' (usually translated as

[10] Scheidle (1993), 15–22 and 209–13. On the cognitive and metaphoric consequences of this idea, Fedriani (2016).

[11] Edwards (1993), 20–2; McDonnell (2006), 105–41; Langlands (2018), 29–45; on the opposition with effeminacy, 161–8 (and Edwards (1993), 64–97). An ideal example of this model is represented by the Sabines (Dench (1996)).

[12] On the link between literature, leisure, and morality, see Toner (1995); Connors (2000).

[13] Among the many references to this episode, we may quote Livy (below, 2.3.2), Valerius Maximus (below, 2.5.1), and Seneca (below, 4.4).

[14] Cf. respectively *TLL* VII 1.1930.37–1933.67 and VII, 1926.10–1930.30, *s.v.* For the adverb *luxuriose*, cf. *TLL* VII 1.1933.68–1934.20. *s.v.*

[15] *DELG*, 444; Beekes (2009), 560. The evidence for the equivalence comes from the correspondences between passages of Greek historiographers (below, 1.4) and Latin ones, such as Sallust and Livy (below, 2.3.1 and 2.3.2). According to Nenci (1983), 1021–2, *tryphe* refers to the eating habits of the upper class. Cf. Gorman/Gorman (2014), 34–65 on *tryphe*; 25–34 on similar terms, such as *hapalos*, 'soft', 'tender', *habros*, 'delicate', and *chlide*, 'delicacy'. Especially on *habros/habrosyne*, Lombardo (1983). To these terms we may add *akolasia* 'license' (cf. Aristot. *EE* 1231a 15–25).

[16] *DELG*, 1085; cf. Cic. *Fin.* 2.23 (below, 2.2.1).

libido) is liklely a coradical of *lagaien*, 'to release'.[17] Further terms may be considered from a philosophical point of view (below, 1.2).

In none of these Greek equivalents of *luxuria* do we find the biological meaning of the Latin noun, which is connected to fertility of the earth. This may be explained by the well-known agricultural origin of the Latin language, but there is also a possibility that it is connected with another Greek term: *Ploutos*, 'wealth, money'. Indeed, according to Hesiod's *Theogony*, this god was born from Ceres and a mortal hero, Iasius, in a fertile field (969–74):[18]

> *Δημήτηρ μὲν Πλοῦτον ἐγείνατο, δῖα θεάων,*
> *Ἰασίων' ἥρωι μιγεῖσ' ἐρατῇ φιλότητι*
> *νειῷ ἔνι τριπόλῳ, Κρήτης ἐν πίονι δήμῳ,*
> *ἐσθλόν, ὃς εἶσ' ἐπὶ γῆν τε καὶ εὐρέα νῶτα θαλάσσης*
> *πάντη· τῷ δὲ τυχόντι καὶ οὗ κ' ἐς χεῖρας ἵκηται,*
> *τὸν δ' ἀφνειὸν ἔθηκε, πολὺν δέ οἱ ὤπασεν ὄλβον.*
>
> Demeter, divine among goddesses, gave birth to
> Ploutus (Wealth), mingling in lovely desire with the hero
> Iasius in thrice-plowed fallow land in the rich land of
> Crete-fine Plutus, who goes upon the whole earth and
> the broad back of the sea, and whoever meets him and
> comes into his hands, that man he makes rich, and he bestows
> much wealth upon him.
>
> (Trans. Most 2006)

Ploutos is therefore related to the fertility of the fields (and also, evidently, with wealth as a result of agricultural activity), as is also the case with *luxuria*.[19] Among the Greek precedents of this idea there is thus also room for mythology.

1.2 Philosophy: *Luxuria* within the Stoic Taxonomy of Vices (and the Platonic Soul)

Luxuria is not part of emotions such as fear, anger, or joy, which might call its status as a passion into question, but it is seen as a vice by all authors—and we know that vice and passions overlap in ancient ethics. This conundrum may be solved if we focus on the idea of desire, which as we have seen is central to its

[17] *DELG*, 611; Beekes (2009), 819. *Lagneia* is the definition of the Christian capital sin translated in Latin by *fornicatio*, and then *luxuria* (below, 5.6). Paul's *aselgeia* is translated by Augustine with *luxuria* (e.g. *Epist.* 93.11; below, 5.4).

[18] Cf. *Od.* 5.125–9; West (1966), 422–4; Tomassi (2010), 251–2.

[19] We may add that for the first Latin occurrence of the term of which we know, in Plautus' *Trinummus*, we may point to a precedent in Aristophanes where we find *Ploutos* (below, 2.1.1).

meaning. Indeed, in Hellenistic and especially Stoic ethics, the taxonomy of vices is grounded in desire, because desire means dissatisfaction and instability, and prevents tranquillity. According to the Stoics, desire derives from a wrong evaluation of appearances, and so vices are originally provoked by a mistake in judgement.[20]

This Stoic taxonomy is most detailed in Stobaeus (esp. *SVF* 3.394 and 395), and a famous list of passions is found in the so-called Pseudo-Andronicus' *Peri pathon* (*SVF* 3.397). Here, passions are all considered as kinds of desire (*epithumia*); we find lust, gluttony, and greediness, which are all specific ways in which *luxuria* can express itself. There is also a word that corresponds to the general idea of *luxuria*, which is *philedonia*, a compound of *philein*, 'to love', and *hedone*, 'pleasure'; its definition is '*epithumia hedonon ametros*', that is, 'excessive desire for pleasures'. Excess and desire both belong to *luxuria*'s etymology; as we have seen, the semantic field of this word includes many kinds of pleasures in addition to those connected with luxury. In my opinion, this is how many Roman writers, and especially the Stoic Seneca, understand *luxuria*:[21] it mixes desire, excess, and pleasures, without specific references, and this makes it fit many different contexts.

In this way, *luxuria* finds a place in the Stoic taxonomy of vices without losing its Roman concreteness. However, we may go even further, and look at the Platonic soul. Indeed, if we read the description of the appetitive part of the soul, the so-called *epithumetikon*, in the *Republic*, we find a passage that would perfectly fit our vice (9.580d–81a):[22]

> *τριῶν ὄντων τριτταὶ καὶ ἡδοναί μοι φαίνονται, ἑνὸς ἑκάστου μία ἰδία· ἐπιθυμίαι τε ὡσαύτως καὶ ἀρχαί. πῶς λέγεις; ἔφη. τὸ μέν, φαμέν, ἦν ᾧ μανθάνει ἄνθρωπος, τὸ δὲ ᾧ θυμοῦται, τὸ δὲ τρίτον διὰ πολυειδίαν ἑνὶ οὐκ ἔσχομεν ὀνόματι προσειπεῖν* [580e] *ἰδίῳ αὐτοῦ, ἀλλὰ ὃ μέγιστον καὶ ἰσχυρότατον εἶχεν ἐν αὐτῷ, τούτῳ ἐπωνομάσαμεν· ἐπιθυμητικὸν γὰρ αὐτὸ κεκλήκαμεν διὰ σφοδρότητα τῶν τε περὶ τὴν ἐδωδὴν ἐπιθυμιῶν καὶ πόσιν καὶ ἀφροδίσια καὶ ὅσα ἄλλα τούτοις ἀκόλουθα, καὶ φιλοχρήματον δή, ὅτι διὰ χρημάτων μάλιστα ἀποτελοῦνται.* [581a] *αἱ τοιαῦται ἐπιθυμίαι.*
>
> 'The three parts of the soul seem to me to have three forms of pleasure, one for each individual part. Likewise three forms of desire, and three forms of rule.' 'Can you explain that?' 'The first element, we say, is the one which allows a man to learn, the second the part which allows him to act in a spirited way. To the third, on account of its diversity, we found it impossible to give its own unique

[20] Above, n. 4; Inwood (1985); Annas (1992); Nussbaum (1994); Sorabji (2000); Brennan (2003), 269–74; especially on Roman Stoics, Reydams-Schils (2005); Fitzgerald (2008).

[21] Below, 4.1.

[22] Cf. Plato, *Phaedr.* 238a–c; *Tim.* 70d–e; *Phaedr.* 246a–b; Vegetti (1999), 60–2. On Plato's partition of the soul, Barney/Brennan/Brittain (2012), with Wilberding (2012) on the appetitive part; Shields (2014). On political implications of this theory, below, 1.3. Especially on the connection between desire, lust, and luxuriant plants, *Tim.* 86.c–d.

> name, [580e] so we gave it the name of its largest and strongest element. We called it desiring (*epithumetikon*)—because of the strength of its desire for food, drink, sex and everything that goes with these—and money-loving, because money is the principal means of satisfying these desires.' (Trans. Griffith 2000)

This part of the soul is fond of food, drink, sex, money, and other pleasures, which is to say that it is an all-round portrait of *luxuria*. This description is echoed by Apuleius in his *De Platone* 1.13.207 (below, 5.3),[23] where *luxuria* occurs, not as a definition but within the examples of vices. Seneca refers to the Platonic division of the soul in *EM* 92.8:

> Inrationalis pars animi duas habet partes, alteram animosam, ambitiosam, impotentem, positam in adfectionibus, alteram humilem, languidam, voluptatibus deditam.
>
> The mind's nonrational part has itself two parts—the one part spirited, ambitious, and wayward, consisting in emotions; the other base, idle, devoted to pleasures. (Trans. Graver/Long 2015)

This division received some attention from Stoics, too, especially Posidonius,[24] even though these parts of the soul, which are ontologically different in Plato, likely correspond to psychological faculties in Stoicism.[25] It is not my intention to tackle this question; to my purpose, it was interesting to note the affinity between the definition of the irrational part of the soul in Plato and the meaning of *luxuria* in its widest sense, in order to stress the relevance of this passion.

1.3 Semantics: A Word for Many Vices; *Luxuria* as the Opposite of a 'Truly' Roman Way of Life

The lack of specific references makes *luxuria* a word for many vices: we find it in reference to love for luxury, gluttony, drunkenness, leisure, and lust, often connected with the lexicon of tenderness and effeminacy: *mollis/mollitia*, 'tender/tenderness', *deliciae*, 'things serving one's pleasure' (*OLD* 2 *s.v.*), and so on. Indeed, these are all intertwined: love for luxury expresses itself mainly on social occasions such as banquets, whence gluttony and drunkenness, which lead to lust;[26] hence

[23] Cf. also Apul. *Pl.* 2.4.225, where this part of the soul is defined as a slave to lust (*libido*), with Fletcher (2014), 81; Simonetti (2017), 381–2.

[24] Frg. A189–95 Vimercati = frg. 32; 38; 142–7 E.-K.; cf. Kidd (1988), 538–51; Vimercati (2004), 627–31.

[25] Inwood (2014), with attention also to Panaetius (77–82). Especially on Seneca, Inwood (2005a), with 38–41 on *EM* 92; Asmis (2015), 228–30; Röttig (2022), 78–83.

[26] Edwards (1993), 173–206, also with reference to prodigality; Weeber (2015), 99–114; especially on banquets, Gowers (1996), 18–21; Vössing (2004), 244–53; 533–9. On the philosophical connections between desire, excess, and lust, Blackburn (2004), 21–7.

the association with *libido*,[27] and the semantic contamination between the two concepts. These are an immoral form of leisure, contrary to that devoted to philosophical speculation. Furthermore, this way of life often squanders a person's assets, which in turn makes him greedy, and he thereby falls into another vice, *avaritia*, which is very often combined with *luxuria*.

In sum, *luxuria* may refer to almost every possible passion related to objects (even in the case of lust, because other people are considered only as objects for the purpose of satisfying one's desires), and not to relationships, as in the case of anger, for example. One might have said that *luxuria* refers to 'private' passions, but this would not be quite true: from the Romans' point of view, private habits, despite being immoral or even disgusting, are scarcely relevant outside the sphere of personal thoughts and rumours. Actual vices are those that affect society—that is, those that have ramifications for social relationships. As Andrew Wallace-Hadrill puts it, 'it is modern, not Roman, thought that restricts "morality" to the private sphere and separates it from "politics"'.[28] Wealth is not dangerous per se, but when it becomes a status symbol, a means of social distinction rather than social benefaction, it may challenge the status quo and arouse the irritation of the lower classes. The same can be said of luxurious banquets. As for leisure, it is blameworthy in that it precludes political commitments, which the Romans valued as necessary for all noblemen, and lust is legitimate if directed at slaves but problematic if it involves noblemen or noblewomen. The private dimension of feelings of guilt did exist, but was not a major issue until the Christian era. Moralistic works in pagan times addressed what we may call 'social vices', those that express a preference for private and individual pleasures over general interest, reversing the idea of personal sacrifice for public benefit in which Roman ethics were rooted.[29] *Luxuria* belongs to these vices: indeed, it is cited as one of the main causes of moral decline by Roman historiographers (below, 1.4, 2.3, and 5.2). The Church Fathers, on the other hand, almost never link *luxuria* to wealth; in their writings, it means drunkenness and lust, and then lust alone (see below, 5.6).

The polysemic nature of the term emerges also through its antonyms, which are numerous. There is *frugalitas*, 'frugality', which is opposed to *luxuria* from the beginning of Latin Literature up to Seneca the Younger and Pliny the Elder, and represents one of the main virtues of the Roman ideal man.[30] *Severitas*, 'austerity', which we find in Valerius Maximus and Pliny the Elder, includes economic issues within a more general ethical picture, recalling archaic sobriety. *Pudicitia*, 'modesty', is opposed to *libido* and also to *luxuria* when these two vices overlap.

[27] *Luxuria et libido* are coupled explicitly since Valerius Maximus (below, 2.5.1); as for the semantic implications of hendiadys in Latin, Rossi (1993), 121–7.

[28] Wallace-Hadrill (1997), 9; cf. Edwards (1993), 4.

[29] Langlands (2018), 33–4.

[30] Gildenhard/Viglietti (2020); more generally on Roman values, Wilkinson (1975), 15–35. Cf. also below, 1.4.

Sobrietas, 'sobriety, chastity', appears with Apuleius, in a period in which *luxuria* not only overlaps with but begins to replace *libido*.

1.4 Pre-History and History of *Luxuria*: Greek Influences and Roman Specifics

As in culture and literature in general, Rome owes much to Greece regarding *luxuria*. The main inheritances are two: *luxuria* as a sign and cause of moral decline, due to sudden affluence through money and luxury from conquered lands; *luxuria* as an allotropic vice introduced by wealthy, effeminate, dissolute Eastern cultures, which affect the originally tough and sober nature of native people.[31] Both motives are especially present in historiographical sources, where we find the Greek correspondent *tryphe*; ironically, the Eastern country singled out as a birthplace of the vice, which is Asia in Greek sources, sometimes becomes Greece itself in Roman ones.[32] Each place has its East. This general opposition appears in further constellations, both spatial, such as that of the sober countryside versus the corrupting city,[33] and temporal, such as that of the good old days versus present decline; the latter is omnipresent in Roman culture.

In Greek and especially Hellenistic historiography, *tryphe*, 'sweet life', represents an evolutive principle, something that occurs because of wealth and that in turn leads to *hybris*, 'arrogance'. It can happen to single persons, such as tyrants, or to a ruling class, such as an oligarchy, or even to a people as a whole (in a democracy).[34] A pivotal text in this regard is in the opening of Thucydides' *Histories* (1.6.1–4):[35]

> *πᾶσα γὰρ ἡ Ἑλλὰς ἐσιδηροφόρει…3. ἐν τοῖς πρῶτοι δὲ Ἀθηναῖοι τόν τε σίδηρον κατέθεντο καὶ ἀνειμένῃ τῇ διαίτῃ ἐς τὸ τρυφερώτερον μετέστησαν. καὶ οἱ πρεσβύτεροι αὐτοῖς τῶν εὐδαιμόνων διὰ τὸ ἁβροδίαιτον οὐ πολὺς χρόνος ἐπειδὴ χιτῶνάς τε λινοῦς ἐπαύσαντο φοροῦντες καὶ χρυσῶν τεττίγων ἐνέρσει κρωβύλον ἀναδούμενοι τῶν ἐν τῇ κεφαλῇ τριχῶν…4. μετρίᾳ δ' αὖ ἐσθῆτι καὶ ἐς τὸν νῦν τρόπον πρῶτοι Λακεδαιμόνιοι ἐχρήσαντο καὶ ἐς τὰ ἄλλα πρὸς τοὺς πολλοὺς οἱ τὰ μείζω κεκτημένοι ἰσοδίαιτοι μάλιστα κατέστησαν.*

[31] Griffin (1985a); Edwards (1993), 22–4; Isager (1993); McDonnell (2006), 259–65.

[32] Dalby (2000), 118–77. On *tryphe* in Greek historiography, above, n. 15; below, n. 34.

[33] In Rome, it is especially frequent in the Augustan age, e.g. in Horace, with the Aesopic tale of the town mouse and the country mouse (*Serm.* 2.6.77–115), and in Propertius (below, 2.4.3). Cf. Harrison (2007).

[34] Passerini (1934), 44–51; Cozzoli (1980); Nenci (1983); Gorman/Gorman (2014). The authors maintain that the link between luxury and corruption is largely a Roman invention, but this goes against literary and historical evidence: Murray (2017). With special regard to Hellenistic historiography, cf. De Martinis (2022).

[35] Hornblower (2003), 25–7. Cf. Eur. *Tro.* 996–7 (Hecuba against Helen): '…Menelaus' palace/ was too small: it cramped your riotous desires (*tryphai*).' (Trans. Shapiro 2009); Dem. 21.159.

> Indeed, all the Hellenes used to carry arms…3. But the Athenians were the very first to lay aside their arms and, adopting an easier mode of life, to change to more luxurious ways. And indeed, owing to this fastidiousness, it was only recently that their older men of the wealthier class gave up wearing tunics of linen and fastening up their hair in a knot held by a golden grasshopper as a brooch…4. An unpretentious costume after the present fashion was first adopted by the Lacedaemonians, and in general their wealthier men took up a style of living that brought them as far as possible into equality with the masses. (Trans. Forster Smith 1935)

Thucydides links the decline of the Athenians to a loosened lifestyle departing from the sober and military attitude that had become limited to the Spartans. This scheme, enriched by Polybius' theory of social decline, will be imitated by almost all Roman historiographers. Indeed, Polybius' account may be considered as the birth date of Roman *luxuria* (31.25.4–7):[36]

> *οἱ μὲν γὰρ εἰς ἐρωμένους τῶν νέων, οἱ δ' εἰς ἑταίρας ἐξεκέχυντο, πολλοὶ δ' εἰς ἀκροάματα καὶ πότους καὶ τὴν ἐν τούτοις πολυτέλειαν, ταχέως ἡρπακότες ἐν τῷ Περσικῷ πολέμῳ τὴν τῶν Ἑλλήνων εἰς τοῦτο τὸ μέρος εὐχέρειαν.* 5. *καὶ τηλικαύτη τις ἐνεπεπτώκει περὶ τὰ τοιαῦτα τῶν ἔργων ἀκρασία τοῖς νέοις ὥστε πολλοὺς μὲν ἐρώμενον ἠγορακέναι ταλάντου, πολλοὺς δὲ ταρίχου Ποντικοῦ κεράμιον τριακοσίων δραχμῶν.* 5a. *ἐφ' οἷς καὶ Μάρκος ἀγανακτῶν εἶπέ ποτε πρὸς τὸν δῆμον ὅτι μάλιστ' ἂν κατίδοιεν τὴν ἐπὶ τὸ χεῖρον προκοπὴν τῆς πολιτείας ἐκ τούτων, ὅταν πωλούμενοι πλεῖον εὑρίσκωσιν οἱ μὲν εὐπρεπεῖς παῖδες τῶν ἀγρῶν, τὰ δὲ κεράμια τοῦ ταρίχου τῶν ζευγηλατῶν.* 6. *συνέβη δὲ τὴν παροῦσαν αἵρεσιν οἷον ἐκλάμψαι κατὰ τοὺς νῦν λεγομένους καιροὺς πρῶτον μὲν διὰ τὸ καταλυθείσης τῆς ἐν Μακεδονίᾳ βασιλείας δοκεῖν ἀδήριτον αὐτοῖς ὑπάρχειν τὴν περὶ τῶν ὅλων ἐξουσίαν,* 7. *ἔπειτα διὰ τὸ πολλὴν ἐπίφασιν γενέσθαι τῆς εὐδαιμονίας περί τε τοὺς κατ' ἰδίαν βίους καὶ περὶ τὰ κοινά, τῶν ἐκ Μακεδονίας μετακομισθέντων εἰς τὴν Ῥώμην χορηγίων.*
>
> Some young men squandered their energies on love affairs with boys, others with courtesans, and others again upon musical entertainments and banquets and the extravagant expenses that go with them, for in the course of the war against Perseus and the Macedonians they had quickly acquired the luxurious habits of the Greeks in this direction. 5. So far had the taste for dissipation and debauchery spread among young men that many of them were ready to pay a talent for a male prostitute and 300 drachmae for a jar of Pontic pickled fish. 5a. It was in this context that Cato once declared in a public speech that anybody could see the Republic was going downhill when a pretty boy could cost more

[36] Walbank (1979), 500–1. On Polybius' theory of cyclical decline, Walbank (2002), 200–8.

> than a plot of land and jars of fish more than ploughmen. 6. These extravagances became disgracefully ostentatious at the period which I am describing; the reason was first of all the belief that after the destruction of the Macedonian kingdom the universal supremacy of Rome had been established beyond dispute, 7. and secondly the fact that after the riches of Macedon had been transported to Rome there followed a prodigious display of wealth and splendour both in public life and in private. (Trans. Scott-Kilvert 1979)

In this passage, the author traces back the introduction of *luxuria* to the war against Perseus of Macedon (168 BCE), and connects it with the transfer of money and habits from the East. As we shall see, other authors will identify the beginning of moral decline with other events, e.g. the definitive defeat of Carthage (146 BCE) according to Sallust, or Manlius Vulso's triumph against Asia (187 BCE) according to Livy.[37] Yet the dynamics are identical: Romans offer a cultural explanation for the fall of the Republic, namely the corruption of *mores*.[38] Even if the specific word *tryphe* is not present, the description of vices (especially homosexual lust and excessive wealth) corresponds to *luxuria*'s main semantic fields. In Polybius, the keywords are *euchereia* (25.4) and *eudaimonia* (25.7), exhibited both in private and in public (another leitmotiv of the Roman moralists).[39] Another interesting detail is the quoting of *Markos* (25.5a) as speaking against luxury. This is of course Marcus Porcius Cato (234–149 BCE), called 'The Censor' not only for having held that magistracy but also for his tireless rigid attitude against vices in general, and Greek vices in particular.[40] Even if we only possess a few fragments from his speeches and works, apart from a technical treatise on agriculture, we find in them all the main subjects on which subsequent Roman literature will blame vices.[41] I think it undoubtable that Cato shaped Latin moralistic literature and acted like a filter through which Latin authors read Greek historiographers. So even though there are no occurrences of *luxuria* in his work, this is probably due to the today fragmentary nature of his speeches and historiographical and moralistic works, and I therefore give him a place in this book (below, 2.1.2).

This model of decline that we find in the historiography is supported in philosophical literature: the connection of *tryphe* with wealth is emphasized by Plato (*Rep.* 4.422a):[42]

[37] Liv. 39.6.7. As for the year 146, we may add Vell. 2.1.1. Of course they draw, in their turn, on other historiographical sources: below, 2.3.2 with n. 146.

[38] Lintott (1972); Edwards (1993), 177–8; Wallace-Hadrill (1997), esp. 9.

[39] See below, 2.2.1 (Cicero) and 2.4 (Augustan age).

[40] Letta (1984), esp. 19–22. At p. 20, Letta theorizes that Cato identified the beginning of the decline with the taking of Syracuse (211).

[41] Below, 2.1.2 with n. 28.

[42] On vices in Plato's *Republic*, Renaut (2020), esp. 80–7; cf. following n. This idea is further developed by Polybius (e.g. 6.7.7–8) and comes back also in Ps. Longinus' *Sublime* (44.7). In general, on luxury in Plato, Berry (1994), 45–62.

> *πλοῦτός τε, ἦν δ' ἐγώ, καὶ πενία· ὡς τοῦ μὲν τρυφὴν καὶ ἀργίαν καὶ νεωτερισμὸν ἐμποιοῦντος, τῆς δὲ ἀνελευθερίαν καὶ κακοεργίαν πρὸς τῷ νεωτερισμῷ.*
>
> 'Wealth and poverty,' said I, 'one produces luxury, idleness and revolution, the other meanness of spirit and poor workmanship—and of course revolution as well.' (Trans. Griffith 2000)

In the same dialogue, Plato attributes to the excess of wealth and to growing social gulfs among the citizens the degeneration from oligarchy to democracy, because the oligarchs' sons are raised in leisure and sloth (*Rep.* 8.556b–c). This way of life makes them weak, unhealthy, and unable to go to war, and when the poor but healthy people realize their feebleness, it becomes easy for them to overthrow the state (*Rep.* 8.556c–e). Already in the *Gorgias*, the aristocrat and sophist Callicles states that true happiness and virtue consist in debauchery, intemperance, and licence (*Gorg.* 492c):[43]

> *ἀλλὰ τῇ ἀληθείᾳ, ὦ Σώκρατες, ἣν φῂς σὺ διώκειν, ὧδ' ἔχει· τρυφὴ καὶ ἀκολασία καὶ ἐλευθερία, ἐὰν ἐπικουρίαν ἔχῃ, τοῦτ' ἐστὶν ἀρετή τε καὶ εὐδαιμονία, τὰ δὲ ἄλλα ταῦτ' ἐστὶν τὰ καλλωπίσματα, τὰ παρὰ φύσιν συνθήματα ἀνθρώπων, φλυαρία καὶ οὐδενὸς ἄξια.*
>
> No, in good truth, Socrates—which you claim to be seeking—the fact is this: luxury and licentiousness and liberty, if they have the support of force, are virtue and happiness, and the rest of these embellishments—the unnatural covenants of mankind—are all mere stuff and nonsense. (Trans. Lamb 1967)

Of course, Socrates shows that this is rather a type of suffering, since it implies permanent dissatisfaction, not very different from that of people doomed in myth; he illustrates the reasoning with the famous image of the soul as a drilled vase, which is impossible to fill (492d–494e). All these themes will be developed in regard to *luxuria*, too, especially by Seneca.

A specific trait of the phenomenology of *tryphe* is environmental determinism: this vice is indeed, as we have seen, associated with Eastern lands, due to a natural influence of the mild weather and the fertility of the land on human complexion, as stated in Hippocrates' essay *On Airs, Waters, and Places.*[44] Again, historiography leads the way: at the end of his *Histories*, Herodotus refers to a link between soft places and weak men.[45] In Greek culture the city Sybaris, in Magna Graecia, was known for its sweet, luxurious life, to the point that a verb was derived from

[43] On this passage, as well as those from the *Republic*, Pontier (2020), 47–53.

[44] See esp. Hipp. *De aere* 12.2–3; 16.1–2; 23.3, who emphasizes in particular the difference between weak Asians and strong Europeans.

[45] Herodot. 9.122.3. On Herodotus' account of this topic, Dorati (2003), esp. 508–13; Gorman/Gorman (2014), 80–94 (but see above, n. 34).

the toponym, *sybarizein*, which meant 'to live in a Sybaritic way'.[46] Roman culture replaced Sybaris with Capua, even if neither this town nor the Campanian seaside, which is referred to as a place of licence, led to a corresponding Latin verb.[47] The analogy between Sybaris and Capua was already established by Polybius (7.1.1–2 = Athen. 12.528a):[48]

> *Καπυησίους τοὺς ἐν Καμπανίᾳ διὰ τὴν ἀρετὴν τῆς γῆς πλοῦτον περιβαλομένους ἐξοκεῖλαι εἰς τρυφὴν καὶ πολυτέλειαν, ὑπερβαλλομένους τὴν περὶ Κρότωνα καὶ Σύβαριν παραδεδομένην φήμην.*
>
> The people of Capua, in Campania, becoming wealthy through the fertility of their soil, degenerated into luxury and extravagance surpassing even the common report of Croton and Sybaris. (Trans. Schuckburg 2002)

These places are not strictly speaking Eastern, of course, but in southern Italy, they are still both perceived as foreign by Greek and Roman writers, who compare them to Asian locations. Besides Capua, we find Baias, located in the same region. Baiae becomes a renowned holiday place from the first century BCE on, and all authors, especially Cicero, Propertius, and Seneca, consider it the ideal location for an immoral life, a location which affects even the wisest person with luxury and lust.[49]

There is thus a theoretical link between the biological and the moralistic meanings of *luxuria*: people's weakness and the softness of life derive from the soil's luxury. The ease of procuring sustenance affects the human body and soul: as many ancient myths report, after the Golden Age, in which everything was easily available, the gods made it difficult for humans to acquire food, and this was the beginning of humanity proper. Places like Sybaris and Capua are disturbing examples of a recreation of the Golden Age, when people did not need to work. Literary tradition, having retraced the mythical history of the fall of pre-historical human beings, points at a licentious lifestyle and consequent arrogance as causes of the fall of these cities.[50]

[46] It is found e.g. in Aristoph. *Pax* 344 (where it has been emended by Meineke to *sybariazein*, which has the same meaning, for metrical reasons). Sybaris was in southern Italy, in today's Calabria. On its legendary story, Gorman/Gorman (2014), 7–25. Among Latin authors, Sybaris as a luxurious place recurs in Seneca (*Ira* 2.25.2) and Quintilian (*Inst.* 3.7.24, quoted below 2.7.2); Ovid (*Trist.* 2.1.417) and Martial (12.95.2) refer to a collection of licentious poems entitled *Sybaritica*. Cf. Hor. *C.* 1.8.1–3. Partially similar meanings were attributed to Lydia and Ionia, two areas in Middle Asia: Dorati (2003).

[47] For Capua, below, 2.2.1; 2.5.2; as for other Campanian locations, below, 4.3. On luxury in these places, see the studies in Aßkamp/Brouwer/Christiansen/Kenzler/Wamser (2008), especially Kloft (2008); Montone (2010); Weeber (2015), 89–98; especially on Baias, below, n. 49.

[48] Walbank (1967), 29–30.

[49] Below, 2.2.1; 2.4.3; 2.5.3; 2.6.2; 4.4; 5.1; 5.2.1; Schmatz (1905); Griffin (1985b); Citroni Marchetti (1991), 121–4; André (1993), 59–63; Stärk (1995); Busch (1999), 230–5; Connors (2000), 499–504; Hönscheid (2004), 16–18; Weeber (2015), 89–98. On the development of villas on the bay of Naples, D'Arms (2003).

[50] For Sybaris, see e.g. Philo, *Spec.* 3.43–4 (a list of the sources in Gorman/Gorman (2014), 23–4); for Capua, above, n. 47.

So the degeneration from sobriety to luxury traces back to the fall from the Golden Age, where want of anything was unknown, to the Silver Age, characterized by desire. This happens in Evander's historical description to Aeneas in the *Aeneid* (8.324–7):[51]

> Aurea quae perhibent, illo sub rege fuere
> saecula: sic placida populos in pace regebat,
> deterior donec paulatim ac decolor aetas
> et belli rabies et amor successit habendi.

Under that king passed the age they called golden: thus, in calm peace was he ruling the nations until little by little, an age, inferior and of duller hue, succeeded it, and the frenzy of war and the love of possessing. (Trans. Fratantuono/Smith 2018)

Evander's expressive narrative concerns Rome and its native inhabitants, *Fauni Nymphaeque* (l. 314), who were uncivilized and strong, and then came to be governed by the god Saturnus, who launched the Golden Age. The degeneration to the Silver Age is described as *decolor* (l. 326), in that silver is less shiny and brilliant than gold, but of course this attribute also expresses a moral judgement, for the Silver Age is characterized by war (l. 327 *belli rabies*) and love for possessions (*amor... habendi*). This periphrasis alludes to the vice of *avaritia*, frequently criticized in the *Aeneid*,[52] but also refers to a more general attitude of excessive desire, which coincides with *luxuria*, which in turn is frequently associated with *avaritia*. Historiographical and moralistic descriptions of the degeneration of Roman morality, from a strong and rigid frugality to an attitude of restless desire for money and pleasure, such as in Sallust,[53] retrace the mythical narrative of the decadence from the Golden to the Silver and Bronze Age, with a key difference: while in the mythical stories war is seen as a sign of degeneration and as a consequence of desire for money and/or power, in the historiographical accounts war appears in the Golden Age, too, and only its consequences, such as excessive booty and money, and lack of discipline in the army, are considered negative for Roman civilization, while peace, with its absence of threatening enemies and with its dangerous state of leisure, leads to *luxuria* itself. This is due to the economic and social ubiquity of conquering wars in ancient civilization, which leads writers to confine peace to legendary places and times, or to identify it with immoral leisure. And this is why both Sybaris and Capua resemble the life of humankind during the Golden Age, as well as the fatal loss of that heavenly condition.

[51] Fratantuono/Smith (2018), 430–3. On this topic, Harrison (2005), 291–6.
[52] Cf. the catchphrase *auri sacra fames* (3.57).
[53] Below, 2.3.1.

Thus far I have listed some common features of the Greek and Roman way of thinking. But, of course, Roman *luxuria* also has more specific and nuanced traits.[54]

First, it appears in several prose genres: historiography, oratory, and more or less philosophical essays. It is very rare in poetry, including satire, surprisingly. This happens not for metrical but for mainly stylistic reasons: poetry generally avoids abstract words; furthermore, *luxuria* is a low-style word, while e.g. *luxus* is part of the poetic lexicon. It is indeed striking that in authors such as Persius and Juvenal, despite their treatment of immorality, luxury, and banquets, *luxuria* receives little attention. Satire seems to *show* rather than to *label*: things and behaviour are more convincing than moralistic exhortation. Despite his prescriptive role, the satirist does not resort to abstract definitions, but prefers to follow the rhetorical principle of *evidentia*: to show things—vices—instead of inveighing against them. He despises abstract terms, because realism is a key feature of satire. Orators, on the other hand, need to level moral accusations against adversaries; historiographers offer explanations for cultural decline and thereby judge generals and emperors from a moralistic standpoint; and Roman philosophers are almost exclusively devoted to ethics. So these three groups are the likeliest to use the word *luxuria*.

Second, the main criterion for identifying an example of *luxuria* is a distinction in its function: if the behaviour in question happens for private reasons, it is a passion; if it happens for the sake of public interest or enjoyment, however, then it is not a vice but an exhibition of magnificence, which is legitimate and even desirable for the Roman Empire. This principle is expressed in the Ciceronian sentence *privata luxuria, publica magnificentia* (*Mur.* 76).[55]

Third, *luxuria* is centred around specific areas: jewels and clothes, and especially banquets.[56] Only a few occurrences regard architecture;[57] this is the case, in my opinion, because in architecture the boundaries between private and public (see the second point) are blurred: most Roman magistrates, not to mention the emperors, performed their professional duties at home, so their houses did in fact have the public purpose of displaying the magnificence of Rome. Banquets are

[54] For a general bibliography, see above, n. 4.

[55] With this statement, Cicero disagrees with Aristotle, whose definition of *megaloprepeia* includes both public and private expenses (*EN* 4.5.1122b19–b22; 1122b35–1123a5), unless, in the case of the latter, they are undertaken for the purpose of showing off one's assets, in which case they are the opposite of *megaloprepes*, i.e. *banausos* (*EN* 4.6.1123a24–7). Cicero may have had Demosth. *Olymp.* 3.25 as a model. Cf. Sall. *Cat.* 52.22 (below, 2.3.1); Hor. *C.* 2.15.13–14 (below, 2.4.1 n. 165); Val. Max. 4.4.9; Plin. *paneg.* 51.1–2. On Cicero's statement, which we also find in Vell. 2.1.2, see Gildenhard/Viglietti (2020), 6–39; below, 2.2.1. On the distinction between private and public, see also above, 1.3.

[56] On precious stones and jewels, Hermann (1959); Naumann-Steckner (2008); Schmauder (2019); Pérez González (2021), 129–43; on pearls, Pérez González (2021), 115–27; on clothes, Maier (2004); Pérez González (2021), 145–70; on perfumes, Pérez González (2021), 171–9; on banquets, Vössing (2004), esp. 244–53; on luxury furniture for banquets, D'Arms (1999); Weeber (2015), 15–36; Lista (2008) (tableware); Bischop (2008) (glasses); Weeber (2015), 137–49 (tables); on foods, Gowers (1996); van der Veen (2003).

[57] Which is a widespread theme: Edwards (1993), 137–78; on luxury architecture, Weeber (2015), 43–62.

without a doubt the main vehicle for *luxuria*. This makes sense: eating is a necessary act, the most natural of all, and its perversion thereby reveals the danger of this vice, since *luxuria* here goes against nature, as it were, and clouds people's reason, reducing them to their beastly and stomach-centred instincts. Furthermore, food and drink in a banquet are short-lived goods lasting only a few hours, which emphasizes the ephemeral nature of pleasure and the waste of money more than e.g. jewels can, which last very long—it is not a coincidence that the jewellery appearing most often in the context of *luxuria* is pearls, which are more fragile than jewels, and especially Pliny the Elder emphasizes the luxury of refined fragile objects, such as glass and earthenware, as an extreme form of vice.[58] As for foods, there is a special focus on fish,[59] not only because it is more expensive and difficult to come by than meat but also, in my opinion, because it belongs to an environment, the sea, that is different from that of humans, the earth. Eating fish exemplifies the breaking of natural rules, since their consumption requires humans to cross environmental boundaries. This is all the more the case with mullets, sea urchins, and so on, which are creatures in between animals and plants, and thus cross the boundaries between species; the same can be said about mushrooms. Furthermore, the aspect of these foods, mysterious and apparently deprived of distinctive animal traits, such as some sort of skin, organs, and so on, and also the fact that they are often mixed together in an indistinct course, presage the disgusting melting together in the stomach (or in the vomit that these foods sometimes provoke): a picture of the filthy appearance of the despicable soul.

Fourth, and last, there is a development in the frequency, evaluation, and even meaning of the term *luxuria*. While it is present but not frequent in archaic literature (which more often involves concrete critique against expenses, *sumptus*), it is often used in the late Republic (especially by Cicero and Sallust), almost disappears in the Augustan age, and then bursts onto the scene as a central theme in Neronian times; subsequently, it retains about an average level of frequency among the vices most discussed. The increasing interest in *luxuria* in the Republican age may be explained both through linguistic reasons—abstract nouns are treated with diffidence and take time to enter common use—and through sociocultural ones: these are the years in which the close contact with Eastern peoples, and the influx of wealth from these new provinces, confront Rome with different ways of life that challenge the rock-solid belief in the *mores maiorum* as the only possible moral compass. This is the period in which *luxuria* spreads throughout Roman culture: Cicero and Sallust describe this phenomenon as the decline of the formerly strong and frugal Roman people. The Augustan age,

[58] Below, 2.5.2. Cf. above, n. 56.

[59] This is evident in Pliny the Elder and Seneca the Younger (below, 2.5.2; 4.3), but we find it in almost all of our authors: already Ennius with his *Hedyphagetica* and Lucilius in his satires, in neither of whom the word *luxuria* occurs, feature fish as a luxury food; cf. La Penna (1989), 4–10.

however, is more reticent on this vice because of political propaganda seeking to focus on the restoration of ancient frugality, and because writers try to justify luxury as being in the public interest. During the Julio-Claudian dynasty, writers face more immediate issues, such as using moral suasion to limit the emperor's absolute power. Fighting *luxuria* here becomes a way to criticize the morality of the court, where the most extreme examples of this vice are found, while still avoiding explicit political dissent. Nero becomes a litmus test in this regard: other emperors are evaluated by comparison with his behaviour. At the turn of the first to the second century CE, after centuries of critique of this vice, or of its luxury-related manifestations, it is no longer labelled as a mark of evil, but is accepted as connatural with nobility and political office, not only de facto but even on a cultural and literary level. This process, which is accelerated through the conversion of the Republic to Empire, is given a further impetus by Tiberius' refusal to promulgate sumptuary laws, and it ends with Pliny the Younger's peaceful acceptance and quiet exhibition of luxury.[60] Hence the disappearance of the term *luxuria* to label wealth, banquets, and so on: it is almost completely absent from Pliny the Younger's writings. Historiography is an exception to this process, both because it looks at the past, and because *luxuria* plays a role in the moral portraits of the emperors, having become a benchmark of Nero's manner—that is, of a tyrannical attitude.

At the same time, *luxuria* begins to overlap with *libido*, 'lust', which at first is only a secondary meaning or a related concept. This semantic twist, which is evident in Apuleius, is further developed by the first Church Fathers, and ends in the classification of *Luxuria* as 'Lust' among the Seven Cardinal Sins of the Christians.

1.5 Concluding Remarks

The Roman fight against *luxuria* lasted as long as their history as a powerful Republic and Empire, and then shifted to the Christian fight against its erotic meaning. The Romans linked *luxuria* with wealth, moral decline, and military weakness, and attributed this passion to the ultimate motivations of every political crisis. This idea was so rooted in their way of thinking that it even imbued the divine sphere: Cassius Dio, while narrating Tiberius' reign, reports a Sibylline prophecy (57.18.5):

> *τρὶς δὲ τριηκοσίων περιτελλομένων ἐνιαυτῶν*
> *Ῥωμαίους ἔμφυλος ὀλεῖ στάσις, χἀ Συβαρῖτις*
> *ἀφροσύνα . . .*

[60] On this process of acceptance, Toner (1995), 65–88; 117–27.

> When thrice three hundred revolving years have run their course,
> civil strife upon Rome destruction shall bring, and the folly, too,
> of Sybaris...
>
> (Trans. Cary 1955)

Civil war and Sybaritic madness (*aphrosyne*) led the Romans to destruction.[61] Vice as a form of mental illness, and as a cause of social and political decline, were seen to last for all of Roman history. Even when Christianity changed the way in which vices were evaluated, lending much more importance to the private and intimate sphere, and focusing on *luxuria* in its erotic sense, this idea of illness and decline persisted, to the point that luxury has remained a challenging issue, despite Enlightenment rehabilitation, capitalism, liberalism, and so on.[62] *Luxuria* is not officially a passion or a vice any more, but we are still afraid of the immoral effect of excess, desire, and luxury, and torn between the seductions of pleasures and a mixed sense of fault, fear, and disgust that may be traced back to Cato the Censor.

[61] Ps.-Pyth. *apud* Stob. 4.1.80 Wachsmuth-Hense—in the cities there is first *tryphe*, then *koros*, then *hybris*, then death—with Novara (1992), 55.

[62] Berry (1994), 99–242.

2
Luxuria: A Short History

Luxuria is an ancient word, frequent in prose works, but with meaningful recurrences in poetry. From archaic comedy to historiography, from satire to encyclopaedic works, it followed the development of Roman literature. This chapter traces a history of the evolution of this concept. It is in the first century BCE that *luxuria* is labelled as one of the worse vices of Roman culture, a sort of capital sin; Augustan age neglects it, while it receives new attention in the Empire, when its secondary meaning, linked to lust, acquires more and more importance. In parallel with literature, Roman law tries to fight this vice, until the emperor Tiberius declares the uselessness of sumptuary measures.

2.1 Beginnings

Luxuria is already present in Latin archaic literature, and especially in comedy. This shows that it was a common word; its meaning fits well in the context of profligate young men and greedy pimps who frequently appear in the plots. The word is absent from Cato the Elder's extant work, but, considering his obsession with frugality and distaste for wealth, this is likely due to the almost complete loss of his speeches. Indeed, Cato offers us all the Roman commonplaces on this vice.

2.1.1 In the Beginning There Was Plautus…

Luxuria makes her first appearance in Latin literature as a grown woman. This is not hyperbole or figurative speech. In fact, in the first occurrence of this word in known literature, we find it personified as a dressed-up mistress, pushing her daughter Poverty to enter a young man's house. She is the narrator of the prologue of *Trinummus*, one of Plautus' last comedies, known for being calmer and less trivial than his most famous plays.[1] Even though personification was a quite common tool in ancient comedies, already in Plautus' Greek models, there is no further example of the personification of *luxuria* (see also below). This prologue has

[1] Bibliography below, n. 16. In general, on Plautus' account of *mos maiorum*, Blösel (2000), 27–37.

Roman Luxuria: *A Literary and Cultural History*. Francesca Romana Berno, Oxford University Press.
 DOI: 10.1093/oso/9780192846402.003.0002

many other exceptional features, such as a dialogue form, as well as a similarity with the divine prologue that is typical of tragedies (*Trin.* 1–22):[2]

LVXVRIA Sequere hac me, gnata, ut munus fungaris tuom.
INOPIA Sequor, sed finem fore quem dicam nescio.
LVX. Adest. em illae sunt aedes, i intro nunciam.—
...
primum mihi Plautus nomen Luxuriae indidit;
tum hanc mihi gnatam esse voluit Inopiam.
sed ea huc quid introierit impulsu meo
accipite et date vocivas aures dum eloquor.
adulescens quidam est, qui in hisce habitat aedibus;
is rem paternam me adiutrice perdidit.
quoniam ei, qui me aleret, nil video esse relicui,
dedi ei meam gnatam, quicum aetatem exigat.
...
huic Graece nomen est Thensauro fabulae:
Philemo scripsit, Plautus vertit barbare,
nomen Trinummo fecit, nunc hoc vos rogat
ut liceat possidere hanc nomen fabulam.
tantum est. valete, adeste cum silentio.—

[*Enter Luxury from the right, followed by Want*]

Luxury: Follow me this way, my daughter, so that you may do your duty.

Want: Yes, but I don't know what I should say our destination is.

Luxury: It's here. There, that's the house, go in at once.

[*Exit Want into the house of Carmides*]

Luxury [*to the audience*]: Now so that none of you will be mistaken. I'll set you on the right track with a few words, if you promise to give me your attention. Now then, first I'll say who I am and who that woman is who went in here, if you pay attention. First, Plautus gave me the name of Luxury: next, he wanted me to have this woman as my daughter, Want. But take in why she went in here at my prompting and give me empty ears while I'm telling you.

There's a certain young man who lives in this house: with my assistance, he squandered his father's possessions. When I saw that he had nothing left with which to maintain me, I gave him my daughter to spend his life with.

[2] Raffaelli (2009), 28–31; on Plautus and Philemon (below, n. 6), Webster (1953), 139–40; Hunter (1980); Lefèvre (1995), 86–8; on the allegories, Petrone (2012), 130–6. As is well known, there is a divine prologue already in Plautus' *Amphitruo.* Bottiglieri (2002), 55–6 sees in this passage a justification for sumptuary laws as a defence of young men's assets.

But don't wait for me to tell you the plot of the play: the old man who'll come here will disclose the matter which to provide for me, I have given him my daughter that he may pass his days with her.... The Greek name of this play is *Thensaurus*; Philemon wrote it; Plautus translated it into a foreign tongue, naming it *Three Bob Day*... (Trans. De Melo 2013, here and below)

Already at first sight the reader or spectator is struck by two elements: first, *Luxuria* explicitly identifies Plautus as the one who named her so (l. 8), with a very rare mention of the poet's name,[3] and this is generally interpreted as a reference to the Greek model, where there was supposedly a personified *Truphe*;[4] second, as is evident from l. 1 on, *Luxuria* is a mother, and her daughter is named Poverty (*Inopia*).[5] This provides us with evidence of *luxuria*'s original semantic connotation, which was deeply connected with money, as is confirmed by the title of the play, both in Latin—*Trinummus*, 'Three coins'—and in its Greek model, the *Thesauros*, 'Treasure', by Philemon.[6] The transposition of the title seems to represent the shift from *Luxuria*, who spends lots of money (a treasure), to *Inopia*, who does not own anything (*Trinummus* alludes to a very small amount of money).[7]

This allegory is given a primary role and a mainly economic sense. And a closer reading shows us how the semantic richness of *luxuria* was already present in its first occurrence. First of all, as Anderson pointed out,[8] this personification of *luxuria*, represented as leaving the house of a young man, alludes to the 'gold-digging *meretrix*' who abandoned him after she realized that he is out of money. This means that lust is implied in Plautus' personification. Furthermore, given the loss of Philemon's original, we may think of two other models for this scene. The first is Aristophanes' *Ploutos*, where we find the allegories of both *Ploutos* ('Wealth') and *Penia* ('Need, Poverty'), even if they do not appear at the same time or in the prologue, but in the middle of the play. Their speeches both deal with entering a character's house: *Ploutos*, despite his initial denial, is forced by Cremilus to enter his house (Aristoph. *Pl.* 231; 234–5; 249);[9] *Penia*, who boasts of

[3] See also l. 19 and *Truc.* 1.

[4] Hertel (1969), 45–8; Segal (1974), 254 n. 7 for the debate; Fantham (1977a), 407–8. While l. 8 may refer to a translation from Greek (*nomen... indidit*), l. 9 seems to refer to a creative act of the poet (*gnatam esse voluit*).

[5] This connection is also in Sallust, with regard to Sempronia (below, 2.3). In Claudian's *Ruf.* 1.37–8, *Luxus* appears within the Night's children, coupled with *Egestas*, 'Want'.

[6] On this New Comedy playwright (fourth century BCE), see Bruzzese (2011), with 58–74 on philosophical parody, and 108–27 on prologues; see also above, n. 2. On the relevance of money in the semantics of Plautus' *luxuria*, Petrone (1993a), 265–70.

[7] Petrone (1993b), 79–90. The title also refers to the trick that solves the plot (ll. 883–4).

[8] Anderson (1979), 336; cf. Petrone (2012), 131–2.

[9] 'Chremilus: "Now, wealth, most puissant of all divinities, please come inside here with me, because this is the house you've got to fill up with riches this very day, by fair means or foul" Wealth: 'By heaven, I really hate going into a strange house; it's never yet brought me any benefit. If I find myself in a pauper's house, he immediately digs a hole and puts me underground... and if I find

having lived there for years (l. 437), is driven away (ll. 426; 604).[10] This source also points to the economic aspects of *luxuria*. But if we focus on the maternal relationship between the two entities, which appears to be Plautine, the mind is drawn to a second model, Plato's *Symposium*, and to its famous tale attributed by Socrates to his schoolmistress Diotima of Mantinea (203c–204b), according to which *Eros* was born from *Penia*, 'Poverty', and *Poros*, 'Trick'. Here we find a personification that is similar to Plautus' *Inopia*[11] and that generates love in the form of desire, one of the most powerful gods in the ancient Pantheon, whom the Romans called, precisely, desire, *Cupidus* (which shares root and etymology with *cupio*, 'I desire', and *cupido*, 'desire'). And we have seen that desire is part of *luxuria*'s etymology.[12] It seems that Plautus is mocking Plato's dialogue, inverting the maternal relationship between poverty and desire, and portraying it in a more down-to-earth way. And this is a first hint of the erotic nuance of *luxuria*.

There are two passages in the play that are relevant for our interpretation of the prologue. The first is l. 28ff., where the old man Megaronides talks about a moral disease in his society. This unspecified disease (28 *morbus*) has grown like a well-watered herb (31 *quasi herba inrigua succrevere uberrime*... 33 *eorum* [*sc. mali*] *licet iam metere messem maxumam*) and expresses itself as pursuit of one's personal interest against the common good. Now, *luxuria* itself also has these vegetal connotations, and appears several times in a sense similar to the adjective *uber* in this passage.[13] We may infer that Megaronides is therefore talking about *luxuria*. Even if we leave aside the herbal image, there is the verb *invado* (l. 28), which is a transparent allusion to the idea of 'getting in', expressed more than once in the prologue, and the reversal of private interest in common ruin (ll. 37–8) recalls the turn from *luxuria* to *inopia* in the first lines. Furthermore, this moral speech, which is significantly connected with the idea of *castigare* (ll. 23 and 26; cf. l. 44), i.e. the typical act of the censors,[14] the magistrates who punished the excesses of expenses and various forms of immorality, recalls Sallust in *De coniuratione Catilinae*, where social decadence is due to *luxuria*.[15] The speech seems to widen the perspective of the prologue, from the individual to the social sphere, and thereby to characterize *luxuria* as primarily a social disease, just as it is in later moralistic literature.[16]

myself in a degenerate's house, I'm thrown away on whores and dice, and in no time I'm out on the street shirtless." ' (Trans. Henderson 2002). Cf. Sommerstein (2001), 5–8 and 151–2.

[10] Cf. Sommerstein (2001), 169. As we have seen (above, 1.1), the semantic root of the Greek word *ploutos* may be connected with those of *luxuria*.

[11] At Plato *Symp.* 204b *Penia* is explicitly labelled as *aporos*, the Greek equivalent to *inops*. Lucian will later show another personification of *Ploutos* in his dialogue *Timon*, modelled after Aristophanes' personification.

[12] Above, 1.1. On the *Symposium* passage on the birth of Eros and its connection with desire, Dover (1980), 141–6; Rosen (1987), 215–21.

[13] Above, 1.1. [14] Lefèvre (1993), 185–6. [15] Below, 2.3.1.

[16] The moralistic issues in this comedy have been widely debated by scholars; see esp. Segal (1974); Fantham (1977a), who refers to Aristotle's *EN* and its definition of *asotia*, 'prodigality'

The second passage relevant to our interpretation of the prologue is the first monologue of the young man Lysiteles (ll. 223–75).[17] After identifying the victim of love as a *cupidus homo* (l. 237), he describes *Amor* as Cupid—a lazy, lusty boy, a liar and a gambler—thus confirming the abovementioned Hesiodic (and Platonic) imagery, and shows how the lover, forced to many useless expenses by the fascinating girl, quickly turns into an *inops amator*, i.e. a man subdued to *luxuria*'s daughter, *inopia* (l. 254). In other words, Lysiteles rephrases the prologue, with *Amor* (also personified) instead of *Luxuria*. And so love and desire are added to the initial couple of opposed (and yet connected) entities, prodigality and poverty, in a circle of interdependent concepts. The same can be said of the only other occurrence of *luxuria* in Plautus, *Asin.* 819, where it refers to the expenses a young man has to undertake in order to keep his erotic relationship alive.

Turning back to the prologue, I would like to focus on the ideas of following (l. 1 *sequere*; l. 2 *sequor*) and getting in (l. 3 *i intro*... l. 7 *abiit intro*).[18] *Luxuria* shows the spectators the same exact attitude she has towards her daughter: right after giving her order to *Inopia*, she addresses the audience with the same image of following a path (ll. 4–5 ...*ne quis erret vostrum, paucis in viam/deducam*...). And, as everyone knows, on a theoretical level, which is implied by the use of personified moral entities, only masters, philosophers, and gods may give others instruction on which path to follow. We think of the famous story of Heracles at the crossroads,[19] where Virtue and Vice, personified as beautiful women, show the hero their ways, and try to convince him to follow them. Heracles chooses virtue's difficult path; Plautus' audience, on the other hand, does not have this opportunity: *Luxuria* is clearly a vice, but one that people have no choice but to follow. The plot is thus characterized as infected by vice, as is confirmed by Poverty's action. Indeed, *Inopia* enters a house (which, as will be explained later, belongs to the young lover Lesbonicus), doing the opposite of what actors usually do:[20] they exit doors and go to the square, since ancient theatres did generally not show internal scenes. This means that *Inopia* will not be an actor like others, but will represent the inner motivation of the protagonist's actions: in other words, she will be the very engine of the plot. And yet she is not independent herself, but acts under *Luxuria*'s influence. So do the spectators, who take orders from her

(*EN* 3.14.1119a32–1120a4); Anderson (1979); Lefèvre (1993), who interprets the plot as mocking Cato the Censor; Petrone (1993b); Sharrock (2014).

[17] On the relevance of this speech for the play, and its connections with Lesbonicus' situation, Anderson (1979), 336–9. 'Lysiteles' probably means 'useful' (Segal (1974), 263). See also Hunter (1980), 225–6 on Lesbonicus' apologia (ll. 657–8) and the connections between *luxuria*, *amor*, and *otium*. The same Lesbonicus says: *insanum malumst in hospitium devorti ad cupidinem* (*l.* 673).

[18] The only model for this scene, which was not in Philemon (Lefèvre (1995), 86–8), has been found in the dialogue of Iris and Lyssa in Euripides' *Heracles*, ll. 843–73, later imitated by Seneca in the prologue of his *Thyestes* (Hertel (1969), 47; Hollmann (2016), 31–3).

[19] Already mentioned in this regard by Fantham (1977a), 408 n. 10.

[20] Sharrock (2014), 177.

about where to go and how to read the play. It is *Luxuria* who plays the authorial role in this comedy.

In its first appearance in Roman literature, *luxuria* already displays many of the features that will become distinctive for it. First, there is the dependence on Greek literature and culture; second, its connotation of wealth, and, secondarily, lust; third, its threatening effects. Furthermore, it is personified and pronounces a prologue, just like a goddess. We may say that *luxuria* makes its entrance in Latin literature as an actual *prima donna*, a role it will retain in the future.[21] As we shall see, even at the very end of our study we shall find it personified again, depicted as an evil creature but without having lost its seductive appeal.[22]

Appendix: Terence

In Terence's plays, *luxuria* does not have the importance Plautus gave it. We find it only once, in hendiadys with *lascivia* (*Heaut.* 945–6... *ut eius animum, qui nunc luxuria et lascivia/diffluit, retundam redigam*...). The association with a term explicitly referring to lust brings to light the richness of *luxuria*'s meanings, while the verb for melting (*diffluo*) alludes to the widespread image of vice as a process of softening and loosening a strong nature. Another passage is interesting, even if here we find *luxus* and not *luxuria* (*Ad.* 760–2):

> Domus sumptuosa, adulescens luxu perditus,
> senex delirans. Ipsa si cupiat Salus,
> servare prorsu' non potest hanc familiam.

The house is wallowing in extravagance, the young man's ruined by luxury, the old man's off his head. Salvation herself couldn't possibly save this house even if she wanted to. (Trans. Barsby 2001)

The sense is exclusively economical, as indicated by the word choice, and it is interesting how the goddess *Salus*, 'Salvation', is called for help. Even if she is intended here in a generic sense of preservation from evil,[23] the original—that is, psychological—meaning is also present, in the sense that luxury is here considered to be a disease from which the young man must be healed. This image, too, will be a *Leitmotiv* of moralistic speeches.

To sum up, in Terence we do not find any peculiar role attributed to *luxuria*, but we find evidence that the imagery of melting and of disease, the two main features of this vice's portrayal, were present and active in Latin literature already at this early stage.

[21] E.g. in Persius (below, 2.6.1), Seneca (4.4), and Prudentius (5.5). Cicero will suggest the personification of vices for delivering powerful speeches, in *De or.* 3.168, citing the following example: *luxuries quam in domum inrupit*; he will also specify that *luxuria* is *avaritia*'s mother (2.171). Cf. below, n. 68.

[22] Petrone (2012), 133–5; below, 2.6.1; 5.5.

[23] Martin (1976), 209.

2.1.2 ... But the True Beginning Was Cato the Elder

Cato the Censor is a sort of prototype of the Romans' restless fight against *luxuria*: he was against Greeks, against luxury, against any kind of excess, and supported frugality and sobriety.[24] We may quote as evidence a passage from Cornelius Nepos' *Life of Cato* (2.3):[25]

> At Cato, censor cum eodem Flacco factus, severe praefuit ei potestati. Nam et in complures nobiles animadvertit et multas res novas in edictum addidit, qua re luxuria reprimeretur, quae iam tum incipiebat pullulare.
>
> But Cato, elected censor together with the L. Valerius Flaccus already mentioned, welded that office with severity. For he both took action against numerous nobles and added many new items to the edict, in order that luxury, which was already beginning to sprout, might be repressed. (Trans. Horsfall 1989)

Plutarch also, in his *Life of Cato*, emphasizes more than once his fighting against 'hydra-like luxury and limpness'.[26] Indeed, he and his descendant Cato of Utica offer many speeches against this vice (recognized by scholars as composed after their actual deliveries).[27] Unfortunately, the extant fragments do not allow us to form a precise idea of Cato's approach to the subject. But there is evidence of his view *of luxuria* in his oratory, which included all the main areas of subsequent moralistic debate: luxury buildings, expensive furniture and clothing, and so on.[28] We may add that the notion that it is impossible for an evil or dishonest man to be a good orator, which was often employed against the corrupting force of *luxuria*, is explicitly modelled after Cato's famous definition of the orator as 'a good man, skilled in speaking'.[29] Furthermore, Macrobius informs us that Cato referred to sumptuary laws as food-related, because they were mainly focused on

[24] Of course, Cato's actual thought was more nuanced than that: Astin (1978), 78–103; Novara (1992), 54–63; Landolfi (1990), 67–73; Blösel (2000), 53–9; McDonnell (2006), 53–6; Passet (2020), 192–201; Vogt-Spira (2022).

[25] Horsfall (1989), 52.

[26] Plut. *Cato M.* 16.7 μετ᾽ ἐκείνου γὰρ οἴεσθαι μόνου τὴν τρυφὴν καὶ τὴν μαλακίαν ὥσπερ ὕδραν τέμνων καὶ ἀποκαίων προὔργου τι ποιήσειν, 'only with the aid of that man [*sc.* Valerius Flaccus] did he think he could make progress towards cropping and searing the luxury and laxity that had sprung up like some Hydra.' (Trans. Sansone 1989). Cf. 4.2–6; 18.2–5; 19.4. See also above, 1.4.

[27] The two most famous examples are Cato of Utica's speech in Sallust's *Catiline's Conspiracy* and Cato the Censor's speech against the abrogation of the *Lex Oppia* in Livy (below, 2.3.1 and 2.3.2). Cf. Berry (1994), 75–7.

[28] For example in Plutarch's *Cato M.* 8.2 = *inc.* 24 Sbl.; cf. Sblendorio/Cugusi (2001), 511; *ORF*[4] 8.133 = frg. 97 Sbl. = Iul. Rufin. *RhLM* 43.21ff. Helm with Sblendorio/Cugusi (2001), 315; *ORF*[4] 8.185 = frg. 139 Sbl. = Fest. p. 282,5 (luxury buildings); cf. Sblendorio/Cugusi (2001), 351–2; *ORF*[4] 8.174 = frg. 218a Sbl. = Gell. 13.24.1 (luxury furniture and clothing); cf. Sblendorio/Cugusi (2001), 410–11.

[29] *Ad Marc.* frg. 18 Sbl. = Quint. 12.1.1; cf. below, 2.7.1.

food expenses and banquets as the main places where *luxuria* is manifested (*ORF*^{4} 8.143 = frg. 210 Sbl. = Macr. *Sat.* 3.17.13):[30] *Cato enim sumptuarias leges cibarias appellat*, 'Cato, in fact, gives that name [*sc.* ratio's law] to sumptuary laws' (trans. Kaster 2011).

The only actual occurrence of our term in Cato, as an adverb, is in a fragment ascribed to the speech *Against the Rhodians*, a sort of Ur-text for the condemnation of luxury (*ORF*^{4} 8.163 = frg. 118 Sbl. = Gell. 6.3.14):[31]

> Scio solere plerisque hominibus rebus secundis atque prolixis atque prosperis animum excellere atque superbiam atque ferociam augescere atque crescere. Quo mihi nunc magnae curae est, quod haec res tam secunde processit, ne quid in consulendo advorsi eveniat quod nostras secundas res confutet, neve haec laetitia nimis luxuriose eveniat. Advorsae res edomant et docent, quid opus siet facto, secundae res laetitia transvorsum trudere solent a recte consulendo atque intellegendo. Quo maiore opere dico suadeoque, uti haec res aliquot dies proferatur, dum ex tanto gaudio in potestatem nostram redeamus.
>
> I am aware that in happy, successful and prosperous times the minds of most men are wont to be puffed up, and their arrogance and self-confidence to wax and swell. Therefore, I am now gravely concerned, since this enterprise has gone on so successfully, lest something adverse may happen in our deliberations, to bring to naught our good fortune, and lest this joy of ours may become too extravagant. Adversity subdues and shows what ought to be done; prosperity, since it inspires joy, commonly turns men aside from wise counsel and right understanding. Therefore it is with the greatest emphasis that I advise and urge that this matter be put off for a few days, until we regain our self-command after so great rejoicing. (Trans. Rolfe 1960)

In this passage, something positive (*res secundae*) causes pride (*superbia*) and a joy (*laetitia*) that springs out excessively (*nimis luxuriose*).[32] This meaning of *luxuria* is vegetal, connected to the luxuriant growing of plants, which is not a negative thing per se but may become dangerous in that it hints at the uncontrollable force of nature that transgresses proper limits. This vegetal dimension adds to the different but intertwining contexts of *luxuria*, but it is a minor semantic area compared to the coupling *luxuria/avaritia* already in Plautus and to the *luxuria/libido* of Imperial times.

[30] On sumptuary laws, below, 2.9.

[31] Sblendorio/Cugusi (2001), 459.

[32] This link with pride is already present in Greek historiography (above, 1.4) and will return in Livy (below, 2.3.2).

2.2 Fixing the Paradigm of *Luxuria*

The first great fresco of *luxuria*, with special attention to oratory, appears in the late Republic, in Cicero, who uses it to attack his personal enemies, above all Verres. Around the same time, Caesar defends himself against the accusation that he suffers from this vice, and instead accuses Pompey of it. The occurrences of *luxuria* in Caesar's work reveals this vice's relevance in historiographical and political debates, as Sallust and Livy will confirm.

2.2.1 The First Great Theorist: Cicero

With *luxuria*, Cicero meant 'an immoderate attachment to physical pleasures and to material splendor'.[33] *Luxuria* is primarily found in Cicero's speeches and, secondarily, his philosophical works, less in his rhetorical and political output. We have a number of occurrences where this vice is related to others, such as *avaritia*[34]—which will be a cue for Sallust—and some where it is related to its Eastern origin (Greece and Asia), in connection with environmental determinism, while there is almost nothing on its philosophical definition. Another feature, which will be confirmed in later authors, is the characterization of bad politicians as prone to *luxuria*: Cicero aims this charge at Sulla, the paradigm of a Roman tyrant, Gaius Verres, a personal enemy whom Cicero turns into the personification of bad government, and Mark Antony, although in his case cruelty is more emphasized than other vices.[35] It is also worth noting that Cicero uses both forms of the noun, that of the first and of the fifth declension, without preferring one to the other, sometimes in the same context, at other times separately (e.g. in the *Verrinae* we find only the first-declension form, in the *Pro Caelio* always the fifth declension). It seems that he is the only one to use both declensions in the Republican age, except for Caesar in a passage in *BC*.[36]

We may also note that, especially in the *Pro Caelio*, Cicero explicitly draws the connection between *luxuria* and lust that will become so productive in Imperial literature.

Furthermore, Cicero has a sentence that will be absolutely pivotal for later authors in that it expresses the general Roman position towards *luxuria*: *privata*

[33] Mitchell (1984), 27; 27–30 on the concept in Cicero, and its connections with *avaritia* (below, following n.). Generally, on moralistic language in Cicero, Citroni Marchetti (1991), 84–92. Cf. Mayer i Olivé (2023).

[34] As happens already in *Sex. Rosc.* 75 and is theorized in *Rhet. Her.* 2.34 *duae res sunt, iudices, quae omnes ad maleficium impellant, luxuries et avaritia.* Cf. Ps.-Longin. 44.6 (where we find *philedonia* and *philarguria*); Calboli (1993), 243.

[35] Cf. Thurn (2018), 160–2; below, 2.5.2; 2.7.1; 4.6.

[36] Above, 1.1; below, 2.2.2.

luxuria, publica magnificentia (*Mur.* 76, quoted below). The Romans thought of private luxury as reprehensible, while they appreciated and even praised public displays of wealth, e.g. in triumphs, celebrations, and relationships with other countries, because these showed the richness, power, and influence of their own country.

We may say that Cicero offers a complete view of the semantic grid of *luxuria*, in all the varieties we find in other authors. For this reason, one would expect some philosophical reflection on *luxuria* as well, but there is none; we shall have to wait for Seneca in this regard.

The most common use of this word in Cicero is indeed oratorical, and we find it in the speeches as one of the main ways to vilify an adversary.[37]

In the *Verrinae* we find two key topics in this regard: first, the representation of *luxuria* as a Greek vice, in line with long-lasting prejudice;[38] second, the first great negative character created by Cicero, namely the former governor of Sicily Gaius Verres, described as a mix of effeminacy and cruelty which will be very influential on later representations of tyrants.[39] Indeed, Verres' name itself offers an ideal starting point, since it means a male pig, an animal that was archetypically considered a symbol of gluttony and more generally of the dependence on the pleasures of the belly.[40] If we read the *Verrinae* as a whole, we find *impudentia*, 'lack of restraint', as Verres' main vice, attributed to him at the outset (see e.g. *Verr.* 1.1.2 and 6), but *luxuria* also plays a relevant part in this picture, because it represents the main way in which Verres' insolence finds expression. Cicero states how he was not simply greed, in fact he valued artworks and manufacturing more than mere money and precious metals:[41] another trait that will long last in Roman *luxuria*, as Pliny shows (below, 2.5.2).

Let us begin in Greece. Since the *Verrinae* are delivered on behalf of Syracusian people, protesting against their former governor Verres, one of Cicero's main concerns is to distinguish between the Sicilian Greeks and the 'original' ones, depicting the latter as lazy and effeminate (Verres, in their mould, wears a tunic and a short Greek mantel, *pallium*, coloured in purple, a totally inappropriate habit for a

[37] Citroni Marchetti (1986); Corbeill (2002), 204–11; specifically on *luxuria* and *avaritia*, Thurn (2018), 148–66.

[38] Above, 1.4; in the *Verrinae* the protagonist's habit is even compared to that of the 'barbarian kings of Persia and Syria' (2.3.76–7), who to the Greeks were the manifestations par excellence of *tryphe*. As is well known, Cicero was actually an admirer of Greece; on his double-edged attitude, cf. Guite (1962); Pollitt (1978), 162–4; Syed (2005), 363–6.

[39] E.g. in Suetonius (below, 5.2.1). Cf. Tabacco (1984–5), 116–25.

[40] See e.g. Plaut. *Mil.* 1058; Cic. *Verr.* 2.1.121; 2.2.191 *videtis... caudam illam Verrinam tamquam in luto demersam esse in litura?* and 2.4.53 *quem* [*sc. Verrem*] *in luto volutatum totius corporis vestigiis invenimus*: Corbeill (2002), 207. On banquets in Cicero, Stein-Hölkeskamp (2001); see also below.

[41] *Verr.* 2.4.46 'you will perceive, gentlemen, that our friend is an art critic, not a money-grubber: precious masterpieces appeal to him, not precious metals'.

Roman governor (*Verr.* 2.5.137)), while the former are morally irreproachable (2.2.7):[42]

> Iam vero hominum ipsorum, iudices, ea patientia, virtus frugalitasque est ut proxime ad nostram disciplinam illam veterem, non ad hanc quae nunc increbruit videtur accedere: nihil ceterorum simile Graecorum, nulla desidia, nulla luxuries, contra summus labor in publicis privatisque rebus.
>
> And then again, the character of the inhabitants is such, so hardy and upright and honest, that it really reminds us of the stern old Roman manners, rather than of those which have come to prevail among us to-day. They have none of the failings found elsewhere among Greeks; they are neither slothful nor self-indulgent; on the contrary, they are industrious, for their own and for the public good. (Trans. Greenwood 1959)

There is a sort of hyperbole by which the Sicilians are represented not only as far removed from Greeks but even as more frugal than Romans. Sicilians are reminiscent of the ancient, sober Romans, just like, we may say, the legendary Greeks of Arcadia. Cicero ascribes to them the virtues of *patientia*, the most Roman of all virtues,[43] and that of *frugalitas*, the exact opposite of *luxuries*.[44] In doing so, he characterizes these provincials as morally, if not legally, worthy of obtaining the rights of Roman citizenship.

Turning to Verres himself, we note among the first charges against him that of being a man *singulari luxuria atque inertia* (2.1.34), two vices already present in *Rhet. Her.* 1.8, on the list of vices to be levelled at an adversary. Cicero repeats the charge later on (2.2.76), with special reference to greediness.[45] Cicero then describes one of Verres' friends, Timarchides, as notable for his *luxuria* and *nequitia*,[46] with special reference to lust (2.2.134 *flagitiosas libidines*), and thus a perfect match for Verres; the same goes for another friend, Apronius, *nequitia, luxuria, audacia sui simillimus* (2.3.22; cf. 2.3.106).[47] Finally he turns to Verres' son, and the connection between *luxuria* and lust emerges yet again (2.3.160):

> Fac enim fuisse in eo C. Laeli aut M. Catonis materiem atque indolem: quid ex eo boni sperari atque effici potest, qui in patris luxurie sic vixerit ut nullum umquam pudicum neque sobrium convivium viderit, qui in epulis cotidianis

[42] Corbeill (2002), 206.

[43] Liv. 2.12.10 *et facere et pati fortia Romanum est.*

[44] So it is in Seneca, e.g. *EM* 51 (below, 4.4). On frugality in Cicero cf. Eisenhut (1973), 64–5, who stresses how it sometimes stands for 'virtue'; Gildenhard (2020), 263–93 (269–76 on *Verrines*).

[45] Cf. Schwameis (2019), 332 and Ricchieri (2020), 298. This reference is also found in the final speech, where *luxuria* is combined with *avaritia* (*Verr.* 2.5.137).

[46] As is another of Verres' friends, Cleomenes (*Verr.* 2.5.87).

[47] As for Apronius' banquets, see Bäumler (2014), 307–8. We may note that *Apronius* may be etymologically connected with *aper*, 'boar'.

> adulta aetate per triennium inter impudicas mulieres e intemperantes viros versatus sit...
>
> Suppose there had been in him the stuff and the disposition to make a Laelius or a Cato of him, what good could be hoped for, or produced from, a boy living amid his father's debaucheries, so that he never set eyes on one decent and sober dinner-party; a boy who day by day for three years spent his adolescence feasting with unchaste women and intoxicated men...
>
> (Trans. Greenwood 1960, here and below)

Had he been as morally strong as Cato, Verres' son would still have been ruined by his father's vices, since he lived among them. So a man polluted by *luxuria* not only naturally bonds with other morally deplorable people but also infects those who live close by. Vice acts just like a virus: it may start from a single man, but soon spreads to his neighbours. This topic, which is rooted in the well-established connection between medicine and ethics, is very productive in moral writings.[48] In this passage, *luxuria* is used as the opposite of modesty (cf. *pudicus*) and abstemiousness (cf. *sobrium*), and the reference to banquets is enriched with shameless men and women (*impudicas, intemperantes*): the emphasis is no longer on money, but on sex and drinking. The special place accorded to the erotic sphere is confirmed at 2.5.80, with the hendiadys *luxuries libidinesque* and the description of Verres' luxurious tent out on a very beautiful and private spot. This description is so appropriate for Verres that Cicero later defines this accommodation as *castra luxuriae* (2.5.96), an oxymoron that perfectly expresses the immorality of the accused: that which should be a most frugal, rigid, and sharp expression of Roman military attitude, i.e. the camp, is turned in Verres' hands into a holiday residence, on a beach with linen tents and so on. The expression *castra luxuriae* also shows the inconsistency between what Verres *should* be, a military chief, and what he *really* is, an immoral person. Indeed, Verres' vice manifests itself in endless and immoral banquets, which break the rules of the average duration of eating and drinking, so that at the end everyone lies down unconscious. Cicero compares it ironically to the most severe Roman defeat in battle, that of Cannae against Hannibal: *Cannensem pugnam nequitiae videre arbitrarentur* (2.5.28). Again, Cicero reaches for military images and examples in order to highlight Verres' distance from the same. Another one of Verres' habits, added to that of Greek clothing, is to be carried around in a litter filled with cushions and rose petals (2.5.27),[49] an effeminate practice antithetical to the virile and military attitude he should have.

As a counterexample, Cicero presents Publius Scipio Africanus, the conqueror of Carthage, and praises him for his respect towards the enemy and especially for

[48] Cf. below, 4.2. [49] On this passage, see below, 3.2.2.

using the artworks and treasures he brought to Rome not for his private luxury, but as ornaments for public buildings and shrines (2.4.98):[50]

> Nam quia quam pulchra essent intellegebat, idcirco existimabat ea non ad hominum luxuriem, sed ad ornatum fanorum atque oppidorum esse facta.
>
> He did understand how beautiful those things were, and for that very reason regarded them as meant not for the luxurious enjoyment of individuals, but for the adornment of temples and cities, and to be hallowed memorials in the sight of future generations.

Here we find the same distinction between public greatness and private luxury that Cicero will express in *Pro Murena* 76 (quoted below), but applied specifically to artworks, about which Scipio was no less learned than Verres. Scipio's generosity towards the public interest turns a potentially dangerous luxury into a way of empowering the image of the Roman Republic.

In the *Pro Murena* (63 BCE), *luxuria* appears four times in the so-called *reprehensio vitae*, i.e. the section in which Cicero names the moral charges against his client and counterattacks them.[51] *Luxuria* is here connected with Asia, in line with the Greek commonplace about it, and also with *voluptas*, the desire that points towards the same etymology as *luxuria*[52] (*Mur.* 11–12):

> Obiecta est enim Asia: quae hoc non ad voluptatem et luxuriam expetita est, sed in militari labore peragrata.... 12.... Et si habet Asia suspicionem luxuriae quandam, non Asiam numquam vidisse sed in Asia continenter vixisse laudandum est.
>
> Asia was cast in his teeth. This province, however, he did not seek deliberately for self-indulgence and high living but traversed in the course of hard service in the field.... 12. If Asia arouses a suspicion of soft living, it is more praiseworthy to have lived modestly in Asia than never to have seen it.
>
> (Trans. Macdonald 1977, here and below)

In these two passages the commonplace is taken for granted but is turned upside down, as it were, in that Murena, with no evidence of questionable behaviour, is held up as an example of heroic resistance to the seduction of the place.[53] The second charge regards dancing, and comes from Cato the Younger, the standard-bearer of Stoic morality, who was part of the prosecution board against Murena (13 *saltatorem appellat L. Murenam Cato*). Here the defence is more sophistic. Since dancing only comes after other immoral activities, such as banquets and lust, and there is no proof for these, the charge of dancing is also without foundation.

[50] Baldo (2004), 461–2. [51] Fantham (2013), 100–4. [52] Above, 1.1.

[53] On the widespread theory of geographical determinism, above, 1.4. A similar reasoning is done by Seneca about who manages to stay sober during *Saturnalia* (below, 4.2).

Both charges against Murena's morality, his stay in Asia and taste for dancing, are labelled *luxuria*: the first as a corruption innate in a place, the second as an umbrella-vice that includes a wide number of inappropriate practices, such as banquets, free sex, drinking, and dancing. In both cases, the term concerns *voluptas*, a physical pleasure, which also defines Epicurean pleasure (e.g. *Fin.* 1.13; see below). So *luxuria* may be external and foreign, or internal and to some degree innate, and it may summarize all the charges against Murena's private life. These must have been quite forceful, since Cicero opens his defence with them.

Four of five occurrences of *luxuria* in the *Pro Murena* are in this section; the remaining one involves Q. Aelius Tubero. A Stoic, and a nephew of P. Scipio Africanus, he was asked to celebrate the anniversary of his uncle's death with a banquet, all while he was running for the praetorship. He offered a very poor banquet, on stools covered with goatskins. People disliked it, and he was defeated at the elections (*Mur.* 75–6):[54]

> Huius in morte celebranda graviter tulit populus Romanus hanc <u>perversam sapientiam Tuberonis</u>, 76. itaque homo integerrimus, civis optimus, cum esset L. Pauli nepos, P. Africani, ut dixi, sororis filius, his haedinis pelliculis praetura deiectus est. <u>Odit populus Romanus privatam luxuriam, publicam magnificentiam diligit</u>; non amat profusas epulas, sordis et inhumanitatem multo minus; distinguit rationem officiorum ac temporum, vicissitudinem laboris ac voluptatis.
>
> The Roman people took hard Tubero's ill-time philosophy in the ceremony commemorating Africanus' death. 76. These goatskins cost this most upright of men and best of citizens the praetorship although he was the grandson of Lucius Paulus and, as I have said, the son of P. Africanus' sister. The Roman people loathe private luxury, but they love public splendour. They do not like extravagant banquets but they much less do they like shabbiness and meanness; they take into account the variety of obligations and circumstances and recognizes the alternations of work and pleasures.

The sentence *odit populus Romanus privatam luxuriam, publicam magnificentiam diligit* stands, as already stated, as a milestone in the Roman struggle to reconcile the magnificence of the Empire, of which they were proud, with the sobriety of archaic times. The debate about luxury in private and public buildings and occasions is a key issue dating back to Cato the Elder, who in his speech *De sumptu suo* defends himself against charges concerning his excessive wealth.[55] Cicero

[54] Richardson-Hay (2009), 72; Fantham (2013), 181–2; Berno (2014a), where I point out how Valerius Maximus (7.5.1) perfectly agrees in blaming Tubero for his inappropriate parsimony, while Seneca praises him (*EM* 95.72–3 and 98.13; below, 4.7); Gildenhard/Viglietti (2020), 66–7 on Tubero; 66–72 on the opposition between public magnificence and private *luxuria*.

[55] *ORF*[4] 8.174 = frg. 218a Sbl. = Gell. 13.24.1 *neque mihi aedificatio neque vasum neque vestimentum ullum est manupretiosum*, with Sblendorio/Cugusi (2001), 519; above, 2.1.2; see also the following note.

represents a key example in this debate, which will be pursued in later times, especially in the Augustan era.[56] *Magnificentia* is the positive counterpart of *luxuria*. As Fantham points out, Tubero's political mistake contrasts with Murena's *magnificentia*, 'expenditure', in organizing public games as an aedile (*Mur.* 38); the games had indeed been *magnificentissimi* (41). So while a superficial listener or reader may consider the frugal Tubero as more virtuous than the prodigal—luxurious—Murena, it is in fact the other way around: since their frugality and prodigality were expressed on public occasions, where it is not only opportune but strongly encouraged to show off the wealth and greatness of the Roman Republic, Tubero appears not frugal but obtusely greedy, while Murena comes across as an ideal representative of the state. Tubero's example is itself cited in order to undermine the moral influence of a radical supporter of frugality, Cato (the future Uticensis), who was one of the prosecutors. Tubero's Stoic belief is labelled *perversa*, 'distorted' (75),[57] and this is consistent with Cicero's strategy of undermining Stoicism in this speech. Cicero, despite his well-known personal admiration for Cato's moral integrity, on this occasion mocks him[58] for his excessive rigidness and his orthodox following of Stoic philosophy, which according to Cicero here is contrary to common sense and also incompatible with the laws.[59] Cicero's words about Cato are general and do not involve any historical example, which is instead supplied by Tubero, who was himself a nobleman and a rigid Stoic, and who lost to Cato in an election. We may say that Tubero is a counterfigure of Cato in this speech. In this way Cicero manages to make Stoic morality, which evidently was not a good fit for Murena, appear too rigid and above all politically self-defeating. This has the advantage of discrediting Murena's prosecutor without offending him directly, and it also justifies Murena's behaviour.

In the *Pro Murena* we thus have a behaviour that might has appeared to be virtuously frugal but is actually considered shameful, and, on the other hand, behaviour that one might have labelled as *luxuria* (expenditure for the games) praised as a virtuous political choice and therefore labelled as something that is without vicious elements, namely *magnificentia*, 'greatness'. This terminological switch demonstrates that there is no moral reprobation at all in regard to *magnificentia*; on the contrary, it is appreciated and praised. The valorization of Murena's behaviour sheds new light also on the charges against Murena in sections 11–14: his greatness as an aedile not only compensates for any limited and momentary concession to pleasure, such as dancing, but also proves that he already as a young man is growing into the role of organizing great public games. The rigid graveness

[56] La Penna (1989), 18–25; Romano (1994), 63–4; Below, 2.4 and 2.4.2.

[57] Berno (2014a), 371–2.

[58] Cf. van der Wal (2007); Del Giovane (2022), 303–6. Cicero will make amends in *Fin.* 4.74.

[59] In this regard, Cicero quotes some Stoic paradoxes such as 'each guilt is the same'. Cf. Berno (2017b), 500–5.

and frugality of Tubero, however, and also of Cato the prosecutor, are not only old-fashioned but also unfit for political government.

In the *Pro Caelio*, the charges of immorality come from one of the prosecutors, L. Herennius. His accusation is first labelled general (25) and then trivial (29). Indeed, Cicero's words almost literally retrace his own precepts in *De oratore*: the expert listener or reader would classify Herennius' speech as a list of commonplaces as presented in a rhetoric handbook,[60] and thus as not specifically related to Caelius' actual way of life but rather as activities shared by all young men of his generation, such as the frequentation of Baiae (27),[61] and more appropriate for some gruff comedy character (such as the father's brother, the *patruus*)[62] than for a prosecutor's speech. If we look at what follows in Cicero's speech, which is famous for its discussion of education and its support for liberality as against the rigid, old-fashioned education of the ancient Republic,[63] we find some unnamed examples of famous contemporary Romans whose young age had been characterized by lust and prodigality but who then rid themselves of those vices (43). And so Caelius has done; indeed, it would otherwise have been impossible for him to launch a glorious career as an orator (44). Once Cicero has defended Caelius from this charge, he uses it himself, against Clodia, whose house is a cave of *luxuries* (twice in 57).

In the *Pro Murena* we had apparent frugality that was in fact greediness (Tubero, but also Cato), and apparent *luxuria* that was in fact a form of greatness devoted to the Republic (Murena). In the *Pro Caelio* we see two kinds of *luxuries*: one a fault of youth that is overcome in adulthood (Caelius, Roman noblemen), the other an innate and well-rooted vice that has ruined a noble family such as the Claudii (Clodia). The moral judgement of the prosecutor (Herennius, who voices Clodia's charges) backfires: Clodia charges Caelius with immorality, but it is she herself who is immoral, and her accusation shows her resentment at having been rejected. In both speeches the charge of vice is hurled by the prosecutors and turned against them by Cicero.

It is also of interest that in the *Pro Murena* Cicero always uses the first declension form, while in the *Pro Caelio* always the fifth declension.[64] While in the first case Cicero makes some concessions to a life of pleasures, in the second he firmly limits it to the young age: the fifth declension form was less frequent than the first declension one, and so it underlined with its very sound the inappropriateness of some behaviours.

[60] *De or.* 2.135; cf. Mortensen (2008), 40 and 45.

[61] That Baiae is the ideal residence for *luxuria* is an enduring commonplace in Latin literature: above, 1.4; below, 4.4.

[62] *Cael.* 25 with Dyck (2013), 99 and Austin (1988), 80; see also following n.

[63] Berno (2013). [64] Dyck (2013), 99.

Our overview of *luxuria* in Cicero's speeches must extend to one further passage: *Agrarian Speeches* 2.95:[65]

> Carthaginienses fraudulenti et mendaces non genere, sed natura loci, quod propter portus suos multis et variis mercatorum et advenarum sermonibus ad studium fallendi studio quaestus vocabantur.... Campani semper superbi bonitate agrorum et fructuum magnitudine, urbis salubritate, descriptione, pulchritudine. Ex hac copia atque omnium rerum adfluentia primum illa nata est adrogantia qua a maioribus nostris alterum Capua consulem postularunt, deinde ea luxuries quae ipsum Hannibalem armis etiam tum invictum voluptate vicit.
>
> The Carthaginians are fraudulent and lying, not because of their character, but rather because of the nature of the place, since because of their harbours, by many and varied discussions with merchants and foreigners, they were called to the desire of deceiving by the desire of gain.... The Capuans have always been proud because of the good quality of their lands and the abundance of crops, the healthiness, layout and beauty of the city. Out of this plentiful supply and abundance of all things first that arrogance was born, which demanded from our ancestors that one of the two consuls be from Capua, then this luxury, which conquered Hannibal himself, at that time still unconquered by arms, by pleasure. (Trans. Manuwald 2018)

Here we find many key issues in the history of *luxuria*: the anti-Greek prejudice, in anti-Campanian and especially -Capuan form, a central commonplace among historical examples, such as that of Hannibal's 'Capuan laziness';[66] a clear statement of environmental determinism (*non genere sed natura loci*) as the origin of the vice, which is generated by too easy and favourable a life, which in turn explains examples related to the Roman army weakened by its stay in the East; a link between two meanings of *luxuria*, that of natural wealth and—consequently—that of excess in any aspect of human life; finally, a link between *luxuria* and *adrogantia*: not only money and sex but also pride is involved in this vice. This last connection, which refers to Cato the Elder,[67] will subsequently be expressed when *luxuria* is either ascribed to the Campanians or is a reaction to a particularly fortunate event, in which case it takes the form of *superbia*. This nexus of meanings will be particularly evident in Livy's work, not only in his account of Capua's history as a town and in the narrative of Hannibal's exploits but also in the historiographical commentary on such events as the exile of Tarquin the Proud, where *luxuria* connects with *superbia* (below, 2.3.2).

Even from a superficial reading of Cicero's speeches it is evident that *luxuria* belonged among his commonplaces, which he used in order to cast aspersions

[65] Manuwald (2018), 394–5. This passage will inspire Livy's account of Campanian people in book 7 (below, 2.3.2 with n. 127).

[66] Below, 2.3.2; 4.4.

[67] Above, 1.4 and 2.1.2.

upon his adversary. Cicero himself explains this in a few passages in *De oratore*, where there are two aspects to the representation of this vice: personification (3.168) and motherhood (2.171, where *luxuria* is represented as *avaritia*'s mother, differently from what had been the case in Plautus). In both instances, the term occurs in examples.[68] Nonetheless, the importance given to the subject of *luxuria* in Cicero's theoretical works on rhetoric is far less than one would expect after having read his speeches.

As for the philosophical works, we find only few but still relevant occurrences of *luxuria*. In *De finibus*, they are concentrated in the second book, in which the character Torquatus explains Epicurus' idea of the perfect good. Torquatus maintains the need of pleasures for a happy life and considers them blameworthy only if excessive. To attack this position, Cicero uses the common Stoic objection: a moderate desire cannot exist, because desire itself is immoderate; one cannot be wise and immoral at the same time, because these two concepts are mutually exclusive. It is interesting for our context that the immoral man is described as *luxuriosus*, someone who lives *luxuriose* (*Fin.* 2.21–2):

> Et tamen quid attinet luxuriosis ullam exceptionem dari aut fingere aliquos qui, cum luxuriose viverent, a summo philosopho non reprehenderentur eo nomine dumtaxat, cetera caverent?... 22. Sed tamen nonne reprehenderes, Epicure, luxuriosos ob eam ipsam causam, quod ita viverent ut persequerentur cuiusque modi voluptates...
>
> Even so, what is the point of granting the indulgent this saving grace? It involves inventing a group of people who, despite their indulgent lives, would escape reproach from our philosopher supreme so long as they avoided the other flaws.... 22. But Epicurus, why are you not reaproaching the indulgents for the very reason that their lives are aimed at attaining pleasures of any kind?
>
> (Trans. Woolf 2001, here and below)

Luxuria is considered directly connected with *voluptas*, 'pleasure' (Greek *hedone*), the keyword of Epicureanism, and with *cupiditas*, 'desire', a craving that defies all barriers. Indeed, here we find in Cicero, implicitly, what will become explicit in Seneca, a definition of *luxuria* as a 'desire for pleasures': not only a desire for luxury and/or lust but generally a desire for every possible kind of satisfaction of physical and morally base instincts, a broad category in which all desires, except that for improving oneself and becoming a wise man, can be placed. Additionally, Cicero offers us a picture of the immoral man devoted to refined banquets at every hour of day or night, with any kind of delicacy and luxury (2.23), a picture that recalls Verres in the *Verrinae*, and also anticipates Antonius in *Philippicae*

[68] *De or.* 2.171 *avaritiam si tollere voltis, mater eius est tollenda, luxuries* (example of argument *ex causis*); 3.168 (example of metaphor), quoted above, n. 21.

2.76.[69] All this is a topical collection of stereotypes. Of course, as Cicero points out, Epicurus would never consider this an example of virtue, but he does not reject *voluptas* per se, which therefore prevents him from labelling such banquets as a vice. This, according to Cicero, leads Epicurus to an inconsistency that shows that *voluptas* cannot coincide with the supreme good (*Fin.* 2.22–3 and 30):

> Unum nescio, quomodo possit, si luxuriosus sit, finitas cupiditates habere. 23. Quid ergo attinet dicere 'Nihil haberem quod reprehenderem, si finitas cupiditates haberent?' Hoc est dicere: 'Non reprehenderem asotos, si non essent asoti.'... Hic homo severus luxuriam ipsam per se reprehendendam non putat, et... ut verum loquamur, si summum bonum voluptas est, rectissime non putat.
>
> There is just one thing I cannot grasp, and this is how the indulgents can ever set a limit on their desires. 23. What, then, is the point of saying 'I would have nothing to reproach them for if they set limits on their desires?' This amounts to saying, 'I would not reproach sybarites if they were not sybarites.'... Here, then, is our strict moralist, expressing the view that sensual indulgence is not in itself blameworthy. If pleasure really is the supreme good... his view is perfectly correct.
>
> 30. Luxuriam non reprehendit, modo sit vacua infinita cupiditate et timore. Hoc loco discipulos quaerere videtur, ut qui asoti esse velint, philosophi ante fiant.
>
> 30. He fails to condemn indulgence so long as it is free of unrestricted desire and fear. In so doing he seems to be on the lookout for recruits. Do you want to indulge? Be a philosopher first!

Cicero alludes to a distinction in Epicurean thought between a licit and an illicit *luxuria*: if free from desire and fear, it is acceptable. But this is a nonsense from both a Stoic and a Roman lexical point of view: indeed, the etymology of *luxuria* points towards desire. There is also a Greek word in this context that Cicero presents as corresponding to *luxuria*: *asotia*, 'prodigality', a term which specifically concerns money (cf. above, 1.1).

A different, more disturbing *luxuria* is that of Sulla[70] (*Fin.* 3.75 *trium pestiferorum vitiorum, luxuriae, avaritiae, crudelitatis, magister fuit*). While we have grown accustomed to the connection between *luxuria* and *avaritia*,[71] that between *luxuria* and *crudelitas* is quite unexpected. Both these vices, however, were also attributed to Verres (as we have seen above), and they evidently characterize the tyrant as a sort of *summa* of all the worst human habits, as a *pestifer*, an adjective applied to Cicero's worst political enemies, such as Clodius or Mark Antony. This triad of vices was thus a commonplace for tyrants. But, as we shall see, it may also

[69] Reid (1925), 132.

[70] For Cicero's characterization of Sulla, Lanciotti (1977) (138–9 on *luxuria*); for Sulla's connection with *luxuria*, see also below, 2.3.1.

[71] Above, 1.3.

describe—if we only replace *crudelitas* with *ambitio*—the moral degradation of Roman society as a whole in Sallust (below, 2.3.1). We here find, in addition to the pessimistic tradition of moral writers, the reception of Plato's theory of the degeneration of the soul in the *Republic*. Plato discusses the soul that, having fallen under the domination of vices, ends up being tyrannical, both on an individual and political level (above, 1.4). And this pattern is present in Latin literature: normal people may degenerate and develop tyrannical habits, while generals and politicians become actual tyrants, but the process is the same in both cases.

We meet *luxuria* again in *De Officiis*, where Cicero, while discussing the virtue of *magnanimitas*, resumes and develops the *Pro Murena* passage on *magnificentia* and *luxuria* (1.92):[72]

> Quae primum bene parta sit…augeatur ratione, diligentia, parsimonia, tum quam plurimis, modo dignis, se utilem praebeat, nec libidini potius luxuriaeque quam liberalitati et beneficentiae pareat.
>
> Such possessions should first of all have been honestly acquired…they should be increased by calculation, care, and thrift, and be devoted not to loose and wasteful living, but to generous act of philanthropy. (Trans. Walsh 2000)

So it is possible to be wealthy without becoming immoral, if one puts one's money to use for other honest people, and not for one's individual and vicious desires. Here, money is clearly an instrument of *luxuria*, which is combined with *libido* in a hendiadys that will recur frequently in Imperial literature.

As in the *Pro Murena*, public attitude is what makes the difference: one may be wealthy as long as one benefits one's country.

2.2.2 Between Historical Example and Propaganda: Julius Caesar

Long before Petronius and Seneca, Caesar was one of the first great characters of Roman history to embody *luxuria* in person. In Suetonius' description, we find some typical traits. As he reports, Caesar had the custom of wearing a loose toga and a fringed narrow-strip tunic (Suet. *Iul.* 45.3), contrary to Roman and closer to Oriental habit. This is also shown by the affinity with Maecenas' way of dressing—himself a sort of personification of *luxuria*—as depicted in Seneca's *Letter* 114.6.[73] Caesar loved collecting gems and artwork (Suet. *Iul.* 47)[74] and was *pronus et sumptuosus in libidines* (50.1), while however he was moderate in drinking, as even Cato publicly admitted (53). Plenty of other sources attest to his taste for excessive, Oriental luxury, among which they count his alleged

[72] While in 1.123 *luxuria* is described as always despicable but in old age extremely disgusting.
[73] Below, 4.6. [74] On the political meaning of this, Flory (1988).

lounging for kingship.[75] Suetonius also refers the commonplace of his being *munditiarum lautitiarumque studiosissimus* (46), to the point that he decorated his camp's floor with mosaics (*ib.*). This issue is particularly of interest, because Caesar himself, during the civil war, accused Pompey of this same vice, while contrasting it with his own and his soldiers' sobriety (*Civ.* 3.96.1–2):

> In castris Pompei videre licuit trichilas structas, magnum argenti pondus expositum, recentibus caespitibus tabernacula constrata, Luci etiam Lentuli et nonnullorum tabernacula protecta hedera multaque praeterea, quae nimiam luxuriem et victoriae fiduciam designarent, ut facile existimari posset nihil eos de eventu eius diei timuisse, qui non necessarias conquirerent voluptates. 2. At hi miserrimo ac patientissimo exercitu Caesaris luxuriem obiciebant, cui semper omnia ad necessarium usum defuissent.
>
> In the camp of Pompeius one might see bowers constructed, a great weight of silver plate set out, soldiers' huts laid with freshly cut turf, and those of Lucius Lentulus[76] and some others covered over with ivy, and many other indications of excessive luxury and confidence of victory, so that it could easily be supposed that they had felt no fear about the issue of the day, inasmuch they had sought out unnecessary indulgences. 2. Yet these men kept taunting Caesar's most wretched and long-suffering army with luxurious indulgence, though it has always lacked every article of necessary use. (Trans. Peskett 1961)

As has been noted, this scene is not reported in any other sources.[77] It seems likely that Caesar describes Pompey's camp as a sort of mock version of the triumphs he celebrated and of the theatre he built, in light of the already well-established prejudice that linked Oriental interests (Pompey's most famous conquests were in Asia) with luxury and moral corruption.[78] This commonplace was already present in the narratives of the Greeks' battles against the Persians.[79] But Caesar also has to defend himself against similar charges, so he attacks them as false and biased, and yet they were widespread, as Suetonius points out (*Iul.* 46). The relevance of the Caesar passage is that it is the only one in the *Bellum civile* in which the terms for luxury appear, and this happens twice: first in relation to Pompey, in the common form of the first declension, *luxuria*, and then in the less frequent form belonging to the fifth declension, *luxuries*, referring to the accusations against Caesar. This choice is not consistent with Caesar's Atticism and famous refusal to use rare words. Given the strong manuscript tradition, it is

[75] Weinstock (1971), esp. 336–40; Rossi (2000), 253–4.
[76] L. Cornelius Lentulus Crus, a powerful political ally of Pompey, is blamed from the very start of *Bellum civile* for his huge debts and his greediness (cf. *Civ.* 1.4).
[77] Rossi (2000), 241.
[78] Cipriani (1990), 123–5; Rossi (2000), 242–53; Grillo (2011), 121–30.
[79] As in Herodot. 9.80.1ff. on the battle of Plataea; cf. Rossi (2000), 243–6. See also above, 1.4.

probably explainable by Caesar alluding to an opponent's source and thus describing the opponent, by means of the declension change, as the actual victim of luxury.[80] I would add, first, that the initial occurrence, describing Pompey's camp, is further stressed by the attribute *nimia*, which strengthens the idea of excess already present in the word's etymology,[81] and, second, that the two superlatives describing Caesar's soldiers, *miserrimus* and *patientissimus*, emphasize not only the virtue opposite to *luxuria* (i.e. *frugalitas* or *sobrietas*) but also the other extreme, namely the lack of necessities (*miserrimus*) and total endurance (*patientissimus*). While Pompey is characterized as an extreme example of luxury, Caesar describes his soldiers as no less extreme in the opposite direction.[82] This stylistic device shows Caesar's firm intention to inscribe himself and Pompey in the well-known paradigm of sober Occidental values versus luxurious Oriental habits.

The only occurrence of *luxuria* in the *Bellum Gallicum* is in the commonplace that luxury makes men feeble and vulnerable (2.15.4):

> Quorum de natura moribusque cum quaereret, sic reperiebat: nullum aditum esse ad eos mercatoribus; nihil pati vini reliquarumque rerum ad luxuriam pertinentium inferri, quod his rebus relanguescere animos eorum et remitti virtutem existimarent; esse homines feros magnaeque virtutis.
>
> When Caesar inquired, as touching the nature and character of these, he discovered as follows. Traders had no means of access to them, for they allowed no wine nor any of the other appurtenances of luxury to be imported, because they supposed that their spirit was like to be enfeebled and their courage relaxed thereby. Fierce men they were, of a great courage. (Trans. Edwards 1963)

This idea is attributed to the Belgian population of the Nervi; they are described like Tacitus' Germani, as pure and strong, as people who shun contact with the corrupted Romans.

So Caesar as a writer inserts himself in the line of moralistic works for which *luxuria* corrupts souls and soldiers, and yet he was notably wealthy and enjoyed luxury himself—not only after his definitive triumph over Pompey but during his whole life. He is the first in a long list of paradoxical characters in Roman history. We may say that, following the Roman tradition about the ideal general,[83] he combined the ostentatious wealth and luxury of a political leader with the effort to avoid, as a military general, any claim to special treatment for himself. He lived the same life as his soldiers, sometimes enduring even

[80] Grillo (2011), 124–5.

[81] See above, 1.1. The expression *nimia luxuries* is extremely rare; we find it in Porphyrion's commentary on Horace (C. 3.1.33) and in the later historian L. Ampelius 11.4, referring to the Oriental king corrupted by all kinds of vice, Sardanapalus.

[82] On the role of frugality in the construction of Caesar's propaganda, Zecchini (2001), 124–5.

[83] On which cf. Cugusi (2005); as for Cesar, Rossi (2000).

worse hardships, and cared for them very much. It is not only he who describes himself in these terms, but Suetonius also credits him the same way (*Iul.* 57–8; 68.1–4), and in general all historical sources agree. As we shall see, in most paradoxical Roman characters we find a doubling of two different spheres; in Caesar's case, this doubling is of the political leader and the general. Caesar already considered the public thing to be his own thing, i.e. himself to be the equivalent of the Roman Republic, and in displaying his wealth he thereby displayed the wealth of the Roman Republic, the wealth that Romans were so proud to show off on public occasions. Parallel to this there is the peculiar world of the army, with its own rules, and exhibiting luxury there is not only morally objectionable but also tactically unwise. It is worth noting that, when Caesar was made a lifelong dictator, he promoted the strictest of all sumptuary laws (46 BCE).[84]

2.3 *Luxuria* as a Corrupting Force of Roman Society: Sallust and Livy

Roman historiography, following patterns in Herodotus and Polybius, presents a picture of decadence due to external and especially Eastern influence, but also to a cosmic law of the cyclical rise and fall of societies.[85] Sallust and Livy both express these issues, focusing on *luxuria.*[86]

2.3.1 *Luxuria* as a Capital Sin: Sallust

In our context, historiography is the field in which the legacy of Greek tradition emerges most clearly. It is here that we find most explicitly the idea of *luxuria* as a foreign vice coming from the East (Asia, from the Greeks' point of view; Asia or also Greece itself for the Romans), a sort of virus that infects the original vigour and integrity of a people upon the contamination with Eastern cultures through wars and commerce.[87] This perspective is of course self-apologetic and self-centred: everything bad comes from the outside and affects a previously perfect people. But there is also the embryo of a socioeconomic theory: luxury comes from a sudden spreading of wealth through wars and commerce; this leads to

[84] Dari-Mattiacci/Plisecka (2010), 13; below, 2.9.

[85] Above, 1.4; Polyb. 31.25.4–7 (decline after the Macedonian wars); 38.22 (fatal decadence); Berry (1994), 67–70; Vassiliades (2019), 109–12.

[86] Velleius Paterculus (1.11.5; 2.1.1–2; 2.33.4; 2.100.3) followed their example, too: cf. André (1965), 308–15; Woodman (1969), esp. 787–8; De Vivo (1984), who stresses how Velleius' moralistic considerations aim to present the emperor Tiberius as a model of frugality. Cf. below, 2.5.2 and 2.7 n. 334.

[87] Above, 1.4; Lintott (1972).

social inequality and thus to a degeneration of social bonding, with an increasing risk of insurrections.[88]

This is what Sallust and then Livy say. In particular, the Romans owe to Sallust the consecration of *luxuria* as a capital sin, with its complementary *avaritia* (and, to a certain degree, the more ambiguous *ambitio*). As is well known, the primary text in this regard is *Catiline's Conspiracy*, where we find this triad in the so-called archaeological digression (ch. 11–12), i.e. the section in which the author explains the reasons why Roman society has degraded to the point that a nobleman may attempt a revolution in order to gain power.[89]

It is at the very beginning of the work that Sallust identifies a moralistic reason for the decline of every people in general, citing Asians and Greeks (*Cat.* 2.5):

> Verum ubi pro labore desidia, pro continentia et aequitate lubido atque superbia invasere, fortuna simul cum moribus inmutatur.
>
> But when hard work is replaced by laziness, self-restraint and evenhandedness by wilfulness and insolence, there is a change in fortune accompanying the change of character. (Trans. Rolfe 2013, here and below)

Here, Sallust lists three polar couples of opposite virtues and vices, *labor/desidia*, *continentia/lubido*, *aequitas/superbia*.[90] These have an only partial semantic overlap with the vices in *Cat.* 11–12, but their way of acting is the same: a brutal attack (indeed the verb *invado* occurs in both passages).[91] I think Sallust uses this kind of language because he is referring to civilizations that affected the Romans from the outside at an early stage, as he says later. So, the Romans have specific vices, in their turn due to the excessive prosperity of Eastern societies. From Sallust's point of view, every people is doomed to decline, as in Polybius' theory;[92] Rome is only the last in a chronological order. We have here an idea of fatal decline that makes history look like a tragic play.

The very first encounter with *luxuria* in *Catiline's Conspiracy* is in the introductory description of the main character (*Cat.* 5.8):

> Incitabant praterea corrupti civitatis mores, quos pessuma ac divorsa inter se mala, luxuria atque avaritia, vexabant.

[88] Especially on Sallust, Shaw (1975); Venturini (1979); Levick (1982). A hint of this is also in Cato's speech in Liv. 34.2–5 (below, 2.3.2).

[89] Harrison (2005), 288–9; Vassiliades (2019), 112–26.

[90] On moralistic language in Sallust, and especially on the connection between struggle for money and aggressive impulses, Citroni Marchetti (1991), 92–100. Specifically on this passage, Mariotti (2007), 155–9.

[91] Ramsey (2007), 60.

[92] This is as true for Livy (Mineo (2015)) as for Sallust; cf. also above, 1.4; Koestermann (1973), 786–800.

> He was spurred on, also, by corrupt public morals, which were being exacerbated by two very destructive evils of an opposite character, extravagance and greed.

Here, *luxuria* and *avaritia* are defined as each other's opposites,[93] but still complementary in that the compulsive desire for luxury implies an increasing need for money. The degeneration of this character, who is burning with desire for absolute power, is partly explained through Sulla's example of tyranny,[94] and then through the general degeneration of society, of which Catiline is but an example. This decline is ascribed to fortune, which Sallust recognizes as the ruling force of human history,[95] a force that had been particularly favourable to Sulla. Sulla is responsible not only for having seized absolute power in Rome by force (11.4) but also for having let his army be corrupted by the delicate Asian style (11.5):

> Huc accedebat quod L. Sulla exercitum quem in Asia ductaverat, quo sibi fidum faceret, contra morem maiorum luxuriose nimisque liberaliter habuerat. Loca amoena, voluptaria facile in otio ferocis militum animos molliverant.
>
> To this was added the fact that Lucius Sulla, so as to secure the loyalty of the army which he had led in Asia, had allowed it luxury and excessive license contrary to our ancestral custom; charming and pleasure-filled places had easily sapped the warlike spirit of his soldiers in their idle moments.

With the aim of making the soldiers grateful and loyal to him (*sibi fidum*), Sulla let them live against their custom, that is, with *luxuria* (*luxuriose*). So *luxuria* is explicitly defined as a way of life antithetical to that of the ancient Romans (*contra morem maiorum*). The degeneration process was facilitated by the fact that the pleasantness of the place itself weakens spirits[96] and softens them (*molliverant*), even if they were previously eager (*ferocis*). The opposition between the hard, vigorous, and manly on the one hand, and the soft, tender, and womanly on the other, perfectly applies to the idea of *luxuria* as a corrupting force that conquers even the strongest, which in Roman culture are soldiers.

[93] Ramsey (2007), 71–2 recalls the speech attributed by Livy to Cato the Elder in 34.4.1 about the sumptuary law (below, n. 134 and 2.9); cf. Mariotti (2007), 223–4. See also Levene (2000), 175–8. Avarice is so dangerous that Sallust compares it to a disease that brings *tabes*, 'putrefaction' (*Iug.* 32.4; Debru (1988), 25). Scheidle (1993), 90–1, emphasizes the fact that vices are viewed as opposed to measure (*Cat.* 5.5 *vastus animus immoderata…cupiebat*; cf. *Iug.* 41.4 *avaritia sine modo modestiaque*).

[94] Cf. Lanciotti (1979), 191–5; Zecchini (2002). On Sulla as responsible for the spreading of *luxuria*, Earl (1966), 14; 46; 105–6.

[95] Cf. *Cat.* 8.1 *profecto fortuna in omni re dominatur*, and 10.1 *saevire fortuna ac miscere omnia cepit*. In general, on Sallust's *archaeologia* in *Cat.* 6–13, Shaw (2022), 119–67.

[96] This is a reference to environmental determinism (above, 1.4; Weiden Boyd (1987), 186) as also in e.g. Sen. *EM* 51 (below, 4.4). Specifically on this passage, Mariotti (2007), 304–6.

The definitive triumph of *luxuria* is celebrated in the subsequent sections, and represented as the direct consequence of a combination of good fortune (*res secundae*) and corrupted habits (*corrupti mores*) (11.6–12.2):[97]

> Ibi primum insuevit exercitus populi Romani amare potare, signa tabulas pictas vasa caelata mirari…8 quippe secundae res sapientium animos fatigant: ne illi conruptis moribus victoriae temperarent. 12.1. Postquam divitiae honori esse coepere et eas gloria imperium potentia sequebatur, hebescere virtus, paupertas probro haberi, innocentia pro malivolentia duci coepit. 2. Igitur ex divitiis iuventutem luxuria atque avaritia cum superbia invasere: rapere consumere, sua parvi pendere, aliena cupere, pudorem pudicitiam, divina atque humana promiscua, nihil pensi neque moderati habere.
>
> There it was that an army of the Roman people first became accustomed to indulge in women and wine; to admire statues, paintings, and chased vessels…8 In truth, prosperity tries wise men's souls; still less could men of depraved character like those temper victory. 12.1. After riches began to be held in honor and led to the acquisition of glory, positions of authority, and political influence, then virtue began to lose its edge, poverty to be considered a disgrace, blamelessness to be regarded as spitefulness malevolence. 2. Therefore, as a result of riches, the youth were suddenly consumed with luxury and greed, together with insolence. They robbed, squandered, valued little their property, coveted that of others; they treated without distinction modesty, chastity, things human and divine; they had no scruples and no moderation.

The triad of Roman capital sins is here *luxuria*, *avaritia*, *superbia*, thus a variation of the first triad, with the elimination of sloth and with the emphasis on wealth and money. The vices are all represented as coming *ex divitiis*, and are personified as a hostile army, as shown by the verb *invado*, already used in 2.5. Conversely, the verbs *fatigo* (11.8) and *hebesco* (12.2) express the effect of the attack: a weakening of the enemy's defence, a prerequisite for victory. The result is excess, the opposite of measure (*nihil pensi neque moderati*), i.e. of virtue of any kind.[98] So the Romans, left without a political and military enemy after the destruction of Carthage,[99] were finally defeated, not by some foreign people, but by an inner enemy, a passion. This passion comes from the outside—ironically from the very countries the Romans have conquered—but takes root in everyone's soul and affects it from the inside.

[97] Mariotti (2007), 311–12 and 315–18. This motif returns in Lucan 1.160–7 (below, 2.8).
[98] Scheidle (1993), 90–1.
[99] This motif is already in Posidonius' *History after Polybius* (*FGrHist.* 87.112 = Posid. frg. B30 V. = DS 34/35.33, with Vimercati (2004), 716).

Sallust later explains that this new wealth is spent on private interests, not public buildings or temples, a theme we have seen in Cicero.[100]

The new situation is due to a state of peace and wellness, which demonstrates, from an axiological point of view, the positive evaluation of war as a way to bring people together against a common enemy and to make them not care for unnecessary goods.[101] It also reveals the ideological origin of the idea of *luxuria* as linked to inactivity: military experience teaches that soldiers, if living in peace for too long, without the threat of an enemy or the obligations of military duties, become lazy, vicious, and uncontrolled. Sallust illustrates this in the passage previously quoted (11.5), and especially in *Bellum Iugurthinum* (below). Unlike the commonplace of the East, and the general idea of a condition of peace and prosperity as morally threatening, which are both Greek,[102] the specific military contextualization is pre-eminently Roman, as is the definition of *otium*, which, again, has a military connection (above, 1.1).

Sallust adds another detail to the characterization of luxury as a way of life more than as a specific attitude (*Cat.* 13.4–5):

> Dormire prius quam somni cupido esset; non famem aut sitim, neque frigus neque lassitudinem opperiri, sed ea omnia luxu antecapere. Haec iuventutem, ubi familiares opes defecerant, ad facinora incendebant: 5. animus inbutus malis artibus haud facile lubidinibus carebat; eo profusius omnibus modis quaestui atque sumptui deditus erat.
>
> They slept before they felt a desire for sleep, they did not await the onset of hunger of thirst, of cold or of weariness, but all such things they anticipated with self-indulgence. These perversions incited youth to crime, as soon as their resources had run out. 5. Their minds, steeped in evil practices, did not at all easily refrain from self-indulgence, and so they abandoned themselves the more recklessly to every means of gain and extravagance.

Luxury expresses itself mostly in anticipating desires, that is, in creating unneeded desires (for eating, drinking, having sex) to satisfy.[103] Things that should have been natural, such as eating and drinking, are thereby perverted in two ways: first, they are indulged in before the body feels the need for it; second, they are exaggerated, because men eat and drink far more than necessary. This twofold transgression of right measure happens because of *luxus*.

[100] Above, 2.2.1.

[101] Fuchs (1958); Kapust (2011), 47–52; Vassiliades (2013). The idea is developed by Seneca, *EM* 90.19 (below, 4.1).

[102] For the former, see above, 1.4; for the latter, also in 51.27; *Iug.* 41.3.

[103] Ramsey (2007), 94; cf. Mariotti (2007), 330–2. The focus on young men is probably inspired by Plato *Rep.* 8.556b–c (above, 1.4).

In this passage, lust is included in *luxuria*: note the recurrence of *lubidines* (13.5). This is also the case when women are involved. There were in Catiline's crew also some prostitutes of a certain age, who lost their charm but not their desire for money (24.3), and there was also the noblewoman Sempronia, who was far too good at dancing, an ability that is listed among *luxuria*'s tools (25.2 *instrumenta luxuriae*). Sallust states that she had been ruined by both *luxuria* and poverty (25.4 *luxuria atque inopia praeceps abierat*).[104] As has often been pointed out, Sempronia represents the extreme expression of the perversion that characterizes Catiline's comrades, in that she exhibits both virile boldness and womanly luxury.[105] In her case also, as is explicitly stated in 13.4, proper measure is exceeded,[106] and *luxuria* leads to poverty, as in Plautus.[107]

The last relevant occurrences of *luxuria* are, not coincidentally, in Cato the Younger's speech against the Catilinarians. As is well known, this rigoristic Stoic, supporter of an old-fashioned morality,[108] in the Senate advocated the death penalty for the conspirers, even though this went against Roman juridical tradition. Before him Caesar had spoken in favour of clemency, warning against the possible legal consequences of the death penalty—and the facts would prove him right[109]—but the Senate sided with Cato. Cato begins by acknowledging his habit of criticizing contemporary *luxuria* and *avaritia* (52.7),[110] and not surprisingly he draws a comparison between the good old times and contemporary corruption (52.22):

> Pro his nos habemus luxuriam atque avaritiam, publice egestatem, privatim opulentiam; laudamus divitias, sequimur inertiam. Inter bonos et malos discrimen nullum, omnia virtutis praemia ambitio possidet.
>
> In place of these, we have extravagance and greed, public poverty and private opulence. We extol wealth, we pursue idleness. No distinction is made between good men and bad, and ambition appropriates all the prizes of merit.

It is interesting to point out the similarity between this characterization of moral decline and Sallust's in 2.5 (quoted above):[111] we find here all the same terms. The

[104] These are the same key concept we find personified in the proemium of Plautus' *Trinummus* (above, 2.1.1).

[105] Weiden Boyd (1987), esp. 185; cf. Mariotti (2007), 409–10.

[106] 25.3...*saltare elegantius quam necesse est probae*. Cf. the allegation against Murena in Cic. *Mur.* 13 (above 2.2.1).

[107] Above, 2.1.1. [108] Above, 2.1.2; cf. Nelson 1950, 66–7.

[109] Indeed, Cicero was sent into exile since in his capacity as consul he was responsible for the convictions.

[110] Kapust (2011), 69. Ramsey (2007), 206 recalls Cato the Elder's speech on behalf of the sumptuary law in Livy 34.4.1–2 *saepe me querentem de feminarum, saepe de virorum... sumptibus audistis*, 2. *diversisque duobus vitiis, avaritia et luxuria, civittem laborare, quae pestes omnia magna imperia everterunt*; cf. Mariotti (2007), 598–9; below, 2.3.2. On this issue, see also Levene (2000), 180–90.

[111] On the similarities between Cato's and Sallust's moral statements, Sklenář (1998), esp. 213–14. Mariotti (2007), 614–15.

Roman people could not avoid the general rule of decline. *Luxuria* is again coupled with *avaritia*, and the sentence *publice egestatem, privatim opulentiam* seems to mock Cicero's words in *Pro Murena* 76 with the image of rich noblemen who act poor in order to avoid taxes and contributions to the state while building major houses and villas for themselves. After the speech, Sallust repeats Cato's words on *luxuria* and *avaritia*, and describes Cato and Caesar as the only great Romans to have escaped the collective degeneration of morality (53.5–6).[112]

The formulation is ambiguous: they both display great virtue, but different habits. While Cato embodies the traditional Roman virtues, and as we have seen also expresses them in a way that resembles Sallust's own view, Caesar's generosity (54.1 *munificentia* and *beneficia*) looks dangerously similar to Catiline's profligacy. Yet they are both considered to be positive models against a condition of general decline and moral degradation.

To sum up, in *Catiline's Conspiracy* we generally find *luxuria* combined with *avaritia*, constantly associated with money and wealth, which in turn are the causes of moral degeneration in Rome. While there is similar material in the *Historiae*,[113] things are quite different in the *Bellum Iugurthinum*, a monography recording the war against Iugurtha in Numidia (112–105 BCE). In this text we find *luxuria* in almost the same places as in the *Cat.*—a philosophical beginning, first encounter with the protagonist, rhetorical speech—but we find *ignavia* instead of *avaritia* in association with *luxuria*, and the barbarian king Iugurtha, far from being part of the general corruption, is very distant from this vice.

The introduction, as is also the case in the *Coniuratio*, focuses on the opposition between body and soul, with the degeneration of the latter following from the *inertiam et voluptates corporis* (*Iug.* 1.4).[114] Again, Sallust blames the perversion of those who dedicate themselves to physical pleasures (2.4):

> Quo magis pravitas eorum admiranda est, qui, dediti corporis gaudiis, per luxum et ignaviam aetatem agunt, ceterum ingenium, quo neque melius neque amplius aliud in natura mortalium est, incultu atque socordia torpescere sinunt.

[112] 53.5–6 *sed postquam luxu atque desidia civitas corrupta est, rursus res publica magnitudine sua imperatorum atque magistratuum vitia sustentabat... Sed memoria mea ingenti virtute, divorsis moribus fuere viri duo, M. Cato et C. Caesar.* Cf. Mariotti (2007), 638–43. This idea is developed by Plut. *Phoc.* 3.1 with reference to Cato: 'I think he fared just as fruits do which make their appearance out of season. For, as we look upon these with delight and admiration, but do not use them, so the old-fashioned character of Cato, which, after a long lapse of time, made its appearance among lives that were corrupted and customs that were debased, enjoyed great repute and fame, but was not suited to the needs of men because of the weight and grandeur of its virtue, which were out of all proportion to the immediate times' (trans. Perrin 1959).

[113] In the fragments in which the issue is tackled, 1.13 McG. = 1.16 M. = Aug. *Civ.* 2.18, and the so-called *Oratio Philippi* (1.67.11 McG. = 1.77.11 M. = Cod. VLat 3864 (V)), Sallust offers reflections analogous to those in the *Cat.* (McGushin (2005), 82–3; 140–1; La Penna/Funari (2015), 140; 266 on *Or. Phil.*).

[114] Paul (1984), 12.

> Consequently, the one has to marvel all the more at the perversity of those who pass their life in luxury and idleness, given over to the pleasures of the body, but allow their intellect, which is better and greater than anything else in man's nature, to grow dull from neglect and inaction. (Trans. Rolfe 2013, here and below)

As we can see, sloth (*ignavia*)—which had been part of the vice triad at the beginning of *Cat.* (*desidia*), but not as thematized as it is here—gains in importance from the start,[115] joined to pleasures and luxury. This combination is interpreted by Koestermann as a polemical allusion to Epicurean philosophy,[116] and it is evidently a key issue here, to the point that Sallust himself is afraid of being charged with Epicureanism (4.3), just like in *Cat.* 3.3–5 he had accused himself of ambition, one of the main vices of his generation. In the *Iug.*, the very first characterization of the protagonist, Iugurtha, is in opposition to this (6.1 *non se luxu neque inertiae corrumpendum dedit*, 'he did not allow himself to be spoiled by luxury or idleness').[117] Whereas *Catiline's Conspiracy* opens with a picture of general corruption in Rome and presents the main character as a victim of moral decline, the *Bellum Iugurthinum* offers a similar description of social degradation but with the protagonist displaying old Roman virtue, despite his being a barbarian enemy.[118] Iugurtha distinguishes himself from the general corruption, which combines sloth and luxury, as is stressed also later in the work (61.3), and the same may be said of his entire people, the Numidians,[119] while the Roman army under the general Spurius Albinus, like that under Sulla in *Catiline's Conspiracy*, as we have seen, is infested with vice and the disgraceful acts arising from them (44.5 *ignaviae luxuriaeque probra*). The Romans as a whole, just like Catiline, represent the embodiment of social degeneration, while the barbarian enemy Iugurtha succeeds in defeating them precisely because he conscientiously resists and despises their vices.

While in *Catiline's Conspiracy* Cato and Caesar were the only ones spared the general decline, in *Bellum Iugurthinum* it is Marius who in his election speech defines *luxuria et ignavia* as mortal dangers for the State (85.43):[120]

> Ita iniustissume luxuria et ignavia, pessumae artes, illis, qui coluere eas, nihil officiunt, rei publicae innoxiae cladi sunt.
>
> Thus, most unjustly do the most abominable practices of luxury and sloth not at all work to the disadvantage of those who practice them, but are the ruin of a blameless nation.

115 On the relevance of this motif in Sallust's account of Roman decline, Wiegandt (2016), 46–7.
116 Koestermann (1971), 32–3. 117 Paul (1984), 29. 118 Koestermann (1971), 45–6.
119 *Iug.* 89.7 *cibus illis advorsus famem atque sitim, non lubidini neque luxuriae erat.*
120 Koestermann (1971), 310–11. On the opposition between Marius and Metellus in light of Roman values, McDonnell (2006), 271–90.

The couple of vices are the same as those mentioned in the opening of the work: as Cato's speech in *Cat.* was similar to what Sallust says in the opening of that work, so too Marius' words in *Iug.*, presenting himself as a role model, reminds the reader of the narrator's introduction. All his acts as a consul and general will show how far he is from these two vices, and how he is able to keep the army away from them.

Against Marius there is Sulla, who in some way falls outside of the dichotomy sloth-luxury vs. virtue: he lived in luxury but was still prominent in war (95.3):

> Igitur Sulla gentis patriciae nobilis fuit...animo ingenti, cupidus voluptatum, sed gloriae cupidior; otio luxurioso esse, tamen ab negotiis numquam voluptas remorata, nisi quod de uxore potuit honestius consuli.
>
> Sulla, then, was a noble of patrician rank...very high spirited, fond of pleasures but more fond of glory. Though a man of luxurious leisure, nevertheless pleasure never showed him down in his undertakings, except that he could have taken a more honourable decision concerning his wife.[121]

Sulla, on whom we have already heard Cicero,[122] is only a secondary character in *Iug.*, a subordinate to Marius, but every reader knows that they would eventually be antagonists in a bloody civil war, and that the former was to be the first example of absolute power in Rome. Sallust's description of Sulla recalls that of Catiline, for its mixing of positive and negative elements; to our point, it is interesting to see that Sulla is *not* affected by sloth, even though he is surrounded by laziness and his life is filled with *luxuria.* So Sulla distinguishes himself from the general corruption, albeit not as neatly as does Marius. Sulla and Marius thus correspond in this context to Caesar and Cato in the *Cat.*: the former two stand apart from contemporary decadence, Marius in a rigid and old-fashioned way (and as the reader knows, he would be the loser in the subsequent civil war against Sulla), Sulla in a sort of ambiguous compromise, but still better than the large mass of people.

Why is *luxuria* mainly connected with greed in *The Catiline Conspiracy*, with sloth in *The War of Jugurtha*? I think it is because of the different circumstances of the two occasions: in *Cat.*, one of the main issues is Catiline's debts, in a word, money, while in *Iug.* the main issue is the inactivity of the army, which only Marius's arrival finally stops. So even if *luxuria* remains a core issue in both works, what we may call its secondary character switches from money to laziness, thus illustrating the polysemic nature of *luxuria* itself.

[121] Sulla divorced his wife Metella and removed her from his house when she was on her deathbed (Cf. Plut. *Sull.* 35.2; Paul (1984), 236).

[122] Above, 2.2.1. On the quoted passage, Koestermann (1971), 340–1.

2.3.2 Missing Archaic Frugality: Livy

In his historical work, Livy pursues Sallust's fight against *luxuria* in similar terms, as is especially evident in his *Praefatio*, whose debt to *Catiline's Conspiracy* is clear.[123] Livy exhibits more pessimism than his predecessor, stating that the Romans as a people have reached a point of no return: *ad haec tempora quibus nec vitia nostra nec remedia pati possumus perventum est* (1.*pr.*10). There seems to be no exception to social decadence. Livy then turns specifically to *luxuria* (1.*pr.*11–12):[124]

> Nulla umquam res publica nec maior nec sanctior . . . fuit, nec in quam civitatem tam serae avaritia luxuriaque immigraverint, nec ubi tantus ac tam diu paupertati ac parsimoniae honos fuerit. 12. Adeo quanto rerum minus, tanto minus cupiditatis erat: nuper divitiae avaritiam et abundantes voluptates desiderium per luxum atque libidinem pereundi perdendique omnia invexere.
>
> No state was ever greater, nor more righteous nor richer in good examples, none ever was when avarice and luxury came into the social order so late, not where humble means and thrift were so highly esteemed and so long held in honour. 12. For true it is that the less men's wealth was, the less was their greed. Of late, riches has brought in avarice, and excessive pleasures the longing to carry wantonness and license to the point of ruin for oneself and of universal destruction. (Trans. Foster 1957, here and below)

This preface contains the two main semantic fields of *luxuria*: money (the connection with *avaritia* and *luxus*, and opposed to *paupertas* and *parsimonia*) and desire (foremost *cupiditas*, then *voluptates*, *desiderium*, *libido*), which yields to lust. These same ideas were also in Sallust's *Cat.* 12.1–2 and 13.4–5 (above, 2.3.1), but were limited to young people, while here they have spread over all of Roman society. Also, while Sallust, after the list of the vices *luxuria*, *avaritia*, and *superbia*, turns to another list, that of the activities to which these vices lead, Livy is more theoretical, and focuses on desire, which is implied but less developed in Sallust. Thus, Sallust's boisterous youthfulness becomes, in Livy, a struggle of self-destruction, a *cupio dissolvi*: *libido pereundi perdendique* is a unique expression,[125] whose alliteration stresses its apocalyptic sense.

Livy is even more insistent than Sallust in his praise of old times: while narrating the rapid creation of an urban army on the occasion of a battle against the Gauls (359 BCE), which would not be possible at his time, he comments that 'so

[123] On intertextuality, Miles (1995), 76–8; Levene (2015), 205–6; specifically on *luxuria* as a cause of decline, Mineo (2015), 142–4. *Contra* Luce (1977), 250–1. On the lexical aspect (*luxuria/luxus*), Adams (1974), 57.

[124] Ogilvie (1965), 28–9; Nagy (1968); Borgo (1991), 306–8; Harrison (2005), 292–3.

[125] It will be imitated by Seneca the Younger, with reference to political suicide (*EM* 24.25 *libido moriendi*) and, in a less dramatic context by Sil. 7.524 *perdendi simul et pereundi ardebat amore.*

strictly has our growth been limited to the only things for which we strive—wealth and luxury' (7.25.9 *adeo in quae laboramus sola crevimus, divitias luxuriamque*). The semantics of *laboro* is here of interest. This verb involves the ideas of working and suffering (*OLD* 1–2 *s.v.*), with emphasis on the latter (*OLD* 3–7 *s.v.*), so this sentence may mean 'we grew better only in that for which we work', as most translations have it, stressing the paradoxical fact that we spend our time and intelligence to increase our vices,[126] not, thus, so as to become better persons, but so as to intensify our degradation. But we may understand the sentence differently, in the sense that 'we grew better only in that for which we suffer': this meaning would lighten our personal responsibility, while pointing to fate as an evil force that burdens us ever more with moral disease: this last sense is at play in e.g. 1.*pr.*4 *quae* [*sc. Roma*] *ab exiguis profecta initiis eo creverit ut iam magnitudine laboret sua*, 'proceeding from slender beginnings it has so increased as now to be burdened by its own magnitude' and 34.4.1 (quoted below). The couple *divitias luxuriaeque* is a variation of *luxuria* and *avaritia*, with a concrete and an abstract noun instead of two abstract ones, and it also condenses the history of decadence: it was money (*divitiae*) that first caused *luxuria*.

Right after this sentence, Livy reports the story of L. Manlius Torquatus and his heroic victory against a giant Gaul—the Roman equivalent to the Biblical fight between David and Goliath. It is an example of pure virtue and devotion to homeland, the exact opposite of the degrading vices just mentioned.

Another topic in which Livy follows his predecessor is his view of *Campania* as a corrupting land of pleasure, whose charming effect has seduced even the fierce Hannibal and his army. This topic is discussed on two different occasions: the first, in the backstory of the first Samnite war, when the Campanians and especially the Capuans, defeated by the Samnites (343 BCE), are described as feeble warriors due to excessive luxury (7.29.5):[127]

> Campani magis nomen ad praesidium sociorum quam vires cum attulissent, fluentes luxu ab duratis in usu armorum in Sidicino pulsi agro in se deinde molem omnem belli verterunt.
>
> The Campanians, however, brought to their allies' defence a reputation rather than a real strength, enervated as they were by luxurious living, and they were defeated in the land of the Sidicini by a side hardened in armed combat. Then they drew upon themselves the whole brunt of the war.
>
> (Trans. Yardley 2013, here and below)

[126] This idea will be developed by Seneca (below, 4.9).

[127] The same idea is repeated later (7.32.7): *Campanos quidem haud dubie magis nimio luxu fluentibus rebus mollitiaque sua quam vi hostium victos esse.* On Campanian pride, already mentioned by Cicero, see Oakley (1998), 305 and Knorr (2012), 871–3; indeed, all the issues tackled by Livy can be found already in Cicero *Leg. agr.* 2.95 (above, 2.2.1). On Cicero's passage as a source for Livy's narrative, Kenty (2017), 64–8. She argues that Livy's account of the event seeks to represent the decline of Capua as a premonition for the Rome of Livy's day.

Not only has wealth made them bad at fighting, but it also affects their war strategy. After their defeat, they send ambassadors begging the Romans for help. The senators consider the privileged status of Capua (7.31.1 *urbs maxima opulentissimaque Italiae, uberrimus ager marique propinquus*, 'Italy's largest and wealthiest city, with a very fertile territory near the sea').[128] The presence of three superlatives (*maxima, opulentissima, uberrima*) points at the idea of exceptionality, but also of excess, which characterizes the city.

Despite the city's attraction, the senators decide to deny the request, invoking their previously settled pacts with the Samnites. The Capuans then declare their total submission to Rome, and the senators react as follows (7.31.6):

> Commoti patres uice fortunarum humanarum, si ille praepotens opibus populus, luxuria superbiaque clarus, a quo paulo ante auxilium finitimi petissent, adeo infractos gereret animos, ut se ipse suaque omnia potestatis alienae faceret.
>
> The senators were deeply touched by the changeability oh human fortunes. Here was an exceedingly wealthy people, famed for its high living and its pride, a people from whom its neighbours had sought assistance a short while ago; and now its spirit was so broken that it was of its own accord placing itself and all its possessions under another's authority.

There is no causal connection here between *luxuria* and decline, but a contrast between the two: *luxuria* is an abundance of means and money that legitimizes pride; what strikes the senators is the 'broken spirits' (*infractos animos*) of those formerly proud people—not the moral decline, but the sudden humility they achieved. But the Capuans' abundance will provoke continued defeat.

In book 23, Livy again takes up the commonplace of 'Capuan laziness' as a symbol of the degrading consequences of inactivity, this time in the context of the second Punic war and the decline of Hannibal after his overwhelming victory at Cannae.[129] The weakening of his previously resistant and dreadful army connects right away with the poisoning effect of Campanian pleasures (23.2.1):

> Inde [*sc.* Hannibal] Capuam flectit iter, luxuriantem longa felicitate atque indulgentia fortunae, maxime tamen inter corrupta omnia licentia plebis sine modo libertatem exercentis.
>
> From there Hannibal veered toward Capua, which had long been basking in prosperity and the favour of fortune, but was most conspicuous in its general decadence and the profligacy of its common people, whose license knew no bounds. (Trans. Yardley 2020, here and below)

[128] Oakley (1998), 290–1.

[129] An example tackled with reference to *luxuria* also by Valerius Maximus and Seneca the Younger (below, 2.5.1 and 4.4).

In this sentence, we find a number of terms related to *luxuria*: both fortune and freedom are experienced without measure or boundaries (*sine modo*), and this is a vice per se; Hannibal's very act of turning (*flectit*) his direction may have a symbolic meaning of changing his habits, from the most rigid discipline to the undue licence of Capua. Indeed, as we have seen, the etymology of *luxuria* relates to the idea of 'turning' in an unnatural or improper way.[130] The process of the decline of Hannibal's rigor is exemplified in a luxury banquet, which was antithetical to military and Carthaginian habit (23.8.6):

> Epulari coeperunt de die, et convivium non ex more Punico aut militari disciplina esse sed, ut in civitate atque etiam domo diti ac luxuriosa, omnibus voluptatium inlecebris instructum.
>
> They began dining in daylight, and the banquet was not at all in line with Carthaginian mores or military discipline but suited rather the wealth and extravagance of the city-state and, indeed, of the house,[131] replete as it was with all sort of titillating delights.

This shows Hannibal's assimilation to the city's worst vices. Later, Livy repeats the reasoning we have already heard from Sallust, according to which the soldiers were softened and weakened by inactivity and pleasures of all kinds (23.18.12).[132] This is illustrated by their disappointing behaviour at the siege of Nola, as observed by the general-in-chief M. Claudius Marcellus (23.45.2):

> Qui pugnent marcere Campana luxuria, vino et scortis omnibusque lustris per totam hiemem confectos.
>
> Those fighting were weak from Campanian excesses and exhausted from drinking, whoring and all manner of depravity throughout the winter.

Livy's remark is harsh: the Punic soldiers were only a pale remnant of what they once had been, and Capua was Hannibal's Cannae (23.45.4 *Capua Hannibali Cannas fuisse*).

Campana luxuria became a catchphrase to define the irresistible pleasantness of that place, which, not coincidentally, was of Greek origin, blessed with an ideal climate, incredible fertility of the soil, and an amazing seaside. This prejudice, in which Hannibal's story fits perfectly, is of course grounded in environmental determinism, but I believe that it is specifically linked to one of the

[130] Above, 1.4.

[131] Hannibal was hosted by two wealthy citizens, Stenius and Pacuvius Ninnii Celeres (23.8.6).

[132] The connection between inactivity and *luxuria* is also found elsewhere, e.g. in 1.19.4; 40.1.4 *luxuria et otio solutam disciplinam militarem esse* (Roman army in Spain). In the last passage, note the participle *soluta*, which alludes to the idea of melting (below, 2.7.2 at Quint. 3.8.28).

original meanings of *luxuria*, which was still alive in the Augustan age, namely that of luxuriance, especially as applied to plants.[133] The exceptional fertility of Campanian soil, stemming from its volcanic activity, is on the one hand a positive quality from the point of view of agriculture and of farmland investment, but on the other hand it represents the natural ground for the corresponding vice: the same (positive) excess we observe in Campanian plants and vegetables, when applied to men, affects morality in a fatal way.

A peculiar connection with Sallust is to be found in Cato's character. In book 34, Livy reports the discussion about the repeal in 195 BCE of the *lex Oppia*, a sumptuary law passed in 215 and specifically directed against women, limiting their jewellery and travel, and forbidding multicoloured dress (34.1.3). Livy quotes a speech attributed to Cato the Censor,[134] who was consul at the time, which recalls the speech of his descendant Cato Uticensis in Sallust's text (above, 2.3.1). Livy's narrative is clearly modelled after the comparison between Cato and Caesar in Sallust. In the *Ab urbe condita*, the part of the 'softer' character is given to the tribune Lucius Valerius, who with the help of a women's uprising ends up the winner (whereas in Sallust the softer character had lost). Cato's speech is a masterpiece of ancient misogyny:[135] from the very beginning he accuses women of *impotentia*, 'lack of self-restraint' (34.2.2; cf. *impotenti naturae* 34.2.13),[136] since they publicly address unknown men (34.2.10), and he bluntly defines this as *licentia* (34.2.13), a word whose erotic allusion would have been evident to the listeners,[137] as already shown by the attribute *blandiores*—comparative of 'seductive'—a few lines before (34.2.10). This becomes even more explicit in the words he claims they used in order to explain the motivation of their protest (34.3.9):[138]

> Ut auro et purpura fulgamus... ut carpentis festis profestisque diebus, velut triumphantes de lege victa... per urbem vectemur: ne ullus modus sumptibus, ne luxuriae sit.
>
> 'So that we can shine in gold and purple... so we can ride our carriages through the city on holidays and ordinary days alike, in triumph, as it were, after the defeat and annulment of the law... and so there may be no limit to our expenditure, no limit to our extravagance.' (Trans. Yardley 2017, here and below)

[133] Above, 1.1 (etymology); 1.4 (commonplaces about Campania); as for the Augustan age, below, 2.4.

[134] On which see Luce (1977), 251–3; Pollitt (1978), 158–60; Chaplin (2000), 97–101; Mastrorosa (2006) with a rich bibliography; Ducos (2010); Bringmann (2015), 403–4. On Cato as historical example and role model in Latin literature, Pasco-Pranger (2015); on the whole episode, Briscoe (1981), 39–42; Bottiglieri (2002), 105–32; Feichtinger (2015); on its political meaning, Habinek 1988, 61–2; below, 2.9.

[135] See Keegan (2021), 88–93; McClintock (2022), 78–80.

[136] A trait with which Tacitus labels Augustus' wife Livia (e.g. in *Ann.* 1.4.5: Goodyear (1972), 124).

[137] Mastrorosa (2006), 597.

[138] Briscoe (1981), 219, stresses the analogies with Cato's actual speeches.

Cato's women portray themselves as triumphant winners in the battle against the law,[139] and consider themselves virtuous. Their habits are costly (*sumptibus*) and exhibit luxury (*luxuria*). As previously (7.25.9, quoted above), *luxuria* is paired with a concrete word that involves money, and these two are described as exceeding the right measure (*modus*), which is the typical definition of vice in antiquity.[140] Cato returns to the idea of measure and boundaries at the end of the speech, where he also offers a sort of prophecy on the unlimited increase of this vice.[141]

Right after the discussion of the women, Cato comes back to his *persona* (34.4.1–2):

> Saepe me querentem de feminarum, saepe de virorum, nec de privatorum modo sed etiam magistratuum sumptibus audistis, 2. diversisque duobus vitiis, avaritia et luxuria, civitatem laborare; quae pestes omnia magna imperia everterunt.
>
> You have often heard me complain about the lavish spending of women, and of men, and not just of private citizen but magistrates, too. 2. You have heard me complain that our state is plagued by two contrary vices, greed and extravagance, afflictions that have been the downfall of all great empires.

This is an almost literal quotation of Sallust (*Cat.* 5.8 *incitabant praeterea corrupti civitatis mores, quos pessuma ac divorsa inter se mala, luxuria atque avaritia, vexabant*),[142] and also of Livy's own preface;[143] it clarifies the sense of the verb *laboro* as 'to suffer'. The two vices *avaritia* and *luxuria* are called plagues that like enemies overturn entire empires. After mentioning the commonplaces of Greece and Asia, he comments (34.4.3): *eo plus horreo, ne illae magis res nos ceperint quam nos illas*, 'the more I shudder at the thought that these things may have been captures us rather than we them'. Again, pleasures, and especially money, are represented as evil enemies who catch us. Of course, the whole consideration of the 'corrupting East' is anachronistic, since the Roman army did not cross into Asia until 190, while the expression with *capio* sound like a rephrasing of the famous Horatian verse *Graecia capta ferum victorem cepit*…(*Epist.* 2.1.156), which itself is likely based on an actual speech of Cato.[144]

Another aspect I would like to highlight in this speech is the allusion to social inequality induced by luxury (34.4.13):

[139] Mastrorosa (2006), 600. [140] Above, 1.1.

[141] Liv. 34.4.19–20 'do not think that matters will stand where they did before the law on this was passed. It is safer for a criminal not to be charged than to be acquitted, and extravagance (*luxuria*) left unchallenged would have been easier to bear than it will be now after it has, like a wild beast, been provoked by its shackles (*ipsis vinculis sicut ferae bestiae inritata*) and then set free.'

[142] Briscoe (1981), 50; above, 2.3.1. [143] Chaplin (2000), 100.

[144] Briscoe (1981), 51–2; below, n. 165 at 2.4.1.

> Pessimus quidem pudor est vel parsimoniae vel paupertatis: sed utrumque lex vobis demit cum id quod habere non licet non habetis.
>
> The deepest embarrassment arises over penny-pinching or lack of means, but the law removes that from you in both cases when you do not have precisely what you are not allowed to have.

In his reply, Lucius Valerius affirms that Cato's critique of *luxuria* is in line with his moral rigor (34.6.2). Valerius in his speech bases his argument on the fact that, first, there is no evidence that the eventual abrogation of the *lex Oppia* led to more *luxuria*; and, second, that this law had been promulgated in a moment of extreme poverty, with the aim of saving women—who were formerly wealthy but became poor due to the Hannibalic war—the embarrassment of going out without jewellery or precious clothing (34.6.15–16). Other statements are only superficially claims for women's rights:[145] Valerius especially points to the shame felt by their husbands at the sight of the luxury exhibited by the allies' wives, who did not suffer the same legal limitation.

Unlike Sallust, Livy does not compare the two orators, but he softens the passionate tone by simply declaring that the women's protest continued until the *Bruti*—the other archetypically rigid family in Roman history—abandoned their effort to maintain the law.

Livy is also original in many respects. First, he dates the turning point of Roman morality not to the destruction of Carthage but to Cn. Manlius Vulso's triumph over Asia in 187 BCE (39.6.7–9; cf. *Per.* 39):[146]

> Luxuriae enim peregrinae origo ab exercitu Asiatico invecta in urbem est. Ii primum lectos aeratos, vestem stragulam pretiosam, plaguals et alia textilia et, quae tum magnificae supellectilis habebantur, monopodia et abacos Romam advexerunt. 8. Tunc psaltriae sambucistriaeque et convivalia alia ludorum oblectamenta addita epulis; 9. epulae quoque ipsae et curae et sumptu maiore apparari coeptae. Tum coquus, vilissimum antiquis mancipium et aestimatione et usu, in pretio esse, et quod ministerium fuerat, ars haberi coepta. Vix tamen illa quae tum conspiciebantur, semina erant futurae luxuriae.

145 Mastrorosa (2006), 610; cf. McClintock (2022), 81–2.

146 Bringmann (2015), 404–5; Briscoe (2008), 225–6. Berti (1989), 45–7, stresses Livy's dependence on the *Annals* by L. Calpurnius Piso Frugi (who in frg. 38 *HRR* = F 9.40 *FRHist.* = Plin. *HN* 17.244 dates the turning point to 154 BCE; cf. Cornell (2013), 218); Zecchini (1982), 176–8, maintains that Livy's source is antecedent to Piso and linked to the *Scipiones*; Feldherr (1988), 42–3; Briscoe (2008), 226 also considers Valerius Antias, but states that Piso's relevance to this passage is unquestionable. According to Carey (2003), 78, who refers to Liv. 25.40.1–3 and 39.6–7, the turning point is anticipated during Marcellus' conquest of Syracuse in 211. Cf. above, 1.4. On Frugi's speaking name, Gildenhard (2020), 254–63.

> For foreign luxury was originally brought to the city by the army in Asia. These men were the first to bring to Rome bronze couches, expensive bedcovers, tapestries and other woven materials, and (things then regarded as luxurious furniture) pedestal tables and sideboards. 8. This was when girls playing harps and lutes made their appearance at dinner party together with other entertainments to amuse the guests; 9. and the dinners themselves began to be put on with greater care and expense. This was when the cook, for the ancients the lowest slave in terms of worth and utility, began to be prized, and what had been menial labor to be regarded as an art. And yet the things that began to appear in those days were barely the seeds of the luxury yet to come. (Trans. Yardley 2018)

This description encloses between two occurrences of *luxuria* a list of luxury items and behaviours, mostly involving clothing, furniture, and banquets, three objective correlatives of *luxuria*. It is interesting that this vice comes from the East with an army, which underscores the connection between military indiscipline and social decadence that we saw already in Cicero.[147] And, as is shown in 36.11.3, it had previously affected Antiochus, the Syrian king, before it infected the people who defeated him, i.e. the Romans. *Luxuria* did not come through commercial exchange, but as a poisoned spoil of a victorious army. Indeed, these are seeds (*semina*): only a tiny thing, but destined to grow enormously in Rome's future. This vice spreads its branches through all layers of society, affecting it as a whole.

A second original feature in Livy is that, while in the preface and from book 23 on he uses *luxuria* with the same meaning as Sallust, in books 2 and 3 we find more than once a meaning of *luxuria* that is quite original and closer to arrogance, something we find in Greek historiography, but is not frequent in the Latin authors that follow.[148] Indeed, a connection between *luxuria* and *superbia* was already present in Cato the Elder (above, 2.1.2) and Sallust, *Cat.* 12.2 (above, 2.3.1), and is a topic in the description of the Campanian attitude (see above). But overall it is not very frequent in Latin literature, which seems more interested in other combinations for *luxuria*, e.g. with sloth, gluttony, and especially lust.

For example, when dealing with Tarquin's death, Livy comments (2.21.5–6):

> Eo nuntio [*sc.* Tarquini mortis] erecti patres, erecta plebes; 6. sed patribus nimis luxuriosa ea fuit laetitia; plebi, cui ad eam diem summa ope inservitum erat, iniuriae a primoribus fieri coepere.
>
> These tidings cheered the Fathers and encouraged the plebs. 6. But the Fathers were too inconsiderate, in consequence of their rejoicing at this event; and the plebs, who up to this time had been most studiously deferred to, began to feel the oppression of the nobles.

[147] Above, 2.2.1. [148] Above, 1.4 and 2.1.1.

This kind of *luxuria* comes with excessive fortune, occurs more than once with *laetus/Laetitia*, and is the consequence of a loss of balance in men's fate. If life becomes too easy and happy, then, through a sort of universal empathy, the excess affects every person's psychology, making his behaviour exceed the limits of decency. We have already seen in Sallust (above, 2.3.1) that the decline of Roman morality is due not only to the wealth following the conquest of Carthage but also to peace itself, the absence of *metus hostilis*. Livy offers evidence for this. Soldiers become lazy and immoral if their licence lasts too long; human beings in general cannot handle a durable state of prosperity without losing their temper. While the risks and dangers stemming from good fortune are a commonplace in antiquity, Livy focuses on a specific aspect, especially from a lexical point of view. Arrogance was the characteristic by which Tarquin was renamed 'the Proud';[149] Roman noblemen risk falling into the same vice as their former Etruscan ruler if they exult too much in his demise.

While in the Preface and in most of his narrative Livy sticks to the connection between *luxuria*, wealth, greediness, and lust, when it comes to the archaic times, a period in which these Oriental vices had not arrived in Rome yet, he turns to a different semantic connection, that with pride. This explains why the meaning involving arrogance is mainly concentrated in a few books in Livy's first decade.[150]

2.4 Augustan Age: The Removal of *Luxuria*

In the Augustan age, we witness a sort of removal process of *luxuria*: after the tirades of Cicero and Sallust, and before those of Valerius Maximus, we find only a few occurrences of the term and of the idea itself, except for in Livy,[151] who is focused on the past. One may think that this is partly due to literary genre: epic in particular, and poetry in general, do not deal with wealth, and specifically *luxuria* is not a poetic word: we find *luxus* instead.[152] But this is not true as far as Augustan poetry is concerned: in Virgil, we find few recurrences of *luxus*,[153] while Horace, Ovid, Propertius, and Tibullus never use this word, while they sometimes use *luxuria/es*. We might have expected something more from Horace's satires and epistles, given the moralistic issues tackled in those works,[154] and also from the

[149] Liv. 1.49.1. For *superbia* in Livy, see Baraz (2008), 379–87; esp. on the relationship between *regnum* and *superbia*, Bruno (1966), 248–9.

[150] Cf. Liv. 2.21.6; 2.48.3; 3.33.2; 3.64.1. We may also add 23.12.12, where the speaking character is Hanno, a Carthaginian general.

[151] Above, 2.3.2.

[152] Cf. Lucr. 5.48, who lists *luxus desidiaeque* among human vices. This poet blames wealth and luxury at 2.20–39, stressing the fact that they do not bring us happiness or tranquillity.

[153] Verg. *G.* 3.135; *Aen.* 1.637; 4.193; 6.605. The recurrences in the *Aeneid* all refer to regal luxury. As for *luxuria*, cf. below, in this same section.

[154] As shown by Persius and Juvenal (below, 2.6.1 and 2.6.2).

detailed Ovidian accounts of women's outfits and makeup; the general impression is that of a quiet reticence on the topic, and this is easily understandable in the light of the historical context. Augustan propaganda was inconsistent in this respect: on the one hand, ancient frugality and sobriety were praised and openly proposed as role models; on the other, luxury had spread all over the Empire, was experienced by Augustan poets,[155] and was especially evident in monuments erected by Augustus himself. The Ciceronian distinction between private and public, with the justification of public luxury as magnificence,[156] was blurred during the Empire. While Horace still stands on it, Vitruvius, who speaks only of *magnificentia*, states that this distinction no longer exists.[157] Architecture is in fact an area in which *luxuria* especially manifests itself in this period.

This inconsistency leads to confused statements, such as that by Ovid's Janus, according to whom clay temples were great, but in marble and golden ones gods feel at home, too (*Fast.* 1.223–6).[158] And perhaps this is the explanation of the general reticence on *luxuria*: it was a sensitive spot for the regime. It is well known that one of the reasons Ovid was sent into exile was the poem in which he wrote *aurea sunt vere nunc saecula* (*Ars* 2.277), ironically referring to the widespread luxury of contemporary Rome.[159]

In Virgil's poems, there are few occurrences of *luxuria*, and they refer to growing plants[160] and—with an original use due to similarity in shape and vigour—to the mane and muscles of war horses;[161] it is perhaps not coincidental that the sole occurrence in the *Aeneid*, which indeed refers to a horse, is inserted in a simile between the animal and Turnus: a brave and strong warrior whose youthful exuberance leads to death. In the *Aeneid*, the more poetic and elegant term *luxus* is preferred for Dido's palace, which for Aeneas becomes a place of lust and

[155] Griffin (1985a). On the 'cultural revolution' in the Augustan era, Wallace-Hadrill (1997); also of interest Morrell/Osgood/Welsh (2019); on the Emperor's moralistic propaganda, Edwards (1993), 64–2; on sumptuary legislation in particular, Romano (2003), 21–2; below, 2.9. On the complex relationships of poetry (in particular, Ovidian poetry) and propaganda, a seminal book is Barchiesi (1994). On the specific theme of love and propaganda, with reference to the relevance of the goddess Venus at this regard, Merriam (2006), 31–56 (Propertius); 57–84 (Ovid).

[156] Above, 2.2.1.

[157] As for Horace, see below, n. 165; Vitruvius deals with the topic in 6.5.2 *bybliothecas pinacothecas basilicas non dissimili modo quam publicorum operum magnificentia <habeant> comparatas, quod in domibus eorum saepius et publica constila et privata iudicia arbitriaque conficiuntur*, on which cf. Romano (1994), esp. 69; Pollitt (1978), 164–7. Pliny the Elder challenges this distinction, too (below, 2.5.2). On *magnificentia*, see also above, 2.2.1; Berno (2019), 118–20; Gildenhard/Viglietti (2020), 72–80. Augustus notoriously put a limit on buildings' height (Strab. 5.3.7; cf. Suet. *Aug.* 89.2), and issued a sumptuary law (Suet. *Aug.* 34.1; below, 2.9).

[158] Barchiesi (1994), 218–25; Berno (2019), 222–3.

[159] A fact to which Ovid himself alludes with the verb *luxurio* (*Trist.* 5.1.43–4, quoted below, 2.4.2). Here, *luxuria* is defined as an excess of joy (*laetitia*), as is the case more than once also in Livy (above, 2.3.2). On the motif of golden age in Augustan age, Wallace-Hadrill (2004).

[160] *G.* 1.112 (*luxuries*) and 191.

[161] In *Aen.* 11.497 and *G.* 3.81, respectively.

time-wasting on his path to Italy.[162] Tibullus has no mention of *luxuria*, while Propertius makes a useless effort to prevent Cynthia from appreciating contemporary luxury.[163] Only Horace and Ovid say something more about *luxuria*, but still in a reticent way.

2.4.1 Horace's Banquet

In Horace's poetry, we find confirmation of the prejudices against the East;[164] furthermore, he blames architectural excess,[165] vanity of riches,[166] and luxury banquets, among which the most famous is that offered by Nasidienus in *Serm.* 2.8,[167] but neither the wealth, luxury, and lust attributed to populations like the Parthians or Egyptians, nor the exotic and incredible dishes offered to Maecenas by this antecedent of Petronius' Trimalchio are labelled as form of *luxuria*. Horace is evidently reluctant to use such a morally loaded term. He prefers the reader to formulate his own moral judgements rather than to receive them from the author. This is in part simply Horace's personality trait, but it is also a way for him to keep a low profile vis-à-vis his powerful friends. He is proud to offer simple banquets to his friends (e.g. *Epist.* 1.5),[168] and stresses that the doctor forbade him to go to Baiae (*Epist.* 1.15.2–3). But he also admits that he appreciates luxurious food when it is served (*Epist.* 1.15.42–6):[169] far from presenting himself as a model of frugality, he tries to balance moderation with an enjoyment of life's pleasures, and uses irony to lighten his existential contradictions.

Only four occurrences of *luxuria* are to be found in Horace, distributed in a satire and two epistles. One of them refers to stylistic choices, as the poet seeks to 'moderate exuberances' *luxuriantia compescet* (*Epist.* 2.2.122), eliminating linguistic excesses thus being a part of Horatian *labor limae*. The occurrence in

[162] *Aen.* 1.637; 4.193. This hint will be developed by Lucan with reference to Cleopatra (below, 2.8). Another occurrence (*Aen.* 6.605) refers to the loaded table which the Fury forbids the Lapiths Ixion and Pirithous to touch, as an infernal penalty.

[163] Hay (2019), 226–7; below, 2.4.3.

[164] La Bua (2013), 276 on *luxuria*. Nenci (1978), 1014, reads the famous sentence *Graecia capta ferum victorem cepit* (*Epist.* 2.1.156) as an allusion to Cato the Elder's speech against the abrogation of the *Lex Oppia* (Liv. 34.4.3), on which see above, 2.3.2 with n. 134. Generally, on moralistic language in Horace, Citroni Marchetti (1991), 100–4.

[165] E.g. in *C.* 2.15, where we find a rephrase of the Ciceronian *privata luxuria, publica magnificentia* (ll. 13–14 *privatus ills census erat brevis,/commune magnum*...); cf. Pearcy (1977), 773–5; Nisbet/ Hubbard (1978), 249–50; Romano (1991–3), 225–8; Edwards (1993), 139–40; Harrison (2017), 175–6 and 181. Cf. also *C.* 2,18; 3,1; 3.24. In general, on architectural luxury in Horace, Pearcy (1977).

[166] E.g. *C.* 2.18 and 3.24, on which Moles (2007b), 171–2.

[167] On the relevance of this satire in light of the whole second book, O'Connor (1990); Gowers (1996), 161–79; Oliensis (1997); Freudenberg (2004), 117–24. Horace focuses on excessive banquets also in *Serm.* 2.2 and 2.4; cf. Gowers (1996), 135–61.

[168] Cucchiarelli (2020), 262–3. On Horace's frugality, Davis (2007); Martino (2008), esp. 6–9; Gildenhard (2020), 295–8.

[169] Cucchiarelli (2020), 422–3.

Ars 214 also belongs to a poetic discussion, but this time refers to its performance: *sic priscae motum et luxuriem addidit arti*, 'so to the early art the flute-player added movement and display' (trans. Rushton Fairclough 1961).[170] This formulation implies the commonplace of modernity as the decline of ancient sobriety, and it also hints at the erotic meaning of the concept *luxuria* (or, as here, *luxuries*).

More interesting are the occurrences in satire 2.3. Here, the speaker is not Horace but the Stoic neophyte Damasippus, who, quoting as a source the philosopher Stertinius,[171] illustrates the Stoic paradox 'all fools are insane', referring to the things people do when subjected to a vice. Scholars agree that the Horace's insertion of a speech into a third-hand speech highlights the distance between the poet's point of view and that exposed in the satire,[172] which is set during the Saturnalia, the feast during which there was a role inversion and a suspension of reality. This literary strategy also makes the reader question the faithfulness of Damasippus' speech.[173] As required by his philosophical credo, Damasippus addresses the main Roman vices: ambition, avarice, *luxuria*[174]—here intended as prodigality—and superstition (2.3.77–81):[175]

Audire atque togam iubeo componere quisquis
ambitione mala aut argenti pallet amore,
quisquis <u>luxuria tristive superstitione</u>
<u>aut alio mentis morbo calet</u>: huc propius me,
dum doceo insanire omnis vos, ordine adite.
...Now, listen
Quietly to me, smooth out the folds
of your toga. Whoever grows unhappy
over sordid ambitions, or
out of greed for money; whoever
burns with the fever for luxury,
or miserable superstitions
or other mental aliments,
come here: draw closer to me,

170 Hooley (1997), 40.
171 According to Pseudo-Acron, he was a wandering philosopher who wrote a 120-book treatise on Stoic philosophy.
172 Castillo (1971), 153; Anderson (1982), 44–5; Bond (1987) and (1998); Freudenberg (2004), 113–17; Reckford (2009), 80–1; Sharland (2009).
173 Cf. previous n. In general, on the relevance of this setting in a satirical poem, Gowers (1996), 133–5. This setting is also meaningful in Seneca's *EM* 18 (below, 4.2); on the relationship between the two texts, Edwards (2017) (83–6 on Hor. *Serm.* 2.3).
174 Fischer (1983); Romano (1991–3), 228.
175 Fedeli (1994), 607; Yona (2018), 271, who stresses the relevance of vices related to the mismanagement of wealth.

in file, all in a row; and
I will demonstrate to you that
you're all mad: every single one of you.

(Trans. Alexander 1999)

All vices are taken into account, including love, even if it is not mentioned in this list.[176] It is interesting that *avaritia* is here meant as pure greediness, i.e. the desire to accumulate money without spending it, and is therefore not connected with *luxuria*. The section on *luxuria* opens with the example of Nomentanus, a famous prodigal who is considered a sort of prototype of this vice.[177] His enormous patrimony, hyperbolically valued at a thousand talents, is totally devoted to a sort of endless banquet in which he collects every most expensive food and thing he can imagine (ll. 224–38). Another example is that of Aesopus' son (ll. 239–42), who will return in Valerius Maximus and in Pliny: he melted a giant pearl in vinegar and drank it.[178] The third, less famous example is that of Quintus Arrius' sons (ll. 243–6), who ate nightingales for breakfast. All three examples are thus connected with banquets, a commonplace in moralistic literature, but also, we may say, a reversal of the philosophical symposium, and of the abovementioned simple dinner of Horace with his friends (*Epist.* 1.5). None of these banquets is called a *convivium*, the Latin equivalent of the Greek symposium and a sober if not strictly philosophical way of spending time with friends. Yet, as it has been long recognized, the poet does not share the speaker's position, and is especially against the Stoic rigidness supported by Damasippus. The examples are presented as a list of worn-out commonplaces, while no one could ever fit the proposed ideal model. The final trick of the satire, when Damasippus turns against Horace, and the poet finally interrupts him, recalls me of a passage in Cicero's *Pro Caelio*, where the orator first pretends to speak with the rigid and severe Appius Claudius Caecus, in order to make him blaming his descendant Clodia for her immorality (*Cael.* 33–4), and then makes him disappear: Cicero was afraid of Appius turning against his own client Caelius (*Cael.* 35).[179] This is Cicero's way to show how old-fashioned and outdated are rigid moral rules.

[176] Avarice: ll. 82–159; ambition: ll. 165–223 (but here also the accent is placed on how to handle money); prodigality: ll. 224–46; love: ll. 247–80; superstition: ll. 281–95. The list is evidently influenced by the so-called (Stoic)-Cynic diatribe: Freudenberg (1993), 84–6.

[177] This man was frequently described as *luxuriosus*, as Horace's commentator Porphyrius notes (Porph. *Ad Serm.* 2.1.22; 2.3.175). Seneca describes him along with Apicius in *De vita beata*: below, 3.2.2. On the whole section about *luxuria*, Fedeli (1994), 632–5; Yona (2018), 276–8.

[178] *RE* 4.1.67, s.v. *Clodius* 16. Cf. below, 2.5.1 (Valerius Maximus) and 2.5.2 (Pliny), with a similar example attributed to Cleopatra.

[179] Cic. *Cael.* 35 'but why, gentlemen, have I introduced a personage so austere, that I am afraid lest that same Appius should suddenly turn and begin to accuse Caelius with that severity of his befitting a censor?' (Trans. Gardner 1958). On the *Pro Caelio* cf. above, 2.2.1.

Food was the less compromising form of *luxuria* for an Augustan poet:[180] indeed, there is neither exception nor perplexity in its evaluation, which is inevitably negative. Augustus was exceptionally restrained in this regard, to the point that he used to participate in banquets without eating anything (Suet. *Aug.* 76.1–2). Horace carefully avoided any delicate subject, such as architecture, private wealth, and even individual outfits, given the care that e.g. his powerful friend Maecenas notoriously put into his attire.[181] He focuses his critique on subjects on which everyone would agree. Furthermore, it is not *his* critique, but Damasippus', who in turn is not a proper philosopher, but is himself repeating the lessons of a not-so-famous philosopher. This distances the speech from Horace, as also seen in the fact that the speaker charges the poet with all vices, including spending beyond his means (ll. 323–4... *cultum/maiorem censu*...). We may say that Horace expresses well the reticence of his age towards *luxuria*.

2.4.2 Ovid's Reticence

In Ovid's entire production, we find fewer than twenty occurrences of *luxuria*. Of course, this is largely due to its being labelled as moralistic, an attitude that does not apply to this poet, even if his personal concern for moderation, a key ethical concept and the very opposite of *luxuria*, is undeniable.[182] Many occurrences refer to plants or animal growth,[183] as in Virgil, with a peculiar use related to muscles (also in Virgil),[184] one reference to excessive fertility as a disease—an observation to which Pliny will pay much attention[185]—one to sheep playing on the grass in springtime,[186] and one disturbing reference to Trojan ground fed by Phrygian blood in Penelope's account.[187]

Penelope offers an interesting description of the suitors who come after her (*Heroid.* 1.87–9):[188]

Dulichii Samiiquie et quod tulit alta Zacynthos,
turba ruunt in me luxuriosa proci;
inque tua regnant nulli prohibentis aula.

The men of Dulichios and Samos, and they whom high Zacynthus bore—a wanton throng—come pressing about me, suing for my hand. In our own hall they are masters, with none to say them nay. (Trans. Showerman 1977, here and below)

180 As we shall see (below, 2.6.2), Juvenal makes the same connection, but in a different context.
181 Griffin (1985a), 22. See e.g. Seneca's description in this regard (below, 4.6).
182 Gibson (2006). 183 E.g. *Met.* 14.629.
184 E.g. *Met.* 7.292; 9.266–7; cf. above, n. 161.
185 *Fast.* 1.689–90; for Pliny, below, 2.5.2. See also *Fast.* 4.644.
186 *Fast.* 1.156 *ludit et in pratis luxuriatque pecus.*
187 *Heroid.* 1.54 *luxuriat Phrygio sanguine pinguis humus*; cf. *Ars* 1.360 *ut seges in pingui luxuriabit humo*; below, 2.7.1.
188 Barchiesi (1992), 95, who notes how *luxuriosus* does not recur in poetry before Ovid.

Here, given the prodigality and lust that characterize these men, we may note that the economic and erotic meanings of the word coincide perfectly, but with the accent on the latter through the expression *ruunt in me* (l. 88), whose erotic implication is clear. The economic meaning is implied by the following line, with its reference to their rule.

A meaning linked to luxury is conversely present in Paris' speech to Helen, when the Trojan prince seduces the queen of Sparta, saying (*Heroid.* 16.193–4):

> Hanc faciem largis sine fine paratibus uti
> deliciisque decet luxuriare novis.

Beauty like yours it benefits to enjoy rich adornment without end, and to wanton in ever new delights.

Sparta's sobriety does not fit Helen's beauty and charm; Eastern luxuries and pleasures are more suitable for her. Here we find the term *deliciae*, which as we have seen is typical of Imperial literature when coupled with *luxuria*, and an ironic reference—given the fact that it is Paris who speaks—to the prejudice of *luxuria* as a vice from the East. Another prejudice, the link between wealth and *luxuria*, is implied in *Rem.* 745–6:[189]

> Cnosida fecisses inopem, sapienter amasset
> divitiis alitur luxuriosus amor.

Hadst thou made the Cnosian poor, she had loved wisely: wanton love is fed of riches. (Trans. Mozley 1979)

In this case, Pasifae's perverse love for a bull is read as due to her being an affluent queen: here as well the two semantic areas of the word overlap.[190]

Another occurrence, in *Ars Amatoria*, goes away from the commonplaces of lyric poetry (2.437–8):[191]

> Luxuriant animi rebus plerumque secundis
> nec facile est aequa commoda mente pati.

Often pride waxes in prosperity, nor is it easy to bear good fortune with equal mind. (Trans. Mozley 1979)

In this case, as more than once in Livy,[192] we find *luxuria* as an excessive reaction to good fortune, which risks becoming a self-destructive attitude.

Yet Ovid was perfectly aware of the erotic meaning of the word, as he shows in his lamentations from exile (*Trist.* 5.1.43–4):

[189] Pinotti (1988), 312–14; Lazzarini (2018), 171; Rimell (2022), 338–9.
[190] Berno (2021a), 28–9. [191] Janka (1997), 331. [192] Above, 2.3.2.

Nec tamen ut lusit, rursus mea littera ludit
sit semel illa malo luxuriata meo.

Yet no writings of mine shall again wanton as once they wantoned: let them have rioted with my jests but once! (Trans. Wheeler 1988)

The commonplace of poetry's lasciviousness, which does not affect the poet's morality, is already present in Catullus (c. 16) and Martial, who also uses *luxuria* in this context.[193] Here it is expressed with the verbs *ludo* and *luxurio*, which are evidently used synonymously: the former identifies the *Ars amatoria* as the cause of his exile, while the latter is described as a sort of overgrown plant that suffocated its owner. Ovid uses participles in a way that is unknown in Republican Latin and typical of declamations.[194]

The more interesting occurrences of *luxuria* in Ovid are to be found in the *Fasti*, and they all point to a compromise: praising archaic frugality and at the same time justifying contemporary magnificence. In book 5, Flora exposes the *aition* of the *Ludi florales* with the fines imposed on noblemen who expropriated lands belonging to the poor. While narrating this event, she states that 'the other modes of luxury did not yet flourish' (*Fast.* 5.279 *cetera luxuriae nondum instrumenta vigebant*, trans. Boyle/Woodward 2000, here and below). *Instrumenta luxuriae* is a Sallustian allusion (*Cat.* 25.2; above, 2.3.1), but more interesting is the fact that the archaic world is here represented as far from flawless: even if *luxuria* was not yet fully present, avarice was still ubiquitous and led to abuse. The other two occurrences of the term *luxuria* are both in book 6, where we find a reference to the Italic goddess Carna, protector of hinges, who, being archaic, does not like rich banquets (*Fast.* 6.172 *luxuriosae dapes*), and a famous passage in which Augustus is presented in the act of razing Vedius Pollio's house, who was guilty of luxury, in order to build a magnificent public porch dedicated by his wife Livia (6.637–44):[195]

Te quoque magnifica, Concordia, dedicat aede
Livia, quam caro praestitit ipsa viro.
Disce tamen, veniens aetas, ubi Livia nunc est
porticus, immensae tecta fuere domus;
urbis opus domus una fuit, spatiumque tenebat,
quo brevius muris oppida multa tenent.
Haec aequata solo est, nullo sub crimine regni,
sed quia luxuria visa nocere sua.
You, Concordia, too, were magnificently enshrined

[193] Mart. 1.4.8; cf. below, 2.5.3. [194] Below, 2.7.1.
[195] Frazer (1929), 304–5; Bömer (1958), 379; Littlewood (2006), 186–91; Roller (2013), 126–9; Berno (2019).

by Livia, who pledged you to a dear husband.
Posterity, Learn. Where the Porticus Liviae is now
was once covered by a massive house.
than one house was a city's labour, and occupied
greater space than the walls of many towns.
It was levelled to the ground, not for someone's attempt
at the throne, but for harmful luxury.

In this case, the relationship between *magnificentia* and *luxuria* is similar to that established by Cicero in *Pro Murena* 76:[196] magnificence is allowed or even desired if it is public and thus for all Romans, whereas it turns into a vice if enjoyed privately. But the boundaries between private and public, licit and illicit, are blurred at a time in which the whole Empire was ruled by a single man, who had a temple in his own house, which Vitruvius' suggestions about noble houses confirm.[197] Ovid's concern, aimed at praising Augustus for his traditional morality, seems to be unsuitable for his time.

2.4.3 Propertius, the Old-Fashioned Elegiac

Propertius is a sort of exception in the Augustan age. Considering the general silence on but actual practice of *luxuria*, he pays much attention to it, mentioning it four times, always in a moralistic sense and with one motif: the resistance of good girls against seduction by money, that is, expensive gifts, luxury villas, and so on. It is well known that the elegiac world recreates, even if in an immoral context—that of free love and illicit relationships—the essence of Roman values, such as loyalty, earnestness, and so on. This is true also for the ideal girl, who should have the moral strength of a Roman *matrona*: exclusive fidelity to her lover, lonely nights without him spent knitting, and so on.[198] The rarity of such loyalty, and the consequent disadvantage for the poor poet, is evident. He therefore exhorts the girl not to let herself be seduced by richer men's gifts, and to be satisfied with poems (1.2.31–2):

His tu semper eris nostrae gratissima vitae,
  taedia dum miserae sint tibi luxuriae.
For these, while I'm alive, you will always be most dear
so long as you've not taste for wretched finery.
(Trans. Lee 1994, here and below)

196 Above, 2.2.1. On this motive, La Penna (1989), 18–25 (18–19 on Horace).
197 Above, 2.4.
198 With specific reference to Rome, Fantham (1997b).

The good girl should be disgusted by luxury items: yet the whole poem, with a list of fancy dresses and jewels to which she is attracted, shows the opposite.[199]

Another poem presents a speaking door, modelled after Catullus 67,[200] which laments the decline of morality and is forced to see the vice of the time, *saeculi luxuria* (1.16.12). This poem is even closer to Sallust's tirades than what we find in Livy. Again, in 3.12.18 Rome is defined as *luxuriae magistra suae*:[201] no longer a victim of Eastern vices, but a master herself, the capital of the Empire corrupts the moral integrity of small and rural villages. The west/east macroscopic opposition finds correspondence in the small-scale countryside/town dichotomy.[202] This attitude matches Augustan propaganda and its eulogy for the traditional old habits of the Romans as farmers and soldiers.

Finally, in 3.13.1, Propertius blames greedy (*avidae*) girls, pointing at Rome as the cause of their vice (3.13.3–4):[203]

> Certa quidem tantis causa et manifesta ruinis:
> luxuriae nimium libera facta viast.
> The cause of such disasters is clear beyond a doubt:
> the road to luxury is too wide-open.

A list of luxury items follows, as well as the comment on the total lack of moderation (l. 13 *reverentia*) in requesting and giving expensive gifts. This leads the poet to an ominous prophecy (l. 60): *frangitur ipsa suis Roma superba bonis*, 'proud Rome is rotten with her own prosperity'. This sentence recalls Livy's preface, which stressed the connection between luxury, wealth, pride, and disgrace,[204] and it surely sounds out of place in a love elegy. Propertius reveals himself to be a more moralistic and traditional Augustan poet, with classic associations between *luxuria* and moral decline. This attitude perhaps granted him, despite the licentiousness of his poetry, the Emperor's benevolence, while the more sincere and ingenuous Ovid was not as lucky.

[199] Curran (1975); Fedeli (1980), 88–91; Baker (1990), 75; Fedeli (2021), 206. After her death, Cynthia's ghost appears to Propertius and laments the lack of luxury in her funeral (4.7.32–4).

[200] On the commonplace link to the motif of *paraklausythyron*, see MacKay (1956); Fedeli (1980), 363–7.

[201] Heyworth/Morwood (2011), 225, who point to 3.5.3–6 and 3.7, both against greediness.

[202] Above, 1.4.

[203] On Propertius' critique of *avaritia* in this poem, see Fedeli (1985), 414–15; Heyworth/Morwood (2011), 230–4, who stress the diatribic tone of the poem (cf. prev. note) Fedeli (2022), 224–5.

[204] Above, 2.3.2.

2.5 *Luxuria*'s Exemplarity: Valerius Maximus and Pliny (with Martial)

In the first century of the Roman Empire, *luxuria* was a widespread and well-known vice, and there were many historical examples fixed by a tradition going back at least to Cicero. The debate about when the decline began was gradually replaced by a sort of contest of vice, where examples of ever more extreme and unacceptable behaviours were put forth. We find something of this already in Horace, subsequently in Seneca and in the satirical tradition.[205] But it is in Valerius Maximus and Pliny that this new tendency is most fully developed, due to the very nature of their works.

2.5.1 Valerius Maximus: When *Luxuria* Meets Lust

The works of Valerius Maximus, traditionally dated to the reign of Tiberius (14–31 CE), is a very lengthy collection of examples of virtue and vices, a sort of handbook or encyclopaedia for when someone needs to enrich his work—a speech, a philosophical essay, and so on—with historical examples on a specific subject. But it also has a political aim in that it constructs a system of moral values for Roman noblemen,[206] with local examples being followed by foreign ones. One chapter is devoted to *Luxuria et libidine* (9.1);[207] it lists nine Roman and seven non-Roman examples. Right from the start, it associates these two vices, which of course anticipates the move from the former to the latter in Christian authors. Valerius clearly explains this association (9.1.*init.*):

> Blandum etiam malum luxuria, quam accusare aliquanto facilius est quam vitare, operi nostro inseratur, non quidem ut ullum honorem recipiat, sed ut se ipsa recognoscens ad paenitentiam impelli possit. Iungatur illi libido, quoniam ex isdem vitiorum principiis oritur, neque aut a reprehensione aut ab emendatione separentur, gemino mentis errore conexae.
>
> Let luxury, that cozening evil, which is somewhat more easily denounced than avoided, be introduced into our work, not to receive any honour but so that recognizing herself she may perhaps be impelled to repentance. Let Lust be joined to her, since she arises from the same vicious origins, and let them not be separated either by way of blame or by way of amendment, connected as they are by a twin psychic error. (Trans. Shackleton Bailey 2000, here and below)

[205] Above, 2.4.1; below, 2.6 and 4.1.
[206] Skidmore (1996), 53–82 (80–1 on 9.1.*init.*); Coudry (1998); Lehmann (1998).
[207] As for lust, cf. Langlands (2006), 123–91.

First, Valerius acknowledges the relevance of *luxuria*, despite its softness (*blandum... malum*): he is evidently thinking more about violent and scary vices like anger, pride, cruelty, and so on. The allusion to repentance (*paenitentia*) is perhaps enriched with a religious nuance.[208] It is noteworthy that, as opposed to Pliny later on,[209] Valerius does not stress the role historiographers ascribe to *luxuria* in the decline of Roman society, a decline at which he only hints.[210] Indeed, as we shall see, he describes this process only regarding foreign countries, all Eastern, and in a Roman context mentions only a few particular examples. *Luxuria*'s relevance is due to its pervasiveness, and its being connected with *libido*, 'lust'. The two vices in fact share the same origin (*principia*) in that they come from the same 'error of the mind' (*mentis error*). This expression may allude to Stoic doctrine, according to which vices are provoked by a mistake in judgement: we are persuaded by appearances and so choose the wrong action, whence the idea of vices as errors of the mind (above, 1.2). And, Valerius states, *luxuria* and lust derive from an almost identical (*geminus*) error. This error is to be seduced by something's or someone's appearances, and to desire this thing or person so much that one will do anything for it. The desire is never quenched but only relit by conquest, and so one is stuck in an endless chain of eagerness.[211]

I find it interesting that, while Sallust states that *luxuria* and *avaritia* only appear contradictory but are in fact related to each other, since a desire for luxury implies a desire for money,[212] Valerius makes a different kind of association. While Sallust considers the consequences of these vices, implying a significant overlap between the two, Valerius considers the causes of *luxuria* and lust, and thereby identifies a common cause, namely improper reasoning, an incorrect choice. This para-philosophical preface is quite original in Valerius' work: he always presents his subject and explains why he treats it, but there are only a few times where he couples two virtues or two vices, and his motivations are generally grounded in aims (e.g. 5.1.1, on mildness and clemency), similarity of expression (9.3, on anger and hatred), or social consequences (4.3, on abstinence and continence),[213] but never in their psychological roots.

Of the nine Roman examples, none is original: we find most of them in Livy or Cicero, and they return in Seneca, Pliny, and Macrobius. Still, Valerius' list merits consideration. Let us present an overview of the characters and subjects: three examples focus on luxury banquets and similar matters (9.1.1: Sergius Orata; 9.1.2: the son of the tragic actor Aesopus; 9.1.5: Metellus Pius);[214] one is the episode also

[208] Müller (2002), 168–9. [209] Below, 2.5.2.

[210] See 9.1.3 *urbi autem nostrae secundi Punici belli finis et Philippi Macedoniae rex devictus licentioris vitae fiduciam dedit.*

[211] See above, 1.1. Seneca will explicate this theory in detail (below, 4.1). [212] Above, 2.3.1.

[213] Why he deals with the associations in 9.5 (pride and despotism) and 9.7 (violence and sedition) is not specifically explained.

[214] Sergius Orata (*c.* 140–91 BCE) has already been mentioned by Cicero (e.g. *Fin.* 2.63) and will be used also by Pliny (*HN* 9.168). See Citroni Marchetti (1991), 111 and Bannon (2014), 178–80 on

narrated by Livy of the abrogation of a sumptuary law, the *lex Oppia* (9.1.3); one is related to a house (9.1.4: Lucius Crassus in competition with Gnaeus Domitius); one concerns prodigality (9.1.6: Curio's family); and three deal with lust (9.1.7: Clodius; 9.1.8: Gemellus; 9.1.9: Catiline).[215] The seven foreign examples are even less original than the Roman ones; all of them concern the decline of armies and reigns due to a combination of these vices:[216] Hannibal and the *Campana luxuria* (9.1.*ext.*1); the Etruscan town of Volsini (9.1.*ext.*2); Xerxes, king of Persia (9.1.*ext.*3); Antiochus, king of Syria (9.1.*ext.*4); Ptolomaeus, pharaon of Egypt, and his subjects (9.1.*ext.*5–6); and the Cyprian people (9.1.*ext.*7).

For the Roman examples, we may observe that Valerius deals exclusively with the Republic, and especially late Republic: the period of Cicero and Sallust, the century in which the moral crisis led to a fatal and irreversible political outcome. The lack of examples from the Empire, which surely were available, is explainable through Valerius' fear of irritating the Emperor.

Valerius considers all the main categories traditionally used to exemplify *luxuria*: houses, banquets, various expenses. We may find substantial overlaps among these. For example, Orata's banquets are made possible by his luxurious house, from whose windows he can catch any kind of fish or mussel (9.1.1). Lust also overlaps with these issues, such as when Clodius' incest with his sisters remains unpunished because of the bribery of the judges, who were evidently greedy and immoral (9.1.7). These overlaps demonstrate that the two vices often coexist.

Another significant trait in Valerius' examples is the observation of decline in single families, from one generation to the next: this happens to Aesopus' (9.1.2) and Curio's (9.1.6) families, but is also alluded regarding Metellus Pius (9.1.5), where the fathers' sobriety was replaced by the dreadful prodigality of the sons, who spent all their money and were overwhelmed by debt. The story has something in common with Plautus' account in the prologue of the *Trinummus*,[217] and of course it is inspired by many statements of Cicero's, who blamed the nobility for its moral decline. But Cicero aims to find fresh and morally stronger forces in the equestrian class, as it happens in the speeches *Pro Murena* and *Pro Caelio* (above, 2.2.1), while Valerius' reasoning is more general, including such diverse groups as actors and noblemen. The decline comes across as unstoppable, since

Valerius Maximus; the actor Aesopus was a contemporary of Cicero, and his son's debauchery has already been mentioned in Hor. *Serm.* 2.3.239–42 (above, 2.4.1), and will return in Pliny the Elder (*HN* 10.142): Citroni Marchetti (1991), 111–12; below, 2.5.2; Metellus Pius (*c.* 130–64 BCE) has been quoted by Cic. *Arch.* 26; cf. Plut. *Pomp.* 18; *Sert.* 22; Macr. *Sat.* 3.13.6.

[215] As for Lucius Crassus (second to first century BCE), cf. Plin. *HN* 17.6; 36.3; we find a detailed description of C. Scribonius Curio's main expense, a wooden theatre with overturning scenes, in Plin. *HN* 36.116–20, who also alludes to his bankruptcy: Schultze (2007); Cicero frequently deals with Clodius' immorality (e.g. in *Att.* 1.16.5; cf. also Sen. *EM* 97.2–5, with Torre (2021)). We do not have other sources about Gemellus (first century BCE), while Catilina is a very frequent example, especially in Sallust (above, 2.3.1).

[216] Vice is thus considered a consequence of bad *otium* (cf. above, 2.3.1): cf. André (1965), 300–8.

[217] Above, 2.1.1.

not even the most important example in life, one's father, succeeds in keeping sons from falling into vices. Considerations such as this seem to negate the very purpose of Valerius' work: if living examples are useless, what can be the point of historical or literary ones? The widespread pessimism of Roman writers is further indicated in passages like this (9.1.5):

> Patet igitur quam celeri transitu luxuria affluxerit: nam cuius adulescentia priscos mores vidit, senectus novos orsa est.
>
> Thus it is evident with how swift a passage luxury flowed int: his youth saw the old morals, his old age began the new.

This is a clear allusion to Sallust's arguments,[218] except that Valerius employs, instead of military images, the idea of a flood: the verb *affluo* and the reference to rapidity (*celeri transitu*) express a metaphor of *luxuria* as a flooding and uncontrollable river. Again, as in Livy,[219] we find the idea of this vice as a fatal and overwhelming force, against which nothing is effective.

The foreign examples are all of Eastern origin, in line with the prejudice that *luxuria* is a vice coming from the East. In the same vein, they are all related to absolute power or tyranny, and to irreversible decline, as their premise shows (9.1.5 *quarum* [*sc. Graeciae et Asiae*] *luxuria severitas ipsa corrumpi poterat*, 'Greece and Asia, whose luxury could corrupt Austerity herself'). *Severitas*, as the devoted chapters show (5.8 and 9.3), is an idea of gravity taken to an excess, so it places itself at the extreme opposite to *luxuria* in an ideal ethical line which would go from rigidness to softness.[220]

The Hannibalic example is clearly modelled after Livy (above, 2.3.2), as its opening shows: 9.1.*ext.*1 *Campana luxuria*... The other examples are also very famous; in each case, the two vices are completely melded together, and often defined as *deliciae* (9.1.*ext.*3 and 6; cf. 9.1.*ext.*7 *delicatus*), one of *luxuria*'s most frequent manifestations in Imperial prose literature[221] and involving any kind of illicit pleasure. Another characteristic of foreign examples is the reference to effeminacy (9.1.*ext.*6–7). In almost most cases, vices are directly connected with decline and defeat of a ruler, and consequently of his country (9.1.*ext.*1–4), and the populations appear only as passive observants of their king's orders and behaviour. The ruler's vices fatally affect his people.

[218] On Sallust as a source for Valerius' chapter 9.1, see Bloomer (1992), 112, Jacquemin (1998), 106–7, and especially Guerrini (1979), 158–66, who notes many lexical and thematic affinities and stresses in particular (158–9) that the example of Metellus Pius in 9.1.5 comes from Sall. *Hist.* frg. 2.59 McG. (= 2.70 M. = Macr. *Sat.* 3.17.7–9). That of Catiline is of course modelled after Sall. *Cat.* 15.2.

[219] Above, 2.3.2.

[220] Cf. below, 2.5.2 (Pliny the Elder) and 2.7.2 (Quintilian).

[221] Above, 1.3.

As for the virtues that Valerius opposes to these vices and that are almost always defeated, we do not find sobriety or frugality among them, but a more generic term: *continentia* 'repression' (9.1.3–4).[222] It is precisely in the chapter on *abstinentia* and *continentia* (4.3) that we find examples of victories over *luxuria* and *libido*, although Valerius says *avaritia* and *libido* (4.3.*init.*1):

> Magna cura praecipuoque studio referendum est quantopere libidinis et avaritiae furori similis impetus ab inlustrium virorum pectoribus consilio ac ratione summoti sint, quia ii demum penates, ea civitas, id regnum aeterno in gradu facile steterit, ubi minimum virium veneris pecuniaeque cupido sibi vindicaverit.
>
> With much care and special zeal must we relate how effectively the onsets of lust and greed, resembling madness, have been repelled by good sense and reason from the hearts of famous men. For a household or a community or a kingdom will hold his ground easily and for all time where and only where the desire for carnal pleasure and for money asserts for itself a minimum of strength.

It is indeed of interest that *luxuria* is not mentioned here. We may say that Valerius considered this all-encompassing term too great, and did not find any virtue capable of fighting it.

Both *abstinentia* 'restraint' and *continentia* are not that frequent in Latin literature, which prefers more specific terms, such as *pudor/pudicitia* and *frugalitas*. The latter is not absent from Valerius (see 4.3.7 and 11). The former is the subject of ch. 6.1, but its specificity to women makes it almost useless in ch. 9.1.[223] These virtues never achieve the relevance and effectiveness of *luxuria*, as can be seen in the various authors.

In the chapter *De abstinentia et continentia*, there are fourteen Roman examples, of which three focus on lust and eleven on frugality. There are only four foreign examples, all Greek, but they include the most famous one of all, namely Diogenes the Cynic, whom Alexander the Great was not able to conquer despite offering him everything he could desire (4.3.*ext.*4; cf. below, 3.3.2). It is perhaps of interest that most Roman examples belong to the third and second century BCE, the ideal time of the Roman Republic, according to Cicero, which comes right before the fatal introduction of *luxuria*, as the first-century BCE examples show. And so Valerius' view of the golden age of the Republic was in my opinion not coincidental, since it was the same as in Cicero, that is, the age of the Scipios. Yet this was also an age of imminent or triggered decline.

[222] Cf. Gildenhard (2020), 298–301; Langlands (2006), cited above, n. 207.

[223] On *pudicitia* in Valerius Maximus, Müller (2002), 21–32; 44–55.

2.5.2 Pliny the Elder and the Phenomenology of *Luxuria*

In Pliny the Elder's encyclopaedic work *Historia naturalis*, moralistic considerations about vices are widespread, with special emphasis on those involving excessive expenses and luxury in general.[224] His concern for ethical issues are well suited to Flavian politics, showing a certain degree of ambiguity in the reuse of traditional motives of frugality, juxtaposed with the celebration of internationality and the absolute power of Imperial Rome.[225] We may say that Pliny offers a sort of phenomenology of *luxuria*, in that he discusses its causes and nature, but not its manifestations. He devotes this aetiology especially to the motif of the *primus inventor*, the first one who, for example, used golden cutlery. Pliny does not neglect secondary issues such as the cost and eventual economic benefits of such inventions.[226] *Luxuria* in fact plays a primary role in the production of wonders, *mirabilia*,[227] which constitute the author's main interest. There are of course the usual manifestations of this vice—banquets, buildings, expensive clothing, and jewellery, along with new historical examples, also from the Imperial Age, especially from Apicius. But some emperors also serve as examples, with Tiberius as an example of frugality and Nero of its opposite.[228] The well-known story of *luxuria* coming from the East due to the conquest of Asia and Carthage is repeated too, with less attention paid to the military aspects, and with a special focus on Pompey and his triumphs as major examples of this vice. As for the distinction between public magnificence and private luxury, Pliny challenges the positive evaluation of the former, stating that public opulence instils in men the desire to have the same for private use.[229]

There are two distinct features to Pliny's treatment. First, *luxuria* is expressed particularly in compounds:[230] making furniture, jewels, and dresses of multiple materials (wood and ivory, pearls and gems)[231] or colours (purple and gold, and so on). These are the habits constantly labelled as manifestations of this vice, habits that are not satisfied with a single, even if expensive, material. Having, say, silver trays is not enough to be *luxuriosus*. They must be silver golden-plated, and so on. This shows that the kind of 'simple' luxury that would have been deplored

[224] Wallace-Hadrill (1990), esp. 85–90; Isager (1998), esp. 52–5; Naas (2002), 97; Beagon (2005), 11–13; Citroni Marchetti (1991) and (2011).

[225] Citroni Marchetti (1991), 73; 175–9; 224–9; 272.

[226] Naas (2002), 436–8; Lao (2011).

[227] Carey (2003), 75–102; cf. Naas (2011).

[228] On Nero, Beagon (1992), 17–18; below, 5.2.1 and 5.2.2. Among historical examples we may also count the northern barbarians who have been corrupted by Roman *luxuria* (*HN* 6.88–9), a theme that Tacitus will treat in his *Germania* (below, 5.2.2).

[229] Plin. *HN* 36.5 *sed publicis nimirum indulgentes voluptatibus. Id ipsum cur? Aut qua magis via inrepunt vitia quam publica? Quo enim alio modo in privatos usus venere ebora, aurum, gemmae? Aut quid omnino diis reliquimus?*

[230] Wallace-Hadrill (1990), 87; Beagon (1992), 75–9.

[231] Isager (1998), 212–20; Weeber (2015), 131–6.

during the Republic was so common in Pliny's day as to be non-luxurious. Pliny's insistence on the mixing and variety of Imperial *luxuria* is the objective correlative of the restless nature of *luxuria* that especially Seneca discusses, stemming from an unsatisfied desire.[232] There is another, related aspect, where *luxuria* is not the simple accumulation and exhibition of money—*avaritia*—and does not focus on precious and durable things such as silver and gold, but on fragile things[233] such as decorated glasses, or even on things that were previously considered humble, such as objects made of earthenware,[234] but that by their contemporary rarity and complexity of processing have become the ultimate kind of luxury. This demonstrates how extreme the vice is, and how its struggle for ever newer pleasures finally reverses the very idea of luxury. This aspect did not appear in Republican accounts of *luxuria.*

A second key element in Pliny's exposition is that he does not ignore the positive meaning of *luxuria*, which involves the fertility of nature and the proliferation of life.[235] Yet this meaning also implies negative consequences: as Pliny often repeats, nature's abundance must be ruled and moderated; if it is not, plants are going to be corrupted and die.

It is also worth noting the absence in Pliny of the erotic meaning of *luxuria*, which we have seen e.g. in Valerius Maximus. It seems that Pliny's use of the word is old-fashioned (although, like Valerius, he sometimes uses *deliciae* in association with *luxuria*, as is common in the Empire), while his references to concrete things and habits are perfectly modern.

The relevance of *luxuria* emerges from *HN* 1, where we find the index of the encyclopaedia: this vice is the only one explicitly mentioned, with five occurrences, regarding shells (1.9), ointments (1.13), silver vases (1.33), marble (1.36),[236] and glass (1.37). This interest is confirmed by the number of recurrences in the treatise, which largely correspond to the listed subjects,[237] with some further specifics: ebony (8.7; 12.5, where it is stressed that it has replaced wood in furniture making), silk (11.76), and turtle shells (9.39)—three expensive, exotic, and vaguely disturbing materials. Indeed, Pliny emphasizes the oddity of considering precious some wild animal's teeth or bones, or a textile made by a sort of spiders.

232 Below, 4.1; Citroni Marchetti (1991), 201–9.

233 Citroni Marchetti (1991), 236–8.

234 Isager (1998), 142–3.

235 Wallace-Hadrill (1990), 88–9. See above, 2.4.2 (Ovid, and more generally Augustan age).

236 Isager (1998), 144–7 and 183–7.

237 Shells, especially as regards pearls (*HN* 9.104; 9.114; 9.119–22; 9.139–40; see below), ointments (12.82; 13.1; 13.20; also 15.19), marble (36.44; 36.51; 36.125), glass (33.5; 36.114). This is less true for silver vases, which are often mentioned but without any particular comments on *luxuria*; there is a condemnation of mines (2.158) as a perverse source aimed at satisfying a perverse taste. Cf. above, 1.4 with n. 56.

Luxuria is first of all a human specific. Of crucial importance is a passage in book 7, where Pliny deals with human beings. He lists the differences between men and animals, with advantage to the latter because of human vice (7.5):[238]

> Uni animantium luctus est datus, uni luxuria et quidem innumerabilibus modis ac per singula membra, uni ambitio, uni avaritia, uni inmensa vivendi cupido, uni superstitio, uni sepulturae cura atque etiam post se de futuro. Nulli vita fragilior, nulli rerum omnium libido maior, nulli pavor confusior, nulli rabies acrior.
>
> To man alone in the animal kingdom is granted the capacity for sorrow, for self-indulgence of every kind and in every part of his body, for ambition, avarice, unbounded appetite for life and superstition; for anxiety over burial and even over what will happen after he is dead. To no animal is assigned a more precarious life, more all-consuming passions, more disruptive fear, or more violent anger. (Trans. Beagon 2005)

In this list of human flaws, which are exclusive of humans as much as rationality, *luxuria* takes second place after grief, and precedes *ambitio* and *avaritia*, the two vices that Sallust combined with it. But *luxuria*'s relative primacy is clear not only from its position but also from the specification: *innumerabilibus modis ac per singula membra*, 'of every kind and in every part of his body'. This original definition emphasizes the desire for variety that is typical of this vice and that has been already witnessed by Seneca (below, 4.3), as well as the fact that it may apply to every body part and to all five senses. Both gluttony and lust are thereby included (even if, as I have already stated, lust is not a major issue in the *HN*), but also more delicate pleasures, such as fine fragrances.

Another striking element in Pliny's list is the insistence on two key ideas, both implied in the very term *luxuria*: that of desire—*luxuria*, *cupido*, *libido* are all related to this semantic field—and that of excess, as shown by the frequency of comparatives and of adjectives that exclude measurability (*in-numerabilis*, *in-mensa*). The entire passage seems to deal with *luxuria*.

A major expression of *luxuria* is, of course, the banquet, which appears frequently in *HN*. There are several references to luxury banquets,[239] especially to macabre foods (8.10: elephant's trunks, eaten to simulate the consumption of ivory), exotic fish (31.95 and 32.144), and ice beverages (32.64), but the main treatment of banquets is in book 9, which is devoted to sea animals and thus demonstrates that fish dishes were the latest fashion at that time, unlike twenty years earlier, in Petronius' work, where Trimalchio offers a luxurious dinner with almost no fish. Roman conquests have led to a magic world of amazing creatures

[238] Beagon (2005), 113–14. See also Vegetti (1982).
[239] *HN* 26.43.

and things for satisfying one's desire for novelty. Book 9 also contains a peculiar concentration of terms related to money,[240] luxury, and *luxuria*, as passages quoted in this section will show.

A peculiar example of a luxury banquet is that of the Hyperborei, a legendary people said to live in the extreme north of the earth. The elderly there commit suicide when they are tired of life (4.89):

> Mors non nisi satietate vitae epulatis delibutoque senio luxu e quadam rupe in mare salienti<b>u<s>; hoc genus sepulturae beatissimum.
>
> Death come to them only when, owing to satiety of life, after holding a banquet and anointing their old age with luxury, they leap from a certain rock into the sea: this mode of burial is the most blissful. (Trans. Rackham 1961a, here and below)

This people represent a living example of the Epicurean metaphor of life as a banquet, to be lived peacefully through satiety. When they judge their life complete, they celebrate it and then jump off a cliff.[241] Pliny states that they do not suffer disease or harm, and that the climate of their land is ideal; they simply have enough of life. There is no negative moral judgement here, but rather a sort of admiration. In this case, a luxury banquet—and here the morally charged word *luxuria* is absent, yielding to the more objective term *luxus*—is the fitting celebration of the end of a serene and satisfied life.

The first great example of luxury banquet is that of Apicius, the well-known hedonist of the Augustan age who was so famous for his banquets as to be identified as the author of a luxury recipe collection. He would become the quintessence of gluttony. His triumph is celebrated in *HN* 9.66–8:[242]

> Mullum expirantem versicolori quadam et numerosa varietate spectari proceres gulae narrant, rubentium squamarum multiplici mutatione pallescentem, utique si vitro spectetur inclusus. M. Apicius, ad omne luxus ingenium natus, in sociorum garo—nam ea quoque res cognomen invenit—necari eos praecellens putavit atque e iecore eorum allecem excogitare. 67. Provocavit—id enim est facilius dixisse quam quis vicerit—Asinius Celer e consularibus hoc pisce prodigos omnes Gaio principe unum mercatus HS VIII mullum. Quae reputatio aufert traversum animum ad contemplationem eorum, qui in conquestione luxus coquos emi singulos pluris quam equos quiritabant. At nunc coco trium horum pretiis parantur et coquorum pisces, nullusque prope iam mortalis aestimatur pluris quam qui peritissime censum domini mergit. 68. Mullum LXXX librarum

[240] Citroni Marchetti (2011), 180.
[241] Berno (2008), 561–2.
[242] Citroni Marchetti (1991), 215–16.

> in mari Rubro captum Licinius Mucianus prodidit, quanti mercatura eum luxuria suburbanis litoribus inventum?
>
> The leaders in gastronomy say that a dying mullet shows a large variety of changing colours, turning pale with a complicated modification of blushing scales, at all events if it is looked at when contained in a glass bowl. Marcus Apicius, who had a natural gift for every ingenuity of luxury, thought it specially desirable for mullets to be killed in a sauce made of their companions, garum-for this thing also has procured a designation-and for fish-paste to be devised out of their liver. 67. With a fish of prices paw, this kind one of the proconsular body, Asinius Celer, in the principate of Gaius, issued a challenge it is not so easy to say who won the match to all the spendthrifts by giving 8000 sesterces c for a mullet. The thought of this side-tracks the mind to the consideration of the people who in their complaints about luxury used to protest that cooks were being bought at a higher price per man than a horse; but now the price of three horses is given for a cook, and the price of three cooks for a fish, and almost no human being has come to be more valued than one that is most skilful in making his master bankrupt.
>
> 68. Licinius Mucianus has recorded the capture in the Red Sea of a mullet weighing 80 lbs; what price would our epicures have paid for it if it had been found on the coasts near the city? (Trans. Rackham 1940, here and below)

This narrative combines most of the categories in which Pliny's *luxuria* expresses itself: banquet, mixing (66 *versicolor*, *varietas*), luxury (expensive fish), and excess leading to perversion (the mullet drawn in the sauce) in a sort of gastric celebration that also involves the sense of sight (the insistence on the dying mullet's colours). Apicius is described as *ad omne luxus ingenium natus*, 'a mind born for every kind of luxury', and this indicates a notion that also Seneca discusses: *luxuria*, far from being an irrational vice, subjects the mind to itself, so that men begin to use their rational faculty in order to excogitate new ways in which to satisfy their desires (below, 4.1). This same mullet episode, albeit without Apicius being mentioned, appeared in Seneca's *Natural Questions*, while Apicius finds himself, and on similar terms, in *De vita beata* and *Consolatio ad Helviam*.[243] Apicius is mentioned also in 19.137, as a model of vice for Drusus Caesar, as against his father Tiberius' *frugalitas*. This reference to Tiberius aligns with the picture of this emperor given by Velleius Paterculus, and differs completely from the more famous one in Suetonius and Tacitus, the latter of whom, incidentally, reports a letter by Tiberius in which he refuses to promulgate a sumptuary law, considering it useless and hypocritical.[244]

[243] Below, 3.2.2; 4.6; 4.9.

[244] Below, 2.9. On Velleius, above, n. 86.

Pearls also receive much attention in Pliny,[245] with some historical examples listed in a *climax*, which shows at best the connection between banquets and luxury. The first is Lollia Paulina, Caligula's wife, and her jewels made by emeralds and pearls, whose value of forty million sesterces exceeded that of the spoils in the triumphs of Curius and Fabricius, two famous examples of frugality (9.117–18).[246] A more shocking example (9.119) is that of Cleopatra,[247] the famous queen of Egypt, who owned the two biggest pearls in the world and, during a banquet at which she seduced Mark Antony, melted one of them in vinegar and drank it, because she had bet that she could eat ten million sesterces all at once (9.121). Still, Pliny comments (9.122): *non ferent hanc palmam spoliabunturque luxuriae gloriam*, 'they will not carry off his trophy, and will be robbed even of the record of luxury!'. And he refers to the story of the son of the tragic actor Aesopus, named Clodius, who did the same thing as Cleopatra, and on an even larger scale, with a more royal attitude.[248]

So, as *luxuria* represents a love of excess, Pliny structures his examples as a descent towards ever greater vice, representing the restless search for something that is always newer and greater.

These examples are particularly significant because they portray a search for pleasure that goes beyond the physical: a melted pearl is surely not tasty or beautiful. The only reason why someone would melt and drink it is to exhibit the ease by which a fortune can be thrown away, even if this entails destroying something that itself had been an object of desire. The story perfectly illustrates in the extreme *luxuria*'s destructive power over those who enjoy it. It is relevant that, despite the space devoted to Cleopatra in the text, the top example comes from the Roman world (and as we have seen, Valerius also lists it with other Roman examples).[249] The disease has now spread all over Roman culture.

Pliny comes back to Mark Antony later, accusing him of both *feritas atque luxuria*, in that he proscribed people only to seize their gems (37.82). These two vices at first seem antithetical, because the former implies violence and irrational frenzy while the latter calls for finer tastes and is more often coupled with effeminate than with brutal habits. But together they form a picture of the worst tyrants, such as of the cruel but effeminate Caligula and Nero (called

[245] Citroni Marchetti (1991), 217–18; 265–7.

[246] Cf. *HN* 16.185 and 33.153. On these paradigms of frugality, already in Val. Max. 4.3.5–6; 4.4.3; 4.4.11, Berrendonner (2001); Vigourt (2001); below, 2.6.2 (Juvenal); 2.8 (Lucan); 4.7 (Seneca).

[247] Citroni Marchetti (1991), 267. Also, Lucan 10.488 defines her palace, where she seduces Caesar, *luxuriosa domus* (below, 2.8). About Augustan propaganda against Cleopatra, which influenced all later authors, Wyke (2002), 195–243.

[248] 9.122 *quo magis regium fiat*, 'which would make it more royal', is Pliny's observation about the fact that Aesopus, unlike Cleopatra, did not do it for a bet, but only to taste an exotic flavour. Aesopus has already been cited, without details, in Valerius Maximus 9.1.2: above, 2.5.1.

[249] Above, 2.5.1.

'enemies of humanity' in 7.45),[250] who coupled a total lack of humanity with a taste for the finest pleasures which we have already find in Cicero's Verres (above, 2.2.1).

Even more interesting is Pompey's case. Pliny stresses the unprecedented luxury of Pompey's triumphal parade, which included a portrait of Pompey made by pearls, and comments (37.14):[251] *illa severitate victa et veriore luxuriae triumpho*, 'here it was austerity that was defeated and extravagance that more truly celebrated her triumph' (trans. Eichholz 1971). Both vice and virtue are personified, following a poetic habit tracing back to Plautus,[252] and which often appears in satire[253] but was already strongly present in Seneca.[254] The explicit representation of the triumph of an abstract entity also anticipates the medieval future of this subgenre.[255]

The allegorical characters themselves are just as interesting. It is not Pompey who won over Asia, but *luxuria* who defeated *severitas*, which is no longer *frugalitas*, the specific virtue of limiting expenses, but a more general and typically Roman attitude of seriousness and sobriety in any field. This shows that *luxuria* is no longer a question of money but of an attitude towards life that perverts the very sense of being Roman. And Pompey is the protagonist in this decline, the general in whom vice is embodied, as Caesar implied in his *Bellum Civile*.[256] Pliny traces the beginning of this decline to the conquest of Asia and destruction of Carthage,[257] but also blames the Greeks more generally.[258] He identifies a complete overturn—not just of a single virtue but of *severitas*, Roman morality itself—with Pompey's triumph over Asia. Pliny thereby voiced a political view that no one had previously expressed so definitively.

Among the expressions of luxury, special attention is given to shells, as they are considered the cause of luxury and moral decline[259] in several respects: as refined food (9.104); as the origin of the luxury colour par excellence, purple (9.105; 129);[260] finally, as the origin of pearls (9.105; 114; 119–22), which, even if sometimes valued as purple by 'mother Luxury' (*mater luxuria*), are much more durable, and this makes them a valuable inheritance (9.124).[261]

[250] Ripoll (1999); above, n. 224.
[251] See also *HN* 37.18; Citroni Marchetti (1991), 282–5.
[252] Above, 2.1.1. [253] Below, 2.6.1. [254] Below, 4.4 and 4.5.
[255] See e.g. Francesco Petrarca's *Triumphs*, a poem which starts with the *Triumphum Cupidinis*.
[256] Above, 2.2.2. [257] *HN* 33.148–50; Citroni Marchetti (1991), 185–7.
[258] *HN* 15.19 (on oil in gymnasia): *usum eius ad luxuriam vertere Graeci, vitiorum omnium genitores*. On Pliny and Greek culture, see Serbat (1987); Wallace-Hadrill (1990), 92–6; Beagon (1992), 18–19.
[259] *HN* 9.104 'but why do I mention these trifles when moral corruption and luxury (*luxuria*) spring from no other source in greater abundance than from the genus shell-fish?'
[260] On purple, see also *HN* 8.197.
[261] *HN* 9.124 'And nevertheless this article is an almost everlasting piece of property it passes to its owner's heir, it is offered for public sale like some landed estate; whereas every hour of use wears away robes of scarlet and purple, which the same mother, luxury, has made almost as costly as pearls.'

Before distinguishing between the two main species of murices from which it is derived, Pliny makes the following remark about purple (9.129):

> Quod si hactenus transcurrat expositio, fraudatam profecto se luxuria credat nosque indiligentiae damnet.
>
> But if having come to this point our exposition were to pass over elsewhere, luxury would undoubtedly believe itself defrauded and would find us guilty of remissness.

Luxuria is here personified,[262] and is imagined to criticize Pliny for his inaccuracy (*indiligentia*). Again, as in Seneca, *luxuria* is related to care for details and perfectionism, and thus with a form of intelligence, far removed from the storm of passions that we find in love and anger. The vice seems to appreciate diligence (*diligentia*), which is indeed a virtue, but one that is here subdued to it. A further key topic of Pliny's *luxuria* are compounds: the mixing of colours (9.139–40) and gems (33.22) and singing voices (16.171), of wood with turtle shell (an innovation of Nero's) and marble inlays (16.232–3; 36.44; 36.51). Also in this case is the origin of the phenomenon natural and related to the biological meaning of *luxuria*, as in the mixture of blossom colours in the spring (16.95), but it is perversely imitated in a restless search for the new, the amazing, and the luxurious. As Pliny says, 'luxury had not thought wood good enough' (16.233): 'normal' luxury, average noble materials are no longer enough,[263] and Pliny is here surely referring to contemporary usage. A significant passage in this context involves the colours of people's attire (9.139–40):

> Sed alia e fine initia, iuvatque ludere impendio et lusus geminare miscendo iterumque et ipsa adulterare adulteria naturae, sicut testudines tinguere, argentum auro confundere, ut electra fiant, addere his aera, ut Corinthia.[264] Non est satis abstulisse gemmae nomen amethystum; rursum absolutum inebriatur Tyrio, ut sit ex utroque nomen improbum simulque luxuria duplex, et cum confecere conchylia transire melius in Tyrium putant. 140. Paenitentia hoc primo debet invenisse, artifice mutante quod damnabat. Inde ratio nata, votum quoque factum e vitio portentosis ingeniis, et gemina demonstrata via luxuriae, ut color alius operiretur alio, suavior ita fieri leniorque dictus; quin et terrena miscere coccoque tinctum Tyrio tinguere, ut fieret hysginum.

[262] This happens quite frequently in Pliny: see *HN* 16.233; 35.3; 35.22; 35.163; above, 1.1 (Plautus); below, 2.6.1 (Persius); 4.1; 4.4 (Seneca).

[263] *HN* 16.233 *luxuria non fuerat contenta ligno, iam ligno et e testudine facit*, 'luxury had not thought wood enough, but now it actually manufactures wood out of tortoiseshell.' (Trans. Rackham 1986). Cf. also *HN* 12.5 (ebony instead of wood).

[264] On these objects cf. Morcillo (2010).

> But every end leads to fresh starts, and men make a sport of spending, and like doubling their sports by combining them and re-adulterating nature's adulterations, for instance staining tortoiseshells, alloying gold with silver to produce amber-metal ware, and adding copper to these to make Corinthian ware. It is not enough to have stolen for a dye the name of a gem, 'sober-stone', but when finished it is made drunk again with Tyrian dye, so as to produce from the combination an outlandish name, and a twofold luxury at one time; and when they have made shell-dye, they think it an improvement for it to pass into Tyrian. 140. Repentance must have discovered this first, the artificer altering a product that he disapproved of; but reason sprang up next, and a defect was turned into a success by marvellous inventions, and a double path pointed out for luxury, so that one colour might be concealed by another, being pronounced to be made sweeter and softer by this process; and also a method to blend minerals, and dye with Tyrian a fabric already dyed with scarlet, to produce hysgine colour.

Modern luxury is not satisfied with merely expensive things: it consists in adding (*addere*), mixing and altering (*adulterare*, *confundere*, *mutante*), redoubling (*duplex*, *gemina*), to create new objects of desire: all these findings show great intelligence (*portentosis ingeniis*). This original expression, repeated for Nero in a similar context in 16.233, is significant: indeed *portentum* in Latin is properly the monster, so the correlated adjective points at something which is more terrifying than admirable for its greatness. Similar points are made regarding glass (33.5; 36.114) and clay (35.163), two fragile and originally cheap materials made precious by fine craftsmanship (in 36.114 we are told of a theatre built entirely in glass;[265] in 35.163 of a giant oven built for Vitellius and his million-sesterces banquet). Another instance are perfumes,[266] which do not even have material longevity and thus represent an ultimate level of insanity (12.82; 13.1; 13.20).

A manifestation of luxury becoming increasingly useless is the fascination for painted surfaces: dresses (22.3–4) and marble decorations (35.3)[267] are covered with artificial colours for the viewer's pleasure, and hides the natural shine of the original materials, a form of perversion that suggests that the shining life of those who are devoted to *luxuria* is mere appearance, under which, as Seneca shows, there is sadness, grief, or disgust for life.[268] Pliny also demonstrates this, when he observes (22.14):

[265] By M. Aemilius Scaurus (*c.* 95–52 BCE); on his theatre, whose stages were mobile and could be swivelled around, Citroni Marchetti (1991), 278–82.

[266] Above, 1.4 with n. 56.

[267] See Malaspina (2020).

[268] Sen. *EM* 115.9 'we marvel at rooms with marble walls, even though we know it is only a thin veneer. We deceive our own eyes: when we gild a ceiling, are we not rejoicing in a lie? For we know that some unattractive wood is hidden under the gold. And the pretense of ornamentation is not only in panelling and coffering. Look at all those who strut about in high places: their prosperity is nothing but gilding (*bratteata felicitas*). Examine it closely and you will see how much rottenness is hidden beneath that thin coating of status.' (Trans. Graver/Long 2015).

Sed quis non mores iure castiget? Addidere vivendi pretia deliciae luxusque; numquam fuit vitae cupido maior nec minor cura.

But who could not with justice censure modern ways? The cost of living has been increased by luxuries and extravagance; never has there been more zest for life or less care taken of it. (Trans. Jones 1951)

Life is valued for its luxury and preciousness; caring for that is seen as caring for one's life, while in fact it is only an ephemeral desire, not a genuine concern for human existence. On the contrary, as Pliny says in what follows, this leads to diseases and injuries, which threaten existence itself.

Besides those referred to *luxuria* as a passion, there are also many occurrences of *luxuria* as a feature of nature: the spontaneous luxuriance of especially plants from the earth. But this emphasis on natural fertility is not at all of the idyllic kind that we see in the opening of Lucretius' *De Rerum Natura*: observations on the wonderful spring of life are balanced by frequent exhortations to temper and control this spring, lest the plants fall sick and die. So natural luxuriance is per se an excess that must be ruled and regulated. To Pliny, even if nature pursues goodness and serves human needs, and despite some passages where nature tries to limit human greed, e.g. by hiding gems underground,[269] this goodness of nature is not innate but requires human effort:[270] farming shows that one needs to guide nature's tendencies. It seems to me that Pliny's passages illustrate that the agricultural meaning of *luxuria* already implies all the negative consequences associated with its moralistic application. The agricultural occurrences of *luxuria* are quite numerous, about fifteen out of a total of below seventy, so more than twenty per cent. They are concentrated, predictably enough, in the books devoted to botany and especially viticulture (17–19). Excessive growth is indeed peculiar of vineyards, and ruinous for this culture.[271] Yet it does not spare corn (18.154):

Inter vitia segetum et luxuria est, cum oneratae fertilitate procumbunt.

Among the vices of corn is also over-abundance, when the stalks fall down under the burden of fertility.

Luxuria is here described as an overwhelming weight, which makes ears falling down; itis here a synonym of *fertilitas*—yet it is not at all positive if excessive. The fact that this concern appears in the discussion of *vitia segetum*, with the word

[269] *HN* 33.1–3; cf. 2.158: a typical moralistic issue, already dealt with in very similar terms by Seneca (below, 4.9).

[270] On the limits and exceptions to Pliny's 'vague Stoicism', see Vegetti (1982), 125.

[271] *HN* 17.178 'Nature is such that she wants to produce off-springs more than she wants to live…the vine on the contrary prefers its own groth to the production of fruit, because fruit is a perishable article; thus it luxuriates ruinously, and does not fill itself out but exhaust itself.' (Trans. Rackham 1961b).

vitium referring to human flaws, is also an indication of the proximity of moral and agricultural discourses. Again, while discussing the oasis of Tacape in Africa, where the soil is exceptionally fertile,[272] Pliny warns (18.189):

> Et nisi multiplici partu exinaniatur ubertas, pereant luxuria singuli fructus. Nunc vero toto anno metitur aliquid, constatque fertilitati non occurrere homines.
>
> And if fertility is not exhausted by multiplied production, each crop would be killed by its own exuberance, but as it is, something is being gathered all the year round, and yet it is an absolute fact that this fertility receives no assistance from human beings.

If not regulated by humans, fertility leads to death: the quoted case is absolutely exceptional. *Luxuria* is connected with two positive terms, *fertilitas* and *ubertas*, but Pliny also stresses its dangerous consequences.

A similar reasoning is made regarding figs, a tree that is notoriously easy-growing (19.113):

> Maturescentium caules depressi in terram obruuntur; ita cavetur, ne in frondem luxurient.
>
> When they begin to ripen, their stalks are pressed down into the earth and covered up: this prevents their making too lush foliage.

The farmer has to prevent the natural growth of suckers from figs fallen onto the ground, which would choke the mother plant. In this case, too, men have to moderate nature's spontaneous fertility, lest it become lethal. These considerations become quite striking in a moralistic light; in particular, they raise the suspicion of an innate tendency of beings towards excess. There is indeed a reason why in the Roman account *luxuria* comes from barbarian, uncivilized people: civilization—that is, moderation and a legal order—are necessary to fight *luxuria*. But Roman laws, as we have seen with the *Lex Oppia*, were not effective in this regard.[273]

Andrew Wallace-Hadrill[274] states that Pliny's insistence on *luxuria* and his attempt to find scientific reasons for criticizing it demonstrates his effort to confirm the validity of Roman values. This is undoubtedly true, but it does not mean that Pliny's moral observations are based on commonplaces, as shown by the fact that, for example, Cato is valued less than his political enemy Scipio.[275] Moreover, the specific objects of *luxuria*—compounds, mixing, fragile and even less valuable

[272] *HN* 18.188 *felici super omne miraculum riguo solo.*

[273] Above, 2.3.2; for sumptuary laws in general, below, 2.9. A reasoning similar to my own above is in Jones-Lewis (2012), who argues that Italy, and specifically Rome, are depicted by Pliny as healing places for the poisons that nature spontaneously produces.

[274] (1990), 90–2.

[275] *HN* 7.100, on which Beagon (1992), 17.

things—show by themselves that this vice has already moved beyond the simple exhibition of wealth, as further emphasized by the lack of its traditional connection with *avaritia*. It is no longer a question of money; it is a contest of *deliciae*, of more and more amazing, unusual, and disturbing habits and things. *Luxuria* has ceased being a mere flaw and has become a monster. Traditional values are no longer effective against this multiform being; something stronger is needed, as Seneca shows.[276]

2.5.3 Martial the Observer

In his large collection of epigrams, dated to the end of the first century CE, Martial exhibits an ironic and somewhat moralistic attitude towards his contemporaries' vices. In his own peculiar way, he offers a list of examples, too, albeit deliberately negative and risible. Our interest in Martial's treatment of *luxuria* lies in the fact that he exploits the full range of meanings of this word, without preference for any one of them. He is indeed perfectly aware of the richness of this word, to the point that he makes it the key to one of his statements on poetics. Comparing his lascivious poems with the modest ones of a colleague, and thus rewriting a well-known commonplace,[277] he declares (3.69.1–4):

> Omnia quod scribis castis epigrammata verbis
> inquie tuis nulla est mentula carminibus,
> admiror, laudo: nihil est te sanctius uno:
> at mea luxuria pagina nulla vacat.

You write all your epigrams in chaste language, there is no cock in your poems. I admire, I commend. You are the purest of the pure. Whereas no page of mine lacks lubricity. (Trans. Shackleton Bailey 1993a)

The poem opposes virtue to vice, specified respectively as chastity (1 *castis... verbis*) and lust (4 *luxuria*). On the one side, the praise of his colleague, who is identified in what follows as Cosconius,[278] is at least slightly ironic, since he is criticized as boring in 2.77. On the other side, the claim of a licentious style belongs to a commonplace in the epigrammatic genre, one that he repeats, famously, at 1.4.8 *lasciva est nobis pagina, vita proba*, 'my page is wanton, but my life is virtuous'.[279] So he treats *luxuria* as a synonym of *lascivia*. Martial juxtaposes with the complete absence of eroticism in Cosconius (3.69.2 *nulla... mentula*) its pervasiveness in his own poems (3.69.4 *luxuria... nulla vacat*), and this contrast is stressed by the

[276] Below, 4.3.
[277] Fusi (2006), 444; cf. above, 2.4.2.
[278] Soldevila/Castillo/Valverde (2019), 162.
[279] In 11.16.3 we find the verb *lascivire*.

repetition of the adjective *nullus* in two different senses: when referring to *mentula*, which is a concrete and specific term defining male genitals, the sense is that there is no erotic language in Cosconius' poems,[280] and when to *luxuria*, which is an abstract and quite generic noun, the allusion is to different and several kinds of vice, something like 'no kind of *luxuria* is missing in my poems'. And indeed, all kinds can be found in Martial's epigrams.

The specific erotic meaning recurs elsewhere, in reference to the god of fertility and specifically to Priapus' *mentula* (7.91.4), and in reference to a young and uninhibited prostitute (9.67.6). And there are many attestations of the other meanings: excessive desire (for breath pills, 1.87.2); luxury, mainly understood as excessive expense (2.63.3–4;[281] 5.19.13; 9.82.4; 11.70.11–12) and splendid banquets (Apicius, 2.89.5;[282] perfumed wine, 14.110.2); natural fertility of fields (11.8.4) and herds (11.41.2); legitimate pride (of a book for its shining cover, 3.2.9; of the poet for his small property, 10.96.6; of someone for his deserved honour, 12.62.10).

A significant example comes from the so-called *Xenia*, from a distich presenting an oyster (13.82):[283]

> Ebria Baiano veni modo concha Lucrino:
> nobile nunc sitio luxuriosa garum.

A shellfish, I have just arrived, drunk with Baian Lucrine. Now in my extravagance I thirst for noble garum. (Trans. Shackleton Bailey 1993b)

The oyster, the luxury food par excellence, is personified, as is usual in epigrams like this, and sums up all the characteristics of *luxuria*: refined food (oysters, fine sauce), drunkenness (1 *ebria*), immoral places (*Baiano*),[284] and most of all restless desire for pleasure: she is drunk, yet she is still thirsty (2 *sitio*), so she may legitimately call herself *luxuriosa*. Furthermore, the ironic image alludes to a noblemen's habit, narrated by both Seneca and Pliny, to prepare fish (especially mullet) drowning in sauce, as a sort of perverse way to imitate nature while also disturbing it, with the sadistic pleasure of watching the animal's agony right before eating it.[285]

All the same, in Martial's multicoloured picture of Roman world, we may say that, despite some classic examples like the omnipresent Apicius, the 'Horatian' sobriety of the poet (10.96.6), and the interest in certain issues found already in Pliny the Elder (seafood, natural fertility, the price of various things),[286]

280 Fusi (2006), 443; cf. 1.35.3–5.
281 Williams (2004), 210.
282 And 3.22, on which see below, 4.6.
283 Leary (2001), 141–2.
284 Above, 1.4.
285 Above, 2.5.2; below, 4.9.
286 With special reference to *Xenia* and *Apophoreta*, see Blake (2011).

and although the poet is far from defending luxury, *luxuria* appears most prevalently in its main second-century meaning, namely lust. More than once it alludes to the emperor's immorality, a trait that is already in Seneca and will become explicit in Suetonius.[287] So Martial seems to be less old-fashioned than his satirical contemporaries.

2.6 Satirical Voices: Those Who Do Not Call Vices by Name (Persius, Juvenal, and Petronius)

The fact that the word *luxuria* implies a moralistic judgement may lead to the conclusion that satirical authors are greatly concerned with this vice, but that would be unwarranted. While this term is frequent in historiographers and orators, we find no occurrences of it at all in the founders of the satirical genre, Ennius and Lucilius (only, in the remains of the first book of Lucilius, a council of the gods who decide how to punish a Lupus who was too devoted to its belly). It is rare in Horace (above, 2.4.1) and in Persius and Juvenal, and there are only two occurrences in Petronius, whose work may be considered a satire only at a certain degree. It is evident that satirical authors avoid calling vices by their names and judging them, preferring instead, in line with the realist nature of their genre, to describe bad habits and to focus on their disgusting consequences. The reader is supposed to arrive autonomously at indignation, the aim of their writings, rather than to be explicitly driven to it by the author; he is thus educated to formulate his own judgement.[288] When we find abstract labels for vices in satire, then the context is in most cases Stoic philosophy, which is particularly interested in the taxonomy and definition of vice.

Generally speaking, from the way in which our vice is treated in Roman satires, we may say that satirical authors look at the past, for models of morality and for ways of presenting it. Leaving aside the formal aspects and the details of the descriptions, which of course reflect the satirists' own society, the transmitted ideas and values are grounded in past times. *Luxuria* is still strictly concerned with wealth (Persius); its favourite place is still the banquet (Juvenal); positive examples are still located far back in the ancient Republic... Reading these texts, it seems difficult to believe that the acceptance of this vice is chronologically imminent (e.g. Pliny the Younger, below, 5.1).

[287] Below, 4.1 and 5.2.1.

[288] See also above, 1.4.

2.6.1 Persius' Personification

As is well known, Persius, who lived in the second half of the first century CE, wrote only six satires, inspired by his Stoic master L. Annaeus Cornutus, who as his name suggests was probably a freedman of Seneca's family. In Persius' slender but dense and conceptual work, we find only one occurrence of *luxus*, as a traditional moralistic subject (1.67), and one of *Luxuria*, personified (5.142).[289] Neither of these two mentions is related to food and banquets, despite the large role these play in the work in illustrating men's degradation.[290]

So *luxuria* does not occupy an important place in Persius' satires: the poet is evidently more interested in the expressionistic, disgusting representations of passion than in theoretical labelling. But the personification in satire 5 is very interesting. The main theme of this satire, which begins with a declaration of apprenticeship to the Stoic Cornutus, is a variation on a Stoic principle:[291] innate slavery, that which stems from vice, is far worse than juridical slavery. Persius personifies vice as the anonymous protagonist's master. He, a new-born Heracles at the crossroads, is the object of a dispute not between Vice and Virtue, as is familiar from the myth, but between two vices, Avarice and *Luxuria.* Both give a persuasive speech, but the hero hesitates, and soon the scene changes, and the passions on stage become Love and Sobriety, but again the protagonist does not choose. He thus becomes the very opposite of Heracles: not only does he not choose virtue, but he is not even able to choose between two different vices.[292] It is worth noting that *Avaritia* and *Luxuria* are characterized in opposite terms, in line with Sallust:[293] the former exhorts a person to work from dawn to dusk in order to make money (5.132–9), while the latter, called *sollers*, 'sly' (5.142), invites the sweetness of life, in a sort of rewrite of Horace's famous ode 1.11, on *carpe diem*, 'seize the day' (5.151–3):

> Indulge genio, carpamus dulcia, nostrum est
> quod vivis, cinis et manes et fabula fies:
> vive memor leti, fugit hora, hoc quod loquor inde est.

Enjoy yourself, let's grab our pleasures, life is all we have, you'll soon be ashes, a ghost, a tale. Live with death in mind. The hour races by and the time I spend talking is subtracted from it. (Trans. Morton Braund 2004)

[289] Bartsch (2015a), 85.

[290] On the symbolic relevance of food in Persius, Gowers (1996), 180–8.

[291] Reckford (2009), 118–24; Bartsch (2012), 218–20; on this satire cf. also Bramble (2009); specific on the personifications of Avarice and Luxury, Hooley (1997), 106–11.

[292] Barr (1987), 149. Satire six is, admittedly, centred around greed, so perhaps that is the ultimate victor. On the story of Heracles at the crossroads cf. above, 1.1.

[293] Above, 2.3.1.

Luxuria resorts to some philosophical commonplaces, such as the brevity of time, the necessity to make the best of it, to convince a man that he ought not to work too hard (another philosophical precept), but its aim is far from proposing a life of contemplative philosophy: it only suggests idleness and physical pleasures. Persius' personification recalls that of Plautus,[294] even if its implications are broader and include laziness and lust, since *dulcia* alludes to the pleasure of the senses, while in Plautus these had only been in the background. A hint at laziness inserts an original and productive agent in the story, but the connection with *avaritia* shows that the economic meaning of the word is still pre-eminent.

Two issues have to be raised: first, as in Horace *Serm.* 2.3, the dissertation on vice is inserted in a Stoic context, thus confirming the impression of a privileged role for that philosophy and its taxonomy of vices, otherwise neglected by satirical authors; second, if we look specifically at Persius' fifth satire, we may say that since the common man's choice is no longer between vice and virtue, but between two vices, morality has clearly degenerated overall, in the author's view. Furthermore, the whole speech, imagined as delivered by a philosopher, is overtly despised by an old soldier (5.189–91) and judged as completely useless for common people. Persius has lost the faith, still alive in Seneca, that people might improve themselves.

2.6.2 Juvenal: The Banquet Obsession

All occurrences of *luxuria* in the sixteen satires of Juvenal, written in the late first century CE, are related to banquets, which are indeed a key subject of satire, whose very name is, as is well known, related to the idea of satiety.[295] The reader would have expected something different in different places, such as *luxuria* referred to women's clothes or jewellery in the famous satire 6, known as 'the satire against women', or perhaps to mine excavation, luxury buildings, and so on, but there is nothing of this. All we have is banquets, which lead to lust in satire 6. We have seen the same focus in Horace, who seemed reticent about other forms of *luxuria*.[296] Juvenal seems to look at wealthy people with the eyes of a parasite, someone waiting for the master to leave some leftovers. He was indeed, as he painfully points out, a client, forced to beg for sustenance from his protectors. It is also from this existence that he constructed his idea of a man reduced to his belly or even to his wide-open mouth (*gula*). Juvenal's *luxuria* is thus a sort of appendix to gluttony. Gluttony itself is mostly seen as an excessive waste of money.

[294] Above, 2.1.1. Reckford (2009), 118–23, stresses the connection not only with comedy but also with Horace's satire 2.3 (above, 2.4.1).

[295] For the food theme in Juvenal, see Gowers (1996), 188–219; Rimell (2005a), esp. 84–5.

[296] Above, 2.4.1.

In this vein, Juvenal offers us: the sordidness of *luxuria* in someone who eats luxury banquets alone, in a paradoxical combination of pomp and misery,[297] which probably hints at the perverse habits of Domitian (1.140);[298] the *luxuria imperii* under Nero (4.137), when massive night banquets were organized,[299] as a precedent to the insanity of Domitian, who arranged a meeting of the Senate to consult on how to cook a giant rhombus fish he had received as a gift; *luxuria* as the main way to ruin someone who refuses to give up banquets, and ends up being sold to a gladiator owner (11.22; 45; 77); the extreme form of *luxuria* expressed in a cannibalistic banquet by some Egyptians (15.45). The vice itself becomes a mouth that swallows everything one owns, to the point of devouring one's very life, or, worse, one's humanity. A man subjected to it is reduced to his ingesting organs and loses any measure or distinction between good and bad. There are some instances of the usual commonplaces: Curius, a legendarily frugal example from the Roman Republic, in satire 11,[300] where we also find Apicius, Baiae, oysters, and so on; Canopus, an Egyptian city that shared with Baiae the title of capital of *luxuria*, in satire 15;[301] Nero, the emperor who truly embodied this vice. The satirist, e.g. in satire 11.56–76, presents himself as a model of moderation and sobriety, and thus as similar to the ancient Republic examples. Here, Juvenal is clearly modelling himself after Horace, but the Augustan poet, despite his celebration of his own frugal banquets, never claims to be a role model in the *Satires*, where, on the contrary, he has himself criticized by self-asserting philosophers.[302]

The sole exception to the ubiquity of banquets is satire 6, which is famous for its attack on women. The satire starts with a proem in which Juvenal laments the disappearing of modesty (*pudicitia*) in modern times (ll. 1–20),[303] linking it to the influence of Greek people (ll. 16–17). Listed among the many flaws of women, *luxuria* is defined as the revenge of conquered enemies on the Romans (ll. 292–300), and is explicitly linked to *libido* (ll. 292–5):[304]

> Nunc patimur longae pacis mala: saevior armis
> Luxuria incubuit victumque ulciscitur orbem.

[297] Plaza (2006), 309 and 333; Stramaglia (2008), 96–7; Mayor (2010), 151–2, both recalling Plin. *Epist.* 2.6.7 (below, 5.1). On the idea of moral decline expressed in this satire, Harrison (2005), 297–8.
[298] Morton Braund (1996), esp. 41–2; Santorelli (2012), 150.
[299] Mayor (2010), 238–9, discusses how night banquets were part of Nero's routine. Seneca states that this habit goes against nature (below, 4.2). On food in satire 4 see also Gowers (1996), 202–11.
[300] Iuv. 11.78–81. Curius is omnipresent in passages that deal with frugality: above, 2.5.2 with n. 246; Courtney (2013), 440–1. On satire 11, see also Felton/Lee 1972; on its connection with Stoicism, Bartsch (2012), 236.
[301] Fredericks (1976), 181–2; McKim (1986), 63; Courtney (2013), 530. Canopus is also quoted in this regard by Seneca (below, 4.4).
[302] Above, 2.4.1.
[303] On Juvenal's rewriting of the myth of the ages, Watson (2012). Cf. below, 2.8 (Lucan) with n. 358.
[304] See Anderson (1982), 264–6; Nadeau (2011), 168–75; Watson (2012), 74.

> Nullum crimen abest facinusque libidinis, ex quo
> paupertas Romana perit...

These days, we are suffering the calamities of long peaces. Luxury has settled down on us, crueller than fighting, avenging the world we've conquered. From the moment Roman poverty disappeared, no crime or act of lust has been missing...

(Trans. Morton Braund 2004)

The idea of vice assaulting Roman society is frequent (cf. Sall. *Cat.* 2.5 and 12.2, above 2.3.1); that of vice as revenge, even if connected, as usual, to the spreading of wealth (ll. 298–300), is an original one. Vice results from fate and is a compensation for excessive fortune (here alluded to by *longae pacis mala*).[305] That this reference to *libido* is meant as lust is shown in the following lines, where there is a reference to Venus (l. 300), and drunk women, after a banquet lasting all night long, are represented while offending the altar of Chastity (ll. 308–11).

So, lust and *luxuria* are connected here, and specifically relate to women, while still involving banquets. Indeed, Juvenal describes an unnamed woman drinking wine[306] and eating oysters at a night banquet, all of which is immoral (as is her consumption of luxury mussels),[307] and which reinforces her primary, sexual immorality (ll. 301–5). It is relevant that banquets are omnipresent and that *luxuria* connects to lust only if women are involved, who according to ancient misogynistic parameters are especially weak-minded and relentless regarding sex.[308] To Juvenal, chastity was guaranteed only by poverty and humble fortune (ll. 294–5; cf. 287–91), such as it happened to virtue according to Roman historiographers.

2.6.3 Mocking Moralists: Petronius

Petronius deserves his own place in this chapter, not for the consistency of his treatment of *luxuria*, but for the lack thereof. Not once during Trimalchio's dinner is this word uttered by any of the guests, even though the occasion is undoubtedly the most extensive description of all the aspects of *luxuria* we have seen so far: excessive banquets, luxury furniture, precious metals, wealth exhibition, lust, luxury buildings. There is only something missing: in this context we do not find an immense waste of money,[309] such as it happens few years later in Pliny's list of immoral banquets (above, 2.5.2): fish and shells play only a secondary role, and

[305] Especially in Sallust and Livy (above, 2.3.1 and 2.3.2). Courtney (2013), 255, cites in this context Polyb. 32.13.6 and Sen. *EM* 73.6.

[306] An action that was absolutely banned in Roman culture: Purcell (1994).

[307] For night banquets, see above, 2.2.1; for oysters, above, 2.5.2 (Pliny on drinking melted pearls).

[308] See above, 2.5.1 (Valerius Maximus) and Cato's speech in Livy 34 (above, 2.3.2). On women as symbol of decadence, Dixon (2001), 56–9 (56–7 on Juvenal).

[309] This has been ultimately stressed by Baratta (2023).

there are no melted pearls of birds' tongues to eat. Trimalchio is not refined in any field, included *luxuria*. This vice is quoted only twice in the remains of *Satyricon*, and both occurrences are in the poetic sections. The first is due to Trimalchio himself, in one of his poetic compositions recited during the banquet. The second and last occurrence, as well as two of *luxus*, are to be found in Eumolpus' poetic improvisations, especially in his poem about the civil war between Caesar and Pompey in the part which represents for us the end of the work. This political background means that both the author and the narrator carefully avoid moralistic judgment of what they describe.[310]

Trimalchio's verses appear among his considerations on the mutability of Fortune, and he attributes them to the first-century BCE mimographer Publilius Syrus, who was famous for his tirade against vice (55.6.1–19):[311]

> Luxuriae rictu Martis marcent moenia.
> Tuo palato clausus pavo pascitur
> plumato amictus aureo Babylonico,
> gallina tibi Numidica, tibi gallus spado;
> ciconia etiam, grata peregrina hospita
> pietaticultrix gracilipes crotalistria,
> avis exul hiemis, titulus tepidi temporis,
> nequitiae nidum in caccabo fecit tuae.
> Quo margaritam caram tibi, bacam Indicam?
> An ut matrona ornata phaleris pelagiis
> tollat pedes indomita in strato extraneo?
> Zmaragdum ad quam rem viridem, pretiosum vitrum?
> quo Carchedonios optas ignes lapideos?
> nisi ut scintillet probitas e carbunculis.
> aequum est induere nuptam ventum textilem,
> palam prostare nudam in nebula linea?
> Quae nova semper amas et mox possessa relinquis
> ecquid Romano sentis te pondere victam
> nec possis ulterior perituram extollere molem?

The walls of Mars crumble beneath the gaping jaws of luxury. To please your palate the peacock clad in Babylonian golden plumage is fed in cages, for you the guinea hen, for you the capon; even the stork, the beloved foreign guest, devotion-filled, graceful-stepping, castanet-dancer, winter's exile, warrant of warm weather, has made

[310] On this issue, which calls the *Satyricon*'s place in the genre of satire into question, see Rimell (2005b). For a traditional view of the whole novel as representation of moral decline, Arrowsmith (1966). On the connection between the *Satyricon* and Nero's habits and vices, Freudenberg (2017).

[311] Setaioli (2011), 117–29, who offers further bibliography; for line 1, Schmeling (2011), 225. Cf. below, 2.7.1.

its nest in the cooking pot of your worthlessness. Why seek costly pearls for yourself, why Indian pearl berries? That your wife adorned with sea spoils might spread her legs, unchecked on the bed of a stranger? For what purpose do you seek green emeralds, the precious crystal? For what purpose the Carthaginian tablished, who is always eager for something new and quickly forsakes his conquests, do you not feel that you are crushed under the dead weight of Rome, and that you cannot raise higher that massive city that is doomed to fall? (Trans. Schmeling 2020, here and below)

These lines deal with two main ways in which *luxuria* expresses itself: banquets (ll. 1–8), outfits, and jewellery (ll. 9–13). Most scholars agree that the poem is an imitation of Publilius and not an original fragment: it is full of Graecisms, which are completely absent from his extant fragments.[312] The second part has been compared with a fragment attributed to Maecenas by Isidore of Sevilla,[313] and Trimalchio's dressing habit, similar to that attributed to Maecenas by Seneca,[314] may suggest a link between the two figures.[315] The connection is limited to the association between pearls and emeralds, which is common in moralistic literature (e.g. Varro *Men.* 382 B. = Ast.; Plin. *HN* 9.117), while the sartorial similarity is probably best explained as a fashion, or perhaps as deliberate emulation on Trimalchio's part of the great Augustan literate.

Putting these exegetic questions aside, I would like to focus on the text. First, Trimalchio considers Publilius as more honest than Cicero (who however was finer in eloquence). So the poem is presented as moralistic, and this is the main issue Trimalchio wants to raise in his struggle to present himself as an embodiment of Roman virtues: indeed he states that he owes his fortune to his frugality (75.10).[316] Second, he uses a tough metaphor, *luxuriae rictus*, which represents the vice not only as a person—something already Plautus did[317]—but as a monster, whose infected bite makes Rome's walls rot. The image is effective, as it mixes two powerful elements: a 'monstrification' of an abstract concept, similar to that used by Ovid for time, *tempus edax*, 'devouring time' (*Met.* 15.234; *Ex P.* 4.10.7), but conveying the idea of rotting instead of consuming, in that vice completely ruins men's lives; and the idea of rotten walls, which probably alludes to Lucretius' expression *putrescere saxa* (*DRN* 5.307), used as evidence of the decline and destruction to which the universe is doomed. Furthermore, the image of Rome as a rock falling on his weight is taken by Livy's preface (above, 2.3.2), a famous

[312] Setaioli (2011), 122–6; Schmeling (2011), 224–5; on the chance that Petronius intends to parody Seneca the Younger's use of quotations from Publilius, Courtney (1991), 21; Setaioli (2014a), 377.

[313] Maecen. frg. Poet. 5 Avallone = 16 Costa = Isid. *Orig.* 19.32.6 *lucentes, mea vita, nec smaragdos/ beryllos, mihi Flacce, nec nitentes/nec percandida margarita quaero/nec quos Tymica lima perpolivit/ anulos neque iaspios lapillos.* Cf. Costa 2014, 291–2.

[314] *EM* 114.6; cf. below, 4.6.

[315] Setaioli (2011), 120–1.

[316] Petr. 75.10 *ad hanc me fortunam frugalitas mea perduxit.* In the same chapter, Trimalchio praises the frugality of his lover (75.4). Cf. Gildenhard (2020), 304–10.

[317] Above, 2.1.1.

passage, too. This verse thus combines two classic moralistic concerns about *luxuria*: that it provokes moral decline, and that this decline is irreversible and leads to doom.

Another interesting feature in Trimalchio's poem is that most of the attacked behaviours are also his own: the poem lists as luxury meat that of peacock, guineafowl hen, capon, and stork; Trimalchio does not offer his guests stork meat, but he makes a joke about peacock eggs, and despises any kind of hens and roosters as too easy to cook (47.10). As for jewels and clothing, the poem talks about pearls, emeralds, rubies, and linen vests; none of these are mentioned elsewhere in the novel, yet Fortunata, Trimalchio's wife, is overloaded by the weight of her jewels (67.7), just like the woman in the poem (55.6.10 *onerata*), and accidentally shows everyone her legs (67.12), just like the woman in the poem with her transparent dress (55.6.15–16). So Trimalchio is in fact unwittingly criticizing himself.[318] This shows his dullness, of course, but also the inefficacy of moralistic injunctions, which are—Petronius seems to imply—regularly mentioned but never actually followed.

The occurrence of *luxuria* in Eumolpus' poem about the civil war is not very different from that in Trimalchio's epigram. Like Trimalchio, Eumolpus is far from being a model of virtue, to the point that he is defined *frugi* in a sarcastic way for his sexual incontinence (140.5); this fact questions from the start the moral intents of his poetic composition.

The context of his poem is that of fatal decline, described as a sort of putrefaction (119.54 *tabes*) and consumption due to luxury (119.56 *detritaque commoda luxu*). The mass of the world is doomed to die (120.83 *perituram . . . molem*),[319] and among a parade of luxury furniture and buildings, while Cato is defeated, Pluto, the king of the dead, asks Fortune to raise a war, almost fulfilling society's desire for self-destruction (120.85–6):

> . . . Aspice late
> Luxuriam spoliorum et censum in damna furentem.

Look about at the plundered riches of wars, extravagance raging to its own ruin.

The vice has become a fury, as happens in extreme cases, now seeming like the goddess of war, Bellona,[320] bent on destruction. The desire for accumulation and

[318] On the complexity of Fortunata's character, marked by the same status anxiety of her husband, Skinner (2012).

[319] A commonplace (Schmeling (2011), 458), but perhaps also another Lucretian hint: *DRN* 5.95–6 . . . *multoque per annos/sustentata ruet moles et machina mundi*. Cf. Star (2021), 57–64; on Trimalchio's poem, Setaioli (2014a), 376–7.

[320] Seneca in *De ira* compares a man subject to frenzied anger to Virgil's account of *Discordia* and *Bellona* (Sen. *Ira* 2.35.6, with quotations of Verg. *Aen.* 8.702–3). Cf. Habermehl (2021), 1023–5. The image of *luxuria* as a triumphant general is also in Demetrius the Cynic's speech as reported by Seneca (*Ben.* 7.9.2; below, 3.3.3); see also 4.6 with n. 113.

exhibition has turned into a frenzy towards total demolition. The main reason Pluto gives for starting a war is that luxury buildings are so ubiquitous and extreme that they have penetrated the underworld too, so that the spirits of the dead aim to rise to the sky (120.27–34). This is an original reading of the topos of men crossing the borders between their element, earth, and the other ones, such as water (travelling over sea), air (trying to fly), and now underground. This appears to go against human nature. So while we are dealing with common literary themes, these are treated in a manneristic way, so to speak.

It is evident that, in Petronius' work, *luxuria* is a highly moralistic word, an annoying and useless commonplace brought forth by improvising philosophers and poets. Only dull and ignorant people, such as Trimalchio, or learned but equally dull ones, such as Eumolpus, may think themselves able to impress. *Luxuria* is a sort of symbol of Roman moralistic rhetoric as a whole, which is old-fashioned and no longer suitable for the current level of degradation. Petronius makes fun of this term as he makes fun of Seneca—according to the pivotal study by Peter Sullivan –[321] representing the word and the man as detached from reality or even hypocritical. He follows Horace, who put *luxuria* in the mouth of a self-described philosopher during the Saturnalia,[322] but Petronius goes much farther. He comes out against moral speech altogether. His moralistic attitude, if he has one, works differently. Encolpius, himself an untrustworthy narrator, only shows, and his sole explicit reaction is astonishment: this is, or may be, a new way of teaching readers something.

2.7 Rhetoric (Seneca the Elder and Quintilian): *Luxuria* between Fathers and Sons

Rhetoric is, together with historiography, the field in which attacks against *luxuria* are most frequent.[323] Compared to historiography, rhetoric generally avoids general statements, and focuses on specific and often peculiar episodes, in a somewhat morbid search for novelty and excess that resembles Pliny's interest in *mirabilia*, with the difference that there is no scientific inquiry into nature and that the extremity of most examples makes declamations look like a mere exercise or a contest of moral voyeurism.

[321] Sullivan (1968), 129–39, argues that some of Seneca's letters are a 'direct contribution for the picture of Trimalchio' (137), and that Seneca may have replied to this mockery in his last epistles (210–13). Cf. Star (2012), 84–113; below, 3.2.2.

[322] Above, 2.4.1.

[323] For considerations on moral decline in these literary genres, Williams (1978), 6–51.

2.7.1 Seneca the Elder: Historiographical and Comic Patterns

In Seneca the Elder's collection of *Controversies*, we find *luxuria* quite frequently; it is even the protagonist of *Con.* 2.6. It is commonly linked with money, to the point that it is often part of abdication lawsuits; its opposite is then *paupertas*, 'poverty'.[324] It sometimes refers to stylistic features, and plays a crucial role in father-son relationships, while it only rarely involves women. The preference for economic nuances is to be explained by Roman legislation, which allows the interdiction of property in case of attested prodigality.[325]

Luxuria is placed at the very beginning of the *Controversiae*, i.e. the preface of the first book, which is addressed to his three male sons (Annaeus Mela, who is Lucan's father; Seneca the Younger; and Annaeus Novatus) and deals with the decadence of oratory, a well-known commonplace. This decline is due to three intertwined causes: the looseness of contemporary morality; the lack of incentive for public speaking; and an inexorable cycle of growth and decline.[326] So Seneca lists an ethical, a political, and a philosophical reason for the decline, which will all be important in later authors such as Tacitus and Quintilian. The turning point is placed at the death of Cicero (1.*pr.*7):[327]

> Quidquid Romana facundia habet quod insolenti Graeciae aut opponat aut praeferat circa Ciceronem effloruit; omnia ingenia quae lucem studiis nostris attulerunt tunc nata sunt. In deterius deinde cotidie data res est, sive luxu temporum—nihil enim tam mortiferum ingeniis quam luxuria est—sive, cum pretium pulcherrimae rei cecidisset, translatum est omne certamen ad turpia multo honore questuque vigentia, sive fato quodam, cuius maligna perpetuaque in rebus omnibus lex es ut ad summum perducta rursus ad infimum, velocius quidem quam ascenderant, relabantur.
>
> Everything that Roman oratory has to set alongside of even above haughty Greeks reached his peak in Cicero's day: all the geniuses who have brought brilliance to our subject were born then. Since, things have got daily worse. Perhaps this is due to the luxury of the age (nothing is so fatal to talent as luxury); perhaps, as this glorious art became less prized, competitiveness transferred itself wholly to sordid businesses that bring great prestige and profit; perhaps it is just Fate, whose grim

[324] On the contemporary debate about wealth and poverty, Migliario (1989), 527–33. On *paupertas* and *frugalitas*, Gildenhard (2020), 301–3.

[325] E.g. Gaius *Inst.* 1.53; *Dig.* 27.10.15. For the father-son relationship in the declamations, Imber (2008).

[326] On this issue, and especially on the correspondence between corrupted habits and corrupted oratory, Sussman (1971), 289–91; Sussman (1972), 203–6; Berti (2007), 212–18; van den Berg (2020). Similar considerations are found in Ps.-Longinus' *Sublime* 44.6–7.

[327] Fairweather (1981), 132–43; 310.

law is universal and everlasting—things that get to the top sink back to the bottom, faster than they rose. (Trans. Winterbottom 1974, here and below)

Here we find a sort of adaptation of historiographical *clichés* of the decline of modern times, as in Sallust and Livy,[328] to declamation: prejudice against the East (*insolenti Graeciae*); irreversible decline; luxury as its cause; fate as the ultimate explanation. This commonplace might also have appeared in Seneca's own and now lost historiographical work.[329] The ethical explanation seems the most relevant, since, following the famous definition of the orator as a 'good man skilled in speaking',[330] which goes back to Cato the Censor, Seneca thinks that an evil man cannot be an orator. This principle, probably of Stoic origin,[331] was already in Cicero and will remain crucial in later authors. So, again, Cato appears as the ultimate source of all kinds of moralistic speeches.[332]

It is worth noting the perfect overlap established by Seneca between *luxus* and *luxuria*, which emphasizes the economic aspect of things. Yet this vice is also characterized as terribly dangerous, indeed it is personified and defined as death-bringing (*mortiferum*), as if it were a poison or a mortal and infectious disease, and so it appears like the overwhelming and evil law (*maligna... lex*) of fate, described right afterwards as a force that casts down everything that has risen. This is another widespread (poetic) commonplace, whose originality here lies in representing fate not as a blind force but as a hateful entity. Seneca's preface thus turns into a tragic scene, where *luxuria* assists evil fate against human progress and brings death and degradation.

To underscore these ideas, Seneca describes the young men of his time, against whom he warns his sons: they are weak, effeminate, and devoted to *deliciae* and every womanly activity and pleasure, such as dancing and singing (1.*pr.*8). This shows that *luxuria* is not always economic, as its connection with *luxus* made it appear, but also affects morality as a form of lust, as happens in Valerius Maximus.[333]

It seems that Seneca with this passage aims to imitate higher literary genres, above all historiography, representing oratory and its decline as a sort of specification of the general principle shown for the development of human history as a whole. While historiographers cite *luxuria* with other vices, such as *avaritia*, and only later come to the subject of fate, Seneca synthetizes and dramatizes the narrative, focusing solely on luxury (*luxus/luxuria*) personified, which is lethal and on the same level as evil fate. So, by elevating the scene with tragic patterns, he compensates for its lesser concerns, which do not involve the macroscopic events of Roman history but only the decline of a specific art.

328 Above, 2.3. 329 On which see Scappaticcio (2020).

330 Cato, *ad M. fil.* frg. 18 Sbl. = 14 Jord. = 370 Sch. *vir bonus dicendi peritus*, quoted in Sen. *Con.*1.*pr.*9, Quint. 12.1.1, and Apul. *Apol.* 94.

331 Kennedy (1963), 293 with n. 49. 332 Above, 2.1.2. 333 Above, 2.5.1.

If we take a comprehensive look at Seneca's *Controversiae*, we find L. Licinius Lucullus, a late Republic nobleman renowned for his luxury banquets, as an emblematic example of *luxuria*;[334] we spot *luxuria* as prodigality (1.1.1) and opposed to sobriety (*paupertas*, 2.1.5–7 and 12–13, quoted below); as a stylistic negative device (attributed to the young Fabianus, *Con.* 2*pr.*2; to Fuscus, *Suas.* 2.10); and as typical of women (*Con.* 2.5.7) and especially young sons: in this case, as in archaic comedy,[335] money and lust are intertwined, since a young man in love (especially if with a prostitute) will waste all the family assets. This motif is frequently present in Seneca the Elder, where an accusation of *luxuria* appears to be a legal reason for disinheritance (e.g. 7.1.26), even if there is no evidence.[336] Sons' *luxuria*, a commonplace since the archaic comedies, also appears in Cicero's speeches; yet this commonplace may lead to paradoxical consequences.

For example, a son who is too involved in war may be pushed by his worried father to calm down, and consider this exhortation as an invitation to vice (1.8.2). We find here a general statement of a certain interest (1.8.5):

> Luxuria, avaritia, desidia, invidia, timor non dediscuntur, et cotidie omnia haec aut castigantur aut puniuntur: tam etiam vitiorum tenaces sumus. Crede mihi, pater, non sum mei iuris cum ille proelii clamor exhortus est...
>
> Luxury, avarice, sloth, envy, fear cannot be unlearned-and every day all these things are either reproved or punished, so tenacious are we even of our vices. Believe me, father, I cannot control myself when the familiar noise of battle has burst out.

The son pictures his fight against enemies as an overwhelming passion, comparing it to 'normal' ones, of which *luxuria* is the foremost, diseases that are untreatable in spite of relentless efforts to eradicate them. Here, as opposed to in the preface, there is no reference to the origin of the passions, which seem innate, and their incurability indicates moral pessimism, but understood in a new and dangerous way: if vices do not heal, moral education is useless, and society is doomed to decline.[337]

[334] *Con.* 9.2.1 and 19 (below, n. 341); cf. Vell. 2.33.4 'as for Lucullus, who was otherwise a great man, he was the first to set the example for our present lavish extravagance (*luxuria*) in building, in banquets, and in furnishings. Because of the massive piles which he built in the sea, and of his letting the sea in upon the land by digging through mountains, Pompey used to call him, and not without point, the Roman Xerxes.' (Trans. Shipley 1961; the anecdote is reported also by Plin. *HN* 9.170). Plutarch also stresses Lucullus' luxury in his *Life of Lucullus*. Cf. Amela Valverde (2023).

[335] On the general connections between declamation and comedy, Bianco (2018), 50–60.

[336] Cf. Bonner (2012), 313–15.

[337] Seneca, on the other hand, believes in the possibility of improving people, even if he is pessimistic about the effect of his own efforts (below, 4.8).

When it comes to fathers' *luxuria*, it is unconventional and absolutely condemned. A case study is *Con.* 2.6, entitled *Pater et filius luxuriosi.*[338] Here is the argument:

> Quidam luxuriante filio luxuriari coepit. Filius accusat patrem dementiae.
>
> A man began to be a debauchee, his son already being one; the son accuses his father of madness.

Even if the son is merged in the same vice as his father, he blames him, because while *luxuria* is tolerated at young age, it is deplorable in old men.

In favour of the father, we have a description of a life devoted to *luxuria*, by Arellius Fuscus senior (2.6.2):

> 'Sed tu' inquit 'senex es.' Unde scis te non futurum luxuriosum senem? Omnia a te vitia: quod unguento coma madet, tuum est; quod laxior usque in pedes demittitur toga, tuum est.
>
> 'But *you* are an old man.' 'How do you know *you* won't be extravagant in your old age? -All my faults arise from you; that my hair is soaked in perfume is your doing. That my toga drops too loosely right to my feet is your doing.

A piece in favour of the son is attributed to Iunius Gallio (2.6.4):

> A laudibus patris incipiam. Fuit hic adulescens temperatissimus, et lubricum tempus sine infamia transit...Iam senex factus est, nisi quod sibi nondum videtur; <in> luxuriam usque eo se proiecit ut accusem. Senex amans, senex ebrius...nonne portentum est? Luxuriosus adulescens peccat; at senex luxuriosus insanit.
>
> 'I shall begin with praise on my father. He was moderate in his youth, and passed through that slippery time without blemish....Now he is old, except that he doesn't think he is. He has flung himself so deep in debauchery that I am prosecuting him. An old man in love, an old man drunk...is this not a prodigy! An extravagant youth is misbehaving; an extravagant old man is mad.'

Gallio ends with a sentence that summarizes a typically Roman idea: a young man devoted to *luxuria* is misbehaving, but an old man who does so is insane, a sort of monster (*portentum*), something exceeding average habits and customs, while intemperance at a young age is tolerated and perfectly normal.[339] The same equivalence between old men's vices and madness is drawn elsewhere. Of another

338 Fairweather (1981), 113; Bianco (2018), 60–72.

339 Cf. also 2.6.7 *utique nulli non nimis luxuriosus sed parum sanus videbatur.*

father, who is accused of insanity by his son, who has adopted a nephew born to another son and a prostitute, Cestius Pius says (2.4.9):[340]

> Oderat luxuriam, vitia castigabat. Hunc tam severum senem putabitis si vobis in lupanari ostendero?
>
> 'He used to hate extravagance, castigate vice. Will you think this stern father sane if I show him to you in a brothel?'

Luxuria here stands in for all vices, with special emphasis on lust, considering the mention of a brothel. The philosophical framework in this passage is Stoic, since Cestius opens his reasoning by saying that *dementia... est sanitati contraria*, 'madness... is the opposite of health' (*ibid.*), which connects with Gallio's sentence quoted above and is also rooted in the idea of a neat opposition between antithetical concepts, a typically Stoic notion (and Seneca, in this same context, calls the passage 'a nice figure').

Luxuria can also be associated[341] with cruelty in historical examples, as in the case in which the proconsul Flamininus, when during a banquet a prostitute said that she had never seen a beheading, immediately ordered an execution (9.2). Argentarius (9.2.1) mentions *luxuria* in his account of the episode, which combines lust, gluttony, and disrespect for humanity. A similar but even more terrifying connection to cruelty involves Mark Antony, whom Pompeius Silo calls *sanguine civili luxuriantem*, 'revelling in the blood of Romans' (*Suas.* 7.5). Antony is depicted as a beast thirsty for human blood, as already in Cicero (*Phil.* 4.11), but with the present participle of the verb *luxurior*, indicating his restless desire and almost erotic enjoyment in killing his fellow citizens.[342]

A more traditional picture of *luxuria*, which is very close to the so-called cynic diatribes and is attributed to Papirius Fabianus, an orator who later turned to philosophy, is the following (Sen. *Con.* 2.1.12–13):[343]

> Ad delicias dementis luxuriae lapis omnis eruitur, caeduntur ubique gentium silvae; aeris ferrique usus, iam auri quoque, in extruendis et decorandis domibus, nempe ut anxii et interdiu et nocte ruinam ignemque metuant;... In hos ergo exitus varius ille secatur lapis et tenui fronte parietem tegit?... in hoc pavimentum tesselatum et infusum tectis aurum? 13. O paupertas, quam ignotum bonum es!

[340] Bianco (2018), 56.

[341] *Con.* 9.2.19, where Votienus Montanus lists four examples of Roman generals whose flaws were tolerated by their people, two (Gurges and Lucullus) guilty of *luxuria*, and two (Manlius and Sulla) guilty of cruelty. Cf. van der Poel (2009), 340–2.

[342] A similar description, with particular attention to drunkenness, is in Seneca's *EM* 83.20–5 (below, 4.6).

[343] Fairweather (1981), 272–5; Migliario (1989), 531–3; Bernstein (2009), 339–43.

> To meet the whims of crazy luxury every stone is quarried, forests are felled throughout the world. Bronze and iron, and now gold too, are set to building and decorating houses-I suppose so that their owners may be able to worry day and night over the risks of fire and collapse.... It is to meet this end that mottled stone is cut to cover walls with its thin veneer? It is for this that the floor is covered with mosaic and gold poured on the roofs? 13. Poverty, how little known a good are you!

This controversy is between a son who refuses to be adopted by a rich man, and his poor father who has disinherited him. Seneca gives Fabianus, who, significantly, speaks only on behalf of the son, while the other rhetors take both sides, a lot of space to tackle this argument, which is expressed in forms similar to that used by many moralistic writers, such as Seneca the Younger, who was one of Fabianus' pupils as a philosopher, and Pliny the Elder.[344] Interestingly, as in 2.1.5–7 (above), it is *paupertas* 'poverty, sobriety', and not *frugalitas*, to be opposed to *luxuria*. The contrast in this case is stronger and sharper.

Also following tradition, Cassius Severus quotes some lines by Publilius Syrus, a mimographer who was famous for his moralistic sentences (7.3.8 = Publil. *Sent.* 236 Meyer): *desunt luxuriae multa, avaritiae omnia.* This sentence is also quoted by Seneca the Younger (*EM* 108.9), who emphasizes *luxuria*'s restless desire and thereby connects it with *avaritia*.[345] This is not a juxtaposition of contraries, as in e.g. Sallust,[346] but different degrees of lack, for greediness is considered as poverty, *luxuria* as need. In this light, the former vice is worse than the latter, and leads more suffering. For once, *luxuria* seems to be dethroned.

On Seneca the Elder, we may conclude that *luxuria* is a frequent topic in his work. Its discussion is linked with a general consideration of moral decline, as in historiography, and with comedy (see the relevance of the father-son relationship), and, at least vaguely, with Stoicism (see the link with Cato, and Fabianus' prevalence among the quoted or mentioned orators).[347]

2.7.2 The Teacher's View: Quintilian

As for Quintilian, *luxuria* is only one vice among many, receiving no special attention, and belongs in the *amplificatio*, the sections one adds to a speech for aesthetic reasons (*Inst.* 4.3.15). While it regularly refers to prodigal sons, especially

[344] Cf. previous n.; for Seneca the Younger, Rolland (1906), 38–9 (38–44 on the general subject of luxury in both authors).

[345] Below, 4.5; Giancotti (1992). Publilius was also quoted by Petronius (above, 2.6.3). While the Younger appreciates and more than once quotes sentences of this kind, in the Elder they are very rare: Fairweather (1981), 311.

[346] Above, 2.3.1.

[347] Fabianus (below, 3.3.3 with n. 64) belonged to the Roman philosophical school of the Sextii, but their ideas were very close to Stoic ones, as Seneca the younger states (*NQ* 7.32.2).

when they are in love with prostitutes, it may also include fathers:[348] this is the case in the collections of the so-called *Major* and *Minor Declamations*, where the debate on this vice often includes a father-son conflict and the sons are generally treated sympathetically.[349] This implies that, just as in Seneca the Elder, *luxuria* almost exclusively involves men. Further, a certain number of occurrences are quotations from or allusions to Cicero,[350] whose treatment of the subject was evidently considered seminal. It is also interesting to note that Quintilian constructs a sort of semantic field around *luxuria*, listing a number of synonyms and antonyms: he thereby offers us a precise view of how this vice was understood in his time.

We find *luxuria* in the context of love (*amor*, *Inst.* 2.4.23), cheating (*adulterium*, 5.10.19 and 20), and lust (*libido*, 12.1.8), as opposed to sobriety (*frugalitas*, 5.10.27 and 73; 12.1.8),[351] as mere generosity, and as a defence strategy (*liberalitas*, 5.13.26; cf. 8.6.36). There is also the following etymological play (3.8.28):

> Tamen quibusdam videtur esse nonnumquam de iucunditate sola consultatio, ut si de aedificando theatro, instituendis ludis deliberetur. Sed neminem adeo solutum luxu puto ut nihil in causa suadendi sequatur praeter voluptatem.
>
> Some however believe that deliberation is sometimes concerned only with pleasure, as in discussions about building a theatre or founding games. But I do not think that anyone is sunk so far in luxury as to consider nothing but pleasure in an advisory speech. (Trans. Russell 2001, here and below)

Quintilian is discussing in a *Suasoria* the case of uselessness in public works or initiatives, and points out that these cannot be only a matter of pleasure, because there is always a serious reason for them, such as honouring a god during public games. The expression *solutum luxu*, 'sunk in luxury' (cf. above, 1.1; Liv. 40.1.4; Sil. 2.502; Tac. *Hist.* 2.99.3; *Ann.* 11.31.2) and its connection with pleasure, illustrate an awareness of *luxuria*'s etymology and its causes: a sort of melting (*solvere*) provoked by excessive wealth (*luxus*), which leads to a restless search for pleasure (*voluptas*). Quintilian knows the Roman tradition regarding this vice also in specific contexts. Literary culture, he says, will be more appreciated in Athens than in Sparta, and then goes on (*Inst.* 3.7.24):

348 E.g. *Inst.* 5.10.47; 11.1.79. In 11.3.74, Quintilian lists the *luxuriosus* young man among the comedy characters.

349 E.g. *Mai. Decl.* 5.11; *Min. Decl.* 252.10; 290.*pr.*; 304; 298.3, 9 and 14; 316; 330; 356.*pr.*1; 367.*pr.*1; 371.1. According to Sussman (1995), this happens because the declamations were supposed to be exercises for teenagers, so this kind of subject matched their interest (and also let them vent their conflicting feelings towards their fathers). Cf. also Vesley (2003), 173–7 specifically on *luxuria*; specifically, on *Major Declamations*, Lamberti (2021), who argues that the smoothening of the father figure reflects the loss of power of the *paterfamilias* in the second to third centuries CE.

350 Especially from the speeches *Pro Caelio* (Quint. *Inst.* 2.4.23 and 4.2.27), *Philippicae* (8.4.25), *Pro Murena* (9.3.82); cf. also 8.3.66.

351 Cf. Gildenhard (2020), 326–9.

> Frugalitas apud Sybaritas forsitan odio foret, veteribus Romanis summum luxuria crimen.
>
> Frugality might seem repulsive to the Sybarites, luxury the worst crime in the eyes of the Romans of old.

Sybaris was an ancient Greek colony near Taranto renowned for licentiousness,[352] and it undoes the classic opposition between Roman sobriety and Eastern luxury with two relevant details: first, there are no hints that the supposed pollution comes from the East, and Quintilian merely mentions this town that in his day had been reduced to a tiny village and whose luxuriousness was lost in a fabulous past; second, he discusses the ancient (*veteribus*), not the contemporary Romans. In doing so he labels the whole issue as old-fashioned, implying that the Romans of his time would not have been critical to *luxuria*. This is the position that Pliny the Younger expresses.[353]

We may conclude that the most relevant semantic element of *luxuria*, from Quintilian's point of view, is economic, as shown by the opposition with sobriety and by the association with the virtue of generosity. The connection with erotic pleasure is taken for granted, since a young man in love will have many expenses; a related passage takes aim at the indecency of luxury and effeminate clothing (12.10.47).[354] The worst consequence of erotic behaviour, from a social point of view, is indeed economic, since it may bankrupt a family, and this explains Quintilian's semantic field.

Quintilian also uses *luxuria* to describe inopportune stylistic exuberance, which should be limited. The positive equivalent of this flaw is 'rich' (12.10.80 *laetus*), and its opposite attribute is 'austere' (9.4.69 *severus*), while the suggested remedy is to 'restrain' it (10.4.1 *adstringere*). Here the semantic field is closer to the biological than the ethical, except for severity, which does belong to the ancient virtues that are *luxuria*'s opposites.

Quintilian shows that, from a semantic point of view, *luxuria* still keeps all its nuances, from lust to luxury, almost indistinguishable from each other, with the added ideas of exuberance and melting. The moralistic paradigm of *luxuria* versus *frugalitas* may be of use in declamations, but does not actually apply to the real world anymore.

2.8 An Eccentric Epic: Lucan

As I have said above (2.4), *luxuria* is not a poetic word: poetry, and especially epic, prefers the more generic *luxus*, and this term is also not very frequent, given its

[352] Above, 1.4. [353] Below, 5.1. [354] Austin (1948), 190–1.

distance from the typical themes of the genre. But in this respect, as in many others,[355] Lucan represents an exception. Indeed in his poem we find, in addition to *luxus*, both *luxuria* and its fifth declension form *luxuries*; he reserves a lot of space for the banquet of Caesar and Cleopatra and models it after many epic descriptions, among which is that of Aeneas and Dido in Virgil's *Aeneid*.[356] But he refers back to other literary genres as well: indeed, in its remake with Mark Antony and Cleopatra, it is tackled as an example of luxury both by Seneca the Younger (below, 4.6) and Pliny (above, 2.5.2). Lucan summons both historiographical and moralistic *clichés* regarding *luxuria*. The former stem from his subject, which is part of recent Roman history and not of a mythical past; the latter are connected to his following Stoic philosophy, like his uncle Seneca the Younger.

Luxus makes its appearance in the opening of book 1, when Lucan analyses the causes of the conflict between Caesar and Pompey, and connects it to the spreading of fortune, thus following the traditional historiographical scheme (1.160–7):[357]

> Namque, ut opes nimias mundo fortuna subacto
> intulit et rebus mores cessere secundis
> praedaque et hostiles luxum suasere rapinae,
> non auro tectisve modus, mensasque priores
> aspernata fames; cultus gestare decoros
> vix nuribus rapuere mares; fecunda virorum
> paupertas fugitur totoque accersitur orbe
> quo gens quaeque perit...

For when Rome had conquered the world and Fortune showered excess of wealth upon her, virtue was dethroned by prosperity, and the spoil taken from the enemy lured men to extravagance: they set no limit to their wealth or their dwellings; greed rejected the food that once sufficed; men seized for their use garments scarce decent for women to wear; poverty, the mother of manhood, became a bugbear; and from all the earth was brought the special bane of each nation. (Trans. Duff 1962, here and below)

In this passage, there is a clear recollection of the myth of virtuous deities who are banished from, or abandon earth because of moral decline (cf. ll. 165–6 *fecunda virorum/paupertas fugitur*), as is the case with Astraea, the goddess of justice.[358] Relevant are also the references to Sallust and Livy and their interpretation of

[355] On Lucan's originality as an epic poet, cf. the recent overviews of Reed (2011), Hardie (2013), and Williams (2017).

[356] Lanzarone (2021), 322, with bibliography. In general, on the affair between Caesar and Cleopatra and its literary sources and fortune, Zwierlein (1974), with 63–4 on Aeneas and Dido; below, nn. 362–4.

[357] Roche (2009), 197–8, who compares Sall. *Cat.* 12.2.

[358] E.g. in Ov. *Met.* 1.149–50. Cf. Iuv. 6.19–20 *paulatim deinde ad superos Astraea recessit/hac* [*sc. Pudicitia*] *comite, atque duae pariter fugere sorores* with Watson (2012), 62–4; above, 2.6.2. Astraea is the deity Virgil sees as returning with a renewed golden age, in *Ecl.* 4. On *paupertas*, above, 2.7.1.

excessive fortune as the starting point of decline. The same idea is expressed at 4.816–19,[359] where Curio's ruin is traced to his corruption by Caesar's gold, and is viewed as an example of Rome's doomed destiny.

In book 4, we find another commonplace, already hinted at in the passage quoted above, but pre-eminently moralistic: the comparison between the current struggle for exotic food and drinks and the simple needs of nature (4.373–8):[360]

> ... O prodiga rerum
> luxuries numquam parvo contenta paratis
> et quaesitorum terra pelagoque ciborum
> ambitiosa fames et lautae gloria mensae,
> discite quam parvo liceat producere vitam
> et quantum natura petat....

Oh Luxury, extravagant of resources and never satisfied with what costs little; and ostentatious hunger for dainties sought over land and sea; and ye who take pride in delicate eating—hence ye may learn how little it costs to prolong life, and how little nature demands.

Luxuria, here in its fifth declension variant, is connected with prodigality as usual (ll. 373–4). Then, in book 9, Cato's eulogy of Pompey after his death stresses that his house was chaste and free from luxury (9.201 *casta domus luxuque carens*...).[361] This creates a sharp contrast to book 10, where Caesar's tyrannical degeneration at the splendid table of Cleopatra, with all kinds of Oriental luxury, is described. As has been noted, the description of the queen's palace, even if modelled on many epic precedents, is ideologically oriented towards moralistic judgement, and, despite the insistence on the barbarian location, is actually reminiscent of the magnificence of Neronian age villas and thereby probably hints at the emperor's love of excess.[362] First, Lucan stresses how the Egyptian queen's luxury was unknown in Rome (10.110 *nondum translatos in Romana saecula luxus*, 'magnificence which Roman society had not yet adopted');[363] he then lists the excesses of her struggle for exhibition and seduction (10.155–8):[364]

> Infudere epulas auro, quod terra, quod aer,
> quod pelagus Nilusque dedit, quod luxus inani

[359] *Perdita tunc urbi nocuerunt saecula, postquam/ambitus et luxus et opum metuenda facultas/ transverso mentem dubiam torrente tulerunt*; cf. Asso (2010), 291; Tracy (2014), 45–6.

[360] Asso (2010), 185; Tracy (2014), 44–5; D'Urso (2022), 557–8.

[361] Wick (2004), 75; Seewald (2008), 130–1.

[362] Lanzarone (2021); on the allusion to Nero and his *domus aurea* in this passage, Morford (1968), 170–1; Voisin (1987), 540; Tracy (2011), 37 and 50; Tracy (2014), 10–12.

[363] Schmidt (1986), 182–3; Berti (2000), 125. On the connection between Egypt and luxury under any respect, Tracy (2014), 31–59.

[364] Schmidt (1986), 237–41; Berti (2000), 151–3, and D'Urso (2022), 752, who stress the affinities between this passage (with 4.373–8) and Seneca the Younger's prose; especially on the motif of seduction, Caston (2011), 149.

ambitione furens toto quaesivit in orbe
non mandante fame...

They served on gold a banquet of every dainty that earth or air, the sea or the Nile affords, all that extravagance, unspurred by hunger and maddened by idle love of display, has sought out over all the earth.

Right before this, Lucan stresses that not only Caesar but even the legendarily austere Fabricius and Curius[365] would have surrendered to such opulence (10.149–54); here, he clearly considers excessive luxury as a form of madness (l. 157 *furens*) due to an ambition that is itself vain (ll. 156–7 *inani/ambitione*; cf. ll. 146–7). This is entirely separate from the natural instinct of hunger, and it makes Cleopatra collect every delicious thing in the world (note the list of three natural elements: earth, air, sea, ll. 155–6) to achieve her aim. As Seneca says, this kind of pursuit is endless, and destined to fail (below, 4.1), but Lucan stops with its initial success, i.e. the conquest of Caesar's heart, which in turn leads to the complete destruction of Rome and the Republic. It is interesting how Lucan reduces the triad of Sallustian vices—greed, luxury, ambition—to two, subsuming the first two under *luxuria* without distinction. This is the logical consequence of the strict connection between greed and luxury that Sallust has already stated.

Not only Cleopatra's banquets, but also her palace is described as a *luxuriosa domus* (10.488), by dint of being extended into the sea:[366] this is an element that moralistic authors such as Seneca consider against nature (e.g. in *EM* 89.21: below, 4.4).

Lucan's treatment of *luxuria* is closer to that of Sallust and Seneca than to that of any epic poet; the very presence of the word indicates this, and is evidence of Lucan's experimental attitude.

2.9 Jurists against *Luxuria*: The Sumptuary Laws

Sumptuary laws have a long history, stretching from ancient Greece to the Enlightenment,[367] or even to the present, if we count under this rubric the additional taxes on luxury goods that are widespread nowadays.

In Rome there was even a magistrate dedicated to this, namely the censor—the office to which Cato the Elder (above, 2.1.2) belonged—and there is a list of senators and even proconsuls expelled by the senate for excessive luxury.[368]

365 Above, 2.5.2 with n. 246.
366 Berti (2000), 322–3.
367 Cf. Berry (1994), 74–84; Bottiglieri (2002); Zanda (2011); Righi/Vettori (2019); McClintock (2022).
368 E.g. Cornelius Rufinus, the consul of 277, expelled by Fabricius, the censor of 275 whose frugality was legendary (Val. Max. 2.9.4; on Fabricius, above, 2.5.2 with n. 246); L. Veturius, expelled by the

Already the XII Tables contain limitations to funeral expenses.[369] The first great measure against luxury was the *Lex Oppia* of 215 BCE, of which Livy narrates the repeal, which occurred in 195 (above, 2.3.2). Its purpose is not entirely clear, but it is evident that it was linked to the second Punic war and the corresponding economic crisis, and it was likely an attempt to limit the exhibition of wealth by newly widowed heiresses.[370] As is noted by ancient sources,[371] after failing to stop the repeal of the law, Cato reacted with a censorial penalty, not just for women but for the whole population, which sanctioned luxury goods and habits.

As noted by scholars, sumptuary laws concern primarily the key landscape of *luxuria*, that is, the banquet.[372] Some such laws are the *Lex Orchia* (182 BC), of which we do not know much; the *Lex Fannia* (161 BCE), which only concerned public banquets during religious festivals and was further narrowed by the *Lex Didia* (143 BCE) and *Lex Licinia* (140 BCE); the *Lex Scaura* (115 BCE); and further ones attributed to Sulla (81 BCE), who revived the issue of luxury funerals, Caesar (46 BCE), who promulgated the strictest of all sumptuary laws, restoring the measures against jewellery and chariots in the *Lex Oppia*, and Augustus (18 BCE).[373] The focus on banquets and public expenditure aimed to limit the number of clients and thereby the personal power that humiliated those members of the senatorial class who could not afford to be patrons, and that also threatened the Republic itself. It is striking that in the last century of the Republic, the issue of luxury involved central political personalities: it was evidently used as part of a general propaganda to convince noblemen of their connection with archaic and sober frugality, with authentic Roman values. In the Republican era they were probably proposed by senators to convey their own social primacy in response to the growing economic power of the equestrians.[374] This limited the profusion of money to the Roman population by magistrate candidates that was typical of

same Cato (*ORF*[4] 8.75 = frg. 65 Sbl. = Gell. 17.2.19). The tribune Duronius was expelled by the censors M. Antonius and L. Flaccus (98 BCE) for having tried to abrogate a sumptuary law promulgated by L. Licinius Crassus in 104 BCE (Val. Max. 2.9.5).

[369] Cic. *Leg.* 2.59 *iam cetera in XII minuendi sumptus lamentationisque funeris traslata sunt de Solonis fere legibus*; cf. 2.64; a detailed list of the measures is in Bottiglieri (2002), 43–4 n. 10; cf. Zanda (2011), 27–36.

[370] Vettori (2019).

[371] Liv. 39.44.1–3; Plut. *Cato Mai.* 18.2–3; Corn. Nep. *Cato* 2.3.

[372] Gowers (1996), 21. Indeed, Cato the Elder named sumptuary laws *cibaria* (above, 2.1.2).

[373] Clemente (1981); Baltrusch (1989), 40–102; Landolfi (1990), 51–67; 76–91; Coudry (2004), 152–68 (synoptic table on p. 170–1); Dari-Mattiacci/Plisecka (2010), 1–15 (synoptic table on p. 11); Zanda (2011), 49–71 (catalogue on p. 113–28). On a *lex Voconia* supported by Cato the Censor, McClintock (2022), 1–55. Especially on the laws promulgated by Sulla and Caesar, Lonardi (2007); especially on Augustus' politics, Marshall (2008), 98–110; Casinos Mora (2015). As for ancient sources: *Lex Orchia*: Macr. *Sat.* 3.17.1–3; *Lex Fannia*: Gell. 2.24.3–6; *Lex Didia*: Macrob. *Sat.* 3.17.6; *Lex Licinia*: Gell. 2.24.7–10; 15.8; *Lex Scaura*: Gell. 2.24.12; Plin. *HN* 8.82; *Lex Cornelia*: Macrob. *Sat.* 3.17.11–12; Gell. 2.24.11; Amm. 16.5.1; *Lex Iulia Caesaris*: Cic. *Att.* 13.7; Dio 43.25.2; Suet. *Iul.* 43; *Lex Iulia sumptuaria*, 18 BCE: Gell. 2.24.14; Suet. *Aug.* 43; see also following notes. On sumptuary laws related to purple, Casinos Mora (2023).

[374] Dari-Mattiacci/Plisecka (2010), esp. 2.

Republican electoral competitions and that represented a strong social bond.[375] With the reduction of such expenses, luxury became pre-eminently confined to the private sphere. Sumptuary laws thus yielded the exact opposite result of the famous Ciceronian sentence, *Mur.* 76 *privata luxuria publica magnificentia* (above, 2.2.1).

The debate on luxury had its zenith during Tiberius' reign, after which, even if it was still probably mentioned in the occasional senatorial discussion, it ceased to be of interest to historians in that context. Tacitus, whose personal interest in the subject is undeniable (below, 5.2.2), is our main source in this regard. He reports a sumptuary law proposal by Octavius Fronto, a former praetor. He and the proconsul Quintus Haterius proposed the prohibition of golden tableware and silk clothing for men. Fronto went further, proposing a limitation on furniture, silverware, and slaves. His speech was opposed by Asinius Gallus, who argued against luxury limitations (16 CE).[376] The speech, which deliberately took a stand against the moral dimension of the issue, was delivered in the presence of Tiberius, who supported the orator; the law proposal was rejected (*Ann.* 2.33.3–4):

> Auctu imperii adolevisse etiam privatas opes, idque non novum, sed e vetustissimis moribus...nisi forte clarissumo [*sc.* fuit] cuique plures curas, maiora pericula subeunda, delenimentis curarum et periculorum carendum esse. 4. Facilem adsensum Gallo sub nominibus honestis confessio vitiorum ex similitudo audientium dedit. Adiecerat et Tiberius non id tempus censurae nec, si quid in moribus labaret, defuturum corrigendi auctorem.
>
> With the expansion of the empire private wealth too had grown, and that was no novelty but in accordance with the most olden traditions...unless perchance all the most brilliant men were required to undertake more numerous concerns and greater dangers but to do without the assuagements of those concerns and dangers. Easy assent to Gallus was provided by his listeners' confessing to similar vices under honorable names. Tiberius too had added that that was not the time for a review, but, if there was any slip in behavior, an instigator of reform would not be lacking and would not fail in his duty.
>
> (Trans. Woodman 2004, here and below)

It is interesting that, while summarizing the speech against luxury, Tacitus pauses at the one point that defends it, evidently because it highlights the moral decline of the senatorial class. Gallus' main argument is cultural: it has been like this for a long time. Further, he maintains, the ruling class deserves luxury as an adequate compensation for its responsibility—and this is a striking idea for a culture that in

[375] Maiuro (2019), 91.

[376] Cf. Dio 57.12.1–2; Woodman/Martin (1996), 376–8; Baltrusch (1989), 155–62; Bottiglieri (2002), 13–19; Maiuro (2019), 92–3.

the late Republic did not pay magistrates for their job, so that political office was not pursued for money.

In *Ann.* 3.53–4, Tacitus reports the aediles' request to limit banquet expenses, as well as the emperor's famous reply in a letter (22 CE).[377] The emperor was for a long time irresolute about how to react (3.52.3):

> Sed Tiberius saepe apud se pensitato, an coerceri iam profusae cupidines possent, num coercitio plus damni in rem publicam ferret, quam indecorum adtrectare quod non obtineret vel retentum ignominiam et infamiam virorum inlustrium posceret, postremo litteras ad senatum composuit...
>
> But Tiberius—having often pondered to himself whether such surging desires could be confined, whether their confinement would inflict a greater loss on the state, and how undignified it would be to handle something which he could not attain or which, if sustained, would entail ignominy and infamy for illustrious men—finally composed a letter to the senate...

Tiberius' concerns are not at all ethical, but political: since the search for pleasure is already widespread (*profusae cupidines*), it is either no longer possible to restrict it or inopportune, because it would create discontent among the upper classes. In his letter, Tiberius repeats some of Gallus' arguments: these vices are by now well-rooted and adult (3.53.2 *praevalida et adulta*). Tiberius lists all the forms of luxury that moralistic works attack (assets, slaves, gold, artwork, clothing, gems), the failure of previous measures, and also the most frequent arguments about the beginnings of moral decline, such as the conquest of a foreign people, and so on (3.54.3). He then shows how insignificant this issue is when compared to the major problems of the Empire, which depends on foreign supplies whose suppression would destroy the whole economy. He presents the matter as simply irrelevant, unworthy of public attention. He reduces this vice to what it originally was: a psychological matter (3.54.5):

> Reliquis intra animum medendum est: nos pudor, pauperes necessitas, divites satias in melius mutet.
>
> For other things the remedy must be within the mind: let ourselves be changed for the better by shame, the poor by necessity, the rich by satiety.

Later, in *Ann.* 4.6.4 and 6, Tacitus discusses the emperor's ethical and psychological decline, chastising him for habits far more vicious than those he refused to consider regarding the senators. He also quotes Plato's famous image of the tyrant's soul teared apart by vices (*Rep.* 9.579d–e: below, 5.2.2). According to

[377] Coudry (2004), 149–52 and 168–70; Mastrorosa (2007); Marshall (2008); Maiuro (2019), 92–6.

Tacitus, the emperor should not go too far in his castigation of the senators, if he does not want them to revolt. But since, at least officially, moral discourse is still in favour of frugality and sobriety, the prince, as the representative of the whole Empire, should display those virtues himself.[378] The senators may be allowed greater assets precisely because they no longer represent the Roman people; their role is irrelevant and at most symbolic, so their behaviour it is not worthy of public concern. But everyone's eyes are on the emperor, so he has as far possible to embody the ideal Roman.

As already stated, after this episode the debate on luxury disappears from the historical record of senatorial meetings. Under Nero, we find it applied to private relationships between the emperor and specific persons.[379] The most famous case is, of course, that of Seneca (below, 3.1), but it was not the only one. Generally speaking, moderation, which naturally entailed refusing the emperor's gifts and also declining to imitate his habits, was a way of forming political opposition. On the other hand, wealth was also dangerous, not only because, if received from Nero, it was an instrument of blackmail but also because it might arouse his covetousness. Many people were in fact charged and condemned mainly because the emperor wanted to get hold of their property. This state of affairs admittedly long predated Nero and can be traced back all the way to the Roman proscriptions.

So the end of sumptuary laws did not entail the end of *luxuria* as a problem, but a shifting of perspectives on luxury as a political instrument: formerly it was a means by senators of eliciting consent from the Roman people, and later it became limited to personal relationships between individual noblemen and the emperor.

The relevance of this issue is also shown by the fact that two authors, Gellius (second century CE) and Macrobius (fourth-fifth century CE), give us a chronological list of sumptuary laws from a more scholarly perspective. Gellius titles his list *De vetere parsimonia, deque antiquis legibus sumptuariis* (2.24.*pr.*1), and the sole occurrence of *luxuria* in this passage refers to an imperial law. He states that he is uncertain whether it was promulgated by Augustus or Tiberius (2.24.15):

> Esse etiam dicit Capito Ateius edictum—diuine Augusti an Tiberii Caesaris non satis commemini— quo edicto per dierum uarias sollemnitates a trecentis sestertiis adusque duo sestertia sumptus cenarum propagatus est, ut his saltem finibus luxuriae efferuescentis aestus coerceretur.
>
> Ateius Capito says that there is still another edict-but whether of the deified Augustus or of Tiberius Caesar I do not exactly remember—by which the outlay for dinners on various festal days was increased from three hundred sesterces to two thousand, to the end that the rising tide of luxury might be restrained at least within those limits. (Trans. Rolfe 1960)

378 Maiuro (2019), 93–6.
379 Maiuro (2019), 96–103.

While other laws are simply described by what they prohibit, this one—the last one—is enriched by the image of *luxuria* as an overwhelming tsunami: this makes us think, even if Gellius does not explicitly say so, that every effort against it is useless. Macrobius, for his part, defines as *luxuria* most of the habits sanctioned by the laws (*Sat.* 3.17), and then devotes a considerable amount of space to the anecdote of Cleopatra and Mark Antony's banquet, where they melted and drank precious pearls (3.17.14–18).[380] The inclusion of this story is due to the fact that Antony himself proposed a sumptuary law, and so Macrobius reports it in order to show how disregarded those laws were even by those who proposed them.

These two writers' scholarly attitude, with the chronological survey of the topic, is something we find only about this kind of law. The list apparently comes from the *Coniectanea* written by the jurist Ateius Capito under Tiberius. Ateius probably argued against the last Roman sumptuary law in 22 CE.[381] And so the circle closes: a complete list of sumptuary measures was collected by a jurist who probably suggested to Tiberius that he block the promulgation of another law of this kind, and who was then cited as a sort of curiosity by two authors afterwards, when luxury was far from being the main issue of Roman society. While Augustus insisted on replicating Republican patterns, pursuing a continuity from that politics with his and so keeping alive a sort of illusion of republic, Tiberius—who explicitly cites Augustus' sumptuary law among the failed measures that made this vice 'more confident' (Tac. *Ann.* 3.54.2 *securiorem luxum fecere*)—acknowledges the truth, and leads the way for these late collectors who look at sumptuary laws as old-fashioned and useless examples of moralism.

[380] Already narrated, among others, by Seneca (below, 4.6), Pliny the Elder (above, 2.5.2) and, in its prequel with Caesar, Lucan (above, 2.8).

[381] Coudry (2004), 140–52.

3
Seneca's *Luxuria*

Seneca is a key author regarding *luxuria*, for two main reasons. First, he was blamed in life, and also by much of posterity, for his excessive wealth, and his inconsistency in preaching frugality while at the same time being almost as rich as the emperor himself. To this vice his accusers add greed, sloth, and lust, emphasizing the excess in any aspect of his life and thereby drawing a complete picture of *luxuria* even without using the word. Second, as a philosopher he thematises this vice as no one before or after him, with a great number of descriptions, representations, and personifications, to the point that it appears not only as the opposite of frugality but as the archenemy of philosophy itself. In this chapter, I will tackle Seneca's real-life association with *luxuria*, that is, the charges of *luxuria* against him (3.1), his reply (3.2), and his position towards Cynic frugality (3.3). In the following chapter, I will deal with Seneca's philosophical theory about this vice.

3.1 Seneca's Inconsistency in Tacitus and Cassius Dio

Seneca's political life, about which he is reticent, finds a place in historiography by being intertwined with all Julio-Claudian emperors, except Augustus.[1] Tiberius disliked him, to the point that Seneca chose to spend a long time with his uncle in Egypt to stay at a safe distance from the Emperor; Caligula was about to kill him, and then one of his lovers told him that Seneca suffered from ill-health and would soon die anyway; Claudius banished him to Corsica, and then, after seven years, pardoned him thanks to Agrippina's intercession. The same Agrippina made him preceptor and, after Claudius' death, counsellor to Nero, with the prefect of the praetorians Burrus. After a few pleasant years the situation deteriorated, until Nero killed Agrippina and, a few years later, Burrus died and Seneca retired. Finally, Seneca got involved in Piso's conspiracy against Nero and was forced to commit suicide. Such an extraordinary existence did not adapt itself to an apologetic historiography. Indeed, Seneca either is regarded with suspicion or is even despised, or ignored, by the three ancient sources that deal with Nero's reign: Tacitus, Suetonius (first to second century CE), and Cassius Dio (second to third

[1] For some recent overviews of Seneca's life, with special regard to Nero, cf. Braund (2015); Rimell (2015a); Star (2016); Wilson (2016); see also following notes.

Roman Luxuria: *A Literary and Cultural History.* Francesca Romana Berno, Oxford University Press.
 DOI: 10.1093/oso/9780192846402.003.0003

century CE).[2] In this section, I will leave the political judgements in the background and focus instead on the passages in which Seneca is explicitly accused of excessive wealth and luxury. These passages revolve around the first years of Nero's reign, that is, the period of Seneca's greatest political influence, as well as around his retirement speech, in which Seneca tries to return to Nero the various assets he has received from the emperor.

Let us start with the charges against Seneca. Cassius Dio does not identify the accuser; he simply lists the accusations (61.10.2–4):

> ...his conduct was seen to be diametrically opposed to the teachings of his philosophy. For while denouncing tyranny, he was making himself the teacher of a tyrant; while inveighing against the associates of the powerful, he did not hold aloof from the palace himself; and though he had nothing good to say of flatterers, he himself had constantly fawned upon Messalina and the freedmen of Claudius, to such an extent, in fact, as actually to send them from the island of his exile a book containing their praises—a book that he afterwards suppressed out of shame. Though finding fault with the rich, he himself acquired a fortune of 300,000,000 sesterces; and though he censured the extravagances of others, he had five hundred tables of citrus wood with legs of ivory, all identically alike, and he served banquets on them. In stating thus much I have also made clear what naturally went with it—the licentiousness in which he indulged at the very time that he contracted a most brilliant marriage, and the delight that he took in boys past their prime, a practice which he also taught Nero to follow.
>
> (Trans. Cary 1925, here and below)

From a formal point of view, this charge is modelled after those against Stoic philosophers for their putative paradoxes. We may find an example of this in an objection reported by Seneca himself (*Const.* 3.1):[3]

> 'Haec sunt quae auctoritatem praeceptis vestris detrahant. Magna promittitis et quae ne optari quidem, nedum credi possint. Deinde ingentia locuti cum pauperem negastis esse sapientem, non negatis solere illi et servum et tectum et cibum deesse; cum sapientem negastis insanire, non negatis et alienari et parum sana verba emittere et quidquid vis morbi cogit audere; cum sapientem negastis servum esse, idem non itis infitias et venturum et imperata facturum et domino suo servilia praestaturum ministeria'.

[2] On the sources, Barrett (2016), xix–xxiii; on Seneca's inconsistencies about his own wealth, Griffin (2003), 286–314; Bartsch (2017), 156–62; on Seneca's hypocrisy in general, Jones (2014); cf. Bartsch (2015b).

[3] A similar passage is to be found in Cicero's *Mur.* 61, also in a context of criticism of Stoic paradoxes.

> 'These are the things that take authority away from your school's teachings. You people promise things greater than can even be wished for, let alone believed. Then, making your huge pronouncements, after saying that the wise person is not poor, you do not deny that he usually lacks a slave, shelter, and food. After saying that the wise person is not insane, you do not deny that he departs from himself and utters words of little sanity, that he dares to do whatever the force of his sickness compels him to do. After saying that the wise person is not a slave, you . . . do not contest that he will be put up for sale and will do what has been commanded and will perform servile duties for his master'. (Trans. Ker 2014)

The structure of the reasoning is identical, and the subjects overlap, in particular regarding wealth (*cum pauperem negastis* . . .) and slavish behaviour (*cum sapientem negastis servum esse* . . .). There was evidently a widespread pattern of criticism against the Stoics, and Seneca's inconsistency offered the ideal opportunity of exploiting it. It has to be noted that the accusations as listed by Seneca himself in *De vita beata* (below, 2.3.2) are more similar to these than to those listed by Tacitus (right below). It seems that Cassius Dio, or his source, has some intimacy with philosophical issues, as is shown also by another passage, about the degeneration of Nero's attitude from joyful and moderate to excessive and pleasure-loving, and finally to perverse and cruel. Indeed, Dio emphasizes that Seneca and Burrus left Nero free to satisfy all kinds of desire and to lead a luxurious life dedicated to *tryphe*, as if they did not realize that this attitude would lead to ever more excessive desires and to perversion (61.4.2):

> *καὶ ἐκεῖνοι συμφρονήσαντες αὐτοὶ μὲν πολλὰ τὰ μὲν μετερρύθμισαν τῶν καθεστηκότων, τὰ δὲ καὶ παντελῶς κατέλυσαν, ἄλλα τε καινὰ προσενομοθέτησαν, τὸν δὲ δὴ Νέρωνα τρυφᾶν εἴων, ὅπως διακορής, ἄνευ μεγάλου τινὸς τῶν κοινῶν πάντων κακοῦ, ὧν ἐπεθύμει γενόμενος μεταβάληται, ὥσπερ οὐκ εἰδότες ὅτι ψυχὴ νέα τε καὶ αὐθάδης ἔν τε τρυφῇ ἀνεπιπλήκτῳ καὶ ἐν ἐξουσίᾳ αὐτοτελεῖ τραφεῖσα οὐχ ὅσον οὐ κόρον αὐτῶν ἴσχει, ἀλλὰ καὶ ἐξ αὐτῶν τούτων προσδιαφθείρεται.*
>
> His two advisers, then, after coming to a common understanding, made many changes in existing regulations, abolished some altogether, and enacted many new laws, meanwhile allowing Nero to indulge himself, in the expectation that when he had sated his desires without any great injury to the public interests at large, he would experience a change of heart; as though they did not realize that a young and self-willed spirit, when reared in unrebuked license and absolute authority, so far from becoming sated by the indulgence of its passions, is ruined more and more by these very agencies. (Trans. Cary 1925)

Nero's moral decline is thus represented as due to his tutors, who fail to limit his exuberance. They thought he would get tired of pleasures, while—as every Stoic knows—this kind of life can only get worse, until it becomes irredeemable. Seneca himself is described as formerly austere and then degenerated (61.10.4).

While Dio presents only once the charges against Seneca, Tacitus refers to them twice. The first time they are attributed to a Publius Suillius, who in turn had been accused in 58 CE (and would later be condemned to death) and had tried to defend himself by claiming that Seneca had behaved even worse in many areas, from sloth (due to 'useless studies') to adultery with women belonging to the Imperial family, to greed: this last in particular is considered as the very opposite of a philosophical attitude (*Ann.* 13.42.4):[4]

> Qua sapientia, quibus philosophorum praeceptis intra quadriennium regiae amicitiae ter milies sestertium paravisset? Romae testamenta et orbos velut indagine eius capi, Italiam et provincias immenso faenore hauriri.
>
> By what wisdom, by which precepts of the philosophers had he procured three hundred million sesterces within a four-year period of royal friendship? At Rome the wills of the childless were being caught (as it were) in his net, Italy and the provinces were being drained by his inordinate usury.
>
> (Trans. Woodman 2004, here and below)

Other accusations, reported in anonymous form, are dated to 62 CE, and are said to have been the cause of Seneca's retirement (14.52.2–3):

> Hi variis criminationibus Senecam adoriuntur, tamquam ingentes et privatum modum evectas opes adhuc augeret, quodque studia civium in se verteret, hortorum quoque amoenitate et villarum magnificentia quasi principem supergrederetur. 3. Obiciebant etiam eloquentiae laudem uni sibi adsciscere.
>
> These rose up against Seneca with various charges, to the effect that he was still increasing his mighty wealth, which had exceeded all private limits, and that he was turning the affections of the citizens toward himself; and in the attractiveness of his gardens and the magnificence of his villas it was as if he were surpassing the princeps. 3. They cast against him too the charge that he was arrogating praise for eloquence to himself exclusively.

We may consider how specific and detailed the accusations in Tacitus are; Seneca's philosophical interests are secondarily considered in the first passage, but entirely ignored in the second, which pays more attention to oratory. The formulation of the charges is different from Dio's, and more varied. Furthermore, it is interesting

[4] Cf. Motto (1966); Seita (1982), with reference also to Dio's passage quoted below.

that in this last passage the emphasis is put on the idea of transgressing limits: 14.52.2 *privatum modum evectas; magnificentia quasi principem supergrederetur.*

All this, and especially the allusion to his buildings' magnificence, portrays Seneca's attitude as an expression of *luxuria.*

Tacitus directly associates Seneca's choice to retire with this last accusation. The passage in question, widely renowned for its rhetorical value and for the report in direct speech of the emperor's no less elaborate reply, is grounded on the idea of moderation, as were the charges (14.53.2–54.3):[5]

> 'Quartus decimus annus est, Caesar, ex quo spei tuae admotus sum... tantum honorum atque opum in me cumulasti ut nihil felicitati meae desit nisi moderatio eius.... 5. Tu gratiam immensam, innumeram pecuniam circumdedisti adeo ut plerumque intra me ipse volvam: egone equestri et provinciali loco ortus proceribus civitatis adnumeror?... Ubi est animus ille modicis contentus? Talis hortos extruit et per haec suburbana incedit et tantis agrorum spatiis, tam lato faenore exuberat? Una defensio occurrit quod muneribus tuis obniti non debui. 54.1 Sed uterque mensuram implevimus, et tu, quantum princeps tribuere amico posset, et ego, quantum amicus a principe accipere: cetera invidiam augent... 2.... Iube rem per procuratores tuos administrari, in tuam fortunam recipi. 3. Nec me in paupertatem ipse detrudam, sed traditis quorum fulgore praestringor, quod temporis hortorum aut villarum curae seponitur in animum revocabo... Hoc quoque in tuam gloriam cedet, eos ad summa vexisse qui et modica tolerarent.'
>
> 'It is the fourteenth year, Caesar, since I became associated with your prospects... you have heaped such honors and wealth upon me that my happiness lacks nothing except its moderation... you have surrounded me with immeasurable favor, with money uncountable, so much so that often within myself I turn over these thoughts: "Am I really counted among the leaders of the community, born as I was in an equestrian and provincial station?... Where is that spirit, content with modestness? Does it construct such gardens as mine and walk through these suburban areas and abound in such large stretches of land and such wide investment?" I am confronted with only one defense, that I was obliged not to defy your gifts. 54.1. "But each of us has reached our full measure—you, as much as a princeps could grant to a friend, and I, as much as a friend receive from a princeps. Every surplus increases resentment... 2.... Order my estate to be administered by your procurators and accepted as part of your fortune. 3. Not that I shall drag myself down into poverty, but, having handed over the things which dazzle me by their flash, I shall reclaim for my mind the

[5] On this speech, Nero's reply speech, and Tacitus' elaboration of both, Dyson (1970), 75–6; Woodman (2012); Ker (2012), 322–4. Cf. also below, 3.3.2.

> time which is set aside for the care of my gardens and villas...This too will redound to your glory—to have conveyed to the heights those who could tolerate modest levels too."

The insistence on measure is evident from the word choice: *moderatio...modicis...mensura...modica*. These words are all denied by their context, except for the last one, which refers to Seneca's strength in bearing frugality. So the words are turned into their opposite, that is, excess, which is also expressed by certain attributes (*in-mensam, in-numeram*, where the negative prefix indicates limitlessness; and *tantis...tam lato*, in a superlative sense), while the final sentence refers to an imposed boundary and to moderation: *praestringor, revocabo*.

Nero's reply is subtle and merciless; about his gifts to Seneca, he affirms the following (14.55.4–56.2):

> 'Et tua quidem erga me munera, dum vita suppetet, aeterna erunt: quae a me habes, horti et faenus et villae, casibus obnoxia sunt. Ac licet multa videantur, plerique haudquaquam artibus tuis pares plura tenuerunt. Pudet referre libertinos qui ditiores spectantur: unde etiam mihi rubori est quod praecipuus caritate nondum omnes fortuna antecellis....56.2...Non tua moderatio, si reddideris pecuniam, nec quies, si reliqueris principem, sed mea avaritia, meae crudelitatis metus in ore omnium versabitur.'
>
> 'And of course *your* gifts to me will be everlasting as long as my life continues; what you have from me—gardens and investments and villas—is susceptible to hazard. And, although it seems a lot, more has been held by numerous men who are in no way equal to your artistic skills. It is too shaming to refer to the freedmen who are conspicuously richer: hence I blush also at the fact that you, the principal in my affection, do not yet surpass all in fortune....56.2...It will be neither your moderation, should you return the money, nor your rest, should you abandon your princeps, but my greed and the dread of my cruelty which will be on the lips of all.'

Nero reuses the arguments of moderation proffered by his former master: material goods are subject to fortune, which was indeed one of Seneca's own lessons, and there are freedmen richer than Seneca, so his excess is not very great. Finally, Seneca's retirement would not be a sign of his *moderatio*, but of the emperor's *avaritia*.

Dio does not mention Seneca's retirement; Suetonius does not add anything to the picture.[6]

[6] In his *Life of Nero*, Suetonius only mentions Seneca thrice; the only hint at his wealth is in 35.5, where the biographer relates that the emperor put him to death despite his retirement: *Senecam praeceptorem ad necem compulit, quamvis saepe commeatum petenti bonisque cedenti*

We may conclude that there was an articulate political opposition to Seneca, with specific and strong accusations, since Seneca himself refers to them in his retirement speech. But he only refers to issues involving money; there is no mention of adultery, flattery, sloth, or anything else not related to wealth. Seneca in fact reduces the accusations against him to those that may be linked to the emperor insofar as his wealth is due to the emperor's gifts. He does the same in *De vita Beata*, as we shall see.

3.2 *De vita beata:* Seneca's Defence against Charges of *Luxuria*

Seneca, as we have seen, was famously wealthy: he owned numerous villas outside Rome, wide estates in the provinces, especially Spain and Egypt, and vast amounts of money.[7] His wealth derived in part from his father, but most of all from Nero and his gifts, as Seneca himself states in his retirement speech.[8] We may assume that his wealth peaked in the so-called *quinquennium Neronis*, i.e. 54–8 CE, the period in which Seneca was preceptor and counsellor to the young emperor. It is indeed in these years, and more precisely in 57–8, that scholars place the composition of *De vita beata*, a dialogue in which Seneca defends himself against the charges of excessive luxury and thus of inconsistency with his philosophy, which his political enemies had brought (Tacitus mentions a Publius Suillius in this connection).[9] In this section, I will explore Seneca's defence strategy, which is exquisitely philosophical. Seneca does not deny the charges, but blames his accusers for their attitude, which is so rigid that no one would escape from their censorship, and he then transforms his personal *luxuria* from a vice (i.e. something totally inappropriate for a philosopher) into what the Stoics called an indifferent (i.e. something that a philosopher may or may not have but that does not affect his morality in any way).

3.2.1 The Dialogue's Structure and Its Semantic Grid

The dialogue, like *De Ira*, is dedicated to L. Iunius Gallio, one of Seneca's brothers, who was involved in politics.[10] Seneca begins by criticizing the opinion of the

persancte iurasset suspectum se frustra periturumque potius quam nociturum ei. All of Seneca's millions are in those *boni* that the philosopher was renouncing.

[7] Griffin (2003), 286–94. See above, 3.1 for ancient sources in this regard.

[8] Tac. *Ann.* 14.53.2–54.3 (quoted above, 3.1).

[9] As already mentioned, the accusations as reported by Seneca look more similar to those in Cassius Dio than to those in Tacitus (above, 3.1). On *DVB* as self-defence, Sullivan (1985), 137–41.

[10] Formerly M. Annaeus Novatus, he was adopted by Junius Gallio, a friend of his father. He was proconsul in Achaia in 51 CE (*RE* 4.335–6, *s.v.*). He is famous for his encounter with Paul on the occasion of the latter's trial.

masses, and extols the Stoic idea of a happy life as 'living according to nature' (1–3), which means pursuing the good of reason, i.e. virtue, and getting rid of pleasures, which lead us to vice and dependence (4–5).[11] Indeed, one ought not to mix virtue with pleasure, as Epicurus does, because pleasure may be connected to moral evil, and because sometimes virtue implies physical pain (6–12). So pleasure and virtue can sometimes be incompatible with each other; pleasure is only a natural but indifferent consequence of being virtuous (13–16). It is only at this point that Seneca turns to his accusers, depicting them as barking dogs who reproach him for his flaws, especially his wealth (17). Seneca's first reply is that they will always find something against anyone, even the most virtuous of human beings, such as the frugal Demetrius or the heroic Cato Uticensis (18–19). The second is that while he is admittedly no sage, and blames himself for his own vices, this is precisely a first step towards a philosophical life. Finally, we should consider wealth as a mere indifferent, which does not make anyone happier. If one manages to do that, and so to detach oneself from material things, then one is approaching wisdom (20–7).

The dialogue is structured alongside the opposition between virtue (*virtus*), corresponding to a happy life (*vita beata*), and pleasures and vice (*voluptas, luxuria*).[12] This is the Stoic scheme, which Seneca sets against Epicureanism, which connected virtue with pleasure, and Seneca demonstrates Epicureanism's theoretical inconsistency. Within this framework, *luxuria* is the main way in which *voluptas* expresses itself—the overlap between these two is so extreme that they are almost identical. Yet at the same time *luxuria* is the vice with which Seneca himself is reproached, and it threatens to remove him from the happy and philosophical life. His escape is subtle, and mainly built on a terminological shift. Whereas in the first part of the dialogue the word *luxuria* recurs frequently, once the charges against him begin to be discussed (17.1) it disappears, and is replaced by generic terms for wealth, such as *divitiae, pecunia* et sim. (e.g. 18.3; 20.4; 21.1–4; 22.1; 22.4–5). This lexical turn represents a shift from a psychological and moral level (the vice of *luxuria*) to a material one (money). And this is where Stoic philosophy comes to the rescue, for the Stoics maintained that all material goods are indifferent (*adiaphora, indifferentia*) for happiness; we may prefer or dislike one or the other, but we are still able to reach happiness with or without them.[13] Read in this light, the charge against Seneca turns out to be an issue of 'indifferents', and no longer an issue of virtue vs vice. Seneca is thus easily able to

[11] On Seneca's theory of happiness, with special focus on *De vita beata*, see Bourgery (1923), 5–9; Asmis (1990); Kuen (1994), 365–79; Bok (2010), 60–6; Dyson (2010); Seal (2021), 86–91.

[12] Eisenhut (1973), 138–40; Kuen (1994), 430. On the connections between pleasure and *luxuria* as opposite to that of virtue and joy (*gaudium*) in Seneca, Evenepoel (2014).

[13] Kidd (1971); Eisenhut (1973), 140–2; Kuen (1994), 366–8; Roller (2001), 64–70; Brennan (2003), 263–4; 287–90; Reydams-Schils (2005), 59–69; especially on Seneca, Mouroutsou (2020), 321–4; on *De vita beata*, Mutschler (2014), 143–4; below, 3.3.4; 4.4.

maintain that he considers wealth as something pleasant but totally irrelevant to his state of mind: once released from the psychological dependence on desire, money loses its connections with vice, and is reduced to a mere object as any other.

3.2.2 *Luxuria* at Pleasure's Court

Let us now focus on the specific contextual use of *luxuria* in this dialogue. The first appearance is in chapter 6, where it refers to the Epicurean evaluation of the happy life (*VB* 6.1):

> 'Sed animus quoque' inquit 'voluptates habebit suas.' Habeat sane sedeatque luxuriae et voluptatum arbiter; impleat se eis omnibus quae oblectare sensus solent, deinde praeterita respiciat ex exoletarum voluptatium memor exultet prioribus futurisque iam immineat...et dum corpus in praesenti sagina iacet, cogitationes ad futura praemittat: hoc mihi videbitur miserior, quoniam mala pro bonis legere dementia est.
>
> 'But the mind also will have its pleasures,' he says. Let it have them, absolutely, and let it preside as arbiter of luxury and pleasures. Let it fill itself with all those things that customarily delight the senses. Then let it look back over things past, and, recalling its erstwhile pleasures, let it revel in what came before. And let it now on the happy life look forward to those pleasures to come...and while the body wallows in its present feasting, let it send its thoughts ahead to the future. So much the more pitiful will it seem to me, since it is madness to count bad things as goods! (Trans. Ker 2014, here and below)

This passage, and especially the expression *luxuriae et voluptatum arbiter*, seems to hint at Nero's famous description of Petronius as *elegantiae arbiter*. Tacitus adds that 'he was considered a man of an educated luxuriousness' (Tac. *Ann.* 16.18.1 *habebatur...erudito luxu*). The sentence refers to the year 65, but there is no reason to exclude the possibility that Petronius had earned his reputation some time before. Seneca may have had the intention to represent Petronius as the very personification of vice; indeed, Petronius, from what we may infer from historical sources, was a sort of anti-Seneca, an example of a life devoted to pleasures but also seriously engaged with politics, who, as Sullivan's book showed, most probably mocked Seneca's learned Stoicism expressed in *EM* in some passages of his novel *Satyricon*.[14]

[14] Sullivan (1968), 129–39; above, 2.6.3 with n. 321.

What Nero defined, with a neutral term, as *elegantia*, is in Seneca's view the realization of desires and pleasures which rule over one's soul. If the historical target of Seneca's words is Petronius, the philosophical one is Epicureanism,[15] according to which happiness is linked to pleasure—in fact, the fictive interlocutor signalled by *inquit* may be an Epicurean supporter—and enriched by memories of good past moments (see *exoletarum voluptatum memor*, a hint at the vice of lust). But Epicureanism makes us prefer the bad to the good, as Seneca goes on to illustrate with a famous description.

The man lies in his fat laziness, which of course symbolizes the degeneration of an Epicurean *otium*[16] but is defined as *sagina*, 'fattening', which alludes to the condition of animals forced to inactivity and overeating in a small cage in order to make their flesh softer to eat.[17] It is a perverse game of mirrors: not only does the human being give up reason and chooses passion, thus reducing himself to an animal-like condition (and this happens with each and every passion, e.g. anger), but he also transforms himself into the filthiest of animals, one whose nature is altered in order to make banquets as luxurious as ever.[18] Thus, he turns into an animal that is actually a creature made of *luxuria*, in order to satisfy his unlimited desire for delicacies. This degradation goes further than in the case of other passions. The *luxuriosus* turns himself into the same being as what he is about to eat, in a horrifying representation of what seems to anticipate Feuerbach's principle: 'You are what you eat.'[19]

Luxuria is here in hendiadys with *voluptates*, as the main means to reach them. There are two more occurrences of *voluptas* in this passage, as well as a specification related to physical pleasure (*oblectare sensus*): all of this is ultimately described, from an ethical point of view, as *mala*: Seneca's intention is indeed to show how Epicurean pleasure can easily be connected with vice, and thus that it is incompatible with virtue.

That *luxuria* is linked with pleasures, especially physical pleasures, and also with vicious laziness, becomes even more evident in a second passage (11.4):[20]

[15] More precisely, its vulgar version (*VB* 12.3–4: see below).

[16] Cf. *Ben.* 4.13.1 *vobis [sc. Epicureis] voluptas est inertis otii facere corpusculum... tenerrimisque cogitationibus, quas tranquillitatem vocatis, animi marcentis oblectare torporem et cibis potionibusque intra hortorum latebram corpora ignavia pallentia saginare*, 'Your idea of pleasure is to give your contemptible body over to idle sloth... to divert the torpor of a lethargic mind with the softest thoughts, which you call "tranquility", and to stuff bodies pallid from idleness with food and drink in the privacy of your garden.' Trans. Griffin and Inwood (2011); cf. Berno (2017a), 68–70.

[17] *EM* 110.13 *alia [sc. animalia delectant te] si diu pasta et coacta pinguescere fluunt ac vix saginam continent suam.*

[18] On banquets in *De vita beata*, Richardson-Hay (2009), 87 and 89; in general on banquets in Seneca, below, 4.3 with n. 47.

[19] 'Der Mensch ist was er isst' (*Sämtliche Werke* 10.5), which originally appeared in a review published by the *Blätter für literarische Unterhaltung* 268 (1850).

[20] Edwards (1993), 187–9.

> Aspice Nomentanum et Apicium, terrarum ac maris, ut isti vocant, bona concoquentis et super mensam recognoscentis omnium gentium animalia, vide hos eosdem in suggestu rosae despectantis popinam suam, aures vocum sono, spectaculis oculos, saporibus palatum suum delectantis; mollibus lenibusque fomentis totum lacessitur eorum corpus et, ne nares interim cessent, odoribus variis inficitur locus ipse in quo luxuriae parentatur. Hosce esse in voluptatibus dices, nec tamen illis bene erit, quia non bono gaudent.
>
> Look at Nomentanus and Apicius, procuring the goods (as they call them) of land and sea, and surveying on their table the creatures of every nation. See these same men gazing down on their banquet from a heap of roses, titillating their ears with the sounds of voices, their eyes with spectacular sights, their taste buds with flavours. Their bodies are stimulated all over with sweet and gentle applications, and to occupy their nostrils while this is happening, fragrances of different kinds are infused right into the room, where sacrifices are being given up to luxury. You will say that these men are immersed in pleasures. Yet it will not go well for them, for they are not rejoicing in good.

In 6.1 there was a plausible reference to Petronius; this passage, in turn, evokes another historical parallel, namely the first Roman character who was obsessed by this kind of pleasures, Gaius Verres, whom Cicero, in his famous and triumphal invective against him, describes as immersed in physical pleasures and odours (*Verr.* 2.5.27):

> Nam, ut mos fuit Bithyniae regibus, lectica octaphoro ferebatur, in qua pulvinus erat perlucidus Melitensis rosa fartus; ipse autem coronam habebat unam in capite, alteram in collo, reticulumque ad naris sibi admovebat tenuissimo lino, minutis maculis, plenum rosae.
>
> Following the custom of the old kings of Bithynia, he rode in a litter carried by eight bearers, which contained a cushion of transparent Maltese embroidery stuffed with rose-leaves, he himself wearing one garland on his head and another round his neck, and putting to his nostrils a fine-meshed bag of delicate linen gauze stuffed with rose petals.[21] (Trans. Greenwood 1960)

This famous image of a Roman official reduced to the baseness of an oriental king, with obvious allusion to his unmanly nature, and especially focused on the delicate colour and smell of the roses, arguably inspired the opening of the scene in *De vita beata* where *in suggestu rosae* is the only specific detail in a context of generic assertions. This detail places Cassius Nomentanus and M. Gabius Apicius in a genealogy of Roman vicious persons right from the start. They surely deserve

[21] See above, 2.2.1.

this place: they both lived after Verres, in Augustan Rome; they both owed their name to a wine variety;[22] they were both known as living examples of luxury.[23] This Senecan scene suggests that, if we connect virtue to pleasure, as Epicurus does, we will end up considering the duty of being 'the foretaster of... pleasure' (*VB* 11.2 *voluptates praegustare*) as virtuous, much as in 6.1 the soul was supposed to be a *luxuriae et voluptatum arbiter*, as we have seen. In that case, there was an unnamed character sitting in his fat flesh. Here, we find the examples of Nomentanus and Apicius, two of the most celebrated Roman pleasure-seekers, previously described as besieged by pleasures (11.3 *voluptatibus obsessi*), as if they were at war: pleasures surround and suffocate them. If in the earlier passage the image was that of a caged animal, here people are still animalized, but in a different way. The loss of human prerogatives is made evident by the fact that they titillate all their senses with different physical sensations and thus blur their own reason: their sense of sight with performances (*spectaculis*), hearing with songs (*vocum sono*), taste with delicious foods (*saporibus*), touch with soft and warm massages (*mollibus... fomentis*), smell with perfumes (*odoribus variis*). Senses are typical of animals, so a performance focused exclusively on sensory experience reduces us to the status of beasts. This whole performance is conceived as a service to a goddess, *Luxuria*: the verb *parentare* refers specifically to religious rituals, properly to those dedicated to the dead or their spirits, *manes*.[24] This leads us a step further from the animalization of the vicious: not only Nomentanus and Apicius become like animals, in that they depend on their senses, but also, in doing so, they officiate at a ritual: they turn into priests of a perverse religion of vice, with a ghost-like goddess who demands absolute devotion. Their condition is described as being *in voluptatibus*, as if pleasures were places in which one can stay; readers are reminded of the opening of *EM* 51, where a personified *Luxuria* chooses to live in Baiae.[25]

We have seen that *luxuria* is connected with *voluptas* in a representation of a morally deplorable Epicurean way of life, but in the subsequent chapters Seneca corrects himself, and tries to absolve Epicurus of the charge of justifying vices. The fault is of those who search for a philosophical justification of their vices, exploiting the ambiguity of the word 'pleasure' used by Epicureans (*VB* 12.3–4):

[22] *Apicius* is a common name for muscat wine; *Nomentanum* was a famous wine produced in *Nomentum*, a town in Latium, where Seneca owned a property (*EM* 104.1).

[23] *Nomentanus* is a character in Horace's famous description of Nasidienus' banquet (*Serm.* 2.8; above, 2.4.1). Apicius is referred to by Pliny *ad omne luxus ingenium natus* (*HN* 9.66; cf. 19.137; above, 2.5.2); as for Seneca, cf. *Helv.* 10.8–10 (below, 4.6); *EM* 120.19. On these characters, Kuen (1994), 166–7; Torre (1997), 381–2.

[24] *OLD* 1 and 2, s.v.; Kuen (1994), 168 *ad l.*

[25] *EM* 51.1 *nos... contenti sumus Bais... locum ob hoc devitandum... quia illum sibi celebrandum luxuria desumpsit.* See below, 4.4. On the personifications of *Luxuria*, above, 2.1.1; 2.6.1; below, 5.5.

> Ille effusus in voluptates, ructabundus semper atque ebrius, quia scit se cum voluptate vivere, credit et cum virtute (audit enim voluptatem separari a virtute non posse)...4. Itaque non ab Epicuro impulsi luxuriantur, sed vitiis dediti luxuriam suam in philosophiae sinum abscondunt et eo concurrunt ubi audiant laudari voluptatem.
>
> That dissolute hedonist, perpetually drunk and belching, because he knows that he is living with pleasure, upon hearing that pleasure is inseparable from virtue...4. They do not, then, indulge in luxury at the urging of Epicurus, but rather, being devotees of the vices, they conceal their luxury in philosophy's lap and make a beeline for where they hear pleasure is praised.

The image is once again that of a pleasure-seeker, this time anonymous, focused on drunkenness (*ebrius*),[26] and obsessed with pleasure: *voluptas* is mentioned three times in two lines; pleasure is, again, a sort of place towards which the pleasure-seeker goes (*effusus in voluptates*), but also a partner with which he lives (*cum voluptate*), something inseparable from his existence. Seneca's final explanation of this attitude is that people like this *ebrius* take advantage of the term 'pleasure' in Epicurean philosophy, where it in fact has a more sober and spiritual dimension, and interpret it as physical pleasure, and use it to excuse their own vices. These include drunkenness, gluttony, lust, and laziness, all of which, as we have seen, are generally labelled *luxuria.* Some people thus try to hide their vices under the surface of Epicurean philosophy, and this is not fair (13.1):

> In ea quidem ipsa sententia sum...sancta Epicurum et recta praecipere et si propius accesseris tristia: voluptas enim illa ad parvum et exile revocatur et quam nos virtutis legem dicimus eam ille dicit voluptati. Iubet illam parere naturae: parum est autem luxuriae quae naturae satis est.
>
> I am myself of the opinion...that Epicurus's teachings are sacred and right and, if you approach more closely, sobering. The fact is that his pleasure is restrained to a small and meager amount, and he imposes the same law on pleasure as we do on virtue. He commands pleasure to obey nature. And what is sufficient for nature is insufficient for luxury.

In fact Epicurus teaches that we should follow nature (*parere naturae*), which is not very different from what Seneca says about his own philosophical school, Stoicism (3.3 *rerum naturae assentior*). *Luxuria* cannot belong in that context, because it represents excess (*parum est...*) against the measure and sobriety of nature. The cover of a philosophical sect allows pleasure-seekers to express their vices in public (13.2 *luxuriatur...aperto capite*), without any trace of shame.

[26] On this vice, see Motto and Clark (1990).

3.2.3 Charge of and Defence against the Accusation of *Luxuria*

We have now seen all discussions of *luxuria* in *De vita beata*: banquets, lust, excess, all of them linked, fairly or not (see above), to Epicureanism—a philosophy that Seneca did not follow. So far there has been no trace of money (at least not explicitly) or of Seneca himself. When he finally comes to the fore, *luxuria* disappears.

The turning point is in chapter 17.1, which opens with the seemingly polemical question *quare ergo tu fortius loqueris quam vivis?* This is only the first in a long series of charges of incoherence and hypocrisy,[27] which anticipates the critique that will often be directed against Seneca in the course of the next two millennia. Seneca's reply consists at first in the admission that he is blaming his own vices (17.3 *non sum sapiens*; 18.1 *cum vitiis convicium facio, in primis meis facio*). He then provides a list of wise men who were nevertheless accused of one thing or the other (18.1–19.1), and states that the aim of wisdom is so noble that the mere attempt at it is praiseworthy (20.2–5). Finally, he accuses his accusers of being morally worse than everyone else (e.g. 19.2–3; 20.6).

The first accusation against Seneca contains a number of individual charges, including that of having wept at his wife's death, but most numerous are the concrete images of luxury,[28] which seem to offer a sharp contrast to the vague and generic descriptions of the previous chapters (17.1–2):

> Si quis itaque ex istis qui philosophiam conlatrant quod solent dixerit: 'quare ergo tu fortius loqueris quam vivis? Quare…pecuniam necessarium tibi instrumentum existimas et damno moveris et lacrimas audita coniugis aut amici morte demittis et respicis famam et malignis sermonibus tangeris? 2. Quare cultius rus tibi est quam naturalis usus desiderat? Cur non ad praescriptum tuum cenas? Cur tibi nitidior supellex est? Cur apud te vinum aetate tua vetustius bibitur? Cur aurum disponitur? Cur arbores nihil praeter umbram daturae conseruntur? Quare uxor tua locupletis domus censum auribus gerit? Quare paedagogum pretiosa veste succingitur? Quare ars est apud te ministrare nec temere et ut libet conlocatur argentum sed perite struitur et est aliquis scindendi obsonii magister?' Adice si uis: 'cur trans mare possides? Cur plura quam nosti? <Cur> turpiter aut tam neglegens es ut non noveris pauculos servos aut tam luxuriosus ut plures habeas quam quorum notitiae memoria sufficiat?'
>
> So if any one of those who bark at philosophy says what they always say: 'Why, then, do you speak more bravely than you live? How is it that you…treat money

[27] 18.1 *aliter…loqueris, aliter vivis.* 20.1 *non praestant philosophi quae loquuntur.* 21.1. *quare ille philosophiae studiosus est et tam dives vitam agit?* For the bibliography on this subject see above, 3.1 with notes 1–2.

[28] Asmis (1990), 246.

> as a necessary resource for you? And that you allow yourself to be disturbed by a loss and shed tears when you hear that your wife or your friend has died? And that you look to your reputation and let yourself be touched by spiteful words? 2. How is it that your country estate is more cultivated than natural use requires? Why do you not dine in accordance with your own prescriptions? Why is your furniture so extravagant? Why is wine consumed at your house that is of an older vintage than you are? Why is there gold everywhere? Why have trees been planted to provide nothing more than shade? How is it that your wife wears in her ears assets equal to those of a wealthy household? How is it that your school of slave boys is decked out in expensive uniforms? How is it that in your house table service is a fine art, and the silverware is not laid out randomly and spontaneously but is expertly arranged, and there is a maestro appointed for the carving up of special dishes?' Add, if you like: 'Why do you have property overseas? Why do you have more than you are aware of? Why are you either so disgracefully negligent that you do not know even a few of your slaves, or so disgracefully luxurious that you have too many for your memory to retain knowledge of?'

Before turning to the accusation itself, I would like to emphasize how Seneca manages to present the prosecutors in a negative light from the start: they do not talk, but bark (*conlatrant*), like rabid dogs eager to bite him (not coincidentally, in 17.3, Seneca adds 'so to feed your malevolence'), with a term that Cicero uses for bad orators.[29] Again, the charges are commonplaces (17.1 'what they always say'; see below), and stem from an evil attitude (17.3 *malivolentia*) rather than fair judgement.[30]

Seneca's list of luxury items includes many aspects of a Roman nobleman's public life, which are here characterized, in most cases, by comparative adjectives expressing excess: Seneca considers money a necessary tool (17.1 *pecuniam necessarium tibi instrumentum*), he owns properties in the countryside which are too cultivated (*cultius rus*), his tableware is too polished (*nitidior supellex*), his wine is of too old a vintage (*vinum aetate tua vetustius*), there is gold everywhere, trees are ornamental rather than fruit-bearing. The list includes all the typical luxury items that are regularly found in satirical texts: in a garden, for instance, one should plant only fruit-bearing trees, because fruitless ones are just an exhibition of wealth.[31] But Seneca's luxury extends to his family and dependents: his wife's earrings, his teachers' clothes, a slave just for cutting meat, more properties across

[29] Cic. *Brut.* 58 *latrant enim iam quidam oratores, non loquuntur.* I thank Andrea Balbo for the reference.

[30] In Martial's *Xenia* 2 we find the poet's reply to accusations, which is structured in a very similar way to that of Seneca here. I thank Silvia Mattiacci for the reference.

[31] Plin. 12.11. Grimal (1969), 415–20; on Seneca, 416–17. Seneca himself criticizes the presence of plane trees by Roman villas (*EM* 55.6).

the sea than he knows and thereby countless slaves there. Excess grows from a matter of degree (*cultius, nitidior*) to infinity (17.2 *plures... quam notitiae memoria sufficiat*), in a suffocating hyperbole.

As Citroni Marchetti points out, this passage is modelled after the diatribe scheme of an inferior (a slave, a *stultus*) accusing a nobleman or a philosopher of inconsistency, as in Horace's *Satire* 2.7.[32] In both Seneca and Horace, the defence does not consist in the denial of the accusations but in the demonstration of their flimsiness, in that they do not take into account the inner disposition of the accused, which is a good one. We may also compare Cicero's description of the corruption of Epicurean *voluptas* (*Fin.* 2.23)[33] and Seneca's own criticism of his contemporary luxury in *Helv.* 10–11 (cf. below, 4.6). This leads to the conclusion that these charges are topical—as Seneca himself notes (17.1 *quod solent*)—which deprives them of their effectiveness; and that they not only are morally insulting but also jeopardize Seneca's well-known affiliation with the Stoics by showing the similarities between his behaviour and that of the immoral interpreters of Epicureanism, such as Nomentanus and Apicius, in this same dialogue (11.4, quoted above, 3.2.2). The latter point may explain why Seneca's attitude to that philosophical school in *VB* is harsher than anywhere else in his works.

A further comparison is also revealing. The whole picture conjured up by Seneca's accusers closely resembles Petronius' portrayal of Trimalchio. This freedman is incredibly wealthy; his dinner is on point in every detail; he owns so much cultivated land that he does not need to buy anything (Petron. 38.1 *omnia domi nascuntur*); his wife is so resplendent in her jewels that, in order to compete with her, he weighs gold bracelets on a scale, while his wife's friend Scintilla wears huge earrings (67.7–9); he owns a slave whose sole job is to cut meat (36.7 *vides illum... qui obsonium carpit: Carpus vocatur. Ita quotienscumque dicit 'Carpe', eodem verbo et vocat et imperat*; cf. Sen. *VB* 17.3 *scindendi obsonii magister*);[34] he owns so many estates that he does not know exactly where they are, and wishes to buy something outside Italy (Petron. 48.2–3; 53.6), although this means that his property is less extensive than that of Seneca; he is so unaware of how many slaves he owns that he asks one of them how he came to enter the *familia* (47.11–12).

The charge levelled against Seneca depicts him like the richest freedman of Petronius' novel, a character whom Seneca would surely find not only morally despicable but also disgusting. Given the impossibility of determining whether

[32] Citroni Marchetti (1991), 124–33. This is the famous satire in which Horace represents himself as accused by the slaves Davus and Mulvius.

[33] Above, 2.2.1.

[34] 'You see the fellow who is carving his way through the meat? Well, his name is Carver. So, whenever Trimalchio says the word, you have his name, and he has his orders.' Trans. Heseltine (1969). Schmeling (2011), 134–5 *ad l.*, recalls Seneca's *EM* 47.6 in which a similar figure is described. On the similarities between Seneca's and Trimalchio's attitudes towards wealth, see Star (2012), 194–201.

De vita beata precedes *Satyricon* or vice versa, we cannot discuss the intertextual genealogy, but the idea that Petronius modelled his luxuriating, ignorant, and morally deplorable character on the learned, powerful, refined, and wealthy Seneca, is a fascinating one. And it is clear that Seneca's enormous patrimony was on the same level as that of the despised category of imperial freedmen.[35] Petronius' readers, Seneca himself included, would have found in the novel a detailed description of those same activities of which the so-called Stoic philosopher and Nero's preceptor had been accused.

Even if this is nothing more than an attractive hypothesis, the fact remains that Seneca was accused of all the commonplace charges against luxury that he himself uses elsewhere,[36] as does his personal admission of fault. Indeed, he does not deny any of these charges; he only says, as we have seen, that he is trying to become a better person: indeed, he is blaming himself, using the verb *obiurgo* ('to reprove' 17.3), a coradical of *ius*, 'right', which represents a fair way of correcting oneself with respect to the insulting talk (17.3 *convicia*, derived from *vox*, 'shout') used by the prosecutors. Seneca is even called—he suggests the label himself—*luxuriosus*, with special reference to the incredible number of slaves he owned. Yet the reasoning suddenly becomes general, and in the following chapters there are no further references to pleasure or luxury, except for some references to money, as in the accusation against Cato the Younger, the Republican and Stoic hero who took his own life,[37] for his excessive wealth (18.3 *nimis dives*), and as in the statement that one ought to spend money with moderation (20.4 *quidquid habebo nec sordide custodiam nec prodige spargam*, 'whatever I have, I will neither guard greedily nor recklessly scatter').

The subject again gains centre stage in 21.1 *quare ille philosophiae studiosus est et tam dives vitam agit?*, 'Why does this one study philosophy and live his life so wealthy?' At this point we expect the concept of *luxuria* to return, but this is not the case. We find instead *dives* and *divitiae*: not vices, but objects. The example of Cato the Younger returns: he was in fact very wealthy, even as compared to Crassus and his legendary assets (21.3),[38] and so we discover that the charge against him (18.3) was true, no less so than those against Seneca. But Seneca neutralizes the charge in two moves. First, there is the implication that if even Cato, who was recognized as a Stoic sage, was rich, Seneca, who is only trying to follow this philosophy, may be wealthy as well; second, Seneca reasons that the substance

[35] 'Suillius says it [*sc.* Seneca's capital] stood at HS 300 million in 58—which put him in the same bracket with the great imperial freedmen' (Griffin (2003), 291, referring to Tac. *Ann.* 13.42.4). As we have seen in his reply speech to Seneca's request for retirement, Nero states to feel ashamed for some freedmen who are richer than Seneca (*Ann.* 14.54.4, quoted above, 3.1).

[36] For silver and gold tableware, see e.g. *Brev.* 12.5; *Helv.* 11.3; for the women's earrings, *Ben.* 7.9.4; for the slaves' dress, *Tranq.* 1.8; for the meat-cutting slave, *EM* 47.6.

[37] Goar (1987), 35–41 and Gäth (2010), 52–8 on Seneca; Drogula (2019), 296–314 (311–12 on Seneca); Gazzarri (2020), 44–7.

[38] Drogula (2019), 254 with n. 93.

of the reproach is not a vice, *luxuria*, which would be unacceptable, but only a material fact, *divitiae*, which belongs not to the category of vice but to that of indifferents (22.4):

> Quis porro sapientium—nostrorum dico, quibus unum est bonum virtus—negat etiam haec quae indifferentia vocamus habere aliquid in se pretii et alia aliis esse potiora? Quibusdam ex iis tribuitur aliquid honoris, quibusdam multum; ne erres itaque, inter potiora divitiae sunt.
>
> Who, indeed, among wise persons—our wise persons, I mean, for whom virtue is the sole good—denies that even these things that we call indifferents have some value in them, and that some are preferable over others? Some of these things are granted some honor, and others are granted much. And, to make sure you do not get it wrong: wealth is among the preferables.

The reasoning flows smoothly: money is indifferent per se, so it does not affect my state of mind, but I may prefer it (indeed it belongs to the *potiora*, the so-called 'preferables' of Stoic philosophy: above).[39] One cannot forbid a sage (*sapientium*) or even a simple philosopher to be wealthy (23.1 *desine ergo philosophis pecunia interdicere*, 'so stop forbidding philosophers to have money')—note that Seneca, writing 'philosophers', now includes himself in this group. Money is not 'good' or 'bad' per se; surely one may prefer to have it, but could be happy even without it (23.1–4). Furthermore, it is the use of money that determines moral value: one may make donations (24.1–3) and thereby keep one's virtue even while being wealthy (25.1–8). It is important to note that this is an attitude that Seneca generally has in all of his works.[40] The difference between the good and the bad man, if they are both rich, is that the former considers money an instrument, like a slave, and masters it; the second is mastered by it (26.1). The dialogue ends with other invectives against his prosecutors, coupled with a declaration of detachment and indifference towards them, with the support of Socrates' example.[41]

To summarize: when it comes to his *luxuria*, Seneca divides his text into two parts. First, he discusses *luxuria* in general, but only so as to define it as far removed from himself, in that it is linked to Epicurean philosophy, while he himself is a Stoic. He then refers to the specific accusations he faces, but minimizes them, shifting from ethics to economics, from vice to objects. While *luxuria* is inadmissible for a Stoic, money is not, but is merely a so-called indifferent; if one makes proper use of it, one may own it, even as a philosopher. Seneca thus avoids lying—he could hardly have denied his wealth, which everyone in Rome knew about—and even transforms his supposed hypocrisy into a philosophical way of

[39] Asmis (1990), 248–9; cf. above, 3.2.1 with n. 13 and 3.2.3.

[40] Griffin (2003), 294–314.

[41] On this rhetorical device see Ker (2010). For a recent overview on Socrates in Seneca, Gazzarri (2020), 40–4.

life, shifting the focus from the inside (the vice of *luxuria*) to the outside (his properties), and then back to the inside again (the good use of money depends on one's psychological disposition). If this strategy does not entirely acquit him, it provides ample evidence of his rhetorical and philosophical skills.

3.3 Seneca and Cynic Frugality: The Case of Demetrius

Seneca's official attitude to poverty is well known:[42] he lists it among the disgraces that may befall a nobleman, along with exile and jail (e.g. *EM* 59.8; 82.10); he sometimes recommends or practices it as an exercise, but still feels ashamed for it; he seldom refers to frugality as a virtue (an exception is in the case of Q. Aelius Tubero, below, 4.7), but at the same time he considers money an indifferent or even a preferable (above, 3.2.3), thus stating that he would prefer to be wealthy rather than poor. From his point of view, it is more a matter of being fine with one has than to settle with little. Furthermore, even when Seneca discusses his personal poverty exercises, as in *EM* 87.2–5,[43] he does not mean actual poverty, since he represents himself in a country wagon with a few slaves, and his momentary and voluntary renouncement of luxury looks more like a *divertissement* for wealthy and bored noblemen than a spiritual exercise: indeed he mentions 'the pauper's cell' among the luxuries of a rich house (*EM* 100.6).[44] Beneath the philosophical motivations there is also fear: Seneca suggests this exercise of 'imaginary poverty' (20.13) in order to be prepared in case of a radical reversal of one's fortunes (18.6). It is in this context that we may view Seneca's position on Cynic frugality. In this section, I would like to tackle this issue with specific reference to Demetrius the Cynic, a contemporary of Seneca, to stress how his position is rooted in his social and cultural environment.

3.3.1 Seneca on Cynic Frugality, and Demetrius the Cynic

Cynic philosophy,[45] founded in the fourth century BCE by a pupil of Socrates, Antisthenes of Athens, proposed an extreme interpretation of the precept that

[42] Rosivach (1995); Gildenhard (2020), 310–25 (317–21 on Diogenes the Cynic); with specific reference to Cynicism, Del Giovane (2015a), 243–75; Pià Comella (2019); Seal (2021), 29–32.

[43] On which see Allegri (2004), 15–29; Inwood (2010), 239–40; Del Giovane (2015a), 248–60; Pià Comella (2019), 409–11. Cf. also *EM* 17.5; 18.5–6 and 9 with Avotins (1977); Pià Comella (2019), 403–6; *EM* 20.12–13 with Pià Comella (2019), 412–13; *EM* 29 with Seal (2021), 41–5; *EM* 123.1–3 with Del Giovane (2015a), 261–75. *EM* 18 represents a peculiar case, for which see below, 4.2.

[44] Cf. Berti (2018), 339. Seneca himself tries to distinguish his temporary poverty exercise from that attitude, to little effect (*EM* 18.7 *non est nunc quod existimes me dicere… pauperum cellas et quidquid aliud est per quod luxuria divitarum taedio ludit: grabattus ille verus sit… non lusus sit sed experimentum*).

[45] Moles (2007a); Desmond (2008); on Cynic frugality esp. 98–103. On frugality in popular philosophy (which was largely inspired by Cynicism), Morgan (2007), 47; 90–4; 119; 274–99.

one should live in accordance with nature: it rejected most signs of human civilization as artificial, ones involving eating, clothing, and sexual relations. They received their name from the dog (*kyon*, *kynos* in Greek), because they had some habits in common with this animal, mainly shamelessness, and fidelity to friends. Their most famous member was Diogenes of Sinope, whose encounter with Alexander the Great was legendary (below, 3.3.2); he lived in a ceramic jar in Athens. Cynicism was famous and widespread in imperial Rome, with many wandering philosophers who lived on the street and delivered moralistic speeches in which they criticized material goods of any kind. This school of thought was not disliked by Stoics. In particular, the Stoics admired its attitude towards wealth, which was categorically rejected without compromise, and the Cynic attitude was in tune with the ideal both of Roman republican virtue and of independence from external goods shared by all Hellenistic philosophical schools. On the other hand, the Cynics' anti-social behaviour and mockery of decency alienated and even disgusted many. Seneca is no exception here.[46] In particular, his attitude towards Demetrius the Cynic and his frugality represents an interesting case study of Seneca's view on the right attitude towards wealth.[47]

Demetrius of Corynthus, named 'the Cynic',[48] was a philosopher who lived in Rome in the first century CE, and had several arguments with more than one emperor, from Caligula to Vespasian, who finally exiled him. Most information about him derives from Seneca, who was a friend of his and apparently pictured him as a sort of Stoic-Cynic sage.[49] He doubtless appreciated Demetrius, as he shows plenty of times, especially in *De beneficiis*, and especially with regard to his frugality.[50] Yet if we carefully read some of these passages, it becomes clear that Demetrius is not as perfect as the first, prototypical Cynic philosopher Diogenes. Diogenes was presented as a superior sage, and his chronological distance from Seneca no doubt allowed the latter to avoid references to his most repellent habits and to focus on the most admirable ones. Demetrius' behaviour, however, is not as spotless as Diogenes'. If we consider his encounter with tyrants, he appears less upright than the founder of his school was towards Alexander the Great, but also than Seneca himself towards Nero. Further, Demetrius' long speech against wealth in *De beneficiis* 7 is questioned by dint of its insertion in a collection of

[46] On Cynicism in Rome, cf. Billerbeck (1982); especially on Seneca, 159–68; Griffin (1996); on the Imperial age, Goulet-Cazé (1990) (2808–12 on its connections with Stoicism). In *Brev.* 14.2, Seneca maintains that the Cynics exceed nature, while the Stoics conquer it.

[47] A version of this paper was delivered at a conference on Roman Cynicism (*Le Cyniques à Rome*, Paris, 3–4 June 2021), and will be published in the proceedings, edited by Marie-Odile Goulet-Caze.

[48] On Demetrius, see Billerbeck (1979); Kindstrand (1980); Desmond (2008), 50–2; following n.

[49] Billerbeck (1979), 12–43; (1982), 159–68; Goulet-Cazé (1990), 2768–9; Sellars (2014), 110; Del Giovane (2015a), 75–100; Pià Comella (2019), 411–18.

[50] Cf. *VB* 18.3 *curet aliquis an istis nimis dives videatur quibus Demetrius Cynicus parum pauper est? Virum acerrimum et contra omnia naturae desideria pugnantem, hoc pauperiorem quam ceteros Cynicos quod, cum sibi interdixerit habere, interdixit et poscere, negant satis egere.*

unnecessary, needless considerations. Finally, Seneca took Demetrius around in Rome not in a friendly way, but as a sort of freak, like Roman noblemen did with dwarfs or fools. In my opinion, this twofold attitude towards Demetrius reflects Seneca's inconsistencies regarding wealth and poverty.

3.3.2 Facing the Tyrant: Demetrius versus Diogenes (and Seneca)

Let us start from a key issue in a Cynic philosopher's life: the meeting with a tyrant. As stated, Demetrius had several arguments with more than one emperor. Seneca focuses on one of them, an encounter between the Cynic and Gaius Caesar Caligula, the prince Seneca despises most. The story is inserted in a long dissertation about Demetrius' thought on wealth, and it is cited as an example of the fact that material wealth is an unsatisfactory illusion, while wisdom represents authentic wealth (*Ben.* 7.11.1–2):[51]

> Itaque cum C. Caesar illi ducenta donaret, ridens reiecit ne dignam quidem summa iudicans, qua non accepta gloriaretur. Dii deaeque, quam pusillo animo illum aut honorare voluit aut corrumpere! 2. Reddendum egregio viro testimonium est; ingentem rem ab illo dici audivi, cum miraretur Cai dementiam, quid se putasset tanti posse mutari: 'Si temptare' inquit 'me constituerat, toto illi fui experiendus imperio.'
>
> And so when Gaius Caesar offered to give him two hundred thousand, Demetrius laughed and refused it, thinking that it was not even worth boasting about rejecting that amount. Great gods and goddesses in heaven! How small-minded Gaius was, whether he was trying to honor him or to corrupt him. 2. Let me bear witness to this outstanding man; I heard him say something magnificent when he was expressing surprise that Gaius was crazy enough to suppose that he could be swayed by that amount. He said, 'If he really wanted to put me to the test, he should have tempted me by offering the entire empire!'
>
> (Trans. Griffin/Inwood 2011, here and below)

The story is clearly modelled after Diogenes' encounter with Alexander,[52] to which Seneca alludes many times; he does not narrate it in detail but expresses unconditional admiration for Diogenes, whose poverty is compared to a divine condition, since it means that he does not need anything.[53] Particularly interesting

[51] Griffin (2013), 330; Del Giovane (2015a), 98–100.

[52] As noticed already by Billerbeck (1979), 167, who points out that in this case, however, the emphasis on *parrhesia* is lost.

[53] *Tranq.* 8.3–5 *tolerabilius autem est, ut dixi, faciliusque non adquirere quam amittere, ideoque laetiores videbis quos numquam fortuna respexit quam quos deseruit. 4. Vidit hoc Diogenes, vir ingentis animi, et effecit ne quid sibi eripi posset.... 5. Si quis de felicitate Diogenis dubitat, potest idem dubitare*

is a passage from the same work where Diogenes is compared to Socrates as a great example of refusing benefits (5.4.3–4):

> At sunt quidam extra omnem subducti cupiditatem, qui vix ullis humanis desideriis continguntur; quibus nihil potest praestare ipsa fortuna. Necesse est a Socrate beneficiis vincar, necesse est a Diogene, qui per medias Macedonum gazas nudus incessit calcatis regis opibus; 4. o! ne ille tunc merito et sibi et ceteris, quibus ad dispiciendam veritatem non erat obfusa caligo, supra eum eminere visus est, infra quem omnia iacebant; multo potentior, multo locupletior fuit omnia tunc possidente Alexandro; plus enim erat, quod hic nollet accipere, quam quod ille posset dare.
>
> But there are those who are withdrawn beyond the reach of all cupidity, who are scarcely affected by any human desires, on whom fortune herself can bestow nothing. Of necessity I shall be outdone in benefits by Socrates, of necessity by Diogenes who passed through the Macedonian treasures naked, trampling on the king's wealth. 4. How rightly did he seem then, to himself and to anyone else whose ability to discern truth was not dimmed, to tower above the man who had the world at his feet. Far more powerful, far richer was he than Alexander, who then had all things in his power; for what Diogenes would not accept was greater than what Alexander could give.

In this case, Diogenes is put on the same level as Socrates, the perfect sage, and his behaviour towards Alexander is regarded as a flawless model. If Demetrius had been on the same level, Seneca would have added his story to the list, but he does not. The two stories do have something in common, e.g. the confrontation between philosopher (Diogenes/Demetrius) and tyrant (Alexander/Caligula), and the terms of *beneficium* (*dare/accipere* for Diogenes, *donare/reicere* for Demetrius). But there is also a striking difference: Diogenes refuses everything: *calcatis regiis opibus* (5.4.3) alludes not only to material stuff but also to regal power and influence. Demetrius for his part refuses a fair amount of money, but his final sentence, even if hyperbolic and ironic, reveals that he might have appreciated political power if offered.[54] This is confirmed by Seneca's comment after the narrative: *sapienti ergo donari aliquid potest, etiam si sapientis omnia sunt* 'therefore a sage can be given something even though all things belong to the sage' (7.12.1). This is the enunciation of a Stoic paradox, but if read in light of Demetrius'

et de deorum immortalium statu, an parum beate degant quod illis nec praedia nec horti sint nec alieno colono rura pretiosa nec grande in foro fenus.

[54] This interpretation is supported by the story in Tacitus about Demetrius defending the corrupt senator P. Egnatius Celer against the Stoic philosopher Musonius Rufus in 70 CE. Tacitus comments that Demetrius acted *ambitiosius quam honestius* (*Hist.* 4.40.3). The reading of this event is controversial; a detailed *status quaestionis* and an attempt to argue for the consistency of Demetrius' behaviour are in Moles (1983).

encounter with Caligula, it becomes more difficult. One may wonder how Demetrius' example can be evidence of the possibility for the wise man to accept gifts although he did not accept anything, but the repetition in the Demetrius story of the verb *dono*, a key term in *De beneficiis*, is revealing. It deals with the importance of gifts as a way of social bonding,[55] and the moral of the story is that there is in fact something that Demetrius would have accepted, which thus distinguishes him from the perfect Diogenes.[56] And if Seneca does not criticize Demetrius' inconsistency, it is, in my opinion, because he was thinking of himself.

Indeed, in writing about this meeting between the emperor Caligula—a Roman tyrant—and the philosopher, Seneca was surely thinking about his meetings with Nero, and especially his acceptance of enormous gifts and properties from the emperor, and about his recent, failed attempt to refuse everything, of which we have a famous narrative by Tacitus. *De beneficiis* was likely written around 64 CE, a year after Seneca's retirement.[57] In his final speech to Nero, Seneca realized that he had been wrong to accept all these goods, and he then tried to act like Diogenes instead and to return everything. But the emperor did not let him do so, precisely in order to prevent him from becoming a sort of hero of the resistance (Tac. *Ann.* 14.53–6; above, 3.1). Seneca's speech presents his wealth as a benefit received through the emperor's generosity (14.53.4 *munificentia*), for which he himself did not offer an equal compensation and which he did not have the chance to refuse (14.53.5 *muneribus tuis obniti non debui*). Nero's reply maintains that Seneca's return of his gifts would not entail the sobriety of the giver, but of greed and cruelty in the recipient (14.56.2 *non tua moderatio... sed mea avaritia, meae crudelitatis metus*). It is evident, first, that Seneca was in a far more difficult situation than Demetrius, because he was forced to accept Nero's gifts, while Demetrius did not suffer any consequence for his refusal; second, that the speech is not only about things, defined in both cases as gifts, but mainly about power and influence (14.53.2 *honores*; 14.53.5 *gratia*), precisely what Demetrius is said to have been likely to accept from Caligula. Seneca was a Stoic, and thus exhorted by his philosophical beliefs to take part in politics; his condition was worse than that of Demetrius, and still he tried to give everything back. Demetrius, on the other hand, who as a Cynic should exhibit a complete detachment from material goods, seems to yearn for political power.

[55] Cf. De Caro (2009); Griffin (2013), esp. 30–74; Coffee (2017), 151–64.

[56] Not all Cynics were that detached from money, as Seneca shows in another, anonymous anecdote in book 2.17.1 of *De beneficiis*: *ab Antigono Cynicus petit talentum: respondit plus esse quam quod Cynicus petere deberet; repulsus petit denarium: respondit minus esse quam quod regem deceret dare.* This story is told by Seneca as an example of a bad way of bestowing benefits, and so his target is the king, not the Cynic philosopher, but it still shows that not all Cynics were like Diogenes. So too, Demetrius himself might not be. Cf. Plut. *Reg. et imp. apopht.* 15.182e; cf. Desmond (2008), 110.

[57] Griffin (2013), 91–6.

Seneca seems to discuss the episode of Demetrius and Caligula as a sort of defence for his own behaviour. At the same time, the comparison with other passages shows that Seneca does not consider Demetrius a role model: not only Diogenes did better, but Seneca himself also tries to do so.

3.3.3 Demetrius' Speech against *Luxuria* in *De beneficiis* 7

In Seneca's prose works, we find several mentions of Demetrius' speeches or sentences, which are always praised both for their content and their rhetorical efficacy, and in most cases are reported in direct speech.[58] We have no evidence that Seneca's quotations are verbatim; it is likely that he altered them in order to soften Demetrius' *parrhesia*.[59] The longest sample of Demetrius' oratory is in book 7 of *De beneficiis*, which opens with a flattering reference to his speaking ability (7.1.3): [60]

> Egregie hoc dicere Demetrius Cynicus, vir meo iudicio magnus, etiam si maximis comparetur: solet plus prodesse, si pauca pracepta sapientiae teneas, sed illa in promptu tibi et in usu sint, quam si multa quidem didiceris, sed illa non habeas ad manum.
>
> Demetrius the Cynic makes the point very well—he is in my judgment a great man even when set beside the greatest—when he says that it is more beneficial if you possess just a few philosophical precepts, but keep them readily available for rapid use, than if you learn many things but do not have them to hand.

A long speech follows, attributed to the Cynic philosopher and directed first against useless competences and then against vices. Scholars have long emphasized the presence in this speech of moralistic commonplaces and the similarities with other Senecan passages (see below).

The praise addressed to Demetrius, if carefully read, is positive, but not unconditionally so; moreover, it is partially negated by the context, for more than one reason.

First, Demetrius is called *magnus*, next to *maximi*: despite the concessive clause (*etiam si*), the parallel between positive and superlative shows that he is something less than the best (the actual wise men, such as Diogenes and Socrates). Moreover, Seneca says 'in my opinion' (*meo iudicio*), which implies that his praise

[58] Cf. *Prov.* 3.3; 5.5; *EM* 20.9–10; 91.19; *NQ* 4a.*pr.*7 (direct speech); *EM* 67.14 (indirect speech).
[59] Goulet-Cazé (1990), 2770–2.
[60] Billerbeck (1979), 20–6; Del Giovane (2014); (2015a), 133–53; Seal (2021), 57–60.

may not be shared by everyone. Finally, it must be pointed out that Seneca presents the book as a collection of remains, whose usefulness is doubtful and that he himself might have passed by: they have been elaborated not for the soul's care, but for the taste of the intellect (7.1.1–2):[61]

> Reliqua hic liber cogit, et exhausta materia circumspicio, non quid dicam sed quid non dixerim...2....quidquid maxime necessarium erat, in primum congessi...Nec mehercules, si me interroges, nimis ad rem existimo pertinere, ubi dicta sunt, quae regunt mores, prosequi cetera non in remedium animi, sed in exercitationem ingenii inventa.
>
> The present book rounds up the leftovers; now that the subject matter is used up, I am looking around not to see what I should say, but what I have left unsaid....2....I piled up at the start all the most important themes....And good heavens! If you ask me, I do not think it contributes much to the topic, once you have dealt with the instructions concerning character, to chase down other themes that have been worked up not to heal the mind but only to give our intellect some exercise.

And this, as Seneca says plenty of times, is a waste of time with respect to spiritual exercise (see e.g. Letter 49). Demetrius' speech serves to support this assertion;[62] indeed, Demetrius' speech goes on listing a wide range of things the knowledge of which does not make us better. Nevertheless, it is worth noting that even if in theory he maintains the same position as Seneca, his long speech, which goes on for page after page, covering almost a third of the book, is in fact *included* in the seventh book, that of useless remains. So there is a suspicion that Demetrius' argument is part of this category.

There are further considerations on Demetrius' value as a speaker, if not as a philosopher (7.8.2–3):

> Non referam tibi Socraten, Chrysippum, Zenonem et ceteros magnos quidem viros, maiores quidem, quia in laudem vetustorum invidia non obstat. Paulo ante Demetrium rettuli, quem mihi videtur rerum natura nostris tulisse temporibus, ut ostenderet nec illum a nobis corrumpi nec nos ab ullo corrigi posse, virum exactae, licet neget ipse, sapientiae firmaeque in iis, quae proposuit, constantiae, eloquentiae vero eius, quae res fortissimas deceat, non concinnatae nec in verba sollicitae, sed ingenti animo, prout impetus tulit, res suas prosequentis. 3. Huic non dubito quin providentia et talem vitam et talem dicendi facultatem dederit, ne aut exemplum saeculo nostro aut convicium deesset. Demetrio si res nostras

[61] Griffin (2013), 114–15; 320.

[62] Del Giovane (2015a), 101–2.

> aliquis deorum possidendas velit tradere sub lege certa, ne liceat donare, adfirmaverim repudiaturum dicturumque...
>
> I will not mention Socrates, Chrysippus, Zeno, and others, great men to be sure—all the greater, in fact, because envy does not get in the way of praise for the ancients. I mentioned Demetrius a while back; it seems to me that nature brought him forth in our age to make the point that he could not be corrupted by us any more than we could be castigated by him. Though he might deny it, he is a man of superb wisdom, with an unbending consistency in carrying out his intentions and the kind of eloquence that suits the most serious matters, rather than the ornamental kind that frets over the niceties of diction—an eloquence determined to pursue its subject with passionate commitment, with true greatness of mind. 3. I am certain that providence gave him the way of life he has and the rhetorical skill he possesses so that our age would have an example to follow and a rebuke to heed. If some god wanted to give our wealth to Demetrius to keep, on the condition that he not be allowed to give any of it as a gift, I venture to claim that he would reject the offer and say...

The formulation here defines Demetrius right from the start as a second-level character with respect to Socrates, Chrysippus, and Zeno, the philosophers and sages of giant stature: 7.8.2 *non referam tibi Socrates...paulo ante Demetrium rettuli...* Demetrius is a good speaker,[63] but he is not on the same level as they, who are the *maiores*—'ancestors' but also 'greater'—but may still be considered an example of virtue. Seneca adds: *rerum natura nostris tulisse temporibus ut ostenderet nec illum a nobis corrumpi nec nos ab ullo corrigi posse.* This is a pessimistic commonplace on contemporary society, but it also implies that Demetrius is ineffective, and his behaviour and speeches useless. And a philosopher who does not manage to change his listeners' lives—the major goal of Seneca's philosophical work—is a failure.[64]

This is shown by what follows: Seneca does not report an authentic speech by Demetrius, but he imagines a fictitious one, which he explicitly ascribes to himself (7.8.3 *si...adfirmaverim repudiaturum dicturumque*). The subsequent moral harangue against luxury and greed is typically declamatory and Senecan, as shown by its similarity with the final passage of *NQ* book 5, which is on the same subject. Moreover, it is exquisitely Roman in its formulation, since it represents both vices, *luxuria* and *avaritia*, as victorious generals who show off their conquests in a triumph. Among '*luxuria*'s spoils' (7.9.2), Seneca's Demetrius lists

[63] Indeed, he lacks *sollicitudo* (7.8.2), which is a flaw in rhetoric (Sen. *Con.* 7.*pr.*6), while has the greatness of mind (Sen. *Ben.* 7.8.2) which is always appreciated (Sen. *Con.* 4.*pr.*6).

[64] We may compare the example of Fabianus, one of Seneca's mentors, whose speeches were not perfect, yet they arouse admiration and emulation, both for his style and his virtues, in his listeners (*EM* 100.12). Cf. Berti (2018), 374–680.

most of the items that Pliny classifies under the same category:[65] turtle shells, wooden inlays, different kinds of crystals, heavy earrings, silk dresses (7.9.2–5). The list is marked by the repetition of the verb *video*, 'I see', which stresses the similarity between the expressions of vice and the spoils shown during a triumphal procession. After this exhibition of *luxuria* follows that of *avaritia*, which concerns not only material goods, especially noble metals and gems which earth has kept hidden, but also symbolic expressions of money, such as debt obligations, certificates, and so on (7.10.1–4). To these we may add estates, flocks, fields, and so on (7.10.5.6). None of them succeeds in satisfying one's desire for possession or luxury. We find these same aspects in a speech attributed to Attalus, another of Seneca's masters, as reported in *EM* 110.14–19;[66] there are some similarities also with the already quoted passage of *NQ* 5.15.[67] Even if we leave aside the moralistic commonplaces, the representation of vices as generals is not common, and illustrates the extent to which Seneca rephrased Demetrius' words. The latter here constitutes an *escamotage* to convey traditional moralistic critiques of wealth. But Demetrius' position in *De beneficiis* is quite conspicuous: it is one thing is to criticize wealth in a discussion of mining, as Seneca does in the first person in *NQ* 5, or to do so in a moralistic essays such as the *Epistles* (e.g. Attalus in *EM* 110); it is quite another to do so in a work devoted to liberality, a word that is close to prodigality, one of the meanings of *luxuria*. The aim of *De beneficiis* is to show how to manage one's liberality in order to build favourable social connections.[68] That is, the whole work presumes a wealthy author and wealthy readers, since liberality is impossible without money. And without liberality, society dies. So a speech against wealth, aligning with the Cynic way of life, outside society, is completely out of place in this work. This is the reason why Seneca gives so much space to Demetrius here: to show, without stating explicitly, how reasonable his arguments are while at the same time being incompatible with social life.

3.3.4 Demetrius as a Freak? Seneca's *EM* 62

One of the most famous quotations of Demetrius is in *EM* 62.[69] Here, Seneca is describing his detachment from public activities that are useless for achieving

[65] Above, 2.5.2. As for the image of spoils, we also find it in Eumolpus' poem *Bellum civile* (Petron. 120.85–6, on which see above, 2.6.3); in the pseudo-senecan tragedy *Octavia*, l. 433, there is a *luxuria victrix* (below, 4.6 n. 113).

[66] The connections with Cynicism in this passage were emphasized already by Billerbeck (1982), 164; Del Giovane (2014); Pià Comella (2019), 418.

[67] A blaming of men's greediness, which pushes them to search for gold underground, as if burying themselves in advance: Berno (2003), 179–207; Williams (2012), 81–4.

[68] Griffin (2013), esp. 30–74.

[69] Del Giovane (2015a), 92–3; Pià Comella (2019); Seal (2021), 45–6.

wisdom, such as court cases. Then he says that he is used to bring Demetrius along, and that he admires him because he does not need anything, and because he despises wealth. This is the typical praise of a Cynic philosopher that we find in almost every passage about him. But there is a noticeable detail in Seneca's narrative. First, he talks about his friends (62.2):

> Cum me amicis dedi, non tamen mihi abduco nec cum illis moror quibus me tempus aliquod congregavit... sed cum optimo quoque sum; ad illos... animum meum mitto.
>
> When I devote myself to friends, I do not even then withdraw from myself. And I don't linger with the people I am thrown in with merely by circumstances... Instead, I choose the very best company; and it is to them that I entrust my mind. (Trans. Graver/Long 2015, here and below)

Seneca loves to spend time with good friends, those who walk with him towards tranquillity and wisdom. He then continues (62.3):

> Demetrium, virorum optimum, mecum circumfero et relictis conchyliatis cum illo seminudo loquor, illum admiror. Quidni admirer? vidi nihil ei deesse. Contemnere aliquis omnia potest, omnia habere nemo potest: brevissima ad divitias per contemptum divitiarum via est.
>
> I carry about with me Demetrius, the best of men. I abandon those clothed in Tyrian purple and converse with him, look up to him, who is barely clothed at all. Why shouldn't I look up to him? I have seen that he lacks nothing. No one can have everything, but there is someone who can despise everything. The quickest way to wealth is to despise wealth.

In the first sentence, the sharp contrast between Seneca's pairs, dressed in purple (*conchyliati*), and the half-naked (*seminudus*) Demetrius is rightly famous. But the context implies another contrast as well, that between Demetrius and Seneca's friends. Seneca describes his relationship with his friends as a mutual self-giving, an intimate closeness, and this is stressed by the repetition of the preposition *cum*, which also recurs as a preverb.[70] Regarding Demetrius, we also have *cum*, twice, as well as *circum-*, but there are no signs of closeness: on the contrary, *circumfero* is properly used of things, e.g. food at a banquet, not of persons. Indeed, it implies the action of carrying in one's hand, or something similar.[71] Seneca thus

[70] As already noted by Pià Comella (2019), 414–15.

[71] Cf. *TLL* 3.1140–3, *s.v.*; Sen. *EM* 94.62 *Philippus... toto orbe arma circumfert.* As for food, cf. Petron. 35.6; 46.8; Plin. *HN* 35.5 *iidem palaestras athletarum imaginibus et ceromata sua exornant Epicuri voltus per cubicula gestant ac circumferunt secum.* In a passage by Ammianus Marcellinus (Amm. 26.9.3 *filiam parvulam... Faustina... lectica circumferens secum*), the verb is referred to a

addresses Demetrius very differently from his friends, in a patronizing way, much like a nobleman speaking about his slaves. We may think of the disabled slaves—usually dwarfs or hunchbacks—or court-jesters that Romans loved to take around for fun.[72] This habit is attested for several emperors: Augustus, Tiberius, Claudius, when he was a private citizen, and Domitian.[73] What princes do with dwarfs or court-jesters, i.e. bringing them along and having serious talks with them, Seneca, who himself states that he does not appreciate fools (50.2) does with a Cynic philosopher, only choosing a more refined and learned jester than princes do. Jesters were appreciated precisely for their vulgar language and jokes (as of the one quoted in *EM* 62), and some slaves even practiced for this precise purpose.[74]

The fact that emperors enjoyed the company of such figures does not mean, of course, that they viewed them as equals. This, I suggest, also applies to Seneca's view of Demetrius. Despite his witty sentences and rejection of luxury, Demetrius belongs to a lower category, far removed from that of noblemen who were passionate for philosophy and from those philosophers who owned their own schools, and were sometimes of Roman origin, as in the case of the Sextii.[75]

This idea is supported by a passage in Lucian's dialogue *Symposium or Lapithae*, which as the title says deals with a banquet. In this context, the jester Satyrion is involved in a challenge with the Cynic philosopher Alcidamas, while the other participants—all representatives of philosophical schools—laugh. The Cynic shows up uninvited, and never sits down on the couches but only on the ground, as servants do, and he is the one who challenges the jester.[76] So in this case it is

person, yet it is a baby in a litter, passively carried around. Recurrencies as Seneca, *EM* 28.2 (*quid miraris nihil tibi peregrinationes prodesse, cum te circumferas?*) refer to a part of the self which is carried around as if it were an object. Cf. also *EM* 108.36.

[72] Barton (1993), 107–8; Stahl (2015), 722–3.

[73] Augustus: Iuv. 5.1–5; Tiberius: Suet. *Tib.* 61.6 *frequenti quodam convivio... interrogatum eum... a quodam nano astante mensae inter copreas*; Claudius: Tac. *Ann.* 12.49.1 *cum privatus olim conversatione scurrarum iners otium oblectaret*; Domitian: Suet. *Dom.* 4.2 *per omne gladiatorium spectaculum ante pedes ei stabat puerulus coccinatus parvo portentosoque capite, cum quo plurimum fabulatur, nonnumquam serio.*

[74] Sen. *Const.* 11.3 *pueros quidam in hoc mercantur procaces et illorum impudentiam acuunt ac sub magistro habent, qui probra meditate effundant, nec has contumelias vocamus sed argutias*; cf. Berno (2018), 168–9.

[75] Below, 4.3 with n. 60.

[76] Lucian. *Symp.* 18–19 'Aristaenetus... ordered the clown to come in and do or say something funny... In came an ugly fellow with his head shaven except for a few hairs that stood up straight on his crown... he began to poke fun at the guests. The rest laughed when they were made fun of, but when he took a fling on Alcidamas in the same way, calling him a Maltese lapdog, Alcidamas got angry: indeed, for a long time it has been plain that he was jealous because the other fellow was making a hit and holding the attention of the room. So, throwing off his philosopher's cloak, he challenged him to fight, or else, he said, he would lay his stuff on him. Then poor Satyrion, for that was the clown's name, stood up to him and fought. It was delicious to see a philosopher squaring off at a clown, and giving and receiving blows at turn. Though some of the onlookers were disgusted, others kept laughing, until finally Alcidamas had enough of his punishment, well beaten by a tough little dwarf. So they got roundly laughed at.' (Trans. Harmon 1913). On Lucian's view of Cynic philosophy, Bosman (2012).

the Cynic philosopher who presents himself and acts as a jester: he puts himself on the same level, and apart from other philosophers.

Demetrius seems to be a peculiar, refined sort of jester: he offers his sentences as jokes, as freaks do; he looks awkward with his badly shaved beard and dirty clothes, and so do freaks; but he has something more, the label of philosopher, which distinguishes him from the more common figures of freaks and fools. Seneca states that he *admires* him, but he feels the need to explain it (62.3 *illum admiror. Quidni admirer?*—just as happens, as we have seen, in *Ben.* 7.1.3 '*meo iudicio*...). Surely Demetrius has something admirable about him, namely his rejection of wealth, but he is not considered an equal or friend of Seneca, or a philosopher who can serve Seneca as a teacher, as Fabianus or Attalus did. He looks more like a slave, from whom only coincidentally the owner can sometimes learn something, or by whose sentences he might be amused. The same may be said of Demetrius' attitude towards wealth: one may appreciate it, but it is that of an outsider, a slave or someone who is excluded from society, while a nobleman has to act differently. As it is well known, in *EM* 5 Seneca warns Lucilius from behaving differently from his peers (*EM* 5.1–2):[77]

> Illud autem te admoneo, ne eorum more qui non proficere sed conspici cupiunt facias aliqua quae in habitu tuo aut genere vitae notabilia sint; 2. asperum cultum et intonsum caput et neglegentiorem barbam et indictum argento odium et cubile humi positum et quidquid aliud ambitionem perversa via sequitur evita. Satis ipsum nomen philosophiae, etiam si modeste tractetur, invidiosum est: quid si nos hominum consuetudini coeperimus excerpere?
>
> All the same, I have a warning for you. There are those whose wish is to be noticed rather than to make moral progress. Don't be like them, altering your dress or way of life so as to attract attention. 2. The rough clothes, the rank growth of hair and beard, the sworn hatred of silverware, the pallet laid on the ground: all these and any other perverse form of self-aggrandizement are things you should avoid.
>
> The word 'philosophy' makes people uncomfortable enough all by itself, even when used modestly. How would it be if we were to begin exempting ourselves from the conventions people usually observe?

And this, as many scholars point out, is a neat refusal of Cynic apparel, which is further stressed by the last part of the same letter (5.5):[78]

[77] Richardson-Hay (2006), 205–9; Dietsche (2014), 42–3. A finest analysis of the whole letter in Pià Comella (2019), esp. 395–402.
[78] Scarpat (1975), 105–6; Richardson-Hay (2006), 207–8.

> Frugalitatem exigit philosophia, non poenam; potest autem esse non incompta frugalitas.
>
> Philosophy demands self-restraint, not self-abnegation—and even self-restraint can comb his hair.

A typical Cynic trait is again considered wrong, or at least inopportune for someone who belongs to Seneca's and Lucilius' social class. Cynic poverty is excessive, to the point that it seems the result of a punishment, not of a free choice. And Seneca's conclusion supports the right to be wealthy (5.6):[79]

> Magnus ille est qui fictilibus sic utitur quemadmodum argento, nec ille minor est qui sic argento utitur quemadmodum fictilibus; infirmi animi est pati non posse divitias.
>
> One who uses earthenware as if it were silver is indeed a great person; equally great, though, is the one who uses silver as if it were earthenware. Not being able to cope with wealth is an indication of weakness.

Seneca's attitude towards Cynicism, and especially towards Demetrius, seems to reflect his defence of the fact that he is an influential and yet wealthy philosopher. He tries to turn the charge of inconsistency directed at him against those philosophers who were coherent in their frugality. He maintains that such frugality is extreme and unnatural, and that a real philosopher, to make society better, has to live within it rather than reject it wholesale. The reasoning is similar to that in *De vita beata*, grounding on the Stoic categories of 'indifferents' (to which both poverty and wealth belong) and 'preferables', which consents us to choose wealth over poverty.[80]

Seneca genuinely admired some traits of Cynicism. But his champion of Cynicism is Diogenes, the almost legendary philosopher who managed to humiliate Alexander the Great and who is thus worthy of comparison with the perfect sage, Socrates. Demetrius is put on a lower level: he confronted Caligula but did not manage to fully reject money and all the things it brings, such as power and influence; his speech on wealth in *De beneficiis* is praised but not fully endorsed; and, finally, Seneca seems to bring him along as a sort of refined freak who utters witticisms. Demetrius was useful to Seneca, as an exhibition of his admiration for poverty to which he laid claim in his retirement speech to Nero—in which, nonetheless, he states (Tac. *Ann.* 14.54.3): *nec me in paupertatem ipse detrudam*, 'not that I shall drag myself down into poverty'. But Seneca did not admire Demetrius unconditionally, and in a way almost despised him, or at least distanced himself from him, as would be expected of a Roman nobleman vis-à-vis a

[79] Richardson-Hay (2006), 219–20.

[80] Above, 3.2.1 with n. 13 and 3.2.3.

dirty, half-naked, badly shaved philosopher. It was far easier to admire a legendary Cynic who lived in the past than to treat as an equal a living Cynic in Rome's Forum. The self-distancing from Demetrius would have to target not only his person but also his ideas about frugality, which were in conflict not only with a luxurious lifestyle but also with Roman society itself, which, as Seneca himself shows in *De beneficiis*, was grounded on liberality as a social bond.

4
Seneca against *Luxuria*

If in real life Seneca may be charged with *luxuria*, in his philosophical works fighting this vice appears to be one of his main purposes—and this is one of his major inconsistencies (above, 3.1). Even when he only hints at a philosophical definition or theoretical discussion about *luxuria*—and indeed his philosophy aims more at showing and convincing than at exposing and demonstrating—it is the vice he targets most often.[1] While he generally avoids to label architectural luxury as such, even if he blames it (below, 4.4), and ignores the discussion of *luxuria*'s starting point in Roman history, he develops other commonplaces (the connection of *luxuria* with banquets and other vices, especially lust, and *luxuria* as a disease) in an original way, intertwining his considerations with references to Stoic tenets such as the theory of indifferents.[2] The importance Seneca accords *luxuria* is shown by his frequent use of personification, a rhetorical device that we have found since Plautus on.[3] In Seneca, it becomes a way of presenting *luxuria* as a sort of siren, a seductive but terrible monster we have to fight in order to avoid reducing ourselves to our stomachs. And this monster is even more dreadful since it hides inside us.

All this makes Seneca a pivotal author for our subject, in that he conveys inputs from many different literary genres, enriches them through a Stoic taxonomy of vices, and offers posterity a set of examples, descriptions, and exhortations to which many subsequent writers, beginning with Pliny the Elder, will refer. In this chapter I will examine Seneca's view of *luxuria*, focusing on some particular issues: the theoretical definition of *luxuria* as the archenemy of a philosophical life (4.1); the world of *luxuria* as upside down (4.2); *luxuria*'s physical location, the stomach (4.3); its homeland, Baias (4.4); its friends (4.5); its champions, Apicius, Mark Antony and Maecenas (4.6); the champions of frugality, Scipio Africanus and Tubero (4.7); the possibility of recovering from *luxuria* (4.8); and 'scientific' attitudes to *luxuria* (4.9). For each issue, I have chosen some case studies in the form of examples and/or texts whose context (e.g. that of a letter) best shed light on the topic.

[1] See Citroni Marchetti (1991), 116–73; Motto/Clark (1993); Borgo (1998), 119–22.
[2] Above, 3.2.1 and 3.2.3; below, 4.4.
[3] Above, 2.1.1; 2.6.1; 3.2.2; below, 5.5. On Seneca's prose works, Armisen-Marchetti (1989), 262–70, who stresses how personification of both virtue and vice creates a sort of theatre of ethical struggles; especially on female personifications of positive ideas, such as the wise man's soul, Dressler (2016), 73–6; 83–6; 124–5; 137–40; 167–204.

Roman Luxuria: *A Literary and Cultural History*. Francesca Romana Berno, Oxford University Press.
 DOI: 10.1093/oso/9780192846402.003.0004

As we shall see, most relevant passages are to be found in the *EM*, Seneca's last work, with the exception of *NQ*, which, despite being a scientific-doxographical work, includes as digressions some short essays on the subject. This in itself is also noteworthy (4.9). In general, the concentration of occurrences of *luxuria* in works written after retirement, with the complete abandonment of Seneca's 'youthful' interest in the subject of anger (as shown by the work *On Anger*), suggests a political dimension: he could discuss anger, the tyrannical passion par excellence, while he did not actually live under a tyranny; but when he did, he had to turn to seemingly lighter and less compromising vices, such as *luxuria*, which does not require explicit references to power relationships. Yet, as historical sources confirm, Seneca's descriptions of luxury-related behaviour still collided with Nero's sensibilities.[4] We may therefore read in Seneca's treatment of *luxuria* a sort of doublespeak,[5] an expression of political dissidence through moralism.

4.1 *Ingeniosa Luxuria* as the Archenemy of a Philosophical Life

If we scour the more than hundred Senecan passages involving *luxuria*, we may formulate some interesting theoretical considerations: this vice goes against nature; it is as old as humankind; it corresponds to Greek *philedonia*; and it shows cleverness and talent. *Luxuria* is, in a word, *ingeniosa* (*NQ* 4b.13.4): and this makes it extremely dangerous and difficult to fight.

First of all, this vice is characterized by its move away from nature (*EM* 90.19):[6]

> A natura luxuria descivit, quae cotidie se ipsa incitat et tot saeculis crescit et ingenio adiuvat vitia. Primo supervacua coepit concupiscere, inde contraria, novissime animum corpori addixit et illius deservire libidini iussit. Omnes istae artes quibus aut circitatur civitas aut strepit corpori negotium gerunt, cui omnia olim tamquam servo praestabantur, nunc tamquam domino parantur. Itaque hinc textorum, hinc fabrorum officinae sunt, hinc odores coquentium, hinc molles corporis motus docentium mollesque cantus et infractos. Recessit enim ille naturalis modus desideria ope necessaria finiens; iam rusticitatis et miseriae est velle quantum sat est.
>
> Self-indulgence has abandoned nature, spurring itself on every day, growing through the centuries, and abetting vices by its own ingenuity. It lusted first for nonessentials, then for things that were harmful; now, finally, it has surrendered the mind to the body, bidding it serve the body's every whim. There was a time

[4] Edwards (2021), esp. 172–6. [5] For this concept see Bartsch (1994), 63–96.

[6] Zago (2012), 258–62; Mazzoli (2017a); Edwards (2019), 273; Armisen-Marchetti (2020a), esp. 327; see also Degl'Innocenti Pierini (2004), 70–88; Seal (2021), 46–57; especially on the golden age in Seneca, Star (2021), 128–33.

> when all that the body got was rations, like a slave; but now, like a master, it has everything provided to it. This is why you find textile businesses here, craft workshops here; here the aromas produced by chefs, there the sensuous movements of dance teachers and sensuous and effeminate singing. The natural limit we once observed, restricting our wants to what is essential and within our resources, has vanished. Nowadays one is considered unrefined and poverty-stricken if one wants just what is enough.
>
> (Trans. Graver/Long 2015, here and below)

Since the Stoics, like most Hellenistic philosophers, considered living according to nature to be the ideal life, *luxuria* is here represented as the exact opposite of ideal behaviour.[7] The personification shows it as a force that, using intelligence (*ingenium*), drives humans in the wrong direction, away from the path to virtue. This definition alludes to the etymological connection of the word *luxuria* with the medical term *luxus*, 'dislocated', in the sense that a joint is no longer in its correct and natural position, but has come into a wrong, painful, and useless one.[8] *Luxuria* is a moral luxation, something that prevents our souls' natural movements. This passage also describes *luxuria*'s evolution, and places it in the sociological context of needs: our desire shifts from necessary and thus natural items to unnecessary, superfluous one (*supervacua*), to the point that we feel the need for things that not only are far removed from nature but even antithetical to it (*contraria*). The result is that souls are enslaved to their bodies, that is, to animal instincts. This sociological analysis, with the shift from necessary to unnecessary, was already present in Sallust (*Cat.* 12.1–2, above, 2.3.1), but Seneca frames these considerations within the Stoic view of the passions, which states that if we choose to behave wrongly, then we slowly descend into vice, and the fall gradually leads to ruin;[9] our rational nature turns into its opposite, that is, we become irrational, no different from animals. These are the philosophical implications of the word *contraria*. And the idea of *luxuria* as behaviour opposed to nature is a key issue in Seneca's conceptualization of this vice. In this passage we also find the explicit reduction of *luxuria*, a generic search for pleasure, to *libido*, lust, the search for sexual pleasure,[10] as confirmed by the quoted examples, which include cooking perfumes,[11] effeminate and seductive chants, and dancing.

Even if this picture implies an evolution of the vice of *luxuria*, it is not a recent one; it has always been so (97.1):[12]

[7] Below, 4.2. This issue is relevant also in *NQ* (4.9). [8] Above, 1.1.
[9] Cf. *EM* 116.3, quoted below. [10] Above, 2.5.1.
[11] On this image and its symbology in Seneca, Gazzarri (2021).
[12] Costa (2013), 66–7; Torre (2021), 74.

> Erras, mi Lucili, si existimas nostri saeculi esse vitium luxuriam et neglegentiam boni moris et alia quae obiecit suis quisque temporibus: hominum sunt ista, non temporum. Nulla aetas vacavit a culpa... pudet dicere, numquam apertius quam coram Catone peccatum est.
>
> You are mistaken, dear Lucilius, if you think that our era is particularly culpable for self-indulgence and for neglect of high moral standards. One likes to blame such deficiencies on one's own times, but in reality it is not the times that are at fault but the people. No era has ever been free of blame. Indeed... I am ashamed to tell you that misconduct has never been more in evidence than it was in the time of Cato and in his very presence.

This reading of *luxuria* seems to be entirely different from the historiographical one. Sallust, Livy, and already Cato and Piso Frugi,[13] identified the beginning of moral decline, and thereby the spread of *luxuria*, with Eastern influence due to military conquest. It does not matter whether the enemy is Carthage, Greece, Macedonia, or Asia: the vice is perceived as coming from outside, which infects the originally sober and virtuous Roman morality. But Seneca goes in a different direction: the vice has always been present, for it is connatural with human psychology. There are no external excuses, because we all carry the germ of vice inside (*Ben.* 4.26.2).[14] The vice, rather, is dependent on our life choices and habits. Again, this is a reference to Stoic philosophy, according to which a human being is either a wise man (a sort of ideal and solitary figure, morally flawless) or a fool (the overwhelming majority of people), who is exposed to all kinds of vice. So the historical evolution is only in the specific expressions of the vice, while the vice itself is innate. Elsewhere, e.g. in letters 86 and 95 (below, 4.7), Seneca turns to the more common idea of society's moral decline, but this is actually not so different: the decline involves specific phenomenological habits and behaviour, which no one doubts, while the human inclination to vice, from an ontological point of view, is always the same.

Seneca refers here to the era of his champion of virtue, Cato the Younger (97.1–10), who together with his ancestor Cato the Elder represented for the Romans, as we have seen, the quintessence of moral integrity[15] and in particular of the struggle against vice. Seneca also alludes to sumptuary laws (97.8–9):

> Et fient et facta sunt ista, et licentia urbium aliquando disciplina metuque, numquam sponte considet. 9. Non est itaque quod credas nos plurimum libidini permisisse, legibus minimum.

[13] Above, 1.4; 2.3.2 with n. 146.

[14] Bellincioni (1978), 15–31; Griffin (2013), 177 and 249.

[15] Above, 2.1.2.; especially on Cato the Younger in Seneca, above, 3.2.3 with n. 37. On Cato in *EM* 97, Torre (2021), 96–9.

> Such things will be as they have been before; but while civic decadence will sometimes subside under pressure and fear, it will never do so of its own accord. 9. You should not suppose, then, that our time has yielded more to lust than any other, or less to the laws.

His words contradict Tiberius' statements about the proposed law (above, 2.9): the emperor states that people may correct their behaviours autonomously, while Seneca rules out this possibility, and says that they need to be forced to act rightly.[16] He goes on to say that we use to be ashamed of our mistakes, except for ethical ones (97.10): 'in other skills, mistakes are an embarrassment to the craftsman, who is upset by his errors; in life, wrongdoing is a source of positive delight'. Seneca carefully distinguishes the sort of pleasure that is natural from that derived through *luxuria* (116.3):[17]

> Inbecillus est primo omnis adfectus; deinde ipse se concitat et vires dum procedit parat: excluditur facilius quam expellitur. Quis negat omnis adfectus a quodam quasi naturali fluere principio? Curam nobis nostri natura mandavit, sed huic ubi nimium indulseris, vitium est. Voluptatem natura necessariis rebus admiscuit, non ut illam peteremus, sed ut ea sine quibus non possumus vivere gratiora nobis illius faceret accessio: suo veniat iure, luxuria est. Ergo intrantibus resistamus, quia facilius, ut dixi, non recipiuntur quam exeunt.
>
> All emotions are feeble at first; then they arouse themselves and gather strength as they advance. It's easier to refuse them entry than to drive them out. No one is denying that all emotions stem from a source that is, in a sense, natural. Nature has endowed us with a concern for ourselves; but once we indulge this concern excessively, it becomes a fault. Nature infused the necessities of life with pleasure, not so that we would pursue pleasure, but so that the supervening pleasure would make what is indispensable more welcome to us. If the pleasure is pursued for its own sake, it becomes self-indulgence. Let us, then, resist emotions as soon as they start to come in, since, as I said, it's easier to refuse them admission than to get them to leave.

In addition to the Stoic exposition of passion as a gradual and irreversible decline, we find here the interesting connection between *voluptas* and *luxuria*. The former, which usually refers to Epicurean (physical) pleasure, is described here as a trick of mother Nature to make us perform what is necessary, an unsolicited but

[16] It is likely that Seneca is here alluding to some sumptuary initiatives taken by Nero during the first years of his reign. (Cf. Suet. *Nero* 16.2 'a limit was imposed on expenditure. Public feasts were reduced to food handouts. With the exception of beans and vegetables, the sale of hot food in taverns was prohibited—previously all kinds of delicacies had been available.' Trans. Edwards 2000.)

[17] Graver/Long (2015), 573. Cf. *Ad Helv.* 10.8–10, with the example of the gourmand Apicius (below, 4.6).

pleasant consequence of our natural behaviour, but not something to be pursued for its own sake, in which case it becomes a dangerous vice, *luxuria*. The connection here between vice and pleasure[18] shows that Seneca, as differently from his predecessors, rather than identifying *luxuria* with the Greek *tryphe* (the historiographical word for luxury), *asotia* (prodigality), or *aselgeia*, considers it as corresponding to *philedonia*, 'love for pleasures'. This word is closer to *luxuria* from an etymological point of view, in that the Latin desiderative suffix *-urus* may well correspond to the theme *phil-* (from *philia*, 'love') of the compound, while *luxus* is more concrete than *hedone*, 'pleasure', since it specifies pleasures as expensive. Seneca thus finds for this Roman vice a place in the Stoic taxonomy of vice, where *tryphe* and similar terms do not appear, while *philedonia* does (*SVF* 3.397; cf. 3.395; 3.422).[19] The emphasis on the connection between *luxuria* and desire is rooted in Stoic ethics, too, according to which every vice is a desire for something: a desire for revenge (anger), a desire for someone else's demise (envy), a desire for money (greediness), and so on.

Further considerations on *luxuria* and desire are to be found in another letter (119.14):

> Ambitiosa non est fames, contenta desinere est; quo desinat non nimis curat. Infelicis luxuriae ista tormenta sunt: quaerit quemadmodum post saturitatem quoque esuriat, quemadmodum non impleat ventrem sed farciat, quemadmodum sitim prima potione sedatam revocet.
>
> Hunger is not ambitious. It is satisfied to stop, and it does not much care what makes it stop. After that are only the torments of a wretched self-indulgence that looks for ways to stimulate hunger after it is sated, to stuff the stomach rather than to fill it, to rouse a thirst that was relieved by the first drink.

Here, the accent is on the contrast between measure, which coincides with nature, and excess, which coincides with *luxuria*: and this excess is not only wrong but painful and unhappy (*infelix*), since it leads to a restless desire for novelty, knowing neither limit nor end, and therefore ultimately becoming a torment (*tormenta*), that is an event which brings an unnatural and so hardly bearable pain.[20] The restlessness of desire is expressed by different rhetorical devices: anaphoric repetition (*quemadmodum*, thrice) to stress the application of vice to each and every aspect of eating, the most natural act at all; emphasis on the *-urus* suffix (*luxuria* but also *esurio*, 'I want to eat, I am hungry', stressed by the alliteration with *saturitas*); and antithesis, where the first element means measure and nature, the second excess (*saturitatem/esuriat, impleat/farciat, sedata/revocet*). The overall

[18] Cf. also 69.4 *luxuria* [*sc. promittit*] *multas ac varias voluptates.*

[19] Above, 1.2.

[20] Courtil (2014); Malaspina (2021). On the metaphorical use of this image, Armisen-Marchetti (1989), 164–5. Cf. 95.18 *supplicia luxuriae*, on which see below, 4.3.

impression is of a sense of nausea, in two ways: as a psychological attitude of despising something, because one is always in search of something better; and a physical, involuntary attitude that comes from unnatural eating habits. When the stomach is not only filled but stuffed, when we eat even while being sated, when we drink without being thirsty, then we feel disgust and nausea, and this may actually be a form of torture (below, 4.3). Seneca's choice of eating as an example not only illustrates this sense of disgust associated with excessive pleasure but also represents the most natural and necessary act of all turned into its opposite—an unnatural, even dangerous event—by vice. And it best expresses the idea of wastefulness, because expensive food and drink are mostly only just tasted briefly, and they expire quickly.

The restless attitude of vice subordinates intelligence and rationality to itself: indeed, *luxuria* is inventive and creative, as well as firm and steady in its purposes.[21] *Luxuria*'s activities subvert natural elements, to the point of self-destruction. This is evident in the case of water, a free element at everybody's disposal which this vice turns into expensive ice drinks to sip in the summer. At this regard, Seneca comments (*NQ* 4b.13.4):

> Hoc quod illa [*sc.* natura] fluere et patere omnibus voluit . . . contra se ingeniosa luxuria redegit ad pretium.
>
> She wanted this stuff to flow and be accessible to everyone . . . but luxury, inventive to its own detriment, has given it a price tag. (Trans. Hine 2010)

Luxuria is smart and clever (*ingeniosa*) and aims this good attitude at the perverse purpose of altering natural rules: being against nature, this turns into a self-destructive behavior, because ice drinks cause stomach diseases. Indeed, nausea is not only a psychological trait, but also a physiological condition of those affected by this vice (below, 4.3 and 4.9 on this passage).

This attitude is shared by other passions, and focused both on the search for exotic items (ivory, purple) and on intervention in what is natural (*Ira* 1.21.1–4):

> Nihil ergo in ira . . . magnum, nihil nobile est. Aut si videtur alicui magnum animum ira producere, videatur et luxuria—ebore sustineri vult, purpura vestiri, auro tegi, terras transferre, maria concludere, flumina praecipitare, nemora suspendere; 2. videatur et avaritia magni animi . . . 3. Videatur et libido magni animi . . . 4. Omnia ista, non refert in quantum procedant extendantque se, angusta sunt, misera depressa; sola sublimis et excelsa virtus est . . .
>
> There's nothing great, then, nothing notable in anger . . . Or if someone thinks anger produces a great spirit, let him think that luxury does too: it wants to be

[21] Citroni Marchetti (1991), 113–18; below, 4.9.

> carried about on ivory, dressed in purple, covered in gold, it wants to move masses of land about, dam up the seas, create waterfalls, hang forests in midair. 2. Let him think that greed, too, is the mark of a great spirit... 3. Let him think that lust, too, is the mark of a great spirit... 4. All such things, no matter how far and wide they reach, are pinched, wretched, base. Only virtue is sublime and exalted... (Trans. Kaster 2010)

As for architectural luxury, the instances Seneca mentions come from the building activity of many emperors of the Julio-Claudian dynasty, from Caligula on.[22] They all stress the subversion of natural environment, with earth and water altered in their own place and function.

To sum up, *luxuria* has all the characteristics of the 'ideal' vice for Seneca: it is linked with desire, the key concept of Stoic ethics, but in a generic way, so that it may be connected with many different attitudes; it is restless in that it seeks ever newer objects of desire, and thereby emphasizes social degeneration; it is easily exemplifiable through widespread and well-known social phenomena, such as the banquet; and it is diametrically opposed to nature, as is excess to moderation and measure. Seneca will develop all these issues, and more, in his *EM*.

4.2 The World Upside Down: Saturnalia (*EM* 18) and Night-Owls (*EM* 122)

A typical feature of Seneca's consideration of *luxuria*, and vice in general, is that it turns the world upside down. According to Stoic ethics, if vice is pursued to an extreme level, reason is enslaved by it, and, given the connection between micro- and macrocosm, nature itself and natural laws are distorted. We find evidence of this in Senecan tragedy, where nights last over days, and planets turn in the opposite direction. The transgression of natural rules reflects the monstrosity of the murders in the tragedies.[23]

Vice creates a sort of counter-nature, a world upside down. Nothing expresses this better than the feast of the *Saturnalia*, where social roles are overturned and everything is allowed.[24] Seneca refers to this celebration, held in December, in *EM* 18 (18.1–4):[25]

[22] As seen in Suetonius (below, 5.2.1). For Seneca's account of this expression of luxury, below, 4.4.

[23] Rosenmeyer (1989), 136–59; Torre (1997), esp. 391–4; Schiesaro (2003), 170–220; below, n. 113.

[24] On *Saturnalia* and their relevance in this letter, Gowers (1996), 27–8; Edwards (2017), with special reference to Horace's satire 2.7, which is indeed placed during the *Saturnalia*; Edwards (2019), 108–9; Soldo (2021), 194–6; 200.

[25] Mazzoli (1991), 79–80; Mazzoli (2005), 130; Edwards (2019), 111–14; Seal (2021), 37–41; Soldo (2021), 198–206.

> December est mensis: cum maxime civitas sudat. Ius luxuriae publice datum est; ingenti apparatu sonant omnia, tamquam quicquam inter Saturnalia intersit et dies rerum agendarum; adeo nihil interest ut <non> videatur mihi errasse qui dixit olim mensem Decembrem fuisse, nunc annum. 2. Si te hic haberem, libenter tecum conferrem quid existimares esse faciendum, utrum nihil ex cotidiana consuetudine movendum an, ne dissidere videremur cum publicis moribus, et hilarius cenandum et exuendam togam. Nam quod fieri nisi in tumultu et tristi tempore civitatis non solebat, voluptatis causa ac festorum dierum vestem mutavimus. 3. Si te bene novi, arbitri partibus functus nec per omnia nos similes esse pilleatae turbae voluisses nec per omnia dissimiles; nisi forte his maxime diebus animo imperandum est, ut tunc voluptatibus solus abstineat cum in illas omnis turba procubuit; certissimum enim argumentum firmitatis suae capit, si ad blanda et in luxuriam trahentia nec it nec abducitur. 4. Hoc multo fortius est, ebrio ac vomitante populo siccum ac sobrium esse, illud temperantius, non excerpere se nec insignire nec misceri omnibus et eadem sed non eodem modo facere; licet enim sine luxuria agere festum diem.
>
> The month is December, and the city is sweating, more than ever. License has been granted to public self-indulgence, and everywhere is a great din of preparations, just as if there were some real diffidence between a day of Saturnalia and a business day. But really there is not a bit of difference—so that I agree entirely with the one who said that what used to be the month of December is now the entire year! 2. If I had you here, I'd like to ask your opinion on what our behavior should be. Should we make no alteration at all in our daily routine? Or should we try not to appear at odds with the general custom, and so make our dinners more festive than usual, laying aside the toga? For what never used to happen except in some time of turmoil, some crisis of the state, we now do for pleasure because of the holiday: we alter our mode of dress. 3. If I know you well, you would stand as intermediary. You would not want us to be exactly like the crowd with the party hats, but neither would you want us to be completely different. And yet it may be that during these days, one ought more than ever to take charge of one's mind, ordering it to abstain from pleasures just when everyone is indulging in them. For if it does not proceed and is not enticed into those luxuries which lead to dissipation, it gives a very sure proof of its own strength. 4. The latter is by far the bolder course, to remain cold sober when everyone else is drunk and vomiting. The former is more moderate: not to hold oneself apart or draw attention to oneself, while still not mingling in every respect—to do as other do, but not in the same manner. For one may celebrate the holiday without dissipation.

Luxuria is the protagonist of this feast, in which every line is crossed. Seneca says that *luxuria* has received a public right (18.1 *ius...publice*), as if it were the king of Rome. There is no precise answer to the question of whether it is opportune or not to celebrate the *Saturnalia*:[26] Seneca proposes both Lucilius' answer—that one celebrate, but only to a limited degree, and his own, which refuses all celebration. Seneca's radical position is an extreme expression of his general attitude: as is well known, he generally urges common habits in clothing and so on (e.g. in *EM* 5, above, 3.3.4). And so he views the *Saturnalia* as illegitimate in that they represent a perversion of all normal habits: first, the feast exceeds the time of the religious celebration and seems to last forever, and forces people to sweat as if it were hot, despite the winter season (18.1); second, it imposes habits that are typical of periods of grief and war, as opposed to a celebration (18.2). The complex nature of Seneca's argument is stressed by the verbs, which first focus on change (18.2 *movendum*, *mutavimus*), then on falling (18.3 *procubuit*), and finally on going and leading (18.3 *it*, *trahentia*, *abducitur*). The whole city is going to celebration and drunkenness, which to resist requires firmness. The term that identifies this virtue, *firmitas*, is surrounded by terms of vice and pleasure: *voluptates*, *blanda*, *luxuria* (18.3). *Luxuria* itself is mentioned three times in four sections. An even stronger attitude (18.4 *multo fortius... temperantius*) is that of the one who does not exclude himself from the celebrations, but manages to remain sober within them. In this case, the abstract opposition between *luxuria* and firmness is replaced by a vivid image of drunkenness (18.4 *ebrio ac vomitante populo*) vs sobriety (18.4 *siccum ac sobrium*): he engages in the same event, but in a different way. The contrast is sharpened by the image of a wet and disgusting crowd vs a dry and decent man, with an expression that comes from comedy and always describes someone who is above trivial and physical pleasures.[27] This is the actual attitude of a wise man. In my opinion, this idea is modelled after Socrates, whose sobriety at banquets was legendary and admired by his friends. To be precise, Socrates adopted a middle way: drinking without getting drunk, but he never lost control and always acted as a sober man among drunk people (e.g. Plato *Symp.* 223b–d; Xen. *Symp.* 24–6). This differs from what is described in letter 7, where being surrounded by a crowd at the public games entails being infected by their vice, such as a taste for human blood. There, Seneca confesses as a personal weakness (7.1) that, especially on festive occasions such as public games, he does not manage to retain his spirit, but feels himself becoming afflicted by vice (7.3). This comes from the Stoic idea of vice as deriving from the influence of bad examples.[28] Letter 18 offers a stronger Seneca, able to resist seductive banquets and wine, but the condemnation of the crowd remains the same, and the terminology used to refer to it is frequent and negative. Indeed, in the opening of the letter (18.1) we find *civitas*, *publice*, and *omnia*, all of them in a negative context: sweating (*sudat*), loud singing (*ingenti apparatu sonant*), *luxuria* itself. Similar terms are repeated

[26] Citroni Marchetti (1991), 132.
[27] Afran. frg. 61 R.[3] = Non. 21.34 *vigilans ac sollers, sicca sana sobria*; cf. 114.3 (cited below, 4.6); *VB* 12.4, where it describes the sober, authentically Epicurean pleasure vs the one trivialized by common men.
[28] Edwards (2019), 82–6; Courtil (2018b), esp. 103–6; cf. below, 4.4 with n. 78.

in 18.2, while in 18.3 we twice find *turba*, the negative noun for 'crowd', etymologically related to the tornado (*turbo*).[29] The crowd is described as *pilleata*, 'cap-bearing', with reference to the cap worn by freed slaves; indeed, during the *Saturnalia* every slave was allowed to act as if he were free, and the noble Seneca appears to despise this license. Again in 18.4 we find *populus*, 'people', and *omnes*, 'everyone'. This plebeian crowd literally surrounds the sage, which increases his heroism in resisting their vice.

The changing of clothes is of interest, too. During these celebrations the Romans used to dismiss the *toga* for the *synthesis*, a fancier dress (cf. Mart. 14.1.1; 14.142).[30] From Seneca's point of view, this dismissal (18.2 *exuendam togam*) is tantamount to giving up dignity itself.[31] He does not even mention the other attire, as if people were naked and ceased to be civilized and polite persons. There is a sort of metamorphosis (18.2 *vestem mutavimus*) of men into drunk, animal-like people, enslaved to their lowest instincts. To lose the toga means to lose every distinctive sign of education and politeness. There is the chance that Seneca had Nero in mind: indeed, Suetonius points out that he used to wear the *synthesina vestis* in public occasions (*Nero* 51):[32]

> Circa cultum habitumque adeo pudendus, ut...plerumque synthesinam indutus ligato circum collum sudario prodierit in publico sine cinctu et discalciatus.
>
> He was so very shameless in his concern for dress and the care of his person, that...he was often to be seen in public dressed in a dinner robe, with a handkerchief around his neck, and his tunic unbelted and his feet bare.
>
> (Trans. Edwards 2000)

Suetonius himself interprets Nero's clothing habits as a moral transgression. It seems that Seneca, by the reference to the changing of clothes as losing morality, is insinuating his own judgement on Nero's ruling, which looks like the overturned world of Saturnalia, a sort of empire of vice.

In the second part of the letter (18.5–13), as is well known,[33] Seneca suggests a sort of exercise of extreme poverty: eating barley bread and polenta and drinking water is unpleasant, except that one may feel satisfaction for having had the firmness to settle for so little (18.10). One might argue that there is a parallel here with the image of the sober sage among drunk people—a demonstration of strength of mind. But the general context does not support the linearity of this interpretation, because during the *Saturnalia* it is natural that everyone should act contrary to his usual habits, and so if a nobleman imitates poverty, this might just be a part of

[29] *Turbo* is a derivative from *turba* (*DELL*, 707–8 *s.v.*).
[30] Leary (1996), 4; 51; 205. [31] Soldo (2021), 202–3.
[32] As for the unbelted tunic, see below, 4.6; in general, on Nero's *luxuria*, below, 5.2.
[33] Above, 3.3.

the celebration rather than a spiritual exercise. Seneca tries to get out of the crowd, but, as in letter 7, it seems that he cannot manage it.

Another, more detailed narrative of a world turned upside down by *luxuria* is in letter 122, where the protagonists are the night owls, those who switch night with day.[34] While in *EM* 18 the reversal of nature was primarily social, in this case it involves two ontological categories, place and time. The letter deals with those who, unsatisfied with 'average' vices, stage banquets and other pleasures during the night instead of the day, turning the natural order of daily activities upside down. And this is called *luxuria* (122.5):[35]

> Omnia vitia contra naturam pugnant, omnia debitum ordinem deserunt; hoc est luxuriae propositum, gaudere perversis nec tantum discedere a recto sed quam longissime abire, deinde etiam e contrario stare.
>
> All our faults contend against nature, they all abandon due order. Self-indulgence makes it a goal to delight in perversity, not just to depart from the straight path but to get as distant from it as possible, and finally take up exactly the opposite position.

Seneca here emphasizes two issues that characterize *luxuria* as an archetypical vice: perversion (*gaudere perversis*), that is, reversing natural rules and reason itself, and its ethical correspondence: deflecting from what is right, to the point of a complete reversal. This alludes to *luxuria*'s etymological connection with *luxus* as 'luxation',[36] and emphasizes its restless search for pleasure, which never ends. Indeed, while virtue offers solid satisfaction, nothing is enough for vice, and this state of affairs leads, as we have seen, to a psychological state of anxiety comparable to torture.[37] The idea of vice as a perversion of nature is rooted in the Stoic concept of *diastrophe*, 'overturning'.[38] Vice constructs a whole upside-down world that goes against nature.

The letter lists many behaviours that go 'against nature', i.e. against rules, common sense, and natural laws: first, switching from a night to a day shift, which is also expressed by the verb *perverto* (122.2 *sunt qui officia lucis noctisque perverterint*)[39] and compared to the legendary figures of the antipodes, people living on the other side of the world and with their heads down, about which there is an ancient tradition.[40] Seneca quotes Virgil and Cato the Elder as authorities (122.2–3), and presents the world of the night as a type of hell. Other comparisons with persons active at night are night owls (122.3 *nocturnae aves*), dead

[34] Moretti (1994), 33–4; 51–2 on antipodes as equivalent to the underworld; Torre (1997), 391–4; Ker (2004), 219–21; Inwood (2010), 347–8; Ker (2020), 198–210. I am grateful to James Ker for his suggestions.

[35] Inwood (2010), 350. [36] Above, 1.1. [37] Above, 4.1.

[38] On this concept in Stoic ethics, Brouwer (2020).

[39] Inwood (2010), 347–8. [40] Moretti (1994), 17–77.

people (122.3), and birds kept in the dark to soften their flesh (122.4). The disgusting image of whitish and flaccid flesh, of which we may find a parallel in the pale complexion of night persons, is still less repulsive than the state of their souls. This correspondence between soft, feeble, sickly bodies and souls matches reflects that between luxurious foods and the inner disposition of the pleasure-seekers who eat them (below, 4.3).

This example of living against nature is the clearest one, since it involves daylight; other examples are the switching out of male and female clothing, imitating young age for the purpose of sexual encounters (122.7), making winter into summer (for example by searching for roses and hot water in the cold season), planting trees over buildings, and building pools within the sea (122.8).[41] All these represent a perversion of time (a person's age, and the seasons) and place (artificial vs natural elements), and thus a perversion of the very roots of nature, since time and place are the *ur*-categories of the Stoic universe.[42]

Seneca then turns again to night persons as an example of the complete reversal of nature (122.9 *totum ab illa* [*sc. natura*] *desciscunt*, 'people finally abandon nature completely') at *luxuria*'s service. We have again the parallel with dead people (122.10 *defunctorum loco sunt*). After a roundup of Roman examples (122.11–13), Seneca resumes the analysis of reversal, employing even further the symbolism of light. It seems that light embarrasses a bad conscience, so evil people logically prefer obscurity, which is why Seneca calls them *lucifugae*, 'those who avoid light'. But *luxuria*, to some degree, needs to exhibit itself, and so holding banquets at night is a way to display one's immoral behaviour while still avoiding light (122.14):[43]

> Praeterea luxuriosi vitam suam esse in sermonibus dum vivunt volunt; nam si tacetur, perdere se putant operam.... Multi bona comedunt, multi amicas habent; ut inter istos nomen invenias, opus est non tantum luxuriosam rem sed notabilem facere; in tam occupata civitate fabulas vulgaris nequitia non invenit.
>
> Moreover, extravagant people want their life to be talked about as long as they live, for if it goes quietly they think they are wasting their efforts.... Many people are big spenders, and many keep mistresses. In order to make a name in this company, you need to go in for notoriety as well as luxury. It's a busy town; common vices get no attention at all.

Luxuria wants fame and notoriety; this is a peculiarity of this vice, as other vices tend to prefer obscurity and elicit a sense of shame in the vicious person. *Luxuria* loves display, and this trait is typical of the Senecan account of it (below, 4.6). Not only does it always seek new forms of pleasure—note the combination of

[41] Winkler (1990), 21; Inwood (2010), 350–1.
[42] Wildberger (2006), 100–32.
[43] Inwood (2010), 352–3.

prodigality, luxury, and banquets on one side (*bona comedunt*, a crystalline metaphor: 'they eat their assets') with lovers on the other (*amicas*, in plural, significantly)—but it has also lost any sense of shame. The extreme degree of this vice is when it yearns for a reputation.

In letter 122, Seneca identifies the cause of this kind of *luxuria*, described as a disease, in the disgust for life (122.18–19):[44]

> Causa tamen praecipua mihi videtur huius morbi vitae communis fastidium... Nolunt solita peccare quibus peccandi praemium infamia est. 19. Hanc petunt omnes isti qui, ut ita dicam, retro vivunt.
>
> But the principal cause of this malady, in my opinion, is a hatred of ordinary life.... People whose reward for wrongdoing is notoriety don't want to commit ordinary offenses. 19. This is the aim of everyone who lives backwards, so to speak.

The equivalence of vice and disease, typical of ancient ethics, is developed in detail in *EM* 95; disgust (*fastidium*) for life is another key issue of Seneca's account of vices, a sort of boredom with more common flaws, and which may also lead to suicide (e.g. in letter 77; below, 4.3). Boredom with normal life and normal vices causes excessive vices, which overturn nature: those who live in this way, in search for bad fame (*in-famia*), live 'in reverse' (*retro*). But in Stoic philosophy this is actually impossible, because everyone is doomed to live in accordance with fate. Living against nature is like rowing against the flow (122.19):

> Ideo, Lucili, tenenda nobis via est quam natura praescripsit, nec ab illa declinandum: illam sequentibus omnia facilia, expedita sunt, contra illam nitentibus non alia vita est quam contra aquam remigantibus.
>
> And so, dear Lucilius, we should stick to the path that nature has prescribed for us, and we should not deviate from it. Follow nature, and everything is easy and accessible; strain against it, and you will live like a rower pulling against the current.

This final image seems to present night persons as destined to fail and to get back to normality, forced by the unbreakable laws of nature. Indeed, breaking natural laws is not possible: it may appear as if one does, but in fact they still hold sway in some way. The situation seems to resemble that of tragic characters like Oedipus: he desperately tries to go against his destiny, but is forced to fulfil the oracle.[45] In the case of letter 122, good habits should correct wrongdoers even against their will. But Seneca does not explain this revenge of nature and of morality over perversion. Furthermore, if we read the letter a second time, we see the exordium in

[44] Inwood (2010), 354.

[45] See also the case of Hippolytus (below, 4.6).

a peculiar light: Seneca's statements about the shortening of daylight, which makes it difficult to finish all one's daily activities (122.1), may betray a measure of envy towards those who do not care about daylight and natural time and thereby have all the time they need for their pleasures, but also for their duties. There is indeed an example, in *EM* 83.14, of the prefect Lucius Piso, who used to drink all night and awake at noon but was very efficient in his work and therefore appreciated by both Augustus and Tiberius. Also Nero, as Suetonius reports, used to have banquets that lasted from noon to midnight (Suet. *Nero* 27.2). On the one hand, Seneca in this letter seems to represent this behaviour as perverse and contrary to nature, as much so as worse vices like cruelty, and so to criticize not only some of his contemporaries but even the emperor; on the other hand, he depicts it as a habit of his time, and thus as in some way inevitable, and also reveals a hint of envy for this life, with its seeming autonomy.

4.3 *Luxuria*'s Location: The Stomach (*EM* 77, 78, 95)

Being a passion, that is, an affect of the soul, *luxuria* may be imagined to also be located inside persons. If it were to be identified with an organ, it would be the stomach, both in the generic sense of an organ that is enslaved to lower instincts, as opposed to those governed by reason, and also in the specific sense of an organ of eating and digestion, basic activities that are repeated again and again, without any final satisfaction.[46] This is exactly the condition into which *luxuria* forces people. The privileged location of *luxuria* at banquets, which Seneca discusses,[47] is here degraded by its close connection with one of the vilest of human organs.

The stomach is treated in Seneca's moral speeches for several reasons. First, the stomach is an instinctual organ, and thus a natural one, which should follow nature above all. And yet it becomes the main instrument of the vice that goes against nature. We find evidence of this in many passages in which simple and natural needs are opposed to the search for excessive and exotic food, e.g. in *EM* 60, where Seneca models his narrative on a Sallustian phrase, the 'slaves of the stomach'.[48] In a similar passage, stressing the insatiability of banquets lovers, he identifies them with their throat (*EM* 89.22 *profunda et insatiabilis gula*,

[46] On the metaphoric relevance of the stomach for ancient emotions, Fedriani (2016), 132.

[47] E.g. in *EM* in 90.7, with artificial pools to raise fish, an example that will also appear in Pliny the Elder's *Natural History* (above, 2.5.2), as well as exotic foods, such as oysters, and inventions like iced drinks (in Seneca, below, 4.9). On food and banquets in Seneca, above, 3.2.2 with n. 18; Gourévitch (1974); Torre (1997), with 389 on the stomach; Stein-Hölkeskamp (2002b), 6–17; Richardson-Hay (2009); Del Giovane (2015a), 277–316; Courtil (2018a); Gazzarri (2021); Berno (2021b).

[48] *Ventri oboedientes* (Sen. *EM* 60.4; cf. Sall. *Cat.* 1.1; Berno (2017a), 62–71). This motif is present also in Lucan's poem, in which the only occurrence of *luxuries* (fifth-declension form) is inserted in a eulogy of frugality (4.373–8; cf. 3.342–8; above, 2.8).

literally 'endless and insatiable throat'): it is indeed their *gula* which 'searches sea and lands in laborious pursuit of culinary fare' (*ib.*). The natural consequence of the identification of human beings with their stomach is the loss of other senses, especially sight (which is the one especially connected with knowledge): indeed, they act as is blind, ignoring all the food at their disposal to search for exotic one.[49]

Second, since the stomach has a function that we share with irrational animals, it embodies the loss of rationality in favour of the passions: if the stomach rules reason, then human beings are no longer different from animals. These persons are completely absorbed by their bodies, despite their miserable dimensions if compared with great animals (*EM* 60.2); even if they expand researches and destroy riches and lands to obtain fine food, they do not manage to enlarge the capacity of their bodies (*Helv.* 10.6).

But, and this is a third key issue, the perversion becomes even more extreme since reason does not disappear but is enslaved by the stomach. And so, the human condition is turned upside down (above, 4.2), with the intelligence being forced to fulfil the lowest functions.

Fourth, also linked with the stomach is the repulsive melting together of different foods, as well as vomit, faeces, and so on, images that are the outcome of the most refined dishes invented by pleasure-seekers, who, as happens in Pliny the Elder,[50] love mixing different foods and specialties. This association replaces the seductive images of sparkling objects, luxurious tableware, and tasty foods with filthy and unsavoury ones, which reveal the true nature of *luxuria*: attractive at first, but ultimately disgusting. And the same association also leads to a physiological explanation of existential nausea.[51]

An example of this nausea is in *EM* 77, in an exhortation to commit suicide attributed to an unnamed Stoic focused on the commonplace of *nihil novi*, 'nothing new' (77.16–18):[52]

> Voluptates ipsas quae te morantur ac retinent consumpsisti: nulla tibi nova est, nulla non iam odiosa ipsa satietate. Quis sit vini, quis mulsi sapor scis: nihil interest centum per vesicam tuam an mille amphorae transeant: saccus es. Quid sapiat ostreum, quid mullus optime nosti: nihil tibi luxuria tua in futuros annos intactum reservavit. Atqui haec sunt a quibus invitus divelleris. 17.... Confitere non curiae te, non fori, non ipsius rerum naturae desiderio tardiorem ad

[49] Cf. *Helv.* 10.5 *sed haec* [*sc. alimenta*] *velut caeci transeunt et omnes regiones pervagantur*... *et, cum famem exiguo possent sedare, magno inritant*; below, 4.6.

[50] Above, 2.5.2; Seneca is often quoted by Pliny as a source.

[51] Cf. Lampe (2008); *EM* 24.26 with Laudizi (2003), 149–53 and Edwards (2019), 153–4; Toohey (2004), 190–2; Kaster (2005), 121–9; Fitzgerald (2016), 137–9. See also below, next section. This kind of nausea is the exact opposite of the image of digestion with which Seneca expresses the assimilation of philosophical sentences (Armisen-Marchetti (1989), 143–4; (2020b)).

[52] Richardson-Hay (2009), 90–1.

> moriendum fieri: invitus relinquis macellum, in quo nihil reliquisti. 18. Mortem times: at quomodo illam media boletatione contemnis!
>
> You linger, you tarry over your pleasures, but you have exhausted even those. Not one of them is new to you; not one is anything but loathsome to you from sheer surfeit. You know what wine tastes like, both with honey and without. It makes no difference whether a hundred gallons pass through your bladder or a thousand; either way you are nothing but a conduit. You know exactly what an oyster tastes like, and a mullet as well. Self-indulgence has sampled everything; nothing remains for future years to try. And this is what you cannot tear yourself away from! 17.... Be honest: it is not any longing for the Senate house or the Forum, or even for the world as a whole, that makes you reluctant to die. What you cannot part from is only your butcher shop-and thanks to you, there is nothing left in it. 18. You fear death, and yet when a platter of mushrooms is before you, how little you care!

The pleasures of life are reduced to the most basic ones, i.e. food and drink, and the world itself to a food market (77.17 *macellum*) with nothing left to buy. All possible food experimentation, exoticism, variety, rarity, have already been experienced; nothing is left for the tireless search for the new that is typical of *luxuria*. The human being is reduced to a bag (77.16 *saccus*) destined to be constantly filled and then emptied, in a replication of the infernal punishment of the Danaids, who were condemned to eternally try to fill a bottomless vase. The nausea of existence, rooted in the disgust of repetition (*odiosa... satietas*), is here expressed most vividly.

A reversal speech is in *EM* 78.[53] Here, the aim is no longer to push someone to commit suicide, but to prevent Lucilius, who has fallen ill, from that temptation. Seneca is speaking (78.23–6):[54]

> 'O infelicem aegrum!' Quare? quia non vino nivem diluit? quia non rigorem potionis suae, quam capaci scypho miscuit, renovat fracta insuper glacie? quia non ostrea illi Lucrina in ipsa mensa aperiuntur? quia non circa cenationem eius tumultus cocorum est ipsos cum opsoniis focos transferentium? Hoc enim iam luxuria commenta est: ne quis intepescat cibus, ne quid palato iam calloso parum ferveat, cenam culina prosequitur. 24. 'O infelicem aegrum!' Edet quantum concoquat; non iacebit in conspectu aper ut vilis caro a mensa relegatus, nec in repositorio eius pectora avium (totas enim videre fastidium est) congesta ponentur. Quid tibi mali factum est? cenabis tamquam aeger, immo aliquando tamquam sanus. 25. Sed omnia ista facile perferemus, sorbitionem, aquam calidam, et quidquid aliud intolerabile videtur delicatis et luxu fluentibus magisque animo quam corpore morbidis: tantum mortem desinamus horrere. Desinemus

[53] In general, on the intertextual relationship between letter 77 and 78, Correa (2021).
[54] Conradie (2010), 266–74.

> autem, si fines bonorum ac malorum cognoverimus; ita demum nec vita taedio erit nec mors timori. 26. Vitam enim occupare satietas sui non potest tot res varias, magnas, divinas percensentem: in odium illam sui adducere solet iners otium.
>
> 'Poor invalid!' Why? Because he does not strain his wine through snow? Because he does not use chips of ice to freshen his hefty schooners of strong drink? Because no one opens Campanian oysters for him right at the table? Because at his meals there is no hustle and bustle of chefs trundling braziers around with the roasts still on them? For self-indulgence has now come up with this device: the very kitchen comes out with the food, to make sure the dishes are not just warm but hot enough to scald the toughest palate. 24. 'Poor invalid!' He will eat only as much as he can digest. The wild boar will not languish to one side as if it were a cheap meat banished from the table; his platter will not be piled up with the breasts of wild fowl because he cannot stand to see a bird served whole. What misfortune has befallen you? You will dine like an invalid—which is to say, in health and sanity.
>
> 25. But as for the liquid diet, the warm water, and all the other things that seem intolerable to those fashionable characters (dissipated, that is—sick in mind rather than in body), we will have no difficulty in enduring them once we stop being frightened by death. And we will stop if we have learned the limits of goods and evils. Then at last will life no longer be tiresome to us, death no longer alarming. 26. For boredom cannot take over one's life when one ponders such a variety of exalted and divine themes: it is when one's leisure is spent in idleness that one is overcome by self-loathing.

There is a comparison between an ill person, who is forbidden from having luxury banquets, and a gourmand, who loves unnatural foods such as iced drinks and oysters—which, not by chance, come from *luxuria's* favourite place, Campania—, and demands that his dishes be cooked in his presence. The description emphasizes the love of excess, for both warm (78.23 *focos, ferveat*) and cold (*nivem, rigorem, glacie*) foods, and *luxuria* is personified as having come up with the idea of bringing cookers into the dining room (*luxuria commenta est*). This is the idea (above, 4.1) of a vice that is not at all irrational but that on the contrary enslaves reason, which is forced to put her skills at its service. As in letter 122, the reference to drinks with ice is not generic or politically neutral, since such drinks were a Neronian innovation, according to Pliny.[55]

The emphasis on temperature is important within medical imagery: doctors used to forbid the sick any food that was too hot or cold.[56] Seneca thus presents the gourmands, who consume icy and boiling foods, as actual sick people, as they

[55] *HN* 31.40. The motif is tackled in detail in *NQ* 4.13 (below, 4.9).

[56] Cf. Gourévitch (1974), 323–5; *Const.* 13.1, with Berno (2018), 174.

are insensitive (cf. 78.23 *palato... calloso*) to normal temperatures and far removed from moderation. Actual sick people, since they are ordered to eat sober and simple food, behave in a far healthier way than the gourmands.

The gourmands are physically healthy, but act insanely, because *luxuria* has taken control of their reason, while the sick, among whom is Lucilius—the letter opens with a reference to his illness (78.1)—are physically unhealthy but psychologically sane, because they avoid dietary excess and act like wise men. The gourmands' world, their idea of a happy life, and physical pleasures in general become mere appearances that hide sick souls. This is an original and counterintuitive use of medical imagery,[57] which expresses the topsy-turvy world of vice in a more refined way than the conventional equivalence between vice and disease.

In this letter there are also images of nausea:[58] the nausea of the pleasure-seekers towards birds cooked whole (78.24 *fastidium*), and existential nausea (78.26 *satietas*), which in this case is avoided by the contemplation of nature. This connects letter 78 with the preceding one: while letter 77 stressed the idea of life as a nonsensical repetition of identical actions, letter 78 only describes immoral people in such terms, not those who devote themselves to philosophy, especially natural philosophy.

A similar image of disgust is the following (*EM* 110.12):

> Non magnam rem facis quod vivere sine regio apparatu potes, quod non desideras milliarios apros nec linguas phoenicopterorum et alia portenta luxuriae iam tota animalia fastidientis et certa membra ex singulis exigentis.
>
> It is nothing much to dispense with royal show, to feel no longing for thousand-pound boars or flamingos' tongues and all the other excesses of the luxurious taste that can no longer stand to eat the entire creature and instead chooses bits of different ones.

Here, as in *EM* 78, the sense of nausea is raised by the habit of eating the entire animal (*tota animalia fastidientis*), and eating only select parts of it becomes the preferred way. This peculiarity, which Seneca seems to be the only one to point out,[59] is connected to the idea of wastefulness. Like spending enormous amounts of money on a single banquet, throwing away the most edible parts of an animal is a form of waste, the most despicable thing at all. In this passage, the expression *portenta luxuriae* describes these behaviours as monsters (*portenta*), things that are abnormal in every respect.

[57] On which cf. Armisen-Marchetti (1989), 136–8; Sjoblad (2015), 27–34; Gazzarri (2020), esp. 183–91 (theoretical ground).

[58] Conradie (2010), 272–4.

[59] Pliny the Elder mentions the habit of eating bird tongue, but without emphasizing this aspect (above, 2.5.2). On this idea cf. also the abovementioned *EM* 60 and *Helv.* 10.1–11 (below, 4.6).

Conversely, when Seneca deals with vegetarianism, which he adopted from his teacher Sotion but then abandoned for health reasons, he reports these considerations, attributed to the Roman philosopher Sextius, whom he genuinely admired[60] (108.18):

> [*sc.* Sextius] adiciebat contrahendam materiam esse luxuriae; colligebat bonae valetudini contraria esse alimenta varia et nostris aliena corporibus.
>
> He also used to say that one should pare away the resources of self-indulgence, and he offered reasoning to show that variety in food is alien to our bodies and detrimental to health.

The reduction of food types implies a limitation to *luxuria*'s expression of its search for excess, and the idea of 'paring away' (*contrahendam*) is linked with the consideration of this vice as something that crosses moral boundaries and needs rules and restrictions.[61] Variety (*alimenta varia*) is another of *luxuria*'s purposes,[62] and is described as noxious for one's health.

The stomach as the ideal location for *luxuria*, and banquet as its ideal expression, are described most fully in *EM* 95, one of the longest of the collection, where Seneca deals, among other issues, with numerous vices of his era.[63] *Luxuria* is the one that takes up the most space, and it is linked, as elsewhere, with disease (95.18–19):[64]

> Quid alios referam innumerabiles morbos, supplicia luxuriae? Immunes erant ab istis malis qui nondum se delicis solverant, qui sibi imperabant, sibi ministrabant.... simplex erat ex causa simplici valetudo: multos morbos multa fericula fecerunt. 19. Vide quantum rerum per unam gulam transituram permisceat luxuria, terrarum marisque vastatrix. Necesse est itaque inter se tam diversa dissideant et hausta male digerantur aliis alio nitentibus.... Inde tam novo aegrotamus genere quam vivimus.
>
> What need for me to mention countless other ailments, the punishment of luxury? These problems did not affect people in former times, when they had not yet become soft by self-indulgence, when they were both their own masters and their own servants.... Bad health was then a simple matter, and its causes were simple: it is multiple courses that have caused multiple ailments. 19. Take note of

[60] On Sextius and his school, Lana (1973); Lana (1992) (110–15 on Sextius); Di Paola (2014) (328–9 on Sextius); Sellars (2014), 100; as for Sotion, who joined the school founded by Sextius, Di Paola (2104), 330–1; Sellars (2014), 101; Del Giovane (2015b), 10 and 13. Even if he abandoned vegetarianism, Seneca maintained some food restrictions, such as avoiding luxury foods like mushrooms and oysters (108.15).

[61] Cf. also 40.5 *inhibenda luxuria.*

[62] Especially emphasized by Pliny the Elder (above, 2.5.2).

[63] Bellincioni (1979), 48–51; Del Giovane (2015a), 288–305; Seal (2021), 60–8. Specific on medicine in this letter, Courtil (2021).

[64] Bellincioni (1979), 250–2.

> the quantity of things that luxury, ransacking land and sea, mixes up for a single throat to swallow down. Inevitably, such different items combine badly and are poorly digested, struggling against one another.... Our illnesses are as bizarre as our manner of living.

While in letter 119.14 the tortures of *luxuria* were linked to its restless desire for pleasures (above, 4.1), in 95.18–19 we find a similar idea of torture (95.18 *supplicia*), but arising from the pain of stomach illness provoked by unnatural eating habits. The focus in this passage, as in the following, is on novelty, variety, and mixing (*multa fericula*, 95.19 *permisceat, diversa, novo aegrotamus genere*), which will appear again in Pliny the Elder.[65] Seneca establishes a direct correspondence between new eating habits and new kinds of illnesses, because the originally resistant human organism 'melts' among delicacies (95.18 *delicis solverant*). This idea of decline is, of course, a commonplace, and frequently described, a degradation of a strong and hard condition (in Roman terms, of virile human nature) to a tender, effeminate, and delicate one.[66] This archetypical structure implies a negative moral judgement of any form of tenderness in men. And *luxuria* is an actor in this process, described in this passage as a *vastatrix*, a *hapax* in the feminine, which in epic language usually referred to wild beasts or warriors.[67] This vice weakens persons, but is itself not weak; on the contrary, it is an invincible, violent enemy, ready to destroy everything.

The emphasis on mixture returns later on, in the words of a gourmand (95.27–8):[68]

> 'Gravest luxuriari per singula: omnia semel in eundem saporem versa ponantur. Quare ergo ad unam rem manum porrigam? Plura veniant simul, multorum ferculum ornamenta coeant et cohaereant.' 28.... Non esset confusior vomentium cibum.
>
> 'It's a burden to indulge ourselves piecemeal. Let everything be served at the same time and blended into the same flavor. Why should I stretch out my hand for individual things? Let the various dishes all come together, with the tidbits of the many courses joined up and united.' 28.... No vomited food could be more jumbled up.

This passage explains why a single dish made of lots of different foods is perceived as perverse: the mixing and melting of different tastes and consistencies make the dish akin to vomit (95.28 *vomentium cibum*). The choice of foods, listed in 95.25–6, is itself revealing:[69] oysters, mussels, sea urchins, and

65 Above, 2.5.2.

66 Gazzarri (2014), esp. 210–12. The passage goes on stating, as an extreme consequence of immorality, that immoral women are affected by typically masculine illnesses (95.20).

67 *OLD s.v.* 68 Bellincioni (1979), 266–7.

69 Gowers (1996), 36 and 123. Gourévitch (1974), 316–17, stresses the detail that oysters are called *inertia*, to point at their slimy and motionless nature. The mention of *garum*, a sausage derived from the fermentation of fish entrails, is itself a sort of anticipation of the image of vomit. On this image see also Citroni Marchetti (1991), 135–7; in general, on the practice and symbology of vomiting, Badel (2012).

mushrooms have in common an indistinct nature—not immediately identifiable as animal or vegetal—and a slimy consistence, which in turn is a prelude to the indistinctiveness of vomit. They are also difficult to digest, so the chance that they induce vomiting is in fact not merely metaphorical. The extreme result of *luxuria*, here expressed by the rare verb *luxuriari*, is not refinement and finesse, but, on the contrary, the disgusting state of a disturbed stomach, perfectly expressed in its perversion of natural habits in a sentence in *Helv.* 10.3 *vomunt ut edant, edunt ut vomant*, 'they vomit to eat, eat to vomit' (trans. Williams 2014). This is, again, the physiological side of existential nausea, but also represents the perversion of morality, normality, and health into their opposites. The fusion in vomit represents the gourmand's soul: behind an exterior of luxury and pleasure is a repulsive mixture of vices where one discolours in another, as Seneca says right after the quoted passage (95.33):[70]

> Voluptas ex omni quaeritur. Nullum intra se manet vitium: in avaritiam luxuria praeceps est. Honesti oblivio invasit; nihil turpest cui placet pretium. Homo . . . iam per lusum ac iocum occiditur . . .
>
> The hunt is on for pleasure from every quarter. No fault is self-contained. Luxury is rapacious. Honor has been forgotten. Nothing is shameful as long as it is profitable. The human being . . . is now killed as a sport and entertainment.

Vice is inextricably linked with the search for pleasure: in this sense, we may say that *luxuria* is vice itself. But it leads into greed, because luxury requires money, and this restless search for ever newer entertainments, where nothing is enough, leads to cruelty. The Stoics maintain that fools (i.e. the non-sages) do not have only one vice, but all of them, to different degrees, and *luxuria* is a manifestation of this principle.

Later on, Seneca turns to the well-known distinction between magnificence and luxury (95.41):[71]

> Quid est cena sumptuosa flagitiosius et equestrem census consumente? . . . Eadem res, si gulae datur, turpis est, si honori, reprensionem effugit; non enim luxuria sed impensa sollemnis est.
>
> What is more outrageous than a banquet that cost as much as membership in the equestrian order? . . . The sum that would be disgraceful if it were merely spent to please the palate escapes criticism when spent on public office. In the latter case, it is not indulgence but an official expense.

Here, Seneca seems to criticize the principle affirmed by Cicero and supported by Augustan propaganda,[72] and to argue that people view what is fundamentally the

[70] Bellincioni (1979), 272–4. [71] Bellincioni (1979), 283–4. [72] Above, 2.4.

same thing—but for the external circumstances—in two different ways, one as morally acceptable and the other not. Seneca supports his radical attitude with the example of Q. Aelius Tubero at the end of the letter (below, 4.7). Right after the quoted passage, Seneca reports the story of a giant mullet presented to the emperor Tiberius, who put it on sale and bet on who would pay the most for it (95.42). Fish have been involved in attacks on luxury since Lucilius' descriptions of banquets,[73] and this commonplace is repeated in letter 95 through not only the giant mullet[74] but also the previously mentioned oysters and mussels (95.27, quoted above).

One of the main topics of *EM* 95 is that to fight advanced and refined vices, such as contemporary luxury, new instruments are needed, and especially a new conception of virtue. This explains Seneca's emphasis on the sage as a warrior, with Cato of Utica compared to a war horse and praised for his military prowess, with a quotation from Virgil's *Georgics* (3.75–85).[75]

It is perhaps not coincidental that Seneca chooses from the Virgil passage two hemistichs to stress the Cato/horse comparison: the first expresses his fearlessness (*G.* 3.79 *nec vanos horret strepitus*, 'not flinching at mere sounds', quoted in *EM* 95.69 and repeated in 95.70), the second his luxuriant strength: *G.* 3.81 *luxuriatque toris animosum pectus*, which concludes his comment on the quotation (95.71):

> Libet admirantem invictam constantiam viri inter publicas ruinas non labantis dicere 'luxuriatque toris animosum pectus'.
>
> In admiration for the man's indomitable resolution, holding his ground while his country collapses, it is a pleasure to quote the words 'his chest is broad for breathing, and is richly muscled'.

Seneca chooses to end his eulogy of Cato, a warrior sage compared to a warlike animal—a war horse—by reaffirming his physical and psychological energy. Cato is not presented as an ethical model, but as a political hero, who fought firmly for the right cause even while knowing that it was doomed to defeat; here we might see an allusion to the ruin of the Julio-Claudian dynasty in Seneca's own day. Furthermore, Cato is described as luxuriant in strength, like the horse in Virgil, with the verb *luxurio* in its positive sense of 'lush'. This sense is unmistakable in the verse, yet the 'richly muscled' epithet is another sign that Cato is far removed from the typical wise man who is serenely detached from the world's vicissitudes,

[73] Above, 1.4 with n. 59; Pliny devotes special attention to the topic (above, 2.5.2).

[74] Mullets have already been mentioned in 95.26, and they are the protagonists of a famous passage of *NQ* 3.17–18 (below, 4.9); the story in *EM* 95.42 is similar to the one about the giant rhombus given to Domitian, in Juvenal 4 (above, 2.6.2).

[75] Cf. Bellincioni (1979), 324–8; Berno (2011), 233–9.

which is no longer what Rome needs. Rome needs, Seneca seems to say, an untiring, even violent struggle for virtue, parallel to the struggle against vice, to the point that he uses the same verb for each. Indeed, *EM* 95.27 is the only Senecan prose passage, except for the one just quoted, where we find the verb derived from *luxuria*, and it is applied, as we have seen above, to the main vice of his own contemporary society. Finally, to highlight the need to radically fight this vice, Seneca ends the letter with an example of excessive frugality, Q. Aelius Tubero (95.72; below, 4.7).

4.4 *Luxuria* at Home: Baias (*EM* 51) and Architectural Luxury (*EM* 89)

Luxuria in architecture is a major theme in most moralistic writers. As we have seen (above, 4.3), in *EM* 95 Seneca refutes the Ciceronian principle of *publica magnificentia, privata luxuria*.[76] Elsewhere, he draws a detailed picture of *luxuria*'s favourite buildings and furniture (e.g. in *EM* 89, quoted below),[77] but in his descriptions of villas, even though he despises excessive luxury, he rarely applies the label *luxuria*. Seneca also presents a new issue, that of environmental determinism. This theory, proposed by the Hippocratic treatise *On Air, Water, Places*, and which maintains that topography and climate influence the inhabitants' health and character, fit Stoic theory well, since according to the latter every being is related to all others through mutual influence (above, 1.4). Seneca applies this theory not only to those who live in a particular place but also to those who spend some time there, such as on holidays. This is a corollary of the Stoic idea of the 'influence of friends': not only people but also places may infect us with vices. This happens all the more in the case of *luxuria*, the most seductive of all passions.[78]

This vice has a favourite place of heart: the seaside (*Tranq.* 2.3), and especially Baias.[79] This town, on the Campanian coast, was a renowned holiday resort for Roman noblemen, along with the Egyptian city of Canopus. It had been a place of excessive license, pleasure, and temptation since the late Republic. So it is not surprising that Seneca locates *luxuria* itself there, in letter 51. This letter deals with an oft-debated philosophical question: are there any places that the wise man

[76] Above, 2.2.1.

[77] Esposito (1993); Delpeyroux (2014); Maruotti (2015); Papini (2021). As a positive example, see *EM* 86 (below, 4.7).

[78] Berno (2014b), 128–30. On the 'influence of friends' in Stoicism, *SVF* 3.228–33; Boeri (2020), 73–80; Brouwer (2020); cf. above, 4.2 with n. 28.

[79] On Baias as a commonplace for vice, above, 1.4 with n. 47. Specific on Seneca's letter 51, Hönscheid (2004), 16–18; Gowing (2013), 240–3, who draws a parallel between Seneca's letter 51 and Cicero's *Pro Caelio* about Baias; Berno (2014b); Fiorini Ripert (2020), with special attention to political implications; Papini (2021), esp. 99–102.

should avoid?[80] Seneca's answer is related to the Stoic doctrine of the preferable: places belong to the so-called indifferent category.[81] Like all external events, objects, and beings, they cannot affect the wise man's equanimity, but there are some indifferents that we may prefer or dislike in certain circumstances, and Baias is of the latter sort, because of *luxuria*'s irresistible seductive power. Indeed, Seneca leaves Baias the day after his arrival (51.1). He presents the vice, personified, as living in Baias, its most fitting home (51.1–3):[82]

> Bais...locum ob hoc devitandum, cum habeat quasdam naturales dotes, quia illum sibi celebrandum luxuria desumpsit....3. Itaque de secessu cogitans numquam Canopum eliget, quamvis neminem Canopus esse frugi vetet, ne Bais quidem; deversorium vitiorum esse coeperunt. Illic sibi plurimum luxuria permittit, illic, tamquam aliqua licentia debeatur loco, magis solvitur.
>
> Baiae...Despite certain natural advantages, it is a place to avoid, and here's why: self-indulgence has adopted it as a party town. 3. Thus a person considering retreat will never choose Canopus for it, although Canopus does not prevent one from living simply. Neither will he choose Baiae: it has become a hostelry of vices. Self-indulgence allows itself more license there; it lets itself go there, as if by some privilege of the place.

This letter is pervaded by the semantic field of softening, melting, loosening. In the quoted passage we find *solvitur*, 'it lets itself go', literally 'it is loosened'; *soluta legibus*, 'unrestricted' (51.4); *blandimentis voluptatum*, 'the allures of pleasures' (51.5); *solverunt, enervaverunt*, 'turned to jelly' (51.5); *delicate, molliter* (51.6); *non est emolliendus animus*, 'it will not do for my mind to be enfeebled' (51.8); *molliter* (51.11). These expressions show the effect of Baias on morality, as Seneca explicitly states (51.10 *effeminat animos amoenitas nimia, nec dubie aliquid ad corrumpendum vigorem potest regio*, 'too much comfort makes the spirit unmanly, and even mere location undoubtedly has some power to ruin one's strength').

Vigor is masculine strength, opposed to the female tenderness and weakness (cf. *effeminat*) introduced by excessively pleasant places (*amoenitas nimia*). The whole idea of softening comes from the fact that Baias, being in a volcanic area, has hot springs, and was famous for its thermal baths, as Seneca himself says, mentioning 'hot lakes' and 'saunas' (51.6 *calentibus stagnis* and *sudatorii*). Hot water relaxes and softens muscles, and is correlative of the equivalent psychological effect of weakening moral strength. A historical example is the so-called 'Leisures of Capua' of Hannibal's army. As is well known from many Roman

[80] Montiglio (2006); Mazzoli (2021), 366–8. [81] Cf. above, 3.2.1 and 3.2.3.
[82] Hönscheid (2004), 19–29; Berno (2014b), 125–7.

sources, the Carthaginian general Hannibal,[83] after many victorious battles in Italy, inexplicably decided to rest in Capua during the winter, after which his army, weakened by Campanian pleasures, was no longer able to fight (51.5):[84]

> Id agere debemus ut inritamenta vitiorum quam longissime profugiamus; indurandus est animus et a blandimentis voluptatum procul abstrahendus. Una Hannibalem hiberna solverunt et indomitum illum nivibus atque Alpibus virum enervaverunt fomenta Campaniae: armis vicit, vitiis victus est.
>
> We should endeavor to put as much distance as we can between ourselves and any incitements to vice; we should toughen our minds and keep them far away from the allures of pleasure. Hannibal was unstrung by a single winter there: the man whom the Alpine snows could not defeat was turned to jelly by the steam baths of Campania. Tough victor in arms, he was vanquished by vice.

Seneca's account focuses on the opposition between cold and warm: the Punic army, strengthened by Alpine snow, was melted by Campanian hot water. This refers to another Stoic tenet, according to which cold water and rigid weather make a man stronger, as they are associated with hardness, while hot water and mild weather make him feebler, because these are associated with melting.[85] Seneca replaces Capua with a generic reference to Campania, because he wants to focus on Baias, but we know that at least since Cicero Capua was itself a luxuriant city.[86]

The example of the rugged and valiant Hannibal defeated by the tenderness of *luxuria* is contrasted other military examples: his arch-enemy Scipio Africanus, who chose for his voluntary exile Liternum a less pleasant place than Baias, and the triumvirs Gaius Marius, Gnaeus Pompeius, and Julius Caesar, who all built villas nearby, but on the top of the hills, in a camp-like position, safely distant from the seaside (51.11). During Republican times one used to build villas far from the sea, while in the Imperial age homes on the water came to be preferred. But while Hannibal is an example of total defeat, the other ones do not actually beat luxury, since their only strategy is to keep at a safe distance from it. This shows how dreadful *luxuria* is, which in turn is confirmed in this letter by the ineffectiveness of its opposite virtue, *frugalitas*.[87]

The ways in which this vice is now manifested do not focus on banquets, as elsewhere;[88] Seneca lists immoral actions that involve eating only peripherally (51.4):

[83] On this historical example in Seneca, Giazzi (2011), 69–72 on letter 51.
[84] Hönscheid (2004), 35–9; Berno (2014b), 127–8.
[85] *SVF* 3.229 = Chalc. *ad Tim.* p. 165 with Vegetti (1983); Brunschwig (1986).
[86] Above, 1.4 and 2.2.1.
[87] *EM* 51.2 *frugalitatem professo*; 51.3 *esse frugi*. Both are hypothetical contexts.
[88] Above, 4.3.

> Videre ebrios per litora errantes et comessationes navigantium et symphoniarum cantibus strepentes lacus et alia quae velut soluta legibus luxuria non tantum peccat sed publicat, quid necesse est?
>
> Why do I need to see drunks weaving their way along the beach, boatmen's revelries, lagoons echoing with band music, and all the other things that unrestricted self-indulgence not only commits but publicizes?

Drunk people on the beach, banquets on boats, concerts on lakes: here, the extravagant element is not the action itself, but the place in which it is located, which is unnatural. Normal eating and drinking should be performed on land and in an enclosed space, but *luxuria*, again, is ostentatious (*non tantum peccat sed publicat*).[89] We may add that *soluta legibus* sums up the breaking of natural laws and the idea of melting that is typical of *luxuria*, but also alludes to the formula that sanctioned the extraordinary position of the Emperor, who stands above the laws.[90] In this case, not only a single habit but *luxuria* itself seems to overlap with the Emperor. The same may be said of Seneca's second description of Baias' pleasures (51.12):[91]

> Habitaturum tu putas umquam fuisse illic M. Catonem, ut praenavigantes adulteras dinumeraret et tot genera cumbarum variis coloribus picta et fluvitantem toto lacu rosam, ut audiret canentium nocturna convicia? Nonne ille manere intra vallum maluisset, quod in unam noctem manu sua ipse duxisset? Quidni mallet, quisquis vir est, somnum suum classico quam symphonia rumpi?
>
> Do you think Marcus Cato would ever have lived there? Why? To count the adulterous ladies sailing by, the many kinds of pleasure boats painted in different colors, the roses floating all over the lagoon? To hear the musicians' nightly racket? Would he not have preferred to remain within some trench works dug by his own hand for a single night's use? What real man would not choose a bugler, rather than a symphony, to interrupt his slumbers?

The fictitious example of Cato is similar to the previous ones: Cato does not fight against the passions; he only prefers to be elsewhere, away from the dissolute women on boats, coloured vessels, roses on lakes, and night concerts. As in the preceding passage, the vice is not so much in the thing itself as in the inappropriate and public place (or time) in which it is shown.

All these instances of vice point to the inappropriateness of certain places for wise men. We may see some political implications in these statements; *solutus*

[89] Below, 4.6.

[90] Fiorini Ripert (2020), 624–6, with reference to the seventh clause of the *Lex de imperio Vespasiani*.

[91] Hönscheid (2004), 68–84; Berno (2014b), 131–2.

legibus, referring to *luxuria* in 51.4, is applied to emperors, as we have seen, and the bad habits Seneca lists are attested for all Julio-Claudian rulers, who owned properties in Baias, not to mention the fact that Agrippina's murder orchestrated by Nero took place there in 58 CE, i.e. only a few years before the writing of the letter.[92] It is possible that Seneca, while criticizing *luxuria* with Republican examples, is in fact making a statement of discontent regarding the contemporary situation. His focus on moral decline, a legitimate subject even under a tyranny, may express political dissent from Nero, who loved night celebrations and boat banquets. Cassius Dio reports, as an example of *akolasia* (license), a luxury banquet with an orgy organized on an artificial lake (62.15.1–6, dated to 64 CE), while Suetonius tells of a water brothel organized for Nero in Baias on the occasion of his arrival by boat (*Nero* 27.3), as well as of a project for a covered pool drawn from Baias' thermal springs (31.3). As already noted for letter 122, Seneca's moralistic claims have political implications in that they point at the emperor's behaviour and that of his court. This was the only possible way to express dissent under a tyranny such as Nero's reign.

Letter 51 is a sort of *aristia* of *luxuria*: the vice is strong as ever, invincible, conqueror of hardened warriors such as Hannibal. This imagery is rooted in the concept of warmth and located next to hot springs. A further reference to this natural phenomenon is in *EM* 89.[93] Here, in a sort of declamation against vices, Seneca lists greed, architectural luxury, and gluttony. *Luxuria* only occurs in the second of these (89.21):[94]

> 'Nunc vobiscum loquor quorum aeque spatiose luxuria quam illorum avaritia diffunditur. Vobis dico: quousque nullus erit lacus cui non villarum vestrarum fastigia inmineant? nullum flumen cuius non ripas aedificia vestra praetexant? Ubicumque scatebunt aquarum calentium venae, ibi nova deversoria luxuriae excitabuntur. Ubicumque in aliquem sinum litus curvabitur, vos protinus fundamenta iacietis, nec contenti solo nisi quod manu feceritis, mare agetis introrsus.'
>
> 'Now I turn to address you people whose self-indulgence extends as widely as those other people's greed. I ask you: how long will this go on? Every lake is overhung with your roofs! Every river is bordered by your buildings! Wherever one finds gushing streams of hot water, new pleasure houses will be started. Wherever a shore curves into a bay, you will instantly lay down foundations. Not satisfied with any ground that you have not altered, you will bring the sea into it!'

[92] Cf. Suet. *Nero* 34.2–4; Tac. *Ann.* 14.4–5; Morford (1968), 173–4; Fiorini Ripert (2020), 612–15; 620–4.

[93] On architectural luxury in this letter, Degl'Innocenti Pierini (2022).

[94] Zechel (1966), 88–91.

Interestingly, *luxuria* and *avaritia* are described as extending widely, with an adverb derived by the word for 'space' (*spatiose* from *spatium*): so, they look like a building which increases progressively, or, as Seneca says in the previous section, as the growth of someone's asset (89.20 *quousque arationes vestra porrigetis, ne provinciarum quidem spatio contenti circumscribere praediorum modum?* 'when are you going to stop spreading out your plantation? You are not even content to limit the size of your own estates by the area of a whole province'). Vices are identified with a real estate which becomes bigger and bigger. This detail is even more meaningful if we parallel it with the previous letter, where it is wisdom to be defined as *spatiosa*, because it needs our soul to be free from other interests (88.33 *magna et spatiosa res est sapientia; vacuo illi loco opus est*, 'wisdom is vast and expansive; it needs room'). On one side, wisdom needs space; on the other, vice is expanding without any limit, so it leaves no room for virtue. Even natural elements, like rivers and lakes, are turned into 'pleasure houses' (*deversoria luxuriae*), an expression which varies the one in 51.3 *deversorium vitiorum*, 'hostelry of vice'.[95]

Here, as in letter 51 (and *Ira* 1.21.1, above 4.1), vice lies in excess, in building something against nature: marble on water, a river inside a house, and so on. This is the realization of an *adynaton*, something that should not exist.[96] Hot springs are viewed as the ideal location for these excesses, for two reasons. First, they are themselves an example of exceptionality, in that water naturally springs out at a cold temperature; second, as we have seen, the idea of warmth brings with it that of softening and of losing firmness and virility.

There is a letter in which Seneca seems to resist this sort of Sirens of pleasure, and therefore incurring Lucilius' admiration. It is letter 56, in which Seneca describes his holiday residence, close to a thermal bath near Baias, and thus exposed to much noise. Seneca depicts his resistance to distractions and describes the opposite situation, in which there is external quiet but a fight of the passions within (56.5). And if one retires, no quiet is enough to stop vices, which may appear to settle but then arise again at the slightest hint of pleasure (56.10). The situation is that of Serenus in the opening of *De tranquillitate animi*,[97] but more pessimistic. *Luxuria* is the subject of this time.

Letter 56 also appears to be a counterpart to 51, offering an example of resistance to external temptations (even if they may be called unpleasant, and not sweet and seductive like the ones in Baias). But at the end of the letter Seneca refutes

[95] The expression comes from Cicero, who defined *libidinum deversorium* (*Phil.* 2.105) a villa in Cassino, formerly owned by Varro, where Mark Antony used to have luxury banquets.

[96] As for architectural luxury in Seneca, cf. also *Ira* 1.21.1 (above, 4.1); *EM* 114.9 (below, 4.6); 122.8 (above, 4.2); 90.9–10 and 90.41–3 with Degl'Innocenti Pierini (2004), 70–88, who compares Suetonius' description of Nero's *domus aurea*. On the *adynata* motif, below, 4.9.

[97] Below, 4.8.

himself, and runs away. Even Ulysses did not stay too long in the vicinity of the Sirens, he says (56.15):[98]

> Fateor; itaque ego ex hoc loco migrabo. Experiri et exercere me volui: quid necesse est diutius torqueri, cum tam facile remedium Ulixes sociis etiam adversus Sirenas invenerit?
>
> Yes, I grant that, and that's why I'm going to leave this place. I wanted to test myself, give myself a workout. But why should I be tormented any longer, when Ulysses found his companions such an easy solution? That was effective even against the Sirens!

It was just an experiment, just like what he did with poverty.[99] The truth is that some temptations are too strong to resist.

4.5 *Luxuria*'s Friends: Related Professions and Vices

Seneca connects with *luxuria* a number of activities, especially related to architecture and decoration:[100] painters, sculptors, and stonemasons are '*luxuria*'s workers' (*EM* 88.18 *luxuriae ministros*; cf. 16.8); architects and decorators were born when luxury spread (90.9), and each of these has a series of luxury objects, which Pliny the Elder will illustrate, within their domain.[101] Cooks are also mentioned in this regard.[102]

As for *luxuria*'s company, Seneca often lists *luxuria* together with one or two other vices, mainly those already discussed by his predecessors: *avaritia*,[103] sometimes also ambition,[104] both of which are cited especially by historiographers. He also refers to the Platonic description of the tyrant's soul teared apart by vices (*Rep.* 9.579d–e), but innovates it describing the human soul (and not only the tyrant's one) as a place where the passions fight each other (*EM* 56.5):[105]

> Animum enim cogo sibi intentum esse nec avocari ad externa; omnia licet foris resonent, dum intus nihil tumultus sit, dum inter se non rixentur cupiditas et timor, dum avaritia luxuriaque non dissideant nec altera alteram vexet. Nam quid prodest totius regionis silentium, si adfectus fremunt?

98 Berno (2006), 304–6; 317–21; Rimell (2015b), esp. 177–8.
99 Above, 3.3 and 4.2.
100 For the topic of luxury buildings, above, 4.4.
101 Citroni Marchetti (1991), 118–19; for Pliny, above, 2.5.2.
102 Above, 4.3.
103 *EM* 7.7; 40.5; 56.5; 69.4; 90.26; 94.23; 108.12.
104 *EM* 7.3; 78.13; *NQ* 1.*pr.*6, quoted below, 4.8.
105 Berno (2006), 279–81. The image of a fighting between vices also recurs in *NQ* 4a.*pr.*2. The passage from Plato is alluded to by Tacitus (below, 5.2.2).

> You see, I force my mind to pay attention to itself and not to be distracted by anything external. It does not matter what is making a noise outside, so long as there is no turmoil inside—as long as there is no wrangling between desire and fear, as long as greed is not at odds with self-indulgence, one carping at one other. For how does it help to have silence in the neighbourhood, when one's emotions are in tumult?

Other associations of *luxuria* are less frequent: with anger (*Ira* 2.21.1–3, with greed and lust; 2.25.4; 3.5.5), with *intemperantia* and *avaritia* (*Ben.* 4.26.2; 4.27.2), with cruelty (*Ira* 3.40.2) and, again, *avaritia* (*EM* 42.4), with lack of self-restraint (36.1 *impotentia*), with lust (100.10), and with madness (115.22). The connection with gluttony is not stated, because in this case Seneca simply stages his critique of *luxuria* at a banquet (above, 4.3; below, 4.9); gluttony is not considered independently, but is simply a manifestation of *luxuria*. But more frequently, Seneca distinguishes one passion from the next, even if he does not rank them, with the exception of anger. Anger Seneca defines as worse than *luxuria*, in that the latter merely enjoys pleasure, while the former enjoys someone else's pain (*Ira* 3.5.5). Another distinction is in the famous story of Vedius Pollio, who had a slave thrown into a pool filled with morays because he broke a crystal cup, and this is labelled cruelty, not *luxuria* (3.40.2). Nevertheless, although anger tops the value scale as the most dangerous vice, along with its degeneration into cruelty, it disappears from Seneca's last writings, while mentions of *luxuria* grow more numerous. Seneca presumably abandons anger and cruelty, which are typical of tyranny, since he himself is living under tyranny. Instead he concentrates on a seemingly minor vice, which admittedly was also widespread at Nero's court, so as to be able to comment on tyranny while more ostensibly speaking of society at large. As for the other vices, comparisons do not establish a degree of importance. For example, while referring to the results of good luck, Seneca differentiates *impotentia* which inflates from *luxuria* which softens (*EM* 36.1), while, as we have seen, Livy considered these to be one single passion, which he called *luxuria*.[106]

The connection with idleness is also of interest; indeed, it is often indirectly recalled in contexts related to places (below, 4.4), but it is explicitly stated in a passage dealing with the ephemeral nature of all things, and of the world itself, although cities as a place are also involved (71.15):

> 'Omnes quae usquam rerum potiuntur urbes...alias destruent bella, alias desidia paxque ad inertiam versa consumet et <u>magnis opibus exitiosa res, luxus</u>.'
>
> 'All cities that have ruled the world...wars will destroy some; others will be swallowed up by desuetude, and peace that turns into idleness, and that which is the most ruinous to great resources—luxury.'

[106] Above, 2.3.2.

This statement, which is attributed to Cato the Younger, echoes historiographical descriptions of decline, with the typical connection between peace, wealth, and ruin that is also frequently attributed to armies.[107] Even more frequent, as we have seen (above, 4.4), is the related idea of environmental determinism, but in this passage also there is a relevant correspondence between places and human beings (71.23):

> Luxurioso frugalitas poena est, pigro supplicii loco labor est, delicatus miseretur industrii, desidioso studere torqueri est: eodem modo haec ad quae omnes inbecilli sumus dura atque intoleranda credimus.
>
> When one is devoted to luxurious living, frugality is a punishment; when one is lazy, work is like a sentence; the fashionable effete person pities the industrial one; the idle finds study a torment. In just the same way, we are all too weak for a task we think of as harsh and intolerable.

The attitudes of luxury and idleness are redoubled (*luxurioso/delicatus*,[108] *pigro/desidioso*) with words similar to those that were used in the context of cities (*luxus*, *desidia*), and are mixed in an ABAB pattern, in order to express the weak spot of each vice. The same habits that lead cities to ruin make human beings feeble and sensitive, and incapable of sustaining any effort. These vices are the wise man's enemies, and he must fight against them to save humanity. But at the end of the letter Seneca moves from luxury and laziness to the more political vices of greed and ambition, which were important in Cato's life,[109] and to fear of death, which Cato, who committed suicide, overcame, and which is ubiquitous in Seneca's *EM*. So *luxuria* and sloth are negative social forces that at first seem less threatening and aggressive than ambition, but that are in fact not less dangerous, since they may destroy not only individuals but entire states. Seen in the light of Seneca's self-censoring attitude with regard to anger, this would support a political reading of Seneca's struggle against *luxuria*: he no longer discusses strictly political passions, but focuses on social ones, showing their political consequences and implications. His sensitive situation—a retirement that the emperor did not officially allow—required an indirect strategy. Though he lived under constant threat to his life, Seneca still tries to send a message to his readers.

Luxuria is frequently surrounded by other vices, and this is not surprising, given the Stoic idea that every fool—that is, every non-sage—has all vices potentially inside himself. A peculiar case is lust, which largely overlaps with *luxuria*: we find it especially in *NQ* (below, 4.9). Furthermore, in some passages *luxuria* seems to include all the passions. In letter 59, Seneca deals with the idea of pleasure, and maintains that true pleasure is only that which is comes with wisdom, while that obtained through material goods is ephemeral and nauseating. Seneca develops

[107] Above, 1.4 and 2.3. [108] Cf. *EM* 5.5 *desiderare delicatas res luxuria est.*
[109] Cf. *Const.* 2.2 *Cato… cum ambitu congressus… et cum potentiae immensa cupiditate.*

this idea, after a list of vices including banquets and *luxuria*, ambition, lust, and also literary interests, all compared to a night's drunkenness which brings illusory fun and then long-lasting nausea (59.15), and he then concludes the letter by describing as *luxuriosi* people who search for seeming pleasures (59.17–18):

> Cum fatigaverunt se vino ac libidinibus, cum illos nox inter vitia defecit, cum voluptates angusto corpori ultra quam capiebat ingestae suppurare coeperunt, tunc exclamant miseri Vergilianum illum versum:
>
> namque ut supremam falsa inter gaudia noctem
>
> egerimus nosti. [Verg. *Aen.* 6.513–4]
>
> 18. Omnes luxuriosi noctem inter falsa gaudia et quidem tamquam suprema agunt.
>
> When people have worn themselves out with wine and lust; when their vices outlast the night; when the pleasures they have consumed beyond the narrow limits of the body begin to suppurate; then in their misery they speak aloud the familiar line of Virgil:
>
> For you know how we spent that night, our last,
>
> Amid deceiving joys.
>
> 18. Indulging themselves, they spend every night amid deceiving joys, as if it were indeed their last.

Luxuriosus, an epithet that Seneca sometimes attributes to himself more than once,[110] is here personified, and summarizes gluttony, drunkenness, lust, and physical pleasures in general, with the idea of nausea explaining his interest in the stomach in his moral speeches. The *luxuriosi* act as anti-sages: they live every day as if it were their last, which would be a wise thing to do, except that they interpret this precept to mean that one should enjoy as many pleasures as possible.[111] Instead of being at peace in their souls and awaiting death, they fill their bodies with filthy pleasures, which are here compared to disgusting infections that begin to fester (59.17 *suppurare*).[112]

4.6 *Luxuria* on Stage: Apicius (*Helv.* 10), Mark Antony (*EM* 83), and Maecenas (*EM* 114)

One of the most famous characteristics of Seneca's tragic protagonists is their urge for notoriety: they want their victims to be aware what has happened, and

[110] *EM* 1.4 (in the sense of 'prodigal'); *VB* 17.2 (in the speech of his accusors); cf. above, 3.2.3.

[111] Something similar happens in *EM* 12.8–9, where the wealthy Pacuvius enacts his own funeral every day, after a Lucullian banquet. Seneca comments that we should to the same, but in good faith. Cf. Berno (2014c), 131–4.

[112] Cf. below, 4.6 (114.25).

the leading passion is usually anger. A relevant example is Atreus in *Thyestes*.[113] This is true also for more trivial passions: 'ambition, luxury, and caprice need a stage' (94.71 *ambitio et luxuria et impotentia scaenam desiderant*).

Indeed, *luxuria* has the same attitude, albeit to a less extreme degree, in Seneca's prose works. The protagonists are in most cases anonymous, not only for political reasons—Seneca avoids criticizing his contemporaries, so as not to incur Nero's wrath—but also for philosophical ones. Since *luxuria* reduces men to their stomachs, their individualities disappear, and they become instead indistinct, animal-like beings, incapable of anything but following their lust for pleasures. But after a certain point, *luxuria* is no longer ashamed and desires ostentation. Beyond many anonymous characters, Seneca cites some historical examples, among which I select as most representative the abovementioned Apicius (*Helv.* 10.8–10), as well as two noblemen who are, opportunely, far removed from Seneca in time: Mark Antony (*EM* 83 20–5) and Maecenas (114.4–8). Two episodes in these passages deal with banquets, which highlights their relevance for the development and display of *luxuria*.

The rich gourmand of the Augustan age, Apicius, is cited several times in moralistic writings; we have already found him in Seneca's *De vita beata* (above, 3.2.2) and Pliny the Elder's *Naturalis Historia* (above, 2.5.2). But it is in the *Consolatio ad Helviam* where he finds his ideal purpose as an example of *luxuria*. In this text, Seneca consoles his mother for his being exiled to Corsica by the emperor Claudius; we thus find the usual commonplaces about the unimportance of wealth and location for happiness. Among these, Seneca inserts quite a long moralistic tirade against *luxuria* and its constant struggle for novelty,[114] with special regard to culinary delicacies (*Helv.* 10.1–7), beginning as follows (10.1):

> In qua [*sc.* paupertate] nihil mali esse, quisquis modo nondum pervenit <u>in insaniam omnia subvertentis</u> avaritiae atque luxuriae intellegit.
>
> But there's nothing disastrous in poverty, as anyone knows who has not yet been driven to the madness of greed and extravagant indulgence, which ruin everything.

Luxuria and greed lead to madness (*insania*) through a perversion: the verb *subverto* literally means 'to overturn' (*OLD* 1, *s.v.*). In this sentence, we find the theoretical ground of Seneca's treatment of passions (above, 4.1). He goes on to describe the restless search for exotic food (10.2; 10.5–7; 10.11), nausea (10.3),

[113] *Luxuria* is not a tragic passion; we find *luxus* three times in the *Phaedra* (204–5, on the inopportunity of exulting too much for good fortune; 456 on vegetation; 517–20 on the dangers of royal luxury, quoted below) and, more interestingly, a *libido victrix* in *Thy.* 46, imitated by *luxuria victrix* at *Oct.* 433. See Mantovanelli (1998) and (2008); Degl'Innocenti Pierini (2001); Ferri (2003), 247–8; Boyle (2017), 122; cf. also De Mitri (2001). On *luxuria*'s triumphs, see above, 3.3.3 (*Ben.* 7.9.2) and 2.6.3 (Petron. 120.85–6).

[114] Meinel (1972), 133–49; Citroni Marchetti (1991), 116–18; Costa (2013), 29–35.

and wasting money, with the example of Caligula (10.4). We have already dealt with all these motifs (above, 4.3), and they now appear as a premise to the story of Apicius (10.8–10):[115]

> 'Scilicet minus beate vivebat dictator noster qui Samnitium legatos audît cum vilissimum cibum in foco ipse manu sua versaret...quam Apicius nostra memoria vixit, qui in ea urbe ex qua aliquando philosophi velut corruptores iuventutis abire iussi sunt scientiam popinae professus disciplina sua saeculum infecit.' Cuius exitum nosse operae pretium est. 9. Cum sestertium milliens in culinam coniecisset...aere alieno oppressus rationes suas tunc primum coactus inspexit: superfuturum sibi sestertium centiens computavit et velut in ultima fame victurus si in sestertio centiens vixisset, veneno vitam finivit. 10. Quanta luxuria erat cui centiens sestertium egestas fuit!...Illi vero tam pravae mentis homini ultima potio saluberrima fuit: tunc venena edebat bibebatque cum inmensis epulis non delectaretur tantum sed gloriaretur, cum vitia sua ostentaret, cum civitatem in luxuriam suam converteret, cum iuventutem ad imitationem sui sollicitaret.
>
> 'Doubtless our dictator, who listened to the envoys of the Samnites as he himself cooked at the hearth the simplest kind of food with his own hand...this man doubtless lived less happily than did Apicius within our own memory, who lectured on cookery in the very city from which philosophers were once expelled on the grounds of corrupting youth, and who defiled his age by his teaching.' It's worth knowing Apicius's end. 9. After he'd poured a hundred million sesterces into his kitchen...he was overwhelmed by debt and then forced for the first time to look carefully into his accounts. He calculated that he would have ten million sesterces left over; and as if doomed to live in extreme starvation if he existed on ten million sesterces, he took his life by poison. 10. What luxury, if ten million counted as poverty for him!...In truth, for a man of such a perverse mindset, that last drink was most healthy. It was when he was not simply enjoying his boundless banquets but boasting of them, when he was ostentatiously displaying his own vices, when he was drawing the city's attention to his own luxurious ways, when he was rousing the young to imitate him...it was then that he was truly eating and drinking poisons.

Apicius, as a contemporary example (10.8 *nostra memoria*), is contrasted with a major instance of frugality in the archaic Republic, the dictator M.' Curius Dentatus,[116] which reproduces the traditional opposition between a frugal past and an immoral present. If we compare this narrative to others on Apicius, what strikes us is the reference to the protagonist's suicide,[117] which Seneca presents as

[115] Favez (1918), 56–9; Meinel (1972), 144–9; Cotrozzi (2004), 89–91; Costa (2013), 34–5.
[116] Above, 2.5.2 with n. 246; below, 4.7.
[117] Also reported by Dio 57.19.5 and Mart. 3.22 (cf. below, n. 120).

a commentary to his own moralistic speech (hence the quotation marks). Apicius is thereby depicted as a perverted Socrates: the story opens with a reference to the potential corrupting force of philosophers, which has led to their banishment in Roman history,[118] but it also reminds us of the well-known allegation against Socrates (Plato. *Apol.* 19b–c; 24b). Like him, Apicius is an expert at his own 'science' (Sen. *Helv.* 10.8 *scientiam popinae professus*)—of cookery—and lectures his contemporaries (*disciplina sua saeculum infecit*). At the end of the passage, Seneca states that Apicius corrupted young people and society as a whole (10.10);[119] furthermore, Apicius committed suicide by poison, as had Socrates (10.9).

Apicius represents vice's perversion of reason in a hyperbolic way: he is an authentic master in vice, someone who not only affects his close ones, as normally happens (above, 4.2), but actually teaches young people and offers himself as an example for all of society to follow. This is a perversion of the idea of education and civil society. And it is all due to *luxuria*: this vice caused not only his gluttony and other luxurious habits but also his death, because he considered his remaining assets inadequate for his lifestyle (10.10 *quanta luxuria erat cui centiens sestertium egestas fuit*). He owes to his vice both his glory and his ruin, just as happens with tragic characters, whose anger leads to bloody revenge and an acquisition of power but ultimately to the destruction of their families and themselves. In a way, this is also true for Socrates, who gained respect and fame through his ability as a philosopher, while this same ability also caused his fellow citizens to condemn him to death.

Given Apicius' perverted nature, the real poison is not that which he drinks to die, which on the contrary turns out to be healthful for him (10.10 *saluberrima*),[120] but the luxurious drinks he had every day, the banquets that fascinated and polluted his contemporaries. This is perhaps the only passage in which Seneca actually says that people subject to *luxuria* deserve to die, because they represent a danger for the community.

Another banquet, a different topic. Letter 83 deals with drunkenness.[121] Even though there are some exceptions (above, 4.2; below, 4.8), drunkenness is considered dangerous, in that it raises vice (83.20):

[118] In 161 BCE (Gell. 15.11.1) and 154 BCE (Epicureans: Athen. 12.547a–b).

[119] Compare Plato. *Apol.* 19b–c 'Socrates is a criminal and a busybody, investigating the things beneath the earth and in the heavens and making the weaker argument 19c. and teaching others (*allous... didaskon*) these same things' (trans. Fowler 2005) and *Apol.* 24b 'Socrates is a wrongdoer because he corrupts (*diaphtheirein*) the youth' with Sen. *Helv.* 10.8–10 'Apicius... who lectured in cookery in the very city from which philosophers were once expelled on the grounds of corrupting (*corruptor*) youth... 10.... he was rousting the young to imitate him (*ad imitationem sui sollicitaret*).'

[120] Cf. Mart. 3.22.4–5 *summa venenum potione perduxti./Nihil est, Apici, tibi gulosius factum*, with Fusi (2006), 231.

[121] Gourévitch (1974), 318–22; Motto/Clark (1990); Russo (2022).

> Ubi possedit animum nimia vis vini, quidquid mali latebat emergit. Non facit ebrietas vitia sed protrahit: tunc libidinosus ne cubiculum quidem expectat...tunc impudicus morbum profitetur ac publicat; tunc petulans non linguam, non manum continet...omne vitium laxatur et prodit.
>
> When an excess of wine has possession of the mind, any fault that was hiding comes into the open. Drunkenness does not create faults—it brings out faults that already exist. It is then that the lustful person does not even wait for the bedroom...it is then that the shameless person admits his infirmity and even boasts of it; it is then that the quarrelsome fellow restrains neither his tongue nor his fist...Every vice is exposed to view.

Wine has the same effect as *luxuria*: if drunk in excess, it erases the natural shame due to which vices prefers obscurity, and makes them show themselves openly. As historical examples Seneca offers Alexander the Great, who, being drunk, killed a dear friend of his, Clitus (83.19),[122] and Mark Antony, Octavian's competitor for succeeding Julius Caesar (83.25):

> M. Antonium, magnum virum et ingeni nobilis, quae alia res perdidit et in externos mores ac vitia non Romana traiecit quam ebrietas nec minor vino Cleopatrae amor? Haec illum res hostem rei publicae, haec hostibus suis imparem reddidit; haec crudelem fecit, cum capita principum civitatis cenanti referrentur, cum inter apparatissimas epulas luxusque regales ora ac manus proscriptorum recognosceret, cum vino gravis sitiret tamen sanguinem.
>
> What was it that destroyed Mark Antony, a man of noble character and exceptional talent? Was it not drunkenness that drove him to foreign habits and the most un-Roman vices? That, and his love for Cleopatra, which was only increased by wine. It was this that made him an enemy to the state, that made him a lesser man than his enemies. It was this that made him cruel, when he used to have the heads of leading statesmen brought to him at dinner—when amid his elaborate feasts and the splendor of kings he would view the hands and faces of the proscribed.

The royal luxury in which Antony is merged, discussed also by Pliny the Elder,[123] also involves Cleopatra, the summit of all possible vices: seductive lust, oriental luxury, kingliness, unrestrained ambition...Wine makes Mark Antony more affected by all this vice, and he turns into a tyrant, displaying his worst passion: cruelty. He is described as bloodthirsty like a beast, as in Plato's *Republic* with its seminal

[122] Seneca cites this example also in *Ira* 3.17.1; cf. *NQ* 6.23.2–3.

[123] With the famous tale of the giant pearl melted in vinegar (above, 2.5.2). Cf. also Lucan's account (above, 2.8).

description of the psychological degradation of tyrants.[124] In this passage we do not have *luxuria* but *luxus*, since the context is socially, and therefore stylistically, elevated, whereas *luxuria* is more appropriate for lower registers. We may quote a passage from the tragedy *Phaedra*, which contains a similar expression (ll. 517–20):

> . . . Regios luxus procul
> est impetus fugisse. Sollicito bibunt
> auro superbi: quam iuvat nuda manu
> captasse fontem . . .
> . . . His instinct is to flee
> royal luxury. The arrogant drink
> from anxious gold; he rejoices to catch
> a spring with bare hands.
>
> (Trans. Boyle 1987)

From a stylistic point of view, the expression *regios luxus* (l. 517) recalls *luxusque regales* of letter 83.25, which puts the two images on the same level as legendary and barbarian luxury. In the *Phaedra*, it is Hippolytus speaking, in a eulogy of a life merged into nature without both exterior goods and social contacts. Even if this attitude first seems good and positive, it is actually excessive and unnatural and will be punished by nature itself.[125] On a philosophical level, as we have already seen (above, 4.2), since in Stoic thought natural laws are unchangeable, every attempt to undermine them results in failure. Specifically, as regards a luxurious life, the tension between a radical refusal and a limited acceptance is evident in Seneca's work and life.[126] But even if Hippolytus' view may be compared with Cynicism for its excessively anti-social attitude, Mark Antony's complete acceptance of and enslavement to a barbarian queen is just as unacceptable. The sum of all possible luxuries and pleasures, worsened by the fact that they are linked with royalty, i.e. an absolute power which the Romans always rejected, at least officially, doomed Mark Antony to degeneration into the worst beast at all: the bloodthirsty tyrant. He, significantly a late Republican example, far removed from the Julio-Claudian dynasty, is one of the few Roman political characters mentioned by Seneca in reference to *luxuria*.

A different context is in letter 114, a very famous epistle on the corruption of verbal style corresponding to that of behaviour, whose protagonist is Maecenas,[127]

[124] Plato *Rep.* 9.572d–73c. The same implication we find in Pliny's account of the banquet of Mark Antony with Cleopatra (above, 2.5.2). On the connections between luxury banquets and habits and the tyrannical soul in Seneca, Citroni Marchetti (1991), 137–9; Torre (1997).

[125] Boyle (1987), 18–24; Mazzoli (2016), 94–7; Mazzoli (2017a), 36–8. On royal luxury cf. also Lucan's account of Cleopatra's palace (above, 2.8).

[126] Above, 3.1.

[127] Graver (1998); Degl'Innocenti Pierini (2013); Berti (2018), 17–30; Edwards (2019), 284–90 on the letter; 72–4 on Maecenas; especially on voice as a sign of moral degeneration, Gleason (1994), 111–13 (generally on the topic, 74–6). On corrupted style, Laudizi (2004).

Augustus' friend and ally in literary propaganda. The images of drunkenness, banquets, and so on are the same, while the focus is on stylistic features, which are seen to mirror a good or bad inner disposition. The parallel between exteriority and interiority postulated by Seneca, which we have seen also in the context of the stomach (above, 4.3), and the pollution by which vices spread all over society in a pandemic way, leads to a connection between *luxuria* and laxity in speech (114.2–3):[128]

> Argumentum est luxuriae publicae orationis lascivia, si modo non in uno aut in altero sit, sed adprobata est et recepta. 3. Non potest alius esse ingenio, alius animo color. Si ille sanus est, si compositus, gravis, temperans, ingenium quoque siccum ac sobrium est; illo vitiato hoc quoque adflatur.
>
> Decadence in language is a sure sign of widespread self-indulgence if it is not found in just one or two but meets with general approval. 3. The condition of the talent cannot be different from that of the mind. If the mind is healthy, well put together, serious, self-controlled, the talent is likewise completely sober; if the mind is flawed, the talent is likewise inflamed.

Lax speech (here *lascivia*, later on also *licentia*, two morally pregnant terms) is not inoffensive, but conditions the public and ultimately provokes *luxuria*. The following series of attributes draws a parallel between speech tone and the soul's disposition, focusing on the term *color*, which means both 'complexion' and 'speech material'. The healthy soul is 'dry and sober' (114.3 *siccum ac sobrium*), the same expression Seneca used in *EM* 18.4 (above, 4.2) to describe sobriety in opposition to drunkenness. Indeed, the correspondence between corrupt eloquence and drunkenness is stated right after Maecenas' presentation (114.4; cf. 144.22):[129]

> Videbis itaque eloquentiam ebrii hominis involutam et errantem et licentiae plenam.
>
> That's what you will see in his discourse; the style of a drunkard—convoluted, wandering, full of liberties.

Maecenas' speech appears the same as that of drunkards: inexplicable, digressive, and licentious. His attitude is judged severely also because he did not want his vices to be hidden (114.4 *vitia sua latere noluerit*, 'Maecenas ... made no effort to hide his faults'), and so he belongs to those whose vice has reached a climax (above, 4.3). Maecenas is a sort of standard-bearer for refined dandies, with sophisticated beards and flamboyant or transparent dresses, on whom Seneca

[128] Berti (2018), 163–6.

[129] Berti (2018), 182–5.

comments (114.21 *qui nolunt facere quicquam quod hominum oculis transire liceat*, 'they don't want to do anything that might be overlooked').[130] There is a whole category of men who live in this immoral way, where vice must be exhibited. This exhibitionism is part of the pleasure.

It is worth noting that Maecenas' look appears to be similar to that of two relevant Roman characters: Julius Caesar, especially by dint of two details underscored by Seneca, the depilated beard and the untied toga, a symbol of loose (sexual) behaviour,[131] and Nero, who according to Cassius Dio goes in public with a linen scarf, a floral dress, and—most extreme of all—ungirdled (63.13.3):[132]

> When he received the senators, he wore a short flowered tunic and a muslin neck-cloth; for in matters of dress, also, he was already transgressing custom, even going so far as to wear ungirded tunics in public. (Trans. Cary 1925)

Cassius Dio calls this habit contrary to the traditional habits, which is the same judgement as Seneca passes on Maecenas. Added to the stylistic correspondences between Maecenas and Nero,[133] this raises the suspicion that in his speech against an Augustan nobleman Seneca is actually referring to his tyrannical emperor.

Seneca does not even appreciate Maecenas' clemency, which he thinks is due not to a good disposition of the soul but to weakness (114.7). He then turns to the general subject of moral decline, with a list of luxury habits (114.9–10):[134]

> Ubi luxuriam late felicitas fudit, cultus primum corporum esse diligentior incipit; deinde supellectili laboratur; deinde in ipsas domos impenditur cura ut in laxitatem ruris excurrant... deinde ad cenas lautitia transfertur et illic commendatio ex novitiate et soliti ordinis commutatione captatur... 10. Cum adsuevit animus fastidire quae ex more sunt et illi pro sordidis solita sunt, etiam in oratione quod novum est quaerit...
>
> When prosperity brings on widespread self-indulgence, the first thing that happens is that more care is given to dress and grooming; next, there is a great fuss

[130] Berti (2018), 180.

[131] Compare Suet. *Iul.* 45. 2 *circa corporis cura morosior, ut non solum tonderetur diligenter et raderetur, sed velleretur etiam* and Sen. *EM* 114.21 *qui aut vellunt barbam aut intervellunt, qui labra pressius tondent et adradunt*; Suet. *Iul.* 45.3 *usum enim lato clavo ad manus fimbriato nec umquam aliter quam <ut> super eum cingeretur, et quidem fluxiore cinctura* and Sen. *EM* 114.4 *quid ergo? Non oratio eius aeque soluta est quam ipse discinctus?*

[132] Cf. Suet. *Nero* 51 *circa cultum habitumque adeo pudendus, ut... prodierit in publico sine cinctu et discalciatus*, already quoted above, 4.2.

[133] Degl'Innocenti Pierini (2013), 61–2; Edwards (2019), 289–90; Edwards (2021), 176–83. Byrne (2007) maintains that Petronius intentionally mocks Seneca's descriptions of Maecenas in his account of Trimalchio; Edwards (2019), 290 does not agree with this hypothesis. Personally, I think that nothing prevents from multiple interpretations in this case: Seneca's Maecenas may allude to Nero, and may also be mocked by Petronius in his novel.

[134] Berti (2018), 109–19; Edwards (2019), 298.

> over household furnishing; then attention turns to the houses themselves: a new wing makes a house into a villa... Next, opulence finds its way to the table. Novelty and changes in the accustomed order became the fashion; what once was dessert becomes an appetizer... 10. Once the mind has taken the habit of rejecting what is customary and holding all traditional usage in contempt, it seeks novelty also in its manner of speech...

The starting idea, of *luxuria* caused by good fortune, is widespread in historiography,[135] but surprisingly rare in Seneca; more frequent is his emphasis on the evolving search for pleasures, which, after bodily care, houses, and banquets, turns to oratory as an ultimate degree of corruption. Note the occurrence of *fastidire*, a verb expressing disgust and nausea, a leitmotiv of *luxuria* at its highest levels.[136]

While in the opening of the letter Seneca criticized laxity or license in speech as a cause of *luxuria*, he later depicts both vices as more or less equal in their display of a morbid soul (114.11):

> Quomodo conviviorum luxuria, quomodo vestium aegrae civitatis indicia sunt, sic orationis licentia, si modo frequens est, ostendit animos quoque a quibus verba exeunt procidisse.
>
> Just as luxury in dress and dinner parties is a symptom of sickness within the society, so an unrestrained style of eloquence, when commonly practiced, demonstrates that the mind from which the words proceed has fallen into decline.

All exterior habits—banquets, clothing, speeches—show the decline of the souls, which 'have fallen down' (*procidisse*: Edwards (2019), 299: 'have suffered a moral collapse').

The letter's conclusion represents the Platonic equivalence between the immoral soul and the tyrant (114.24), and stresses the increasing effects of a more and more developed vice (114.25):[137]

> Cum vero magis ac magis vires morbus exedit et in medullas nervosque descendere deliciae, conspectu eorum quibus se nimia aviditate inutilem reddidit laetus, pro suis voluptatibus habet alienarum spectaculum, subministrator libidinum testisque, quarum usum sibi ingerendo abstulit.
>
> But when this tyrant's sickness erodes his strength more and more, when the indulgences work their way down into the bones and tendons, then it finds enjoyment in the sight of those to whom it has made itself useless through

[135] Above, 2.3. [136] Above, 4.3.

[137] Citroni Marchetti (1991), 137–9; Berti (2018), 194–7; Edwards (2019), 304–5.

> excessive greed: it takes vicarious pleasure in observing the pleasure of others, becoming an accomplice and a witness to their lusts, since in surfeit it has robbed itself of the use of its own.

The passage is characterized by expressions of excess (*magis ac magis*, *nimia*), and is focused on the inability to enjoy pleasures when certain limits have been exceeded (*quarum usu sibi ingerendo abstulit*). Again (above, 4.5: *EM* 59.17), pleasures (*deliciae*) are considered a disease (*morbus*) and an infection that weakens natural strength (*vires...exedit*) and spreads all over the body (*in medullas...descendere*), until it leads it to death, here identified with insensitivity. The love for personal ostentation is replaced by that for looking at others' vices as a spectacle (*spectaculum*). And the final image is, as in letter 95.19,[138] that of a single stomach (114.26 *unum...ventrem*) that devours the products of numerous kitchens, entire cellars, and fields: a sort of faceless monster or storm that can only destroy other people's work, without any satisfaction for itself.

4.7 Frugality on Stage: Scipio Africanus (*EM* 86) and Q. Aelius Tubero (*EM* 95)

Then there are the heroes of frugality,[139] whom Seneca tries to present as smart as the formers. Apart from the foreigner Demetrius the Cynic (above, 3.3), they are Roman, and come from the golden age of the Republic, the second and first century BCE: Scipio Africanus and Quintus Aelius Tubero.

Scipio Africanus is the protagonist of a famous and deeply studied letter, *EM* 86,[140] in which Seneca relates his visit to Scipio's property, stressing the sobriety and moderation—almost poverty—of the building and the bathroom (86.5–11). Of course, this impression was mostly due to the state of architectural use and fashion in Scipio's day, so it is easy for Seneca to present Scipio as a sort of venerable hermit, all while ignoring the fact that he retired to Liternum to avoid a case of embezzlement brought against him by the archenemy of luxury, Cato the Censor, who is casually mentioned in a list of frugal aediles in 86.10, together with Fabius Maximus (the 'delayer', who won the first Punic war) and the Cornelii, i.e. Scipio's family. Seneca praises Scipio's frugality and criticizes contemporary luxury (86.4–10):

[138] Above, 4.3. See also *EM* 60.2–3.

[139] On the relevance of this virtue in Seneca, Gildenhard (2020), 310–25.

[140] Henderson (2004), 93–170; Del Giovane (2012); Costa (2013), 225–44; Rimell (2013); Maruotti (2015), 351–4; Rimell (2015b), 178–98; Edwards (2019), 234–54; Bessone (2018); Fucecchi (2019); De Maria (2021); Papini (2021), esp. 103–12.

> Vidi villam extructam lapide quadrato . . . balneolum angustum, tenebricosum ex consuetudine antiqua: non videbatur maioribus nostris caldum nisi obscurum. 5. Magna ergo me voluptas subiit contemplantem mores Scipionis ac nostros: in hoc angulo ille 'Carthaginis horror' . . . abluebat corpus laboribus rusticis fessum. . . . Sub hoc ille tecto tam sordido stetit, hoc illum pavimentum tam vile sustinuit: at nunc quis est qui sic lavari sustineat? 6. Pauper sibi videtur ac sordidus nisi parietes magnis et pretiosis orbibus refulserunt, nisi Alexandrina marmora Numidicis crustis distincta sunt, nisi illis undique operosa et in picturae modum variata circumlitio praetexitur . . . 7. . . . Eo deliciarum pervenimus ut nisi gemmas calcare nolimus. . . . 9. At olim et pauca erant balnea nec ullo cultu exornata: cur enim exornaretur res quadrantaria et in usum, non in oblectamentum reperta? Non suffundebatur aqua nec recens semper velut ex calido fonte currebat, nec referre credebant in quam perlucida sordes deponerent. 10. Sed, di boni, quam iuvat illa balinea intrare obscura, et gregali tectorio inducta . . . Nam hoc quoque nobilissimi aediles fungebantur . . . utilem ac salubrem temperaturam, non hanc quae nuper inventa est similis incendio . . .
>
> I have seen the villa built of squared masonry . . . and the cramped bathing quarters. These last was dimly lit, as the old ones generally were, for our ancestors thought a bathhouse couldn't be hot unless it was dark. 5. So I took great pleasure in pondering the habits of Scipio—and our habits. In this little nook, the famous 'terror of Carthage' . . . would wash his body, worn out from working in the fields . . . This shabby roof was over his head; this cheap tile floor was under his feet.
>
> But nowadays who could stand to bathe in such a style? 6. A man now thinks himself a shoddy pauper unless his walls gleam with large and costly mirrors, unless his Alexandrian marble has a contrasting inlay of Numidian and a border all around of many colors laid out like a painting . . . 7. . . . We have reached such a pitch of luxury that we don't even want to walk unless we tread upon precious stones! . . . 9. In the old days, there were only a few bathhouses, and they had no kind of décor . . . there were no water jets below the surface, no constant supply of fresh water as if from a hot spring, and no one cared whether the water that washed away dirt and grime was crystal clear. 10. And yet, in all truth, how delightful it is to enter those dark bathhouses with their plain stucco . . . aediles from the noblest families used to . . . ensure cleanliness and a serviceable and healthy temperature—not the temperature you find now, which is more like a furnace.

Seneca seems aware that most of the seemingly frugal details are due to building conventions in use in Scipio's time (86.4 *ex consuetudine antiqua*), but he considers this very fact a proof of the ancients' sobriety. Houses are made luxurious by the addition of expensive materials and fine workmanship (86.5–7), as the repetition of *nisi* underlines, which emphasizes an exotic provenience (Alexandria, Numidia, etc.), by excessive preciousness (gems not for jewellery but for floors), and by fragile materials (glass). Luxury is no longer a question of money alone, but also of a restless search for things that are expensive not so much for their material as for their remote provenance, difficult workmanship, or fragility. These are the same issues that Pliny will tackle in his *Natural History*.[141] This process of accumulation is emphasized by the further comparison, among wealthy people, between plebeians and freedmen (86.7): the latter represent the apex of luxury. Related to this apex is the idea of warmth, which as we have seen characterizes luxury (above, 4.4): here, hot springs, which are dangerous per se, are artificially reproduced, and the temperature is so high that they are comparable to a fire (86.10). The idea of the high temperature melting what was previously strength is here taken to an extreme degree, the image of burning being often associated with destructive passions, such as anger and love.

As for ancient bathhouses, Seneca opens the description with a list of negative connotations: they are small and dark (86.4 *angustum*, *obscurum*, this last repeated in 86.10), and shabby and cheap (86.5 *sordido*, *vile*). He then enumerates comforts they do *not* have (86.9 *non... nec... nec*). The general impression of this exhibition of frugality is indeed negative, and is confirmed by another image (86.12–13), also connected with bathrooms, namely that of perfumes, another luxury object,[142] which Seneca judged to be a worse alternative to plainly sweating. Seneca overturns the common-sense opposition between good and bad smell, because the latter comes from actual manly work, while the former comes from vicious habits, which is why 'now that fancy bathhouses have been invented, people are much filthier' (86.12 *spurciores*).

Despite his declarations of enthusiasm at the thought of entering Scipio's bathhouses (86.10), Seneca seems to share the reader's perplexity, to the point that he himself admits that they are 'excessively severe' (86.14 *nimium tristia*). Scipio remains a positive example for his ethical choice of abandoning Rome, as Seneca affirms in 86.1–2, but as far as architecture and way of life are concerned, Seneca is aware that times have changed and that some comforts nowadays are necessary.

During his 'archaeological walk', an aspect Seneca praises is agricultural work, one of the key characteristics of the ideal Roman. There are some literary models for this encounter with an idealized past, including Virgil and Cicero.[143] But perhaps the *ur*-source of this scenario is Cato the Elder's encounter with

[141] Above, 2.5.2. [142] Above, 2.5.2.

[143] Bessone (2018) draws a parallel between Seneca's visit to Scipio's villa and Aeneas' visit to Evander, and spots a correspondence between Sen. *EM* 86.5 *sub hoc ille tecto tam sordido stetit...* and Verg. *Aen.* 8.622–3*... haec... limina victor/Alcides subiit, haec illum regia cepit.* Del Giovane (2012), esp. 159–60 compares Cic. *Sen.* 51 and 55 and his idealization of rural life, with the example of M.' Curius Dentatus. Seneca's narrative, though, is closer to Plutarch's description than to Cicero's.

Manius Curius Dentatus. As Plutarch reports in his biography of the Censor (*Cato M.* 2.1–2):[144]

> Near his farm was the villa that had belonged to Manius Curius, a man who had celebrated three triumphs. He would always wander over to this place and gaze at the grounds and the dwelling. The insignificance of the one and the simplicity of the other gave him some idea of the character of this man who, though he had attained pre-eminence among the Romans...lived in this farmhouse. 2. Here it was that the ambassadors of the Samnites found him, seated in front of the fire, engaged in boiling turnips. They had come to offer him a large sum of money, but he sent them away saying, 'A man who can be satisfied with such a meal has no need of gold....' With his head full of these things Cato would return home and, when he contemplated instead his own house, his estate, his servants, his way of life, he would exert himself all the more and would cut back inessential expenses. (Trans. Sansone 1989)

Curius' assets were modest, and his house almost a hut, and yet he was the conqueror of Pyrrhus, and he triumphed thrice. While the following story, about Curius' refusal of a rich gift from the embassy of the Samnites (*Cato M.* 2.2), is well known—it is mentioned, for example, by Valerius Maximus 4.3.5—and contributes to make Curius, along with Fabricius, into an archetypical example of Roman frugality (above, 2.5.2 with n. 246), his encounter with Cato is less known, but represents, in my opinion, a relevant precedent for Seneca. Cato meditates on his meeting with the great general, and decides to dedicate more time to agriculture and to cut his expenses. Seneca does not connect this example to himself, but only makes a general speech against contemporary luxury. But in the second part of the letter he discusses the agricultural tips he learned from Egialus, the actual owner of Scipio's property, and he thereby shows that he is making an effort within agriculture, the most frugal Roman activity (86.14–20). The truth was actually, as some recent studies have pointed out, that he was there in order to conclude an economic speculation on some vineyard assets, but the reader is left with the impression of a nobleman who occupies himself with the frugal and sober activity of oil cultivation. Seneca thus presents himself as the ideal inheritor of Scipio's model, not only in the choice of frugal occupation but also, we may add, in voluntary retirement after a controversial accusation.

The second, more radical example of frugality is Q. Aelius Tubero, who used goatskins and clay tableware for a public banquet, and was thus defeated in the elections.[145] This event, dated to 129 BCE, is recorded by Cicero, Valerius Maximus, and Seneca; there are evident intertextual relationships among these

144 This passage was already been paralleled to Seneca's description of Scipio by Ker (2009), 351.

145 On this historical example and its versions, see Passet (2010); Berno (2014a); above, 2.2.1.

reports, but their evaluations differ: while Cicero (*Mur.* 75) and Valerius Maximus (7.5.1) criticize Tubero's behaviour as offending against the magnificence that is due on public occasions, and therefore consider his political defeat just, Seneca exalts his nonconformist behaviour as evidence of superior moral integrity, in spite of, or perhaps even because of, Tubero's defeat (*EM* 95.72–3):

> Proderit non tantum quales esse soleant boni viri dicere formamque eorum et liniamenta deducere sed quales fuerint narrare et exponere, Catonis illud ultimum ac fortissimum vulnus...Laeli sapientiam...alterius Catonis domi forisque egregia facta, Tuberonis ligneos lectos, cum in publicum sterneret, haedinasque pro stragulis pelles et ante ipsius Iovis cellam adposita conviviis vasa fictilia. Quid aliud paupertatem in Capitolio consecrare? Ut nullum aliud factum eius habeam quo illum Catonibus inseram, hoc parum credimus? censura fuit illa, non cena. 73. O quam ignorant homines cupidi gloriae quid illa sit aut quemadmodum petenda! Illo die populus Romanus multorum supellectilem spectavit, unius miratus est. Omnium illorum aurum argentumque fractum est et [in] milliens conflatum, at omnibus saeculis Tuberonis fictilia durabunt.
>
> It will be helpful not only to state a good man's typical qualities, with a description of his character and features, but to give an account of what such men have been like—Cato's final and supremely courageous wound...Laelius' wisdom...the splendid deeds of the other Cato at home and abroad; Tubero's wooden couches when he was spreading them out for a public feast, with goatskins in place of coverlets and earthenware utensils laid out for the banquets in front of Jupiter's very shrine. In a word, he gave poverty a sacred place on the Capitol. Although I know no other act by Tubero to rank him with the Catos, do we find this one insufficient? He was not throwing a party but practicing official parsimony. 73. People lusting for glory are so ignorant of what it really is or how it should be sought. On that day there were many whose furnishings were viewed by the Roman public, but only one at whom they marvelled. The gold and silver of all the others has been broken up and melted down countless times, but Tubero's earthenware will last forever.

As are many passages on *luxuria*, this one, dealing with its opposite, *paupertas*, is also focused on an object, in this case earthenware. Tableware made of clay is the poorest material of all, which Roman literature considered as a symbol of a sober age in which wealth was not valued.[146] Seneca compares it to its opposite, gold, at the very end of the letter, thereby reversing common sense: gold, a resistant material, will remain but only to be reused, while Tubero's earthenware, even though it is

[146] There were also refined clay objects, which were highly valued precisely for their fragility (cf. Plin. *HN* 35.163, above, 2.5.2), but this is not the case here.

fragile, will last forever. The symbolic value, which is the highest one according to Seneca, is contrasted with economic value. While Cicero describes Tubero's behaviour as an example of 'perverted wisdom' (*Mur.* 75 *perversa sapientia*), alluding to the Stoic idea of vice as a perversion,[147] Seneca states that it was a sort or religious gesture, which consecrated poverty in the most reverential Roman place of all, the Capitol (*EM* 95.72 *paupertatem in Capitolio consecrare*). And this is enough to rank Tubero with the Catos.

And all this is at the end of *EM* 95, the letter in which Seneca seemed to criticize Cicero's view on private luxury and public magnificence (above, 4.3), a view that is in the same speech, the *Pro Murena*, as Tubero's story. It seems to be a unique moment in which Seneca praises a behaviour that breaks the rules and habits of Roman society: as we have seen, he always exhorts people to follow common rules, at least on the surface, which for example leads him to reject Cynic ideas.[148] Athenaeus, in a context inspired by Posidonius, lists Tubero among the few Romans and Stoics who respected sumptuary laws;[149] he does not explicitly mention this episode, but since the context clearly refers to it—indeed, most sumptuary laws regarded banquet limitations: above, 2.9—there is a possibility that Posidonius himself did. Either way, it seems plausible that Seneca took inspiration for his eulogy of Tubero from Posidonius. This may explain the peculiarity of his reading of the episode.

Furthermore, the general aim of letter 95, as we have seen (above, 4.3), is to maintain that vice in general, and especially *luxuria*, has reached such a level of complexity that there is the need of an equally evolved virtue to face it. In this context, the 'luxuriant' Cato, compared to a vigorous war horse, was a fitting example of a sage. Tubero, with whom the letter ends, may be a second example, explicitly put on the same level as Cato, despite his lesser fame, since the Tubero example deals with *luxuria*, the main vice in the letter: this vice is so developed that frugality needs to be just as extreme in order to be effective. Only a radical and publicly exhibited poverty, like Tubero's, may fulfil this need.

4.8 Can You Recover from *Luxuria? Tranq.* 1.9 and *EM* 112

Most of Seneca's work is considered protreptic, and it features students disposed to philosophy.[150] Seneca's struggle towards his and the readers' moral improvement

[147] Above, 2.2.1; 4.2 with n. 38. [148] Above, 3.3.

[149] Athen. 6.274c–e 'Mucius Scaevola, for example, was one of the three men in Rome who respected the Fannian law, the other being Aelius Tubero and Rutilius Rufus…The law stipulated that no one was to entertain more than three people from outside his household…it prohibited buying fish that cost more than two-and-a-half drachmas…' (Trans. Olson 2008). Athen. 6.274a, about the archaic Romans' frugality ('According to Posidonius, the Roman tradition involved endurance, frugal diet, and the modest and limited use of other material possessions…'), is ascribed to Posidonius' *History* as frg. 59 J. = 266 E.-K. = A 269 V. (cf. Kidd (1988), 910–12; Kidd (1999), 339; Vimercati (2004), 676).

[150] For a critical orientation on this key issue, Bellincioni (1978); Cooper (2004), 309–34; Inwood (2005b); Roskam (2005), 60–98, Cooper (2006); Hadot (2012), 273–356; Dietsche (2014), 120–56; Setaioli (2014b); Wagoner (2014).

is not always successful. There are two relevant cases regarding *luxuria*: Serenus in the opening of *De tranquillitate animi*, and an anonymous friend of Lucilius in *EM* 112.

The first case is famous: Serenus is the interlocutor of the dialogue, and also of *De constantia sapientis*, and he opens the work talking in the first person, with a long speech about his stressful struggles to stay frugal and sober against the seductive appearances of his friend's luxurious habits. As has been noticed, he is structurally inconsistent, not only in his purposes but even in his name, whose meaning is 'serene, quiet'. Seneca's aim is to make him return to his true nature, which is expressed by his name. Serenus' wavering regards oratorical and political ambition, but most of all *luxuria*, which he treats in detail, describing his discomfort with other people's magnificence (*Tranq.* 1.7–8), which has a seducing effect on him (1.9):

> Circumfudit me ex longo frugalitatis situ venientem multo splendore luxuria et undique circumsonuit: paulum titubat acies, facilius adversus illam animum quam oculos attollo; recedo itaque non peior sed tristior, nec inter illa frivola mea tam altus incedo tacitusque morsus subit et dubitatio numquid illa meliora sint. Nihil horum me mutat, nihil tamen non concutit.
>
> As I emerge from the prolonged inattention induced by thrift, this extravagance with its immense splendor has engulfed me and reverberated all around me. My gaze trembles and I raise my mind toward it more easily than my eyes. So I depart not worse but saddened, and I walk less tall among my possessions, and an unspoken sting comes over me, and uncertainty whether those luxuries are not better after all. None of this changes me, but it does not fail to disturb me.
>
> (Trans. Fantham 2014)

Luxuria is an enemy that surrounds Serenus without leaving him any escape route, as expressed by the repetition of the preverb *circum*, 'around' (*circumfudit*, *circumsonuit*), further emphasized by *undique*, 'everywhere', and by the opposition between the brightness of luxury (*splendor*) and the dark, boring sadness of frugality. *Luxuria*'s seduction primarily affects sight (*acies*, *oculos*): the sense of vision, which is the most important for knowledge but also the most impressionable, is subdued by the glare of this vice, which is also characterized as a biting animal (*morsus*, 'bite'). This situation weakens Serenus' motivation and makes him sad (*tristior*) for, instead of proud of, his frugality. As he states later on, he is not overthrown by vice, but he suffers from nausea, a sort of discontent or disgust for his way of life (1.17).[151]

Seneca tries in many ways to renew Serenus' enthusiasm for philosophical life: in the end of the dialogue, he also admits—uniquely, in his works—the legitimacy

[151] Lotito (2001), 24–68; Schofield (2015), 78–9. Cf. also above, 4.3.

of some pleasures, such as dancing and drinking (17.8).[152] We may infer from the deep affection he shows Serenus, whose abrupt death he mourns in *EM* 63, that his friend managed to resist the temptations.

Letter 112 tells a different tale. It deals with a friend of Lucilius whom Seneca does not appear to appreciate very much.[153] As in *EM* 29, Seneca considers the man a lost cause: he is weak, soft, and broken by his bad habits (112.1). Seneca imagines Lucilius' protests that his friend is disposed to improve, and here is his reply (112.3–4):

> Hic de quo scribis et mandas non habet vires: indulsit vitiis. Simul et emarcuit et induruit; non potest recipere rationem, non potest nutrire. 'At cupit ipse.' Noli credere. Non dico illum mentiri tibi: putat se cupere. Stomachum illi fecit luxuria; cito cum illa redibit in gratiam. 4. 'Sed dicit se offendi vita sua.'...Homines vitia sua et amant simul et oderunt. Tunc itaque de illo feremus sententiam cum fiedm nobis fecerit invisam iam sibi esse luxuriam: nunc illis male convenit.
>
> This fellow you are writing to me about with all these instructions has no strength in him; he has indulged in his faults. He is at one and the same time both enervated and hardened: he can neither accept reasoning nor provide it with nourishment. 'But he himself wants this.' Don't believe it. I don't mean that he is lying to you: he thinks that he wants it. He is fed up with self-indulgence; soon he will be reconciled to it again. 4. 'But he says he is tired by his way of life.'...People love their faults and hate them at the same time. So let's reserve judgement about him until he supplies us with proof that he and self-indulgence have become enemies. Right now, it is just that they are not getting along.

The analogies with the opening of *De tranquillitate animi* are evident: the man wishes to get rid of his vices, but does not manage to do it; he tries to abandon *luxuria*, and then returns to it. His feeling is similar to that of nausea (112.3 *stomachum*), as in Serenus' case. Seneca is convinced that he will not succeed, because he is at the same time too softened—almost rotten (*emarcuit*)—and hardened (*induruit*) by vices. *Luxuria* has had a double and contradictory effect on him: it has made him weaker and softer, as it always does, and it has hardened him, in the sense of becoming a habit.[154] As a consequence, he is unable to follow good advice, because his hardness in vice makes him insensible to it, and his softness deprives him of the requisite moral strength. He says he is dissatisfied by *luxuria*, but does

[152] A condemnation of drinking, even if with some exceptions, is in *EM* 83.20 (above, 4.2 and 4.6). On the problematic ending of *Tranq.*, Giusti (2017), 244–56. Cf. also Ker (2020), 184–96.

[153] Cf. e.g. *EM* 29.1–8; 36.1–7.

[154] We have seen this in *EM* 78.23–6 (above, 4.3), and will find it again in *NQ* 4b.13.11 (below, 4.9). Cf. *EM* 85.8 'we can never trust that our faults have been subdued.'

not really mean it; it is as if he had had an argument with a lover (112.4 *male convenit*), not that he actually despises her (*invisam*). The sentence *homines vitia sua et amant simul et oderunt* is clearly an allusion to Catullus' famous distich (*C.* 85.1 *odi et amo*...), and supports this idea.

We have seen two examples, an optimistic and a pessimistic one, of persons affected by *luxuria*; in both cases *luxuria* was personified as a seductress with a sparkling appearance, and with whom they are involved in a toxic relationship, typical of lyric poetry, where the man is no longer able to act or live right. This rhetorical device, which adopts the well-known pattern of unhappy love, expresses why it is so difficult to get rid of vices.[155]

Lucilius himself is at a higher level than his friend, of course, but also than Serenus. Seneca states his achievements in a preface to *Natural Questions* (*NQ* 1.*pr.*6):

> Effugisti vitia animi; non est tibi frons ficta, nec in alienam voluntatem sermo compositus, nec cor involutum, nec avaritia quae quicquid omnibus abstulit sibi ipsi neget, nec luxuria pecuniam turpiter perdens quam turpius reparet, nec ambitio quae te ad dignitatem nisi per indigna non ducet: nihil adhuc consecutus es; multa effugisti, te nondum.
>
> Have you broken free from moral vices? Your face does not have a feigned expression, your speech is not designed to please somebody else, nor are your feelings concealed, nor do you harbor greed, which denies itself what it has taken from others, nor luxury, which squanders money shamefully only to recoup it even more shamefully, nor ambition, which will bring you honors only by dishonorable means? You have not yet achieved anything: you have broken free from many things, but not yet from yourself.
>
> (Trans. Hine 2010, here and below)

Lucilius no longer has any problem with vices, but he must still overcome his own individuality in order to reach the perfection of wisdom. There is no risk of a relapse, as in the previous examples, but he still has not completed the path to virtue. The reference to Lucilius can perhaps be questioned, since the 'you' may be generic, but this passage is close to the dedication of the treatise to him (1.*pr.*1), and in this same work Seneca notes that Lucilius suffered from flattery (4a.*pr.*3–22), to which the first vice listed in the quoted passage may allude (1.*pr.*6 *frons ficta*). So it is quite certain that the advanced pupil in the passage is Seneca's dear friend, about whom Seneca is more positive than about anyone else.

[155] Cf. Berno (2022).

4.9 Scientific *Luxuria:* Moral Digressions in Seneca's *Natural Questions*

Seneca's meteorological treatise *Natural Questions*, written around the same time as the letters and also addressed to Lucilius, strikes the modern reader for its digressions on moral topics, which at first sight seem out of place. Seneca's aim is to help men get rid of passion, most of all fear, by explaining the natural processes that cause earthquakes, rainbows, eclipses, floods, and so on. As in Lucretius, rational explanations exclude divine intervention and thus reduce the fear of natural phenomena.[156]

A lot of space in *Natural Questions* is indeed reserved for fear (*NQ* 2.53; 6.1–3; 6.32), but greed is considered regarding mines (5.15), lust and erotic games regarding mirrors (1.16) and the idea of progress (7.31–2); to these we may add flattery, which as we have mentioned above was Lucilius' flaw (4a.*pr.*3–22). *Luxuria*, apart from some casual mentions in the prefaces (1.*pr.*6; 3.*pr.*16; cf. above, 4.8), is thematized twice, both times in connection with water (rivers, 3.17–18, and hailstorms, 4b.13); it is also mentioned in connection with lust, in 1.17 and 7.31.

Natural Questions deals with almost all main vices; only anger is absent, the subject of a three-book dialogue written under Claudius' reign, *De ira*, an absence that is also noticeable in the letters and that might be explained by the tyrannical degradation of Nero's reign in those years (62–65 CE). Since anger is the main passion of a tyrant, Seneca probably avoided this subject so as not to irritate the emperor. Nevertheless, the vices he mentions in *Natural Questions*, and especially those connected with *luxuria*, are typical of Nero's court, as we have already seen in every section of this chapter. We may thus infer that Seneca is expressing his discontent for the regime in the only way he could: by shifting from a political to a moralistic field.[157]

The account of *luxuria*'s in this work deserves particular attention, for more than one reason: first, Seneca is more detailed here than in the letters; second, he develops some issues linked with the literary genre, especially the ideas of technological progress and invention, applying them to vice;[158] third, the overlap between *luxuria* and lust, which will become important in the subsequent history of *luxuria*, appears here with greater force than in the other prose works.

In the preface of book 1, Seneca states that Lucilius got rid of vices, including *luxuria* (*NQ* 1.*pr.*6).[159] At the end of the same book (1.17), we find *luxuria* in a moral digression related to the use of mirrors.[160] Mirrors may have a moral intent,

[156] Williams (2012), 1–16.

[157] Berno (2003), 327–35; above, the introduction of this chapter.

[158] As we have noted, this issue is scarcely present elsewhere, with the relevant exception of *EM* 90, which deals with Posidonius' theory (above, 4.1).

[159] Above, 4.8.

[160] Citroni Marchetti (1991), 159–61; Limburg (2007), 276-89.

of showing men how they look, and so he suggests that men, if handsome, should not profit from it, and if not handsome, should work on their minds instead (1.17.4). *Luxuria* plays a double role in this context: first, as a sort of mean inventor who distorts nature's gifts; second, as a cause of excessive luxury and expenditure. The first aspect is typical of *NQ*: Seneca maintains that, while nature gave men plenty of things, including suggestions for inventions, these never led to vice. For example, men had the idea of mirrors from their images reflected in water, yet the use of mirrors for seduction has nothing to do with nature, but is a manifestation of *luxuria* (1.17.2–5):

> Non in hoc scilicet ut ad speculum barbam velleremus aut ut faciem viri poliremus—in nulla re illa [*sc.* natura] luxuriae negotium gessit—sed primum omnium, quia imbecilli oculi ad sustinendum comminus solem ignoraturi erant, formam eius hebetato lumine ostendit. . . . 4. Inventa sunt specula ut homo ipse se nosset, multa ex hoc consecuturus, primum sui notitiam, deinde ad quaedam consilium: formosus, ut vitaret infamiam; deformis, ut sciret redimendum esse virtutibus quicquid corpori deesset; iuvenis, ut flore aetatis admoneretur illud tempus esse discendi et fortia audendi; senex, ut indecora canis deponeret, ut de morte aliquid cogitaret. . . . 5. Fons cuique perlucidus ac leve saxum imaginem reddidit . . . Aetas illa simplicior et fortuitis contenta nondum in vitium beneficia detorquebat nec inventa naturae in libidinem luxumque rapiebat.
>
> It was not, surely, so that we could pluck our beards in front of a mirror, or so that we men could make our faces smooth: she has never in any way served the interests of luxury. No, first of all, because our eyes were too feeble to tolerate looking straight at the sun and would not have known its shape, she displayed it with a weakened light. . . . 4. Mirrors were invented so that human beings might know themselves, and this leads to many benefits—first of all self-knowledge, then guidance for particular circumstances: for the handsome person, to avoid dishonor; for the ugly person, to realize that virtue must compensate for bodily imperfections; for the young man, to be reminded by his youthful beauty that this is the time for learning and for courageous enterprises; for the old man, to put aside what is inappropriate for gray hairs and to reflect on death. . . . 5. A clear spring or a smooth rock offered each person a reflection . . . That more innocent age, which was content with what came to hand, did not yet distort benefits into vices and did not appropriate nature's discoveries for the sake of lust and luxury.

Seneca stresses the idea of discovery (1.17.4 and 5 *inventa*), which is not immoral but has been distorted over the years by men's evil attitude; he characterizes an earlier age as more innocent than the present (1.17.5 *simplicior*) and as satisfied (*contenta*) with what it had: the exact opposite of the restless desire for ever more refined pleasure that characterizes his contemporaries. The context is that of the philosophical suggestions on the correct use of mirrors, as witnessed by Phaedrus (3.8.14–16),[161] Diogenes Laertius (2.33), and Apuleius (*Apol.* 15), among others. Mirrors are indeed considered a means to follow the Delphic exhortation to 'know thyself'.[162] In this case, the Delphic precept is limited to the physical aspect: Seneca maintains that young people must often look at their image in a mirror, so that, if they are handsome, they will behave as worthy of it, and if ugly, they will try to hide their appearance behind noble habits. Despite this edifying picture, the reference to the Delphic precept, along with the reference to springs, which offer physical reflections, trigger in the reader's mind the memory of the tragic myth of Narcissus,[163] and this casts a dark shadow over the whole argument on mirrors as something originally positive.

Also in book 1, interestingly, Seneca couples *luxuria* and *libido*, in a hendiadys that appeared already in Valerius Maximus (9.1).[164] This happens right before the last quoted passage, in the context of the licentious story of Hostius Quadra, narrated in the previous chapter of *NQ* 1, in which mirrors are instruments of lust (1.16.1–9).[165] This example of a good invention that has been turned into a way of satisfying one's lowest cravings leads to the moral considerations of 1.17, and matches the conclusion involving luxury, where Seneca asserts that nowadays mirrors are needed for any sort of vice (1.17.8–10):

> Postea, iam rerum potiente luxuria, specula totis paria corporibus auro argentoque caelata sunt, gemmis deinde adornata; et pluris unum ex his feminae constitit quam antiquarum dos fuit, nempe illa quae publice dabatur imperatorum pauperum liberis.... 10. Processit enim paulatim in deterius opibus ipsis invitata luxuria et incrementum ingens vitia ceperunt, adeoque omnia indiscreta sunt diversissimis artibus ut, quicquid mundus muliebris vocabatur, sarcinae viriles sint; omnes dico, etiam militares. Iam speculum ornatus tantum causa adhibetur? Nulli non vitio necessarium factum est.
>
> Later, as luxury gained control, mirrors as big as the whole body were made from engraved gold and silver, and later on they were decorated with jewels. One of these cost a woman more than the value of the dowries of her ancient counterparts, including the dowries given at public expense to the children of impoverished generals.... 10. For luxury has gradually got worse, enticed

[161] A father to his children (an ugly girl and a handsome boy): *'cotidie' inquit 'speculo vos uti volo/tu formam ne corrumpas nequitiae malis/tu faciem ut istam moribus vincas bonis.'* Cf. Arr. *Epict. Diss.* 2.14.21.

[162] Courcelle (1975), 30 with nn. 60–1 and 33. An echo of this commonplace is to be found in Plaut. *Epidic.* 382–7 and Ter. *Ad.* 415–16 *inspicere..., tamquam in speculum, in vitas omnium/iubeo atque ex aliis sumere exemplum sibi.* Ovid frequently alludes to it, ironically, in his *Ars amatoria* (e.g. 2.497–512; 3.261-2).

[163] In Ovid's account of the myth, the oracle says about Narcissus that he would have had a long and happy life 'if he did not get to know himself' (*Met.* 3.348... *si se non noverit*...).

[164] Above, 2.5.1.

[165] Berno (2003), 31–63; Limburg (2008); Williams (2012), 55–60.

> onward by wealth itself; vice has increased vastly; and so indiscriminate is recourse to all sorts of treatments that what used to be called female toiletries are now standard male equipment—for all men, I tell you, even soldiers. Is a mirror now used just for the sake of our appearance? No, it has become essential for any and every vice.

Luxuria here is described as a constantly increasing and unstoppable force, and does not exclude lust; indeed, Seneca underscores that luxury mixes female and male ornaments, which in turn indicates effeminacy and immoral sexual behaviour. The observation that a mirror is essential for any vice alludes to the desire to be seen, which, as we have witnessed (above, 4.6), characterizes passions at their highest degree.

The connection between *luxuria* and *libido* is emphasized in another passage, inserted in a speech about the slowness of scientific progress. Seneca states that this slowness is due to a lack of engagement, while the commitment devoted to vice is always strong (7.31.1):[166]

> Tarde magna proveniunt, utique si labor cessat. Id quod unum toto agimus animo nondum perfecimus, ut pessimi essemus; adhuc in processu vitia sunt. Invenit luxuria aliquid novi, in quod insaniat; invenit impudicitia novam contumeliam sibi; invenit deliciarum dissolutio et tabes aliquid adhuc tenerius molliusque quo pereat.
>
> Great enterprises progress slowly, especially if effort falters. We have not yet completed the one task to which we apply our whole minds—becoming as immoral as possible. Vice is still in progress. Luxury discovers something new to go crazy over, sexual immorality discovers a new indignity to inflict on itself, the moral collapse and corruption that stem from self-indulgence discover something more voluptuous, more sensuous, to die for.

Luxuria is a brilliant inventor, together with lust and pleasure: note the repetition of *invenit* in reference to the three passions. Not only, as in book 1, are the discoveries (*inventa*) turned into instruments of vice; it is vice itself that creates (*invenit*) them. Thus, there is progress in vice, as there is in technology, but the former progress is faster, because evil persons are fully devoted to their goals. The following examples all involve sexual aspects, both pertaining to appearance, such as effeminate clothing, gait, and jewellery (7.31.2), and to a person's inner nature, such as emasculation (7.31.3). As we have seen elsewhere, Seneca is far more interested in the development of vice than in identifying a hypothetical beginning point of decline, as happens in historiography (above, 4.1).

166 Berno (2003), 294–306; Limburg (2007), 372–6; Williams (2012), 85–7.

There are two other passages in which *luxuria* plays a primary role. In the third book, announced in its preface (3.*pr.*13), the subject is rivers. The discussion of underground rivers and fish is interrupted by Lucilius: we will go fishing with a spade, he says in disbelief (3.17.1). Rhetorically speaking, this is an *adynaton*, that is, something impossible, which goes against natural laws, and which gives Seneca the opportunity to turn to *luxuria*'s breaking of natural laws, in a far worse way than underground fish do. But underground fish are only an apparent *adynaton*, because these do in fact exist in nature, while *luxuria* alters nature in an incredible way (3.17.2–3):[167]

> Hoc miraris accidere; quanto incredibiliora sunt opera luxuriae, quotiens naturam aut mentitur aut vincit? In cubili natant pisces et sub ipsa mensa capitur qui statim transferatur in mensam. Parum videtur recens mullus, nisi qui in convivae manu moritur. Vitreis ollis inclusi afferuntur et observatur morientium color, quem in multas mutationes mors luctante spiritu uertit. Alios necant in garo et condiunt vivos. 3. Hi sunt qui fabulas putant piscem vivere posse sub terra, et effodi, non capi. Quam incredibile illis videretur, si audirent natare in garo piscem nec cenae causa occidi sed super cenam, cum multum diuque in deliciis fuit et oculos ante quam gulam pavit!
>
> Are you surprised by this? How much more incredible are the achievements of luxury! How often it either fakes or surpasses nature! Fish swim on a couch, and one is caught beneath the table to be transferred onto the table immediately. A mullet does not seem fresh enough unless it has died in the guest's hand. They are put in glass bowls and brought in, and as they die people watch their color; death causes many alterations to it, as their breathing struggles. They kill other fish in the fish sauce, and marinate them while still alive. 3. Where does that leave people who think it just a tall story that a fish can live under the earth and be dug up instead of caught? How incredible it would seem to them if they heard of a fish swimming in fish sauce, and being killed not *for* dinner but *at* dinner, after it had been treated like a pet for ages and had fed the eyes before it fed the gullet!

Luxuria's inventions not only imitate (17.2 *mentitur*) nature but surpass it (*vincit*): it is the aim of every scientist, achieved by a vice. The story of mullets (itself a luxury fish) swimming and dying in a sauce, and over a table, represents two *adynata*: a river *inside* a house, and made of sauce. A briefer discussion of mullets is also in Pliny the Elder (above, 2.5.2). Seneca insists on the concept of the unbelievable (17.2 *incredibiliora*; 17.3 *incredibile*) to stress the fact that *luxuria*'s creations are far more incredible than any oddities of nature. This is a commonplace

[167] Citroni Marchetti (1991), 163–7; Torre (1997), 394–6; Berno (2003), 65–110; Gauly (2004), 96–104; Williams (2012), 75–80.

of ancient scientific treatises, i.e. to show the logical reasons behind amazing phenomena. On the one hand, the extraordinary behaviour of those who make fish drown in sauce renders the existence of underground fish more believable: from a didactic point of view, the vice turns to be useful. On the other hand, the exceptional creativity in going against nature is terrifying, because it reproduces on a small scale the destruction of the *cosmos* as it is.

The *adynata* demonstrate *luxuria*'s effectiveness in going against nature, its creativity overwhelming nature's own, as well as its taste for excess in every field. Its behaviour involves many dimensions: expense (the mullet comes straight from the sea, so it costs much more than usual), time (it is killed during the banquet and not before it), place (a river inside a house; a river made of sauce), decency (the sadistic pleasure of watching a dying creature), taste boundaries (especially sight and taste). After the *adynata*, Seneca, apologizing for his literary boldness, ends the digression with synaesthesia—a propos of taste boundaries (3.18.7):

> Non tempero mihi quin utar interdum temerarie verbis et proprietatis modum excedam. Non sunt ad popinam dentibuset uentre et ore contenti; oculis quoque gulosi sunt.
>
> I cannot stop myself from using words recklessly from time to time and crossing the boundary of propriety: in an eating-place they are not content with teeth, and stomach, and mouth; they are gluttons with their eyes as well.

Seneca crosses the lines of stylistic decorum because he needs to transgress rules in order to adequately express this vice; *adynaton* is not enough, because the confusion also involves taste, and so synaesthesia is needed. These *luxuriosi* eat with their eyes, thereby perverting the natural role of each organ. The image corresponds to synaesthesia used by Cicero to describe Cato the Younger (*Fin.* 3.7 *quasi helluari libris, si hoc verbo in tam clara re utendum est, videbatur*, 'he appears to be gorging himself on books, if I may apply this term to so honourable an occupation' trans. Woolf 2001). The senses that are being mixed are in both cases sight and taste; both Seneca and Cicero apologize for their linguistic boldness. But Cicero is referring to the incarnation of a sage, while Seneca uses the same rhetorical tool to describe the perversity of vice.

In this long passage of *NQ* book 3, *luxuria* is again described as an inventor making things that are more amazing than natural wonders (17.2 *quanto incredibiliora sunt opera luxuriae*), but at the same time as lazy and sleepy (18.1 *longa somniculosae inertisque luxuriae neglegentia*), and finally, with an oxymoron, as active and dying (18.3):

> Tantum ad sollertiam luxuriae pereuntis accedit, tantoque subtilius cotidie et elegantius aliquid excogitat furor usitata contemnens.

> How the resourcefulness of deadly luxury has increased! Madness that despises the familiar devises each day something so much more subtle and more elegant!

This vice is represented as inactive and almost dying, and at the same time as animated by an inventive spirit. This is possible because *luxuria* is usually nauseated by its restless search for pleasures: it quickly gets used to each of them, to the point that it grows numb, but at the same time it stays hungry for transgressions and further novelties. Thus we get the image of an inert corpse that suddenly reanimates at the idea of new pleasure.

Another opportunity of seeing *luxuria* in action regards iced drinks in book 4b.[168] We have already seen them in *EM* 78.23, and Pliny the Elder informs us that they were Nero's invention (*HN* 31.40; above, 4.3): this is an instance of what appears to be a generic moral sermon turning into a declaration of political dissent.

The digression, as in book 3, is justified by an intervention of the addressee, who exhorts Seneca to discuss not how snow-ice is created, but why one should not buy it (4b.13.1). Seneca answers with the expression *cum luxuria litigare*, which is also present in book 3 (18.1) and is recalled at the end of *EM* 51.[169] It is a both colloquial and juridical expression, and it personifies *luxuria* as a political enemy who is too strong to be legally attacked (4b.13.1 *cotidianum istum et sine effectu iurgium est*).

The detailed description of this vice focuses on two points: first, it may turn every natural element, even a basic one like water, into something perverse (4b.13.4).[170]

This is the same as what happens with inventions, such as mirrors in book 1.17 (quoted above). Second, the opposition that expresses this anti-natural element, both here and in letter 51, is the one between cold and warmth. Cold should be good, as we know, in that it is related to moral strength (above, 4.4), but in this case it is perverse, because it is created in the warm season and is therefore against nature (another *adynaton*), as well as very expensive (cf. above, 4.3). Also, the excessive cold corresponds to an excessive warmth of the stomach due to an excess of eating (4b.13.6–7):

> Quibus nullum intervallum umquam quo interquiescerent datum est, sed prandia cenis usque in lucem perductis ingesta sunt, et distentos copia ferculorum ac varietate comessatio altius mersit; deinde numquam intermissa intemperantia quicquid animi decoxerat efferavit et in desiderium semper novi rigoris

[168] Berno (2003), 145–77; Gauly (2004), 104–15; Limburg (2007), 224–42; Williams (2012), 136–44.

[169] 51.13; above, 4.4.

[170] This passage has been quoted above, 4.1. Cf. Citroni Marchetti (1991), 167–70, who compares Plin. *HN* 19.52.

> accendit. 7. Itaque... stomachus ille solutus et aestu suo languidus quaerit aliquid quo erigatur.
>
> They are never given any pause for rest: after dinners lasting till dawn, lunches are stuffed in, and when they are bloated with the quantity and variety of the courses, partying sends them into deeper decline. Then the unremitting self-indulgence, which has already overcooked their minds, drives what is left of them into a state of frenzy and inflames them with longing for something ever colder. 7. So... that stomach, weakened and enfeebled by its own heat, seeks something to revive it.

In this passage, the stomach (13.7 *stomachus*) is personified as master of the person's actions and choices (above, 4.3), and is also described as *languidus*, a term similar to one that refers to *luxuria* in book 3 (3.18.1 *iners*); *languidus* combines the ideas of soft and lazy and fits within the context of idle effeminacy. Again, vice is at the same time idle and active, dying and creative in always finding new ways to satisfy its desires. Here, as in book 7, the accent is on the idea of innovation (4b.13.6 *semper novi*), in this case specified as a restless search (13.6 *nullum intervallum, ingesta sunt, numquam intermissa*) which ends in drowning (*mersit*) the subject in food and drink. Extreme *luxuria*'s tendency toward self-destruction is particularly evident in this case.

The end of the chapter emphasizes that *luxuria*, turning everything upside down, changes herself too, from something delicate and tender to something rough and resistant. It is compared to a fever and described as 'an inconquerable evil that develops from soft and pliant to hard and enduring' (13.11 *luxuria invictum malum et ex molli fluidoque durum atque patiens*). As in *EM* 95 (above, 4.3), it is not as weak as it seems, but in fact very strong and a formidable opponent, with the same qualities of strength and resistance as the wise man himself: *invictus*, *durus*, and *patiens* are among the ideal sage's main characteristics.[171] But since *luxuria* constantly seeks new pleasures and is incapable of settling, it runs into a problem: there is no form of water colder than ice and snow, so what comes next? So while this vice is difficult to beat, it is also doomed to dissatisfaction.

[171] Cf. e.g. *EM* 95.71; *Prov.* 6.6; Berno (2003), 163–5.

5
From *Luxuria* to Lust

The turning from the first to the second century CE is crucial for the semantics of *luxuria*. During this century, we witness a process of legitimization of luxury, banquets, and the expensive pleasures of life,[1] and consequently the negative label *luxuria* in this regard disappears (Pliny the Younger). Historiographers still use it for an emperor's immorality and waste of public money, and Nero had been an especially pivotal figure here[2] (Suetonius, Tacitus). But in the second century, *luxuria*, having freed itself from that context, becomes more frequently used in reference to lust. There had already been an overlap between luxury and lust, more or less vividly, in almost all Latin authors. We have seen, for example, that Valerius Maximus couples the two vices, devoting a chapter to them (above, 2.5.1). But during the second century CE the word *luxuria* switches more fully to lust, replacing *libido* in most instances. This happens in some Church Fathers, but the key author is a pagan and, to some extent, a licentious one: Apuleius. The fact that this shift happens in Roman Africa (Apuleius was born in Madaura, the converted Christian Tertullian in Carthage), a province in which there was no tradition that could resist literary innovations, is perhaps of interest. In the period from the second to the fourth century, most Latin authors come from this continent, which was evidently an ideal cultural soil for both pagans and Christians.

5.1 Pliny the Younger: Condoning *Luxuria*

In his epistolary work, Pliny traces a picture of the nobleman as a politician who also claims his right to spare time and to pleasures, and among these, *luxuria* is very prominent.[3] Pliny the Elder's nephew is indeed the first author who not only does not criticize this vice but who also justifies it as a status symbol of his social class. Of course, this is not stated explicitly, but only implied. The term itself, which as we know has negative connotations, is almost entirely absent from his works:[4] apart from some theoretical occurrences in the *Panegyric* in lists of vices,[5] we find it only in one letter (2.6), which deals with the satirical motif of an

[1] Toner (1995), 65–88; 117–27.
[2] Kragelund (2000).
[3] Leach (2003); Myers (2005).
[4] Leach (2003), 149.
[5] In opposition to *frugalitas* (*Paneg.* 3.4; 44.8); *luxus* is, associated with *stupra* (82.9) and laziness (*segnities* or *otium*, 82.6 and 9).

Roman Luxuria: *A Literary and Cultural History*. Francesca Romana Berno, Oxford University Press.
 DOI: 10.1093/oso/9780192846402.003.0005

average vs an inopportune dinner.[6] The letter is addressed to Iunius Avitus, a young *protégé* of Pliny who died suddenly at a young age, as Pliny narrates in *Epist.* 8.23.[7] Pliny emphasizes Iunius' good nature and willingness to be morally guided. This explains the parenetic tone of epistle 2.6. The whole letter warns against a peculiar form of vice, the mixing of *luxuria* and degradation (*sordes*), exemplified by the one who invites friends to a banquet and then offers different kinds of food and drink according to their social status. Pliny overtly despises this behaviour, and supports a moderate expense for a dinner that must be the same for everyone (2.6.5–7):[8]

> Et hercule si gulae temperes, non est onerosum quo utaris ipse communicare cum pluribus. Illa ergo reprimenda, illa quasi in ordinem redigenda est, si sumptibus parcas, quibus aliquanto rectius tua continentia quam aliena contumelia consulas. 6. Quorsus haec? ne tibi, optimae indolis iuveni, quorundam in mensa luxuria specie frugalitatis imponat. Convenit autem amori in te meo, quotiens tale aliquid inciderit, sub exemplo praemonere, quid debeas fugere. 7. Igitur memento nihil magis esse vitandum quam istam luxuriae et sordium novam societatem; quae cum sint turpissima discreta ac separata, turpius iunguntur.
>
> Indeed, if you are abstemious it is not a heavy expense to share with a number what you yourself enjoy. What must be suppressed and 'reduced to the ranks' is economizing on expenses, for you will attend to this more honourably on your own modest appetites than by insulting others.
>
> 6. Why do I recount this? To ensure that the extravagance at table of certain men, by masquerading as frugality, does not deceive you, a young man of noble disposition. It befits my affection for you, whenever such an incident occurs, to exploit it as an example to warn you what you should avoid. 7. So bear in mind that there is nothing you should avoid more than the novel alliance of extravagance and meanness, traits most demeaning when distinct and separate from each other, but still more so when they are merged.
>
> (Trans. Walsh 2009, here and below)

In the first quoted section, the lexicon is typically moralistic, with the ideas of measuring (2.6.5 *temperes*), limiting (*reprimenda, parcas, continentia*), and straightening (*in ordinem redigenda, rectius*) pleasure excesses. In the second, the traditional motif of mixing different vices is renewed by the association of a vice with its antonymic virtue, such as luxury and an apparent frugality (2.6.6 *specie frugalitatis*),

[6] Marchesi (2015).

[7] *CIL* VI.10229.20 preserves his will, in which Pliny and Tacitus are quoted.

[8] Sherwin-White (1966), 152–3; Philips (1976); Whitton (2013), 120–8. On Pliny's idea of frugality, Gildenhard (2020), 329–36. Cf. following n.

which, however, turns out to be sordidness:[9] and this mix leads to a result which is even more revolting (2.6.7 *turpissima*, *turpis*) than the single immoral habit.

This moralistic tone is due to the young age of the addressee, whom Pliny wishes to educate. But in a context like this, which requires a critique of luxury, Pliny prefers not to dwell on the traditional sermon against banquet expenditures, but on the unfair behaviour towards the guests; it is not waste of money but greed that is taken to task. He states that gluttony has to be controlled, but without making an example of it; in his opinion, it is more important to satisfy all the guests than to spend too much. Indeed, when it comes to banquets at his own house, Pliny describes them as less expensive than others, and yet, while criticizing dishes like oysters in other houses, he mentions the presence of snow at his own banquet, which both Seneca and Pliny the Elder classify as *luxuria*.[10]

This parenetic letter, as said above, is the only one in which *luxuria* makes an apparition in Pliny's epistolary work. Elsewhere, he praises a friend's 'fat retirement' (1.3.3 *pingui secessu*), and his own 'delightful leisure', his private quiet, which he appreciates more than any occupation (1.9.6 *dulce otium*; 1.6.1 *inertia mea et quite*; 5.6.46),[11] as he does his munificence (1.8.9 *munificentia*) and his many luxury villas (e.g. 2.17; 9.7), some of which are similar to those in Baias (5.6.14–46).[12] A significant example of his attitude is a letter in which he describes some of his properties, expressing his preference for the one located in Tuscany (5.6.45–6):[13]

> Altius ibi otium et pinguius eoque securius: nulla necessitas togae, nemo accersitor ex proximo; placida omnia et quiescentia, quod ipsum salubritati regionis ut purius caelum, ut aer liquidior accedit. 46. Ibi animo, ibi corpore maxime valeo. Nam studiis animo, venatu corpus exerceo.
>
> I enjoy there a leisure more profound and more rich, and therefore more carefree. I need not wear a toga, no neighbour summons me, and all is peace and

[9] Bütler (1970), 119–20 (119–22 on frugality in Pliny). Another kind of noblemen's fake frugality is witnessed by Seneca (e.g. *EM* 100.6: above, 3.3. with n. 44).

[10] Plin. *Epist.* 1.15.2; above, 2.5.2 and 4.9. As for the commonplace of the moderate banquet, cf. also *Epist.* 3.12.4. On this topic and its political implication, Stein-Hölkeskamp (2002a).

[11] Cf. also 1.10.10; 4.3.1–2; 7.3.4–5 (to exhort a lazy friend to undertake some visits); 8.21.1. Pliny was indeed admired for the activity of his uncle Pliny the Elder, and considers himself *desidiosissimus* as compared to him (3.5.19). For the bibliography cf. following notes.

[12] There is an enormous bibliography on Pliny's villas, among which Du Prey 1994; Hoffer (1999), 29–43; Riggsby (2003); Gibson/Morello (2012), 200–34. Specifically on the motif of the artificial landscape, Pavlovskis (1973), 25–33; Re (2021). On Pliny's self-praise, Gibson (2003). On the connection between villas and leisure, Myers (2005), 111–23, who highlights the correspondence between Pliny's and Statius' attitudes (cf. *Silv.* 1.3.91–3, where the poet praises a *fecunda quies*, 'fruitful relief', free from excessive luxury and pleasures, *luxuque carentes/deliciae*, on which Myers (2005), 108); Gonzales (2014). As is well known, Statius praises villas, which are expressions of Epicurean leisure and pleasure, such as those of Pollius Felix (*Silv.* 2.2) and Manlius Vopiscus (*Silv.* 1.3). On Statius' fascination for artificial landscapes, Pavlovskis (1973), 2–25; Delarue (2014).

[13] Sherwin-White (1966), 330.

> tranquillity; this very fact enhances the health-giving atmosphere of the region, as if the sky were more cloudless, and the air clearer. 46. When I am there I am supremely healthy in mind and body, for my books exercise my mind, and hunting my body.

His leisure is described in both Epicurean (5.6.45 'fatter', *pinguius*) and Stoic ('more carefree', *securius*) terms.[14] Indeed, *pinguis* is a physical term referring to someone who is happily satisfied with food, and more generally with life's pleasures, and hence the link with the trivial interpretation of Epicurean happiness, as in Horace's assertion that 'I am a pig from Epicurus' hare'.[15] It is this sort of inactivity that Seneca criticizes.[16] *Securus* comes from *sine cura*, 'without concern', and thus expresses the positive state of mind achieved by the overcoming of every destabilizing thought. The two faces of well-being are represented by the two activities Pliny mentions, studying and hunting, the former for the soul, the latter for the body.

This ideal condition of Pliny, even if described in somewhat philosophical terms, is more properly a general 'feeling good', which excludes the attainment of wisdom; it is underscored by the tranquillity (*placida*, *quiescentia*) and healthiness of the place (*salubritati*, *purius*, *liquidior*). Pliny's view that connects quiet and salubrious villas with a peaceful state of mind contrasts with Seneca's opinion that external conditions do not influence psychological attitudes, and cannot soothe anxiety (*EM* 56.6; cf. above, 4.4):

> Nulla placida est quies nisi quam ratio composuit; nox exhibet molestia, non tollit, et sollicitudines mutat...Illa tranquillitas vera est in quam bona mens explicatur.
>
> There is no restful calm but that which is settled by reason. Night doesn't take away our cares; rather, it exposes them to view, exchanging one anxiety for another...Only as the mind develops into excellence do we achieve any real tranquillity.

The terms (*placida*, *quies*) are almost identical to those used by Pliny, whose leisure is made 'more carefree' (*Epist.* 5.6.45 *securior*) by places like this. Pliny's *securus* opposes Seneca's worries (*sollicitudines*). As we have seen, Seneca's independence

[14] Cf. also 9.3.1. Specifically on *pingue otium*, Méthy (2007), 366–9. On Pliny's idea of leisure, another topic in which the distance from Republican ideals is evident, Bütler (1970), 41–57; Ussani (1984); Pani (1992); Hoffer (1999), 111–18, with special reference to Plin. 1.9; Méthy (2007), 353–78; Page (2015), 154–63; on its relationship with Seneca's idea of leisure, Gibson/Morello (2012), 169–99. For Pliny's moderate interests in philosophy, André (1975); Griffin (2007), 462–8 on his refusal of excessive Stoic rigor.

[15] Hor. *Epist.* 1.4.16; cf. Berno (2017a), 60–2.

[16] *Const.* 3.4, with Berno (2018), 100. *Pinguis* always has negative connotations in Seneca, except for an ambiguous occurrence in *EM* 73.10, where he refers to the leisure granted by the emperor; cf. preceding n; Berno (2024).

from exterior conditions is not as strong as may appear to be the case in the quoted passage; indeed, at the end of the same letter, he runs away from a noisy location; moreover, in letter 55.7, after criticizing the retirement of the former politician Servilius Vatia in Campania as a sort of premature death, he admits that he chose an ideal place for his retirement—one that is healthy and pleasantly windy.[17] Pliny overcomes Seneca's inconsistencies by admitting the pleasures of wealthy leisure and tempering the *securitas* of Stoic contemplation with an attribute that alludes to pleasures without shame. Pliny the Elder's moralism, not to mention Seneca's, seems ages away. Pliny the Younger shows how one may enjoy pleasure and still serve the state.

He overcomes the tension between traditional Roman values, such as moderation and frugality, and the contemporary social conditions of noblemen. There is no shame in being wealthy or in enjoying leisure; one should only avoid sheer exhibition. This attitude is visible already in Horace (above, 2.4.1). Very little is asked of the reader; the message is of an economic, social, and psychological satisfaction that accepts the Empire for what it is, leaving Republican longings and philosophical concerns to old literature.

5.2 Suetonius and Tacitus: *Luxuria* as an Emperor's Vice

Roman historiography, from Sallust to Livy, considered the starting point of moral decline and the Eastern origin of *luxuria*. From the late first century on, Imperial authors no longer have these concerns: *luxuria* is either one among many vices in the emperors' psychological portraits (Suetonius) or evidence of endemic degradation (Tacitus). Tiberius' letter reported by Tacitus, in which the emperor admits the uselessness of sumptuary legislation (above, 2.9), signals the end of the hypocritical situation in which the Senate officially condemned attitudes pursued by the senators themselves. But while Pliny the Younger finds a solution to hypocrisy by avoiding the embarrassing term *luxuria* as he describes his habits, ones that moralistic writers would have thus labelled, both Suetonius and Tacitus keep criticizing this vice, primarily as part of a tyrannical attitude, and secondarily as contrary to authentic Roman values. It is expressed mainly in banquets, which blur the boundary between liberality and lavishness,[18] and in architecture. Historiography looks at the past, and shows how old attitudes persist.

[17] Sen. *EM* 55.7 *esse illam [sc. villam] totius anni credo: occurrit enim Favonio*... *non stulte videtur elegisse hunc locum Vatia in quem otium suum pigrum iam et senile conferret*; cf. Berno (2006), 219.

[18] Schulz (2019), 11–32, with attention to the idea of transgression. She points out how the same behaviour is labelled as liberality by the panegyrical tradition, and as *luxuria* by authors with different political aims (35; 47; 331–2), in line with rhetorical manipulation in epideictic speeches (368–9).

5.2.1 *Luxuria* and the Caesars: Suetonius

Despite Suetonius' known penchant for listing the emperors' vices, according to the biographical use of rubrics,[19] in his *Lives of the Twelve Caesars* we find only a few occurrences of *luxuria*.[20] No references regard Augustus,[21] Claudius, Galba, Otho, or Domitian; in the book devoted to Julius Caesar, *luxuria* is used for those who asked Caesar for help (*Iul.* 27.2). This, in my opinion, is because in Suetonius' time this vice was already widespread, tolerated, and at least implicitly accepted, as Pliny the Younger shows. Far more dangerous for Roman society, to Suetonius, were pride, cruelty, and a lack of care for the state. *Luxuria* is in most cases confined to private license, and is therefore no danger to public affairs; its threatening aspect emerges only when it is combined with other tyrannical traits. Public efforts to limit it are of course praised, as tradition requires: Vespasian is lauded for his legal struggle against vices (*Vesp.* 11):[22]

> Libido atque luxuria coercente nullo invaluerat; auctor senatui fuit decernendi, ut quae se alieno servo iunxisset, ancilla haberetur.
>
> With no measure to curtail them, lust and luxury had flourished. At his instigation, the senate decreed that if any woman should have a relationship with someone else's slave, she was to be considered a slavewoman.
>
> (Trans. Edwards 2000, here and below)

The intent of this law was not so much to recall matrons to modesty as to avoid the fractioning of an asset by sharing it with illegitimate sons, but Suetonius lists it among the procedures aimed at restoring the ancient moral code. In this passage, as in the case of Cesonia, to be discussed below, *luxuria* is connected with lust, which in both cases plays the bigger part; this will be a constant semantic trait of *luxuria* in the second century CE. But Vespasian's frugality was more than that: born in a Sabine village, he was raised at a small farm to which he loved to return (*Vesp.* 2.1)—an example of truly Italic virtue, modelled after the

[19] Hurley (2014). On the structural and ideological functions of virtue and vice rubrics, Cizek (1977), 106–18; Wallace-Hadrill (1983), 142–74; Gascou (1984), 787–98; Schulz (2019), 273–7.

[20] On the meaning of this vice in the context of emperors' biographies, Wallace-Hadrill (1983), 157–8.

[21] Even if Suetonius refers the emperor's passion for luxury vases: *Aug.* 70.2 'He was also notorious for his passion for precious tableware and Corinthian bronze... Indeed, in the time of the proscriptions, the following words appeared on his statue: 'My father dealt in silver, I deal in Corinthian,' for it was thought that the names of some men had been included among those proscribed because of their Corinthian vases.'

[22] Grelle (1980), 352–9; Langlands (2006), 257–63; Langlands (2014), 119. On Vespasian's frugality, Gildenhard/Viglietti (2020), 84–5. The restraint of luxury and lust is indeed one of the virtues Suetonius appreciates most: Wallace-Hadrill (1983), 152. On Vespasian's attitude towards banquets, Vössing (2004), 310–11.

archetypical Manius Curius.[23] Despite his appreciation of Vespasian's sobriety, Suetonius is not able to value his care for the economy of the Empire, and labels it as 'lust for money' (16.1 *pecuniae cupiditas*), the sole vice he attributes to this emperor.

The case of Titus, Vespasian's privileged son, is of interest, too, because Suetonius reports the allegations of vices made against him—*saevitia, luxuria, libido*, and even the label *alius Nero*—but only as unconfirmed suspicions (*Tit.* 7.1 *suspecta*).[24] An admirer of the Flavian dynasty from its beginning, Suetonius himself does not allege these things, and in the same passage he emphasizes how Titus refuted all these charges with his irreproachable behaviour as a prince.[25]

An antithetical example is Caligula, and it is an interesting one: despite the fact that the only occurrence of *luxuria* refers to a dissolute woman, Cesonia, the emperor's mistress (*Cal.* 25.3, in association with *lascivia*), Gaius is remarkable for his waste of money, especially at banquets (*Cal.* 37.1):[26]

> Nepotatus sumptibus omnium prodigiorum ingenia superavit, commentus novum balnearum usum, portentosissima genera cibarum atque cenarum, ut calidis frigidisque unguentis lavaretur, pretiosissima margarita aceto liquefacta sorberet, convivis ex auro panes et obsonia apponeret, aut frugi hominem esse oportere dictitans aut Caesarem.
>
> His ingenuity in extravagant expenditure outdid that of all other prodigals ever; he invented a new kind of bath and the most outlandish varieties of food and drink-he used to bathe in hot and cold perfumed oil and would drink the most precious pearls dissolved in vinegar and offered his guests loaves of bread and savouries made out of gold. He used to remark that a man should either be frugal or a Caesar.

The luxury habits here are the same as those listed by Seneca and Pliny the Elder: expensive foods, immoderate use of cold and hot facilities, melted pearls (reminiscent of Mark Antony and Cleopatra). Suetonius, like Seneca before him, stresses the effort of reason (*ingenia, commentus*) in search for novelty (*superavit, novum…usum*) and excess (*prodigium, portentosissima, pretiosissima*), in addition to thermal baths, also mentions something new, namely golden bread and food. The latter turns the poorest and most basic of foods, bread, into a luxury item, and replaces the nutritive function of nourishment with a mere exhibition of luxury. The recollection of the myth of Midas is evident, the king who turned

[23] Above, 2.5.2; 4.7.

[24] Martinet (1981), 66–7; Tatum (2014), 172–3. On Titus' banquets, Vössing (2004), 311–12; 487; 503.

[25] Schulz (2019), 322–3.

[26] Dalby (2000), 13–16; Vössing (2004), 297–302; 324–6; 336–7; 378.82; 428–38; 486–7; 499; 514–18; 530.

everything into gold as a god's gift, and starved because of it. Caligula comments on these banquets with the sentence 'you should be either a frugal man, or a Caesar.' It is the only occurrence of *frugi* in Suetonius, which suggests that the sentence is reported verbatim; it implies the need for an emperor to be the opposite of frugal, i.e. *luxuriosus*.

Other emperors in Suetonius—Tiberius, Vitellius, and Nero—are indeed charged of *luxuria*, with Nero, unsurprisingly, taking the idea to its zenith.

As we have seen, Tiberius, exhibiting a fair amount of *Realpolitik*, refused to promulgate a sumptuary law (above, 2.9). Suetonius does not mention this, listing instead, without the slightest sign of admiration, some examples of frugality ascribed to him (*Tib.* 34.1),[27] from which we may infer, as also from his book on Vespasian, Suetonius' essential acceptance of the luxury of the times. Nevertheless, he does report an insulting letter against the emperor written by the Parthian king Artabanes, who reproaches Tiberius with all his vices, to the point that he suggests that the emperor ought to commit suicide (*Tib.* 66):[28]

> Quin et Artabani parthorum regis laceratus est litteris parricidia et caedes et ignaviam et luxuriam obicientis monentisque, ut voluntaria morte maximo iustissimoque civium odio quam primum satis faceret.
>
> Indeed, he was even attacked in a letter from Artabanes, the king of the Parthians, who accused him of parricide, murder, cowardice, and luxury and advised him to end his own life as soon as possible to appease the most intense and well-justified hatred felt by his citizens.

Luxuria is here linked not to lust, despite Tiberius' personal inclination towards this vice, but to laziness (*ignaviam*) and cruelty (*parricidia et caedes*). This makes sense, since the accusation comes from another ruler and thus takes into account which vices are more dangerous for an empire: indeed they have social consequences, while lust is a private thing. It also of interest that the critique comes from an Eastern absolute king, i.e. the embodiment of *luxuria* in historiographical commonplaces. Roman society is so degraded that even a Parthian king may accuse it of those same vices his people transmitted to the West.

The place of honour in Suetonius' narrative on *luxuria* is, of course, reserved for Nero.[29] In the book devoted to him, there are two occurrences of the term,

[27] Gunderson (2014), 142. On Tiberius' attitude towards banquets, Vössing (2004), 293–7; 374–7; 394–7; 427–8; 485–6; 497–9.

[28] Cf. Tac. *Ann.* 6.31.1.

[29] Cizek (1977), 126–9, stresses the fact that Nero represents Suetonius' most successful example of a *crescendo* in vices. As for Nero's *luxuria*, Heinz (1948), 68–70; Gildenhard/Viglietti (2020), 82–3; on its connection with *avaritia*, Schulz (2019), 290–1. On Nero's love for transgression, Sauron (2005); specifically on banquets, Dalby (2000), 10–12; Goddard (1994); Stein-Hölkeskamp (2002b); above, n. 22.

and one of *luxus*, while in the other books we find only one of *luxuria*. Suetonius lists with *luxuria* other vices—*petulantia*, *libido*, *avaritia*, and *crudelitas*—as those that seemed but childish fancies but that in fact turned out to be integral parts of Nero's nature (*Nero* 26.1):[30]

> Petulantiam, libidinem, luxuriam, avaritiam, crudelitatem sensim quidem primo et occulte et velut iuvenili errore exercuit, sed ut tunc quoque dubium nemini foret naturae illa vitia, non aetatis esse.
>
> At first the signs he showed of insolence, lust, luxury, greed, and cruelty were gradual and covert and could be put down to the errors of youth, but even then it was clear to all that these vices were due not to his age but to his nature.

Cassius Dio will also emphasize this, pointing out that Seneca and Burrus underestimated the young emperor's excesses and realized only too late that they were actual vices (61.4–5).

Naturae vitia: Nero's soul was corrupted by the start, and thus incurable. He is the only emperor about whom Suetonius says this. His narrative starts from juvenile mean habits, like riotous behaviour at night, and goes on to the 'increasing vices' (*Nero* 27.1 *invalescentibus vitiis*), among which he mentions night banquets,[31] boat feasts and orgies at Baias (maybe alluded to by Seneca in *EM* 51: above, 4.4), sexual promiscuity and wild erotic games (*Nero* 28–9), and insane expenses, comparable to Caligula's (*Nero* 30.1–3), seen especially in architectural luxury: the *domus aurea* (*Nero* 31.1–2)[32] and an open pool from Misenus to Avernus lake, watered by Baias' thermal spring (*Nero* 31.3).[33] This expenditure made him poor and therefore drove him greedily in search for taxes and rich people's assets.

Nero's house (*Nero* 31.1–2) is described as a sort of reproduction of the universe. It contained every kind of environment: sweet and salt water, forests, fields, pastures; everything was covered in gold or gemstones; the dining room's ceiling let roses and perfumes fall down, and, since it swivelled on its own axis, represented the switch from night to day and the heavenly orbits. Elements, earth zones, stars, orbits, daylight...every major phenomenon of the universe was reproduced there, showing how Nero was ruler of the whole world. This is not just luxury: it is arrogance, pride, limitlessness.

[30] This list is imitated in the fifth century by Orosius in his *Histories against Pagans* (7.7.1); cf. Lefebvre (2017), 83–4.

[31] Vössing (2004), 306–8; 326; 384–5; 439–56; 500–1; 520–2.

[32] Morford (1968) who stresses the distortion which political anti-Neronian propaganda made on the description of this palace; Voisin (1987); Beste (2011); Panella (2011); Viscogliosi (2011); La Rocca (2017); Lefebvre (2017), 122–38; Schulz (2019), 67–9 and 284–6. In general, on Nero's buildings, Beste/Hesberg (2013).

[33] Seneca may have alluded to this enterprise, too (above, 4.4). In general, on Nero's architectural luxury, Elsner (1994).

Suetonius shows Nero's pertinacity by discussing the fact that he did not give up any of his luxurious habits in spite of the uprisings in Spain and the consequent threat to his power (*Nero* 42.2), and that his health was very good, even though his life was full of excess (51):

> Fuit...valitudine prospera: nam qui luxuriae immoderatissimae esset, ter omnino per quattuordecim annos languit, atque ita ut neque vino neque consuetudine reliqua abstineret.
>
> His general health [*sc.* was] good-for despite his luxurious and most excessive way of life, he was only ill three times in fourteen years, and even then not so as to have to abstain from drinking or his other habits.

The superlative *immoderatissimae*, in its turn derived from the negation of measure (*in* + *moderatio*), is a *hapax* in Latin literature, and expresses Nero's life of excess. Nero's vice emerges in a list of physical attributes that are harmful to health and associated with shameless clothing habits,[34] and Suetonius almost admires the emperor's physical resistance. *Luxuria* evidently means more than banquet expenses, since Suetonius mentions wine and 'other habits' (*consuetudine reliqua*), which allude to food but also to sexual license, another cause of ill health. The passage just quoted comes right before the narrative of Nero's death (*Nero* 57.1–2), and so *luxuria* stays with Nero all his life, as opposed to cruelty, which seems to disappear along with his absolute power.

A last instance of *luxuria* is referred to Vitellius, one of the protagonists of the year 69, in which four emperors succeed one to each other (cf. below, 5.2.2). Vitellius is accused by Suetonius himself of cruelty (*saevitia*) and *luxuria* (*Vit.* 13.1).[35] In his case, this vice is expressed in a very specific way, namely gluttony:[36] the emperor had three or four banquets per day, and he did not eat all the delicacies listed by Pliny the Elder, but, as happens in Seneca's *EM* 95.27-8 (above, 4.3), he melted all of them together into a unique dish, created with foods brought from the farthest reaches of the Empire (*Vit.* 13.2). He only managed to keep up this lifestyle thanks to his habit of vomiting (13.1). All these details paint a picture not only of disgust but also of an immense waste of money: all this food was very expensive, and much of it was thrown away. Suetonius calls him a 'bottomless throat' (13.3 *profunda gula*...),[37] stressing once more Vitellius' disgusting habits and shamelessness by narrating that during the sacrifices he ate the victims' entrails, and in the taverns the leftover foods. This beastly habit, which shows a

[34] For which see above, 4.6. [35] Venini (1977), 129.
[36] Dalby (2000), 7–10; Vössing (2004), 326–7; 404–5; 502.
[37] This epithet is already in Seneca, *EM* 89.22 (above, 4.3), and is applied again to Vitellius in Suet. *Vit.* 7.1.

lack not only of decency but of human propriety altogether, is a prelude his heartless cruelty (*Vit.* 14).

5.2.2 The Mark of Degradation: *Luxuria* in Tacitus

The grave moralistic Tacitus frequently, especially in his *Annals*, quotes and criticizes luxury (*luxus*), less often *luxuria*. But a close reading of the passages shows that the meanings of these two terms overlap: *luxus* is also frequently connected with lust, excess, and a desire for pleasure. In my opinion, this happens for stylistic reasons: since the *Annals* are Tacitus' last work, in which the style is more solemn and refined, he decides to use the poetic primitive word *luxus* instead of the prosaic derivative *luxuria*.[38] There is no doubt, in any case, that he is old-fashioned in this regard:[39] no one would suspect that he was a contemporary and personal friend of Pliny the Younger. The loss of a part of Tacitus' work prevents us from fully comparing his treatments of the various emperors, as is possible in Suetonius' *Lives*, but there are some signs of Tacitus' moral view of the first century of the Empire,[40] which is rooted in the traditional idea of an opposition between virtuous moderation and immoral excess.[41]

Few recurrences of *luxuria* are to be found in Tacitus' essays. In the *Germania*, he says that 'our *luxuria*' (*Germ.* 45.5 *luxuria nostra*) gave a name to amber, which would have remained a waste product of the sea if it were not for the Germans. This passage, which conflicts with archaeological evidence,[42] also collides with Tacitus' presentation of Germans as similar to archaic Romans in their fierce and uncorrupted morality, as opposed to his own contemporaries who are so used to luxury and vice that it would be easy to beat them in a war. Similarly, in the *Agricola* Tacitus points out that the Germans made war for defending their homeland, while the Romans were pushed to do so by their *luxuria* (*Agr.* 15.4).[43] Certain other barbarians, such as the Thracians, are also criticized for their luxury (*Ann.* 4.48.1).

In the *Histories*, almost every occurrence of *luxus/luxuria* refers to an emperor (namely Otho and Vitellius) who is blamed for his similarity to Nero. Indeed, while cruelty is not specifically linked to any emperor, it seems that Nero is a touchstone of *luxuria*: every excessive banquet, immoderate lust and luxury, is

[38] Indeed Woodman/Martin (1996), 379 notes that Cicero, Livy, and both Senecas use *luxuria*, while Lucan, Silius, and Statius prefer *luxus*.

[39] Cf. Burgeon (2017).

[40] As for the parallels with the genre of satire, and especially with Juvenal, cf. Keane (2012), 412–20.

[41] Schulz (2019), 96–101. Cf. above, 1.3.

[42] Rives (1999), 318–20.

[43] Agricola himself is praised for keeping away from that vice (*Agr.* 6.4).

traced back to him as an archetype of vice.[44] Even his fall is ascribed to it, in the words of his successor Galba (*Hist.* 1.16.2):[45]

> Nero ... non Vindex[46] ... sed sua immanitas, sua luxuria cervicibus publicis depulerunt: neque erat adhuc damnati principis exemplum.
>
> It was not Vindex ... but his [*sc.* Nero's] own monstrous character, his own extravagance, that flung him from the neck of the people; yet never before had there been a precedent for condemning the emperor.

Immanitas is, in combination with *luxuria*, a novelty; it is linked with the idea of excess leading to extreme impiety (it comes from the negative prefix *in* and *manus*, 'good' [*OLD*, *s.v. manus*^{2}]). Nero has been ruined by his excessive behaviour, which made him noxious in the eyes of his people. Such a thing has never happened before, according to Tacitus.

A second peculiar trait is that Tacitus abandons the traditional explanation, typical in Roman historiographers, of moral and political decline as the result of a lack of fear of an external enemy and an excess of money and luxury from the East.[47] Instead, Tacitus favours a more realistic view, of increasing struggle for personal power (*potentiae cupido*) and correspondent carelessness for public interest (*Hist.* 2.38.1). The prejudice against Eastern weakness and indulgence, as well as its political application, do appear in Tacitus as well (e.g. *Ann.* 2.57.4),[48] but there is no theoretical explanation for decline comparable to that in Sallust or Livy. I venture to say that this happens because the Flavians, the sober and solid dynasty to which Tacitus owes his career (*Hist.* 1.1.3), made their whole fortune in the East: Vespasian was even pronounced emperor by the Eastern legions, and not in Rome. It would have been inopportune to ascribe to the East the spread of corruption and vice, given that the restoration of the principate after the bloody end of the Julio-Claudian dynasty and the year of civil disorder in which three emperors—Galba, Otho, and Vitellius—were elected and soon thereafter brutally killed, came from that region.

[44] And, as is well known, he is also to become an archetype of the tyrant in Western culture: Gwyn (1991).

[45] Kragelund (2000), 494–5; Schulz (2019), 96. This passage is imitated by Augustine in *Civ.* 5.229; cf. Lefebvre (2017), 66.

[46] Gaius Iulius Vindex was a Gallic nobleman, governor of the province of Gallia Lugdunensis, who rebelled against the emperor Nero between 67 and 68 CE. This episode contributed markedly to the end of Nero's reign.

[47] Harrison (2005), 297 on *Hist.* 2.38; cf. above, 1.4; 2.3; Koestermann (1973), 800–9. A topos that does appear in Tacitus is the degradation of an army if kept in inactivity (e.g. *Hist.* 2.7, where we find the only occurrence of the fifth-declension *luxuries*; 4.36; *Ann.* 1.16; 3.33.1–4, where the soldiers are negatively affected by the presence of women in the camps).

[48] Here, Gnaeus Piso blames Germanicus for oriental luxury, as he accepted some golden crowns from the king of the Nabataei. Cf. also *Ann.* 2.78.1.

From this dense narrative of civil and external wars emerge some characters marked by *luxuria*. The first is a paradoxical character, Licinius Mucianus, who plays a primary role in Vespasian's attainment of power but remains controversial. Tacitus describes him as follows (*Hist.* 1.10.2):

> Luxuria industria, comitate adrogantia, malis bonisque artibus mixtus; nimiae voluptates cum vacaret; quotiens expedierat, magnae virtutes. Palam laudares, secreta male audiebant.
>
> He displayed a mixture of luxury and industry, of affability and insolence, of good and wicked arts. His pleasures were extravagant if he was at leisure; whenever he took the field, he showed great virtues. You would have praised his public life; but his private life bore ill repute. (Trans. Moore 1956, here and below)

This portrait recalls Cicero's and Sallust's Catiline.[49] Tacitus' judgement of Mucianus is ambiguous, but this initial characterization outweighs his subsequent notable political and military enterprises. When compared to Vespasian, whose sole vice was greed, as in Suetonius, Mucianus is singled out for his magnificence and for his lifestyle which exceeded that of any private man (2.5.1), and he is later considered similar to Vitellius' worst courtesans (2.95.3).

Then comes Otho, who emulates Nero's luxury (1.13.3):

> Namque Otho pueritiam incuriose, adulescentiam petulanter egerat, gratus Neroni aemulatione luxus.
>
> For Otho has spent his boyhood in heedlessness, his early manhood under no restraint. He had found favour in Nero's eyes by imitating his extravagance.

This *luxus* extends to lust. Nero entrusted Otho with his mistress Poppaea, but then Otho apparently fell in love with her, and so was sent to Lusitania.[50] And Plutarch describes him with three terms that are all possible equivalents of *luxuria*: *tryphe*, *philedonia*, *asotia* (Plut. *Galba* 19.2–3).[51] The emulation goes so far that, after his election to the principate, common people and soldiers call him 'Nero Otho' (*Hist.* 1.78.2). As a private man he is still classified among those who, when requested by Galba to return Nero's luxurious gifts, have already been

[49] Cic. *Cael.* 12: *erant apud illum inlecebrae lubidinum multae; erant etiam industriae quidam stimuli ac laboris.... Neque ego umquam fuisse tale monstrum in terris ullum puto, tam ex contrariis diversisque et inter se pugnantibus naturae studiis cupiditatibusque conflatum.* Cf. Sall. *Cat.* 5.1–8.

[50] The affair is mentioned in *Ann.* 13.45.3. On the different versions of this episode, Audano (2021), 154–9.

[51] Plut. *Galba* 19.2: 'Marcus Otho, now, was a man of good lineage, but from his very childhood corrupted by luxury and the pursuit of pleasure (*tryphe*, *philedonia*) as few Romans were... 3. For because of Otho's lavish prodigality (*asotia*) Nero made an intimate friend of him, and was well pleased to be rallied by him often for parsimony and meanness.' (Trans. Perrin 1926). On Otho's banquets, Vössing (2004), 309.

spoiled by vice (1.20.1). His extravagance was indeed such as would have burdened an emperor (1.21.1 *luxuria etiam principi onerosa, inopia vix privato toleranda*).[52] This dissolute way of life, which also extended to his followers, caused a combination of physical weakness and psychological ambition (1.22.1):

> Non erat Othonis mollis et corpori similis animus, et intimi libertorum servorumque, corruptius quam in privata domo habiti, aulam Neronis et luxus, adulteria matrimonia ceterasque regnorum libidines avido talium, si auderet, ut sua ostentantes, quiescenti ut aliena exprobrarent.
>
> Otho's mind was not effeminate like his body. His intimate freedmen and slaves, who had more licence than prevails in private houses, constantly held before his eager eyes Nero's luxurious court, his adulteries, his many marriages, and other royal vices, exhibiting them as his own if he only dared to take them, but taunting him with them as the privilege of others if he did not act.

Nero's mixture of luxury and lust, stressed by the poetic use of the plural of *luxus*,[53] is not only pursued by Otho but also suggested by others, for whom Nero's behaviour and Imperial rule go together.[54] On the opposite political side, Piso, designated as Galba's successor, criticizes Otho precisely for considering the Empire as the fulfilment of his quest for pleasure and for masking *luxuria* as liberality (1.30.1). Indeed, Piso's chopped off head will be what Otho will soon contemplate with insatiable eyes (1.44.1).

Freed from Galba and Piso, the scene is immediately refilled by Vitellius; and Tacitus comments (1.50.1):

> Tum duos omnium mortalium impudicitia ignavia luxuria deterrimos velut ad perdendum imperium fataliter electos... vulgus quoque palam maerere.
>
> Then the thought that two men, the worst in the world for their shamelessness, indolence, and profligacy, had been apparently chosen by fate to ruin the empire, caused open grief... even to the common people.

Otho and Vitellius, seen as fatal disgraces for the Roman empire, are here coupled through their vices: lust, laziness, and *luxuria*. All these, trapping men in a chain of banquets, pleasures, and delicacies, prevent them from properly ruling the Empire, but Vitellius, too, seems to identify the supreme power with excessive luxury and especially banquets (1.62.2), while Otho at least dissimulates his vices under a veneer of integrity (1.71.1). A further comparison is in favour of Vitellius (2.31.1):

[52] Again we may spot a parallel with Catiline (Sall. *Cat.* 5.7).
[53] Also in *Ann.* 12.12.3; 13.20.1; cf. Goelzer (1920), 52.
[54] As for the connection between kingship and luxury, see below; *Ann.* 2.4.3.

> Minus Vitellii ignavae voluptates quam Othonis flagrantissimae libidines timebantur... Vitellius ventre et gula sibi inhonestus, Otho luxu saevitia audacia rei publicae exitiosior ducebatur.
>
> The indolent pleasures of Vitellius were less feared than the fiery passions of Otho... the sensuality and gluttony of Vitellius were regarded as disgracing him alone; Otho's luxury, cruelty and daring seemed more dangerous to the state.

Here, Vitellius' gluttony is considered less dangerous, because it is private, while Otho's luxury and cruelty affect the Empire. Nevertheless, as Tacitus anticipates in this same passage, the end of the conflict would have reversed this judgement.

Vitellius' banquets (*epularum foeda et inexplebilis libido*) are criticized for their huge expenses, due to exotic foods and wine, and for the negative example given to the soldiers, who get used to pleasures and begin to despise their leader (2.62.1).[55] The insatiability (*inexplebilis*) that characterizes the emperor's vice shows that it is incurable.[56] The emulation of Nero is, again, explicitly pursued (2.71.1):[57]

> Namque et Neronem ipsum Vitellius admiratione celebrabat, sectari cantantem solitum, non necessitate... sed luxu et saginae mancipatus emptusque.
>
> For Vitellius cherished great admiration for Nero himself, whom he had been in the habit of accompanying on his singing tours, not under compulsion... but because he was the slave and chattel of luxury and gluttony.

Here emerges a second key issue of *luxuria*, the enslavement of one's rationality and dignity (*mancipatus*, *emptus*; cf. above, 4.1). Despite the widespread knowledge of his vices, Vitellius tries to dissimulate them in his speeches (2.90.1). When his political situation deteriorates, he lies in morbid inactivity, soothing his anxieties with luxury (3.36.1; cf. 3.55.2). Vitellius seems to retrace Otho's path, with Nero as a model. And this, of course, leads him to self-destruction.

The ruin is not limited to the Emperor and his circle, but affects the Empire itself, continuing through even the most extreme circumstance: the fight against Vespasian gets to the point that in Rome there exist the cruellest battle and the most dissolute lust side by side (3.83.2):[58]

> Saeva ac deformis urbe tota facies:... quantum in luxurioso otio libidinum, quidquid in acerbissima captivitate scelerum, prorsus ut eandem civitatem et furere crederes et lascivire... inhumana securitas et ne minimo quidem temporis voluptates intermissae.

[55] Cf. *Hist.* 2.76.5; Vössing (2004), 309–10.
[56] Cf. *Hist.* 2.95.2–3.
[57] Gildenhard/Viglietti (2020), 83.
[58] Schulz (2019), 150.

> Horrible and hideous sights were to be seen everywhere in the city…There were all the debauchery and passion that obtain in a dissolute peace, every crime that can be committed in the most savage conquest, so that men might well have believed that the city was at once mad with race and drunk with pleasure.… men showed inhuman indifference and never relaxed their pleasures for a single moment.

This horrible scene reflects the highest level of moral perversion, when rationality is absent and every vice, even if contrary to another, is mixed together: *furere*, 'to rage', expresses the full degree of anger, that of insane frenzy, and *lascivire*, 'to lust', conveys the full degree of licentiousness, lust, and laziness. Two opposite habits coexist and cooperate in the destruction of Rome's society and dignity. The same word, *facies*, 'appearance' but also 'face', seems to personify the city, as its inhabitants are unnamed and unidentified: not coincidentally, their irrational confidence is labelled as 'inhuman' (*inhumana*).

As it is well known, even if Tacitus here describes events which happened before those narrated in the *Historiae*, the *Annales* have been written afterwards, so they represent the last stage of the historiographer's thought. In this work, luxury may be a way to ruin someone, inducing him to take up vice and ambitions (as the senator Firmius Cato did with his friend Libo Drusus, *Ann.* 2.27.1), or it is used, as happens frequently in Roman history, in political propaganda, or to characterize someone, such as when Sallustius Crispus, descendant of the historiographer, is compared to Maecenas for his wealth and political influence.[59]

As in all extant Roman historiographers, luxury is not attested regarding Augustus, but only some of his courtesans (1.10.5). Tiberius, whose letter against sumptuary law is still not divorced from moral concerns,[60] sends his son Drusus to Illyricum in order to correct his inclination towards pleasure (2.44.1: *urbano luxu lascivientem*, 'living a reckless life of urban luxuriousness'), which the Roman noblemen appreciate (3.37.1).[61] His senators, who are still nostalgic for the *lex Oppia*, discuss whether the natural tendency of women to luxury is more dangerous if they follow their husbands to military camps (3.33.2) or stay alone in Rome (3.34.5).[62] The senators upset the emperor because they bother him with futile

[59] *Ann.* 3.30.3 *Maecenatem aemulatus…diversus a veterum instituto per cultum et munditias copiaque et adfluentia luxu propior.* Cf. Woodman/Martin (1996), 269–72. *Luxu* as a dative is a Sallustian feature (*Iug.* 6.1). Similar habits are reported for Cotta under Tiberius (Tac. *Ann.* 6.7.1), and for Sextus Papinius, also under Tiberius, who committed suicide to escape the shame (6.49.1–2); Aurelius Cotta and Haterius Antoninus are supported by Nero despite their dramatic prodigality (13.34.1); other examples of profligacy are Tigellinus, for his banquets (15.37.1–4), Scaevinus, one of the conspirators (15.49.3). Clodius Quirinalis, head of the navy in Ravenna, was charged with *luxuria saevitiaque* (13.30.1), because he ruled Italy as if it were a humble province, and committed suicide to prevent the conviction.

[60] Above, 2.9.

[61] Woodman/Martin (1996), 316, compare Sulla in Sall. *Iug.* 95.3.

[62] Woodman/Martin (1996), 293–4 and 306.

questions; he himself, once retired in Capri, wastes away in immoral leisure (4.67.3):[63]

> Quanto intentus olim publicas ad curas, tanto occultior in luxus et malum otium resolutus.
>
> His former attentiveness to public concerns contrasting with his more concealed relaxing into luxuriousness and evil inactivity.
>
> (Trans. Woodman 2004, here and below)

Tacitus credits Tiberius with some merit in ruling the Empire, while considering his retirement as an abandonment of his duties. A few chapters later, after quoting the famous letter in which the Emperor admits his inability to do or decide anything, Tacitus comments (6.6.2):

> Neque frustra praestantissimus sapientiae firmare solitus est, si recludantur tyrannorum mentes, posse aspici laniatus et ictus, quando ut corpora verberibus, ita saevitia libidine malis consultis animus dilaceretur. Quippe Tiberius non fortuna, non solitudines protegebant, quin tormenta pectoris suasque ipse poenas fateretur.
>
> Not without reason did the most outstanding man of wisdom customarily affirm that, if the minds of tyrants could be opened up, mutilations and blows would be visible, since, just as bodies were mauled by lashings, so was the spirit by savagery, lust, and evil decisions. In Tiberius' case neither his fortune nor his solitude protected him from admitting the tortures of his soul and his own punishments.

The reference is, of course, to Plato and his famous description of a tyrannical soul and its sufferings; it is debated whether the reference is to a passage of the *Republic* (9.579d–e) or *Gorgias* (524e–525a).[64] The image of *tormenta* also recalls some passages by Seneca, who uses the same word (above, 4.1).

A more obvious example of the vice in Tacitus is Messalina, Claudius' dissolute first wife, whom Tacitus calls *non alias solutior luxu*, 'never more dissolute in her

[63] Woodman (2018), 309–11. On this topic cf. Blänsdorf (1996).

[64] See Woodman (2017), 113, who also compares Sen. *EM* 97.15, for a *status quaestionis*. The emphasis on psychological torture is more evident in *Gorg.* 524e–525a: 'Rhadamanthus ... surveys the soul of each ... often when he has laid hold of the Great King or some other king ... he perceives the utter unhealthiness of his soul, striped all over with the scourge, and a mass of wounds, the work of perjuries and injustice; 525a. where every act has left its smirch upon his soul, where all is awry through falsehood and imposture, and nothing straight because of a nurture that knew not truth: or, as the result of an unbridled course of fastidiousness, insolence, and incontinence, he finds the soul full fraught with disproportion and ugliness.' (Trans. Lamb 1967). That this is a reference to Plato is supported by a passage from Apuleius' *De Platone et eius dogmate*, where the author ascribes to Plato the idea that *tyrannidis genus ex luxuriosa et plena libidinis vita, quae ex infinitis et diversis et illicitis voluptatibus conflata mente tota dominatur* (Apul. *Pl.* 2.15.241–2). As for the typical figure of the tyrant in Tacitus and his moral descriptions, Dunkle (1971), 17–20; Galtier (2011), 183–91. Cf. also above, 2.9.

luxuriousness' (*Ann.* 11.31.2 cf. above, 2.7.2), in reference to her organizing a sort of private bacchanal with her new husband Silius. In this passage, Tacitus clearly implies with this word much more than the Republican meaning of 'luxury'. Later, Vitellius supports the incestuous marriage of Claudius and Agrippina with a paradoxical argument: indeed, the emperor would have needed to officialize his affair, because he was *non luxui aut voluptatibus adsuefactus*, 'unaccustomed... to luxuriousness or pleasures' (12.5.3).

Atte, the freedwoman who becomes Nero's lover and confidante, together with Otho and the freedman Claudius Senecio *penitus inrepserat per luxum et ambigua secreta*, 'had crept his way in thoroughly by the techniques of luxuriousness and ambiguous secrecy' (13.12.2). In this passage, *luxus* definitely indicates lust,[65] and is now becoming interchangeable with *libido*. The girl is tolerated because Nero's senior friends (probably Seneca and Burrus) thought she might satisfy the prince's lust (*cupido*) and keep him away from noblewomen. Again, *inritamenta luxui*, 'spurs to luxuriousness' (14.15.2),[66] is used for the brothels and taverns by the artificial lake Augustus built for the naumachie. Another luxury water banquet is ascribed to Nero's *factotum* Tigellinus (15.37.1–4). Nero is passionate for extravagance (*nimia luxus cupido*) in his restless search for new pleasure, which leads him to impiety (14.22.4). A further indication of this is, as in Suetonius, the *Domus aurea*: according to Tacitus, the most remarkable thing about this house was the reproduction of natural environments inside (15.42.1–2).[67]

Gaius Piso, the head of the conspiracy against Nero and his would-be successor, is also not free from *luxus*, but in his case it is justified as suitable for the times: a severe and sober emperor would never have been appreciated (15.48.2):[68]

> Is Calpurnio genere ortus ac multas insignesque familias paterna nobilitate complexus, claro apud vulgum rumore erat per virtutem aut species virtutibus similis. 3. Namque facundiam tuendis civibus exercebat, largitionem adversum amicos, et ignotis quoque comi sermone et congressu; aderant etiam fortuita, corpus procerum, decora facies: sed procul gravitas morum aut voluptatum parsimonia; levitati ac magnificentiae et aliquando luxu indulgebat, idque pluribus probabatur qui in tanta vitiorum dulcedine summum imperium non restrictum nec perseverum volunt.
>
> Born of Calpurnian lineage and incorporating through his father's nobility many distinguished families, he enjoyed a brilliant reputation among the public for his virtue—or displays which resembled virtues. 3. He employed his fluency for the protection of citizens, and lavishness toward his friends; and with strangers too

[65] We find the same sexual meaning in *Ann.* 13.20 (where Paris the freedman turns on Nero's lust).

[66] *Inritamenta* with genitive referring to vices is quite frequent in Tacitus (e.g. *Hist.* 1.88; 2.62; *Ann.* 3.9), and also appears once each in Valerius Maximus (2.6.1) and Seneca (*EM* 51.5, above, 4.4).

[67] Ash (2018), 193–4.

[68] Ash (2018), 223–4.

> he was affable in conversation and encounter. He also had the chance advantages of a lofty physique and a handsome appearance. But gravity of behavior and frugality in pleasures were alien to him: he indulged in levity, magnificence, and sometimes luxuriousness, and that earned him the approval of the numerous persons who, given the sweetness of the vices surrounding them, do not wish the supreme command to be either restrictive or oversevere.

Largitio, levitas, magnificentia: three substantially positive qualities balance that inclination to luxury (*aliquando luxu*) that accords with the general 'sweetness of vices' (*vitiorum dulcedo*) of the times. *Perseverus* is an intensified version of the already hard *severus*, 'rigid', while *restrictus* is a derivative of the verb usually applied to the limitation of luxury, *restringo*, 'to limit'.

Luxuria makes its last appearance in Tacitus' work in *Ann.* 16.3.1,[69] in the context of the fictitious legend of a cave in Africa filled with gold and precious stones. Fortune mocked Nero, says Tacitus (16.1.1 *inlusit...Neroni fortuna*), and so the waste of public money continued onward to financial ruin.

There is also Petronius, Nero's master of luxury, *erudito luxu*, 'a man of educated luxuriousness' (16.18.1), whom Tacitus seems to admire even more than Seneca.

In sum, we may say that Tacitus confirms Nero's pre-eminence in *luxuria* among the emperors, even more so than is the case in Suetonius: Nero embodies everything an emperor should *not* be, and acts as a negative model for Otho and Vitellius. Tacitus avoids general speeches about luxury, except in the context of sumptuary laws; he is the first to use *luxus* synonymously with *luxuria*, including the meaning of lust, and he probably does so for stylistic reasons. There are no theoretical digressions; there is only the admission of an embedded habit, and the view that it is a threat to the empire when it wastes public funding and compromises the emperor's dignity.

In subsequent Roman historiography, Nero remains an archetype of vice: he is cited, along with his copycats Otho and Vitellius, as a model for the most *luxuriosus* of all the emperors in the *Historia Augusta*, Heliogabalus.[70] He embodies all the key features of this vice: luxurious clothes and jewellery, banquets, and sexual promiscuity.

[69] Cf. Lefebvre (2017), 257.

[70] *SHA*, *Heliogab.* 18.4 'Concerning his life many filthy anecdotes (*obscena*) have been put into writing, but since they are not worthy of being recorded, I have thought I ought to relate only such deeds as illustrate his extravagance (*luxuria*). Some of these, it is said, were done before he ascended the throne, others after he was made emperor; for he himself declared that his models were Apicius among commoners and, among emperors, Otho and Vitellius.' (Trans. Magie 1980). As for Apicius, above, 3.2.2; 4.6. See Neri (1999), 219–25 and 230–2. Other emperors guilty of *luxuria* in the *HA* are Helius Verus, Gallienus, and Carinus: Haehling (1991); Neri (1999), 234–6.

5.3 *Luxuria* Turning into Lust: Apuleius

The final transformation of *luxuria* into lust begins in Africa with Apuleius, the fascinating orator devoted to Isis. It is indeed quite common that provinces show a freer use of language than the motherland: it is easier for the former to ignore norms crystallized in centuries of literature. I do not wish to impute any specific feature to *Africitas* here, but only to suggest that a provincial, imbued with Greek language and literature and living in a country with plenty of different cultural stimuli, may use Latin with a more original attitude than his colleagues in Rome, and attribute 'new meanings to existing words'.[71] Apuleius is many things: an orator, a philosopher, perhaps a magician, an initiate in the mysteries of Isis—and also an experimenter in the Latin language.

As a philosopher, he provides a definition of *luxuria*, linked as usual to avarice and prodigiousness (*Pl.* 2.4.226–7):[72]

> Cupiditatibus luxuria, id est appetitus applicat voluptatum 227. et desideriorum ad fruendum potiendumque haustus inexplebiles. Ex hac manat avaritia atque lascivia, quarum altera liberalitatem coercet, altera immoderatius fundendo patrimonia prodigit facultates.
>
> Plato adds to this list of desires luxury, that is, appetites 227. for pleasures and desires in order to enjoy and possess insatiable thirsts. From this place avarice and prodigiousness flow, of which the former restrains generosity; the latter, by more immediately wasting one's inheritance, squanders opportunities.
>
> (Trans. Fowler 2016, here and below)

The link among *luxuria*, desires (2.4.227 *cupiditatibus*, *desideriorum*), and pleasures (*voluptatum*) is evident, and so is *luxuria*'s link to insatiability (*inexplebiles*), represented as endless thirst (*haustus*), like an infernal punishment.[73] Apuleius also locates this vice in the worst part of the human soul, the one addicted to desires (*Pl.* 1.13.207):[74]

> Postremam mentis portionem, infernas abdominis sedes tenere ut popinas quasdam et latrinarum latebras, deversoria nequitiae atque luxuriae.
>
> And, last, desire and longing, the last part of the soul, hold the lowest seats of the belly and are, just like certain taverns and secret corners of the bathhouses, the storehouses of wickedness and wanton excess.

[71] Cf. Mattiacci (2014), 102.

[72] Fowler (2016), 192–3. On the authenticity of this work, Dal Chiele (2016), 23–7.

[73] Cf. above, 4.3 (Seneca).

[74] For the platonic tripartition of the soul in Apuleius, Hijmans (1987), esp. 452–3; Dal Chiele (2016), 139–42. Specific on this passage, Fowler (2016), 176.

Apuleius here chooses to imitate Seneca's expression *deversorium luxuriae*, which the latter had used for Baias (*EM* 51.3: above, 4.4), to define this humble part of the soul. The connection between Plato's theory of an irrational part of the soul, enslaved to earthly desires, and Roman writers' description of persons affected by *luxuria* is undeniable, despite the differences between Stoic monism and Platonic pluralism of the soul.[75]

As an orator of the Second Sophistic, Apuleius does not use the word *luxuria*—contrary to the case in Latin Declamations, for example—with the exception of two contrapositions, between philosophers and *luxuriosi* (*Apol.* 27, with reference to the search for rare fish),[76] and virtue and *luxuria* (*Flor.* 3.12, with reference to Apollo's skills).[77] It is worth noting that here *luxuria* stands for 'vice' in general, in opposition to such categories as virtue and philosophy, as also is the case more than once in Seneca.[78] Apuleius in the *Apologia* rebukes the charge of poverty (*paupertas*), emphasizing that frugality is a philosophical virtue and that it prevents luxury and 'gastronomic and sexual pleasures' (*Apol.* 18 *delicias ventris et inguinum*, trans. Hunink (2001a)). In this speech, he evidently struggles to appear as an authentic and serious philosopher.

But it is as a novelist that Apuleius shows most clearly his innovative use of the term *luxuria*. First, from a stylistic point of view, he is the only one, apart from Cicero, who alternates the forms of the first with those of the fifth conjugation; he also ignores the word *luxus*.[79] *Luxuries* seems to be preferred in 'higher' contexts, such as when referring to Cupid, and in ironic ones, e.g. when Lucius is called a donkey. In general, most occurrences of the term involve Cupid, and this already points to an erotic meaning of this word. Elsewhere, *luxuria* describes the virtuous Plotina, who avoids urban pleasures (*Met.* 7.6),[80] a malicious wind that sticks the gown to a girl's body (*Met.* 10.31), and the donkey's erotic (*Met.* 7.23 *luxuriem lasciviamque*)[81]—of course in this case it could not be a chance of spending money. Finally, it has to be noted that we find several recurrences of *libido* in the novel, yet this term is never referred to Psyche or Cupid, but to trivial, vulgar, or illegitimate forms of sexual intercourses.[82]

[75] Above, 1.2 For the tyrannical soul as victim of *luxuria*, above, 5.2.2.

[76] A typical luxury food, as we have seen (above, 2.5.2); cf. Costantini (2019), 83–7. The fish have strange names, which identify male and female genitals: *veretilla* and *virginal* (*Apol.* 34); Costantini (2019), 112–19.

[77] Cf. Hunink (2001b), 77. For the dispute between Marsyas and Apollo in this passage, and its reading in the light of Middle Platonism, Fletcher (2014), 229–34. There is also an occurrence of *luxus* as 'luxated' (*Flor.* 16.20), while in *De deo Socratis* 23 Apuleius quotes, in reference to Socrates, the passage about the war horse from Virgil's *Georgics* already quoted by Seneca (above, 4.7).

[78] Above, 4.1.

[79] Except once, where the protagonist describes himself: *in luxum nepotalem... pererro* (2.2).

[80] This is the elegiac meaning of the term: above, 2.4.3. On Plotina's character (and her possible political implications), Müller-Reineke (2008).

[81] Puccini-Delbey (2003), 107–8.

[82] See below. Cf. *Met.* 2.10; 2.11; 2.17; 3.14; 3.20 (Photides and Lucius); 6.22 (Jupiter on Cupid's effects on him); 8.3; 9.24; 10.4; 10.5 (illegitimate relationships); 7.21; 7.23; 10.19; 10.21; 10.22

At the very beginning of his presentation, Cupid is described by Pan, who addresses Psyche crying about her husband's disappearance, as a 'lascivious boy' (*Met.* 5.25):

> Hircuosus deus... Psychen... permulcet verbis lenientibus: '... Luctum desine et pone maerorem, precibusque potius Cupidinem deorum maxime percole, et utpote adulescentem delicatum luxuriosumque blandis obsequiis promerere.'
>
> The he-goat divinity... soothed her [*sc.* Psyche] with comforting words: 'Stop grieving and mourning, and instead pray to Cupid and give him your full devotion, because he's the greatest god there is. He's a spoiled, self-indulgent kid, but do whatever he wants and get on his good side, and eventually he'll give you credit.' (Trans. Ruden 2012, here and below)

Pan is the deity of fertility and sexual exuberance, so we may assume an erotic subtext for those 'comforting words' (*verbis lenientibus*), and for the whole sentence in general; he calls Cupid 'the greatest God of all', an epithet usually reserved for Jupiter, and also a young, delicate boy. This double definition seems to represent the double meaning of the novel itself, as a joke (cf. 1.1) and as a story of spiritual elevation. *Luxuriosus*, here as often connected with *delicatus*, cannot refer to spending money on banquets or luxury, but its same reference to the deity of sexual desire implies an erotic nuance.

Luxuria is then mentioned by the very goddess of love, Venus, along with its new competitor, which is no longer frugality (*frugalitas*) but chastity (*sobrietas*). The scene resembles a prosecution *de moribus* against her son (5.30):

> 'Sed nunc inrisui habita quid agam? Quo me conferam? Quibus modis stelionem istum cohibeam? Petamne auxilium ab inimica mea Sobrietate, quam propter huius ipsius luxuriam offendi saepius? At rusticae squalentisque feminae colloquim prorsus horresco.'
>
> 'I'm some kind of a joke now, so what recourse do I have? How do I get control of this snake in the grass? Should I look for help from my rival, Sobriety? I don't know how many times I've gotten the better of her, and it was always when my son here was running wild. I absolutely shudder at the thought of dealing with this woman from the sticks, who doesn't know the first thing about taking care of her looks.'

Imitating the great oratorical (and theatrical) commonplaces on the topic *quid agam?*, Venus calls a personified Chastity (*Sobrietas*) her enemy (*inimica*): she is

(Lucius as a donkey). More than once, *libido* is coupled with *voluptas* or *lascivia* (e.g. 2.17). Only few recurrences refer to excessive desires other than sexual: 2.22 (the witches' perversions); 5.27 (the envy of Psyche's sister).

rough and shabby (*rusticae squalentisque*), that is, the opposite of her own delicate and refined appearance. Cupid's *luxuria* is the very means by which he offended Chastity. It is evidently a mixture of luxury and sexual pleasures, which Venus seems to consider from a moralistic point of view, despite her distaste for sobriety.[83] Indeed, the goddess of love plays the role of a severe parent who tries to teach morality to his reluctant son, which was typical of ancient comedy and of imperial declamation.[84]

After Venus' outburst, Ceres and Juno try to calm her (5.31):

> 'Quid tale, domina, deliquit tuus filius, ut animo pervicaci voluptates illius impugnes, et quam ille diligit tu quoque perdere gestias?...Mater autem es et praeterea cordata mulier, filii tui lusus semper explorabis curiose, et in eo luxuriem culpabis et amores revinces, et tuas artes tuasque delicias in formoso filio reprehendes? Quis autem te deum, quis hominum patietur passim cupidines populis disseminantem, cum tuae domus amores amare coerceas et vitiorum muliebrium publicam praecludas officinam?'
>
> 'What great harm has your boy done, lady? Why are you so stubborn about this? It's as if you were waging war on his good times. You're even trying to destroy the woman he loves!...Be that as it may, you're his mother, and an intelligent woman besides. Are you going to go on like this endlessly, reconnoitering your son's amusements, censuring his friskiness, running roughshod over him if he has a love affair-and condemning your own expertise and your own pleasures when it comes to your gorgeous son? There's not one of the gods, or a single mortal, who would put up with your scattering passion over every nation if you undertake this unlovely repression of love in your own home and bar up what until now has been a factory supplying naughtiness for women at large.'

The goddesses are themselves linked to fertility, as a sort of female correspondence of Pan, Ceres being devoted to fields and agriculture, Juno to women as birth-givers. In this respect, they represent a manifestation of Venus, the goddess of love as a generative force of the universe: they cannot underestimate these prerogatives, even if the author, who adds a touch of irony to every scene, says that they are in fear of Cupid's vengeance. The goddesses list all terms related to *luxuria* and love: pleasure (*voluptas*), love (*diligit*, *amores* [twice], *amare*), pleasures (*delicias*), desire (*cupidines*, whose etymology traces back to Cupid); *luxuria* itself is coupled with love. All these are women's vices (*vitiorum muliebrium*), but there is no moral judgement in this: on the contrary, Ceres and Juno show their

[83] Venus in the novel seems to vacillate between her chaste and heavenly manifestation (*Venus caelites*) on the one side, and her lascivious and erotic one (*Venus vulgaris*) on the other, in accordance with the Platonic myth (*Symp.* 180c–181e), which is reported in Apul. *Apol.* 12.

[84] Cf. above, 2.1.1 (Plautus); 2.7.1 (Seneca the Elder).

appreciation for Venus' (and Cupid's) prerogatives and their pleasant implications for women, emphasizing Venus' inconsistency in blaming actions that she herself inspires.

Later in the story, while Psyche and Cupid suffer Venus' vengeance, Psyche having to pass some tests and Cupid being locked in his mother's house, the lovers happen to spend the night in the same place, but in separate rooms; the reason for Cupid's punishment is expressed as follows (6.11):

> Partim ne petulanti luxurie vulnus gravaret, partim ne cum sua cupita conveniret.
>
> In part to keep him from indulging his lust and worsening his wound, in part to bar him from any encounter with the object of his desire.

The wound here is twofold: it is physical, due to the boiling oil of the lamp with which Psyche accidentally burnt Cupid's shoulder, and emotional, due to Cupid's love for her. *Luxuries* here represents the manifestation of his desire to scratch both wounds, worsening the situation. The past participle *cupita*, which is rare and mostly archaic, refers again to Cupid's etymological connection with desire.[85]

The *Deus ex machina* in this story is Jupiter himself, who suggests an official marriage, including the divinization of the wife, to put a brake to Cupid's juvenal exuberance (6.23):[86]

> 'Dei conscripti Musarum albo, adolescentem istum quod manibus meis alumnatus sim profecto scitis omnes. Cuius primae iuventutis caloratos impetus freno quodam coercendos existimavi; sat est cotidianis cum fabulis ob adulteria cunctasque corruptelas infamatum. Tollenda est omnis occasio et luxuria puerilis nuptialibus pedicis alliganda. Puellam elegit et virginitate privavit: teneat, possideat, amplexus Psychen semper suis amoribus perfruatur.'
>
> 'Divine senate, duly enrolled in the Muses' register, I'm sure you're all acquainted with this young man, who was reared under my guardianship. His early youth has given rise to certain overheated, impetuous exploits, and I've decided to put a specific bit between his teeth and rein him in. We've had enough scandal, with these daily stories of his adulteries, seductions, corruptions, etc. We must eliminate any opportunity for more and bind his boyish friskiness with the hobbles of matrimony. He's chosen a girl and made himself free of her virginity. Let him have, hold, and wrap himself around Psyche, and enjoy her as his beloved for all time.'

[85] Puccini-Delbey (2003), 101; 38–9 on the lexical family of *cupido* in the *Metamorphoses*.

[86] Haskins (2014), 263–4. She translates *luxuria* as 'self-indulgency'. On Jupiter's speech and the motif of the Council of Gods, Harrison (2013), 247–50. On Cupid as a boy growing up, Morwood (2010).

Cupid's behaviour is labelled *luxuria puerilis*, and must be bound (*alliganda*): his is the same aim as Venus', who as we have seen chained her son because of it, but Jupiter finds a more reasonable and lasting solution to the problem. Furthermore, every moralistic writer in Rome says that *luxuria* has to be restrained and limited. Jupiter acts like every wise father with a reckless son: he asks him to marry a girl whose virginity he has taken.

While in Apuleius' oratorical and philosophical works *luxuria* has a quite traditional meaning, in the novel—a freer literary genre—it never refers to banquets or excessive expenses, but to love's pleasures. Interestingly, *libido*, the term that Valerius Maximus uses synonymously with *luxuria*,[87] is rare in Apuleius, and it refers there to a violent, uncontrollable sexual desire,[88] such as that of Psyche's sister, who is envious of her fortune (*Met.* 5.27), and that of Jupiter, inspired by Cupid, in his adulteries (6.22).[89] It seems that *libido* is sexual desire that goes against nature—through a violation of marriage (Jupiter) or innate boundaries (the intercourse between the donkey and a girl, 7.21)—while *luxuria* is the search for a pleasure legitimized by youth and/or marriage. In the case of youth it is not a vice, but more of a juvenile and forgivable fancy. Yet the semantic turn from the economic to the erotic sphere is relevant, and Christian culture will embrace it, and construct on it one of its most hated and feared capital sins.

5.4 An Overview of Tertullian (and Augustine): *Luxuria* against *Pudicitia*

Among the Latin Church Fathers of the first centuries, Tertullian (*c.* 155–230 CE), and Augustine (354–430 CE), both born in Africa, make relevant considerations on *luxuria*. Tertullian shares with Apuleius the same 'Asian' rhetorical background,[90] which strives for new ways to utter old concepts, but also a general overview of the Church Fathers reveals that they offer interesting considerations on *luxuria*. In some of their works we find several occurrences of *luxuria* as lust, while in others it has the traditional reference points of greed and expenses.

Some common features may be emphasized: lust and luxury are no longer conjoined, so we find *luxuria* either with *avaritia* or with *libido* (Tertullian)[91] or *fornicatio* (Augustine),[92] which in Christian Latin tends to replace the classical term *libido* (and initially stands for the capital sin of lust);[93] sometimes *luxuria* is

[87] Above, 2.5.1. [88] Above, n. 82; Puccini-Delbey (2003), 39–41.

[89] Puccini-Delbey (2003), 101–2.

[90] Mattiacci (2014), 90. Of course, between Apuleius and Christianity, the values differ (cf. Bradley (2012), 104–25).

[91] Tert. *Nat.* 1.5.16 (*avaritia*); 1.10.28 and 1.16.3 (*libido*); *Adv. Marc.* 1.330 and 2.360 (*libido*).

[92] *Epist.* 93.9; see below. On Augustine's view of this vice, Berry (1994), 89–94; on his personal experience of it, Brown (1988), 387–408.

[93] Below, 5.6.

opposed to chastity (*castitas*);[94] another idea frequently associated with *luxuria* is drunkenness, which becomes a more important aspect of banquets than food or luxury tableware, a fact that again connects *luxuria* with lust, given the disinhibiting effect of wine.[95]

Tertullian and Augustine are both prolific writers. I would like to focus on a specific area for each of them: Tertullian's *On the Apparel of Women* (*De cultu feminarum*), which reproaches women with luxury and lust, adopting some commonplaces already present in Cato the Elder, and Augustine's commentaries on Paul's letters.

Tertullian has a special interest in women's education. In his essay *De cultu feminarum*, in which echoes of classical moral writings (especially those by Seneca and Pliny the Elder) have been long recognized,[96] are all the commonplaces of morally reprehensible female luxury: jewels and especially pearls, giant earrings, colourful clothing, fine makeup, which are all desirable by dint of their exoticism and expense.[97] And yet we do not find traditional *luxuria* here, which indicates the loss of the economic application and meaning of this word in Christian culture. Tertullian uses the peculiar word *pompa* with a similar meaning as the classical *sumptus*, *deliciae*, which also remain,[98] and *concupiscentia* for the classical *libido* or *cupido*.[99] *Luxuria* itself occurs in a strictly erotic sense, opposed to *pudicitia* and linked to *licentia*. While Tertullian's opinion is the same as that of Cato the Elder in his support of the *Lex Oppia* (above, 2.3.2 and 2.9), except for some specifics linked to Christian tenets, the lexicon has changed.[100]

The virtue of modesty seems to exclude not only lust but also beauty in general (*Cult.* 2.3.1–2):

> Nam ubi pudicitia, ibi vacua pulchritudo, quia proprie usus et fructus pulchritudinis corporis luxuria, nisi si quis aliam messem decori corporis arbitratur. Illae sibi formositatem et datam extendant et non datam conquirant, quae quod ab illa flagitatur, sibi quoque praestare se putant, cum alteri praestant. 2. Dicet aliquis: Quid ergo non, et exclusa luxuria, et admissa castitate, laude formae sola frui et de bono corporis gloriari licet? Viderit quem iuvat de carne gloriari.
>
> For, where modesty exists there is no need of beauty, since, strictly speaking, the normal use and effect of beauty is wantonness, unless, of course, someone can think of some other good that flows from bodily beauty. Let those women

[94] Tert. *Cult.* 2.3.2; *Castit.* 13. [95] Cf. e.g. Tert. *Pud.* 17.
[96] Isetta (1986), 33–41.
[97] Cf. *Cult.* 1.5.1–7.2 (gold and jewels); 1.8.1–5 (colourful clothing); 2.6.1–7.3 (dyed hair/wigs).
[98] E.g. *Cult.* 2.9.1–2 (*pompae* and *deliciae* are opposed to *frugi*); 2.9.7 and 13.3 (*deliciae*).
[99] E.g. *Cult.* 1.9.2: *concupiscentiam... habendi*. *Libido* is used in the restricted sense of 'sexual desire' (e.g. 2.2.1; 2.12.1).
[100] We may add that in a work inspired by Tertullian's *De cultu*, Cyprian's *De habitu virginum*, there are no recurrences of *luxuria*.

> enhance the beauty they possess or seek for beauty they do not possess who think that they bestow upon themselves what is demanded from beauty when they exhibit it to others. 2. But someone will say: Suppose we exclude wantonness and give to chastity its rightful place. Why should we not be permitted to enjoy the simple praise that comes to beauty and to glory in a bodily good? Let whoever takes pleasure in glorying in the flesh see to that.
>
> (Trans. Quain 1959, here and below)

Even though Tertullian later specifies that Christian spouses do not have to be ugly and shabby (2.5.1), here he makes a direct connection between a woman's beauty and the vice of lechery, which is called *luxuria*. He admits that the desire to be appreciated is an innate tendency, and which affects men, too, but the encounter with God should negate it, as well as luxury itself (2.8.2):

> Tamen, cognito Deo, adempta placendi voluntate, per luxuriae vacationem omnia illa ut otiosa ut hostilia pudicitiae recusantur.
>
> Are not all of these things quite idle and hostile to modesty once we have known God, have put aside the desire to please others and foresworn all lasciviousness?

Again, *pudicitia* is opposed to *luxuria*, which is the natural consequence of the desire to please (*placendi voluntate*). *Luxuria*'s etymological link with desire is still evident, even if in this case it is not the desire for pleasure that is at the root of sexual sin, but the desire to please.

The following chapter contains some remains of the old connection between *luxuria* and luxury (2.9.2):

> Hae pompae quam de proximo curent luxuriae negotium et obstrepant pudicitiae disciplinis dinoscere in facili est, quod gratiam decoris cultus societate prostituant.
>
> To be sure, there is no difficulty in recognizing how close the connection is between these pomps and the business of lasciviousness and how they must interfere with the principles of modesty: such frills adjoined to fancy dress prostitute the grace of true beauty.

Luxury and expenses prostitute (*prostituant*) natural beauty, for the purpose of lust (*luxuria*) and against *pudicitia*. Tertullian's final exhortation is for women to wear the purple of modesty, the silk of sobriety, and so on, in order to gain God as a lover (2.13.7 *taliter pigmentatae Deum habebitis amatorem*). Of course, this expression is intended in a purely spiritual sense,[101] but, even though it avoids the word *luxuria*, it transmits an undeniably erotic feeling.

[101] Isetta (1986), 202–3.

As far as Augustine is concerned, in his *Confessiones*, a text that owes much to classical pagan literature—and especially to Seneca[102]—we find the classical *libido* more often than the 'Christian' *fornicatio*, and a few occurrences of *luxuria* together with avarice (e.g. *Conf.* 2.5; 8.10). A review of the occurrences of *luxuria* in his whole work shows that it is often a translation of the Greek word *aselgeia* (one of its Greek equivalents already in classical time)[103] in Paul's epistles. More than once in Augustine's work is *luxuria* indeed listed among the *opera carnis*, the 'works of the flesh'. This expression is found in Tertullian, too, but without reference to *luxuria*. In Augustine it is modelled on a passage of Paul's *Epistle to the Galatians* (5.19): *ta erga tes sarkos.*[104] In that context, the expression is followed by a list of vices, among which we first find πορνεία, ἀκαθαρσία, ἀσέλγεια, which in *Epist.* 93.11 Augustine translates as *fornicationes* ('sexual sins'), *immunditiae* ('impurity'), *luxuria* ('debauchery'), and repeats several times in different works.[105] The *opera carnis* are all those activities that end in vice because they are aimed at the satisfaction of some bodily desire, which is something morally deplorable per se in Christian thought. Another instance of these words is Paul's *Second Epistle to the Corinthians*, whose conclusion is (*Cor.* 2.12.21):

> ... and I would mourn for many of those who have sinned before now, and not repented of the uncleanness and sexual immorality and lustfulness (*akatharsia, porneia, aselgeia*) which they committed. (Trans. Johnson 2020)

While in the *Vulgata* the three vices in this passage are translated as *immunditia, fornicatio*, and *impudicitia* (2 *Cor.* 772a M.), Augustine switches *fornicatio* to the third place, and replaces *impudicitia* with *luxuria* (*Epist.* 265.7):

> Et lugeam multos ex his qui ante peccaverunt, et non egerunt poenitentiam super immunditia, et luxuria, et fornicatione quam egerunt.
>
> I mourn many of them that sinned before and have not done penance for the uncleanness and lasciviousness, and fornications they have committed.
>
> (Trans. Parsons 1981)

This list of vices frequently returns in his writings, with evident reference to Paul's words.[106]

[102] Cf. e.g. Byers (2015), 64 on the young Augustine's lust. [103] Above, 1.1.

[104] In the so-called *Vulgata* translation of the New Testament, we find *ta erga tes sarkos* translated as *opera carnis* too, and *aselgeia* as *luxuria* (*Gal.* 777a M.).

[105] E.g. *Fid. et op.* 15.25; *Octo Dulc. quaest.* 1.4; *In ps.* 143.6. Augustine wrote a commentary on Paul's *Letter to the Galatians*, in which he discusses the quoted passage (section 48).

[106] E.g. *Spec.* 37.18; 162; 351.3–5; *C. Faust.* 21.92. Cf. prevoius n.

Augustine's translation choice, especially evident in his sermons and epistles, orients the semantics of *luxuria* towards lust (below, 5.6), while luxury plays no major role.

5.5 A Final Allegory: Prudentius

It is not without reason that our journey along the path of *luxuria* ends with a personification—the rhetorical figure with which this passion first appeared in Latin literature, in Plautus (above, 2.1.1).[107] This concluding personification is in the work of an author born in Spain, as was Seneca the Younger, who lent so much importance to *luxuria*. Personifications have been frequent in this history, and illustrate the fear that this vice it inspires, making it appear almost as a monster against which we engage in mortal combat. Seneca played a primary role in all this by employing, in his prose, several poetic tools to emphasize how tragic the situation is for those who try to follow virtue.

The Christian Aurelius Prudentius Clemens was born in Spain, probably in Calahorra, in 348 CE; his *Psychomachia* was published in 405. It is an allegorical poem,[108] in which we find conflicts between virtues and vices: Faith against Polytheism, Modesty (*Pudicitia*) against Lust (*Libido*), Patience against Anger, Humility against Pride, *Luxuria* against Sobriety (*Sobrietas*), Greed against *Ratio*, Concord against Discord. Most vices have fierce allies, and these add some variety to the one-on-one fighting in a landscape that recalls tournament scenes. The virtues are no less cruel than the vices: they aim to inflict painful and bloody death, and rage against their enemies with harsh speeches. Prudentius completely ignores Pity and Clemency. The poem's literary models belong to two different areas: epic (Virgil, Ovid, and Statius, among others),[109] and sacred writings (above all the book of *Genesis*),[110] but it also owes much to pagan culture, which dedicated temples to abstract figures such as Faith, Fortune, and Concord.[111] It is a unique experiment that what is merely a rhetorical tool, usually confined to few images in a broader context, covers an entire poem.

Although he is original in his literary choices, Prudentius is more traditional than Apuleius in his use of semantics: indeed he distinguishes Lust from *Luxuria*. *Libido* tries to attack Modesty with her torches,[112] and then gets slaughtered in a lake of blood (ll. 40–52). The fight is quick and ends with a long, incensed speech by Modesty (ll. 53–97), who cites biblical and Christian examples of chastity, such

[107] On the connection between these two personifications, Petrone (2012), 33–5; Mazzoli (2017b), 54.

[108] On the nature of Prudentius' allegories, and their relationship with ancient rhetoric on personification, Haworth (1980), 12–115; Machosky (2003); Bardzell (2009), 32–42; Di Serio (2018).

[109] Mastrangelo (2008), 14–40; specifically on Virgil, Smith (1976), 234–300 (290–1 on *Luxuria*); Hardie (2017) and (2019).

[110] Hannah (1977); Bureau (2003).

[111] Haworth (1980), 55–73.

[112] Hardie (2017), 5–6, and Mazzoli (2017b), 52–3, compare it with Virgil's description of Fury.

as Judith and Maria,[113] and then purifies her sword from her enemy's blood, consecrating it in a church (ll. 98–108).[114] From a narrative point of view, the combat is simple; from an allegorical point of view, flesh is a symbol of corruption, opposed to the sanctity of God's incarnation,[115] and blood is a symbol of (sexual) pollution and contamination. The fight between *Luxuria* and *Sobrietas* (and not frugality, as it was until the end of the first century CE; note that already Apuleius formulates the opposition in these terms)[116] is narrated in much more detail; it is the most original part of the poem. The description of *Luxuria* begins with its foreign origin, as also happens in classical Latin[117] (ll. 310–25):[118]

> Venerat occiduis mundi de finibus hostis
> Luxuria extinctae iam dudum prodiga famae,
> delibuta comas, oculis vaga, languida voce,
> perdita deliciis, vitae cui causa voluptas,
> elumbem mollire animum petulanter amoenas
> haurire inlecebras et fractos solvere sensus.
> At tunc pervigilem ructabat marcida cenam,
> sub lucem quia forte iacens ad fercula raucos
> audierat lituos atque inde tepentia linquens
> pocula lapsanti per vina et balsama gressu
> ebria calcatis ad bellum floribus ibat.
> O nova pugnandi species! Non ales harundo
> nervum pulsa fugit...
> sed violas lasciva iacit foliisque rosarum
> dimicat et calathos inimica per agmina fudit.

From the western bounds of the world had come their foe Indulgence, one that had long lost her repute and so cared not to save it; her locks perfumed, her eyes shifting, her voice listless, abandoned in voluptuousness she lived only for pleasure, to make her spirit soft and nerveless, in wantonness to drain alluring delights, to enfeeble and undo her understanding. Even then she was languidly belching after a night-long feast; for as it chanced dawn was coming in and she was still reclining by the table when she heard the hoarse trumpets, and she left the lukewarm cups, her foot slipping

[113] Bureau (2003), 107; Franchi (2013), 93–104.

[114] On the whole episode, Nugent (1985), 27–32; Corsano (2004); Bardzell (2009), 44–6; Franchi (2013), 79–122; Pelttari (2019), 105–15; Frisch (2020), 199–231.

[115] Nugent (1985), 29.

[116] Above, 5.3; Frisch (2020), 283.

[117] With the difference that *Luxuria* is imagined as coming from the West, not the East. This is probably due to a symbolic connection: the West is where the sun (the light of reason and virtue) sets, as the word *occiduis* (l. 310) shows; cf. Pelttari (2019), 144; Frisch (2020), 285–7. I would add that Prudentius could be alluding to the legend of the town of Sybaris, which was located west of Greece (above, 1.4).

[118] Pelttari (2019), 144–6; Frisch (2020), 277–91. On *Luxuria*'s personification, Mazzoli (2017b), 54; Frisch (2020), 282–3.

as she stepped through pools of wine and perfumes, and trampling on the flowers, and was making her drunken way to the war. Yet it was not on foot, but riding in a beauteous chariot that she struck and won the hearts of the admiring fighters. Strange warfare! No swift arrow is sped in flight from her bowstring...but as if in sport she throws violets and fights with rose-leaves, scattering baskets of flowers over her adversaries. (Trans. Thomson 1949, here and below)

I would like to highlight two literary allusions here: Venus' seducing appearance in the opening of Lucretius' *De rerum natura* (the pleasant flowers, the atmosphere of seduction and desire, etc.),[119] and the depraved monster/tyrant's hangover, e.g. the Cyclops in the *Odyssey* or Mark Antony in Cicero's second *Philippic* (the burping, the wine, etc.).[120] These two figures represent the two main aspects of *luxuria* through Roman history: the erotic and seductive, grounded in desire, and the 'material', grounded in banquets and (especially for Christian authors) drunkenness. As in every other Christian text, luxury seems to be absent from the picture. The profusion of words related to pleasure and desire retraces the whole semantic field we have come to know: *deliciae, voluptas* (l. 313), *mollire, petulanter* (l. 314; in Apuleius there was *petulans*), *solvere* (l. 315), *lasciva* (l. 324). This list is further enriched by *languida, vaga* (l. 312), *amoenas* (l. 314), all terms related to sweetness and seduction: even if *Libido* has been beaten, lust is still somewhere here. The whole collection of fascinating images represents a 'new way of fighting' (l. 321 *nova pugnandi species*): instead of using weapons, *Luxuria* throws perfumed flowers to her enemies and seduces them (ll. 326–7), to the point that they lose all their aggressive habits (ll. 328–43):[121]

Inde eblanditis Virtutibus halitus inlex
inspirat tenerum labefacta per ossa venenum
et male dulcis odor domat ora et pectora et arma
ferratosque toros oblitos obliso robore mulcet.
Deiciunt animos ceu victi et spicula ponunt
turpiter heu dextris languentibus obstupefacti,
dum currum varia gemmarum luce micantem
mirantur...
Et iam cuncta acies in deditionis amorem

[119] Compare Lucr. 1.1–20 and Prud. *Psyc.* 310–15 and 324–5. Pelttari (2019), 145–6, compares the character of Venus in Claudian's Greek *Gigantomachia* (ll. 43–54), while Nugent (1985), 41, points out a striking resemblance with Prudentius' description of the saved soul in his *Hamartigenia* 856–8: *illic, purpureo latus exporrecta cubili,/floribus aeternis spirantes libat odores./Ambrosiumque bibet roseo de stramine rorem...*

[120] Compare *Od.* 9.371–4, Cic. *Phil.* 2.63, and Prud. *Psyc.* 316–20. See also the passages quoted below.

[121] Pelttari (2019), 146–7; Frisch (2020), 291–4. The danger here is comparable to that of avarice, which presents itself as the virtue of frugality: Bureau (2003), 113.

sponte sua versis transibat perfida signis
Luxuriae servire volens dominaeque fluentis
iura pati et laxa ganearum lege teneri.

So the Virtues are won over by her charms; the alluring breath blows a subtle poison on them that unmans their frames, the fatally sweet scent subduing their lips and hearts and weapons, softening their iron-clad muscles and crushing their strength. Their courage drops as in defeat; they lay down their javelins, their hands, alas! enfeebled, all to their shame struck dumb in their wonder at the chariot gleaming with flashing gems of varied hue…And by this time the whole array, its standards turned about, was treacherously submitting of its own will to a desire to surrender, wishing to be the slaves of Indulgence, to bear the yoke of a debauched mistress, and be governed by the loose law of the pot-house.

This scene also recalls Lucretius' proemium, where Venus manages to calm Mars' warlike attitude (Lucr. 1.31–40); victory is not due to violence but to sweetness: *eblanditis virtutibus* (Prud. *Psyc.* 328), *tenerum, labefacta* (l. 329), *dulcis* (l. 330), *obliso robore mulcet* (l. 331), *dextris languentibus* (l. 333).[122] The image of 'soft poison' (l. 329) recalls the literary descriptions of love in general, and Cupid's arrows in particular. These echoes do not fit the context of the poem and weaken the position of the virtues, which begin to look bad and aggressive, while *Luxuria* comes across as calm and loving. This shows the extremely dangerous nature of this vice.[123] Other traditional traits of this vice are that it is an outlaw (l. 328 *inlex*; l. 341 *versis…signis*; l. 343 *laxa…lege*), enslaves those who follow it (l. 342 *servire volens*), and exhibits luxury (ll. 335–9), which inspires not so much a desire for expensive things as a struggle for a life of pleasures (ll. 342–3). The expression *Luxuria domina*, 'debauched Mistress' (l. 342), sums her commanding attitude and her soft, seductive apparel: this comes close to the *dura puella* of elegiac poetry, who inspires passion and then reduces her lover to a slave.

Again, it is *luxuria*'s erotic nature that makes her so difficult to fight. Against this irresistible enemy, only Sobriety reacts. First, like all brave generals facing the risk of defeat, she delivers an encouraging speech to her army. She despises scented flowers (ll. 354–5), perfumed hair (ll. 358–9), effeminate walking (ll. 362–3), banquets with a profusion of wine (ll. 367–70). All these traits of *luxuria* are compared to the hardness and pure joy of faith, just as in classical texts they were compared to the challenges of virtue. Finally, Sobriety defines her enemy (ll. 377–80):[124]

[122] The insistence on looseness is connected by Nugent (1985), 43–4, to the idea of sin as a wandering of the soul.

[123] Smith (1976), 180; Nugent (1985), 42; Machosky (2003), 27–8. Compare the episode of Hannibal at Capua (e.g. Sen. *EM* 51.5, above, 4.4).

[124] Pelttari (2019), 151; Frisch (2020), 302, who compares some passages from the section on *Libido*.

His vos inbutos dapibus iam crapula turpis
Luxuriae ad madidum rapuit importuna lupanar,
quosque viros non Ira fremens, non idola bello
cedere compulerant saltatrix ebria flexit!

And it is after tasting of *this* banquet that you let shameful debauchery carry you relentlessly to the drunken den of Indulgence, and soldiers whom no raging Wrath nor idols could force by war to yield have been prevailed on by a tipsy dancer!

Criticism of the enemy, a commonplace in military speeches, leads to a new definition: *luxuria* is no longer referred to as a sort of seductive princess surrounded by pleasant things, but degraded to the owner of a brothel (l. 378: *lupanar*). The brothel itself is described as *madidum*, 'moist (with wine)', but the idea of soft and wet not only is related to wine but also includes all kinds of pleasures of the flesh. The final label 'tipsy dancer' (l. 380) points in the same direction: already in Cicero, this meant someone who is morally reprehensible in any respect. Cicero reports (*Mur.* 13) Cato of Utica's words to the young Murena: *saltatorem appellat L. Murenam Cato*,[125] and this is perhaps the source of Prudentius' line. Cicero defends Murena by arguing that this is not an accusation but an insinuation, although he himself uses it elsewhere to label someone as dishonourable (e.g. in *Sen.* 13; *Pis.* 22).

Sobriety then moves against *Luxuria*. Her weapon is the Christian cross:[126] it scares *Luxuria*'s horses, which overturn her chariot. This scene is inspired by the myth of Hippolytus, where a monster from the sea frightens the young man's horses.[127] And as in that myth, accepted meanings are challenged: Hippolytus was pure and innocent, the victim of a false accusation of incest made by his stepmother Phaedra, while the sea monster was the expression of an undeserved and cruel punishment requested from the gods by his father. In Prudentius, *Luxuria* plays the role of Hippolytus, and Sobriety that of a blind and erroneous divine judgement. Furthermore, while the enemy lies wounded, Sobriety, pitiless as all other virtues in the poem, delivers the final hit, throwing a rock at her neck. The rock as a weapon is Homeric, and we find it also in Virgil;[128] hitting the neck is also frequent in epic, and it is interesting that *Libido* in Prudentius dies in a

[125] As we have seen (above, 2.2.1), the *Pro Murena* is a speech where, for his client's benefit, Cicero maintains the need to abandon the rigidity of archaic habits.

[126] Pelttari (2019), 147–8, emphasizes the analogy with Constantine's use of this sacred symbol. Cf. also Bureau (2003), 106 and 110; Frisch (2020), 307.

[127] On the Hippolytus myth in Prudentius, without reference to this passage, Romano (2011), 265–7. Mastrangelo (2008), 137–42, reads the images of horses and chariot with reference to the Neoplatonic myth of the fall of the soul, modelled after Plato's *Phaedr.* 254e.

[128] Cf. e.g. *Il.* 12.445–50; 21.403–6; Verg. *Aen.* 12.896–902; cf. Pelttari (2019), 155; Frisch (2020), 308.

similar way, as we have seen. *Luxuria* dies eating her own blood, while the victor mocks her 'final pleasures' in a perfectly epic style (ll. 423–31):[129]

> Dentibus introrsum resolutis lingua resectam
> dilaniata gulam frustis cum sanguinis implet.
> Insolitis dapibus crudescit guttur et ossa
> conliquefacta vorans revomit quas hauserat offas.
> 'Ebibe iam proprium post pocula multa cruorem'
> virgo ait increpitans. 'Sint haec tibi fercula tandem
> tristia praeteriti nimiis pro dulcibus aevi.
> Lascivas vitae inlecebras gustatus amarae
> mortis et horrifico sapor ultimus asperat haustu!'

The teeth within are loosened, the gullet cut, and the mangled tongue fills it with bloody fragments. Her gorge rises at the strange meal, gulping down the pulped bones she spews up again the lumps she swallowed. 'Drink up now thine own blood, after thy many cups,' says the maiden, upbraiding her. 'Be these thy grim dainties, in place of the too much sweetness thou hast enjoyed in time past. The taste of bitter death in thy mouth, the savouring of this final, ghastly draught, turns to gall the wanton delights that allured thee in thy life.'

The bloody image presents *Luxuria*'s death as a sort of failed self-consumption: she swallows her teeth, blood, and tongue, and then vomits them out. Her death, and also *Libido*'s, have been interpreted as a reversal of the prosopopeia, in other words as a cancelation of the personification of vice:[130] the virtues' victory over passions is so complete as to annihilate the rhetorical tools by which the poet represented vice. I would add that, once again, the model is the Homeric Cyclops, an embodiment of beastly pleasures, who, drunk after eating some of Ulysses' mates, vomits human flesh (*Od.* 9.373–4).[131] Sobriety views *Luxuria*'s death as retaliation for her too sweet (Prud. *Psyc.* 429 *nimiis*... *dulcibus*) experiences, and her end must therefore be bitter (ll. 430–1... *amarae/mortis et horrifico*... *haustu*...), to compensate for her illicit, licentious pleasures (l. 430 *lascivas*... *inlecebras*). Sobriety seems to feel a hint of resentment—perhaps even envy?—for all of *Luxuria*'s pleasures.

The poet then comes to the flight of *Luxuria*'s allies, and lists 'Jest and Sauciness' (l. 433 *Iocus et Petulantia*), Desire (l. 436 *Amor*), Ostentation (l. 439 *Pompa*), Allurement (l. 441 *Venustas*), Pleasure (l. 444 *Voluptas*), and finally Luxury (l. 455

[129] Pelttari (2019), 155–7; Frisch (2020), 308–10.

[130] Paxton (1994), 66–9.

[131] Hermann (1978) compares Verg. *Aen.* 5.468–70 *ast illum* [*sc. Daretem*] *fidi aequales genua aegra trahentem/iactantemque utroque caput crassumque cruorem/ore eiectantem mixtosque in sanguine dentes.* The passage refers to the end of the boxing match between Entellus and Daretes.

Luxus), who leads the way to the following fight, that between Avarice[132]—who collects the remains of *Luxuria*'s army—and Charity.

The composition of this army confirms the aspects that Prudentius' narrative has already revealed, including both the erotic and the luxurious, with a focus on desire and physical pleasure.[133] At this stage, *luxuria* is still a complex and nuanced vice, and this makes it very dangerous. Seduction is something more complex and irresistible than mere lust.

5.6 Conclusion

In Roman classical world, *luxuria* is a key topic, especially for historiographers, who connect it with the decline of society. Its impressive apparel, made by luxury banquets, jewels, shiny dresses, eased both its personification and its crystallization in some iconic historical examples, such as Hannibal, Cleopatra, and Apicius. Among Roman emperors, Nero stands as a touchstone of this vice; not by chance, it is in Nero's times that flourished Seneca, the author who offered the most detailed account on it. During the second century CE, a secondary meaning of this term, lust, becomes the main one.

Having become lust, *luxuria* slowly enters into the list of the Christian cardinal sins.[134] This list has several classical antecedents, among which we may mention Cicero and Horace.[135] The 'inventor' of these moral archetypes is Evagrius Ponticus (345–399 CE), who uses the Greek word *lagneia* (*Pract.* 6–14), and he is followed, in Latin literature, by John Cassian (360–435 CE) who in his fifth *Conlatio* calls lust *fornicatio*, and couples it with gluttony (*Conl.* 5.2; 5.3; 5.4; 5.10; 5.16).[136] To the best of my knowledge, the 'consecration' of *luxuria* as a capital sin is due to a pope and saint, Gregory I (540–604 CE).[137] In the same period, it appears also in the works of the bishop Isidore of Seville, who defines *luxuriosus*

132 Mazzoli (2017b), 54–5, retraces the story of the opposition and connection between *Luxuria* and *Avaritia*. Prudentius defines luxury as *edax* (*Psyc.* 455): cf. Petron. 55.6.1 (above, 2.6.3).

133 I would add that Prudentius connects luxury with effeminacy in his *Hamartigenia* (ll. 279–99).

134 For the fascinating story of this cultural scheme, Bloomfield (1952), 1–104 on the ancient to medieval tradition; Wenzel (1968); Casagrande/Vecchio (2000), 181–224 (149–80 on lust); Newhauser (2007), 1–9; specific on *luxuria/libido*, Conte (2005), esp. 404–18; on the persistency of these categories in contemporary times, Schimmel (1992), 1–26; specific on lust, 111–37. On the relationship between ancient passions and Christian vices, Casagrande/Vecchio (2015), 165–85.

135 In both cases, the vices are diseases of the soul, and the lists are supposed to be referred to human beings in general, and not to Roman society, as it happens e.g. in Sallust (above, 2.3.1): Cic. *TD* 4.26 *avaritia, ambitio, mulierositas, pervicacia, liguritio, vinulentia, cuppedia, et si qua similia*; Hor. *Epist.* 1.1.38 *invidus, iracundus, iners, vinosus, amator* (in the same passage, Horace also refers to greed and ambition). Cf. Bloomfield (1952), 45–6; Cucchiarelli (2020), 188–91.

136 Cassian considers *luxuria* as linked to *philargyria*, i.e. greed (*Coll.* 22.3), while e.g. in 7.32 he couples it with *libido*.

137 *Moral.* 31.45. In this passage, Gregory lists vices derived from *luxuria* as follows: *de luxuria, caecitas mentis, inconsideratio, inconstantia, praecipitatio, amor sui, odium Dei, affectus praesentis saeculi, horror autem vel desperatio futuri generantur.*

as 'melted in pleasures'.[138] Gregory, given his authority and influence,[139] provided the ultimate theological structure for the vices that, from then on, became known as 'the seven cardinal sins'. This was the beginning of a long story of censure: even though in most cases *luxuria* is not considered the worst sin (Dante deems it a light one in his *Commedia*), it is undoubtedly the most seductive and hated of all vices. *Luxuria* remains connected with gluttony as a vice linked to desire, although it is deprived of its social and economic aspect, and now includes the additional meaning of *libido*. The neglect of the economic aspect can probably be explained by the early Christian state of mind. For the pagan Romans, society was foremost in the scale of values, and so they ranked vices insofar as they challenged the stability of the state. This is why lust, whose consequences are in most cases private, was not given much importance per se, while luxury was attacked because it threatened social relationships. The move from Republic to Empire affected this situation, but did not overturn it. Christian religion has a completely different point of view.[140] Here, the private sphere is the most important, because sin lies inside the heart, and God may inspect and judge it: hence the relevance accorded to lust, while wealth as ostentation loses importance: money are culpable *per se*, independently from their being spent or accumulated.

The erotic meaning of *luxuria*, prevailing in medieval Latin, is continued in most Romance languages, both by lexical definition and in the common language: see, for example, French 'luxure', Spanish 'luxúria', and Italian 'lussuria'. This may be explained by the pre-eminence of Christian (and especially Catholic) religion in these countries. Cultures that are less bound to the Roman curia name this sin with a different etymology ('lust' or 'lechery' in English, 'Wollust' in German), while terms derived from *luxuria* keep the original economic nuance, as do 'luxury' (cf. the German adjective 'luxuriös').[141] This multifaceted word has led to multiple etymologies, and has demonstrated its durable semantic richness.

138 Above, 1.1. Cf. Greg. M. *Moral.* 31.97; Isid. *Lib. num.* 9.51 *denique et octo principalia vitia describuntur, ex quibus multitudo omnium vitiorum exoritur, id est, invidia, iracundia, tristitia, avaritia, ingluvies, luxuria, inanis gloria, superbia*. In the same period, bishop Eutropius in his *De octo vitiis* still follows Cassian, using *fornicatio*. The number of cardinal sins oscillates in the beginning between eight and seven, and is then fixed at seven with Gregory, even if e.g. Alcuin, in the eighth century, still names eight of them, including Gloom (*tristitia*), with *fornicatio* as Lust (*Virt. ac vit.* 29).

139 Bloomfield (1952), 73–5.

140 Cf. Hopkins (1999), esp. 178–86.

141 Cf. Romanian 'lux' ('luxury') and 'luxuriă' ('lust'). In English, we find also the verb 'to luxuriate' and the adjective 'luxuriant', both focused on the biological meaning of (excessive) growth; in German there is also 'Luxus' as luxury and exuberant fertility, and the rare and learned terms 'Luxuria' ('conscious carelessness', such as *luxuria* in Sen. *EM* 1.4), the verb 'luxurieren' 'living a luxury life' and the noun 'Luxese', a compound of 'Luxus' and 'Askese' which refers to a life mixing luxury and frugality, which has been replicated by the French 'luxèse'.

Bibliographical References

Adams, J. N. (1974), 'The Vocabulary of the Later Decades of Livy', *Antichton* 8: 54–62.

Alexander, S. (1999) (ed.), *The Complete Odes and Satires of Horace*, with a Forward by R. Howard (Princeton).

Allegri, G. (2004), *Progresso verso la* virtus. *Il programma della lettera 87 di Seneca* (Cesena).

Amela Valverde, L. (2023), 'La *luxuria* romana a finales de la República: el caso de Lucio Licinio Lúculo', in Pons Pujol, L., Pérez González, J. (eds.) De luxuria propagata romana aetate. *Roman luxury in its many forms* (Oxford) (forthcoming).

Anderson, W. S. (1979), 'Plautus' *Trinummus*: The Absurdity of Officious Morality', *Traditio*, 35, 333–45.

Anderson, W. S. (1982), *Essays on Roman Satire* (Princeton).

André, J. (1975), 'Pensée et philosophie dans les *Lettres* de Pline le Jeune', *RÉL* 53: 225–47.

André, J.-M. (1965), *L'*otium *chez Valère Maxime et Velleius Paterculus*, *RÉL* 43: 294–315.

André, J.-M. (1993), *La villégiature romaine* (Paris).

Annas, J. (1992), *Hellenistic Philosophy of Mind* (Berkeley).

Armisen-Marchetti, M. (1989), Sapientiae Facies. *Étude sur les imgaes de Sénèque* (Paris).

Armisen-Marchetti, M. (2020a), 'Le statut moral de l'homme primitif chez Sénèque: anthropologie, éthique, théâtre', in Aygon, J.-P., Courtil, J.-C., and Ripoll, F. (eds.), Seneca saepe noster. *Articles de Mireille Armisen-Marchetti sur l'oeuvre de Sénèque (1981–2013) réunis en son honneur* (Bordeaux), 319–29.

Armisen-Marchetti, M. (2020b), 'La digestion du philosophe: le commentaire des citations finales dans les vingt-neuf premières *Lettres à Lucilius* de Sénèque', in Aygon, J.-P., Courtil, J.-C., and Ripoll, F. (eds.), Seneca saepe noster. *Articles de Mireille Armisen-Marchetti sur l'oeuvre de Sénèque (1981–2013) réunis en son honneur* (Bordeaux), 258–71.

Arrowsmith, W. (1966), 'Luxury and Death in the *Satyricon*', *Arion* 5.3: 304–31.

Ash, R. (2018) (ed.), *Tacitus, Annals, Book 15* (Cambridge).

Asmis, E. (1990), 'Seneca on the Happy Life and Stoic Individualism', *Apeiron* 23: 219–55.

Asmis, E. (2015), 'Seneca's Originality', in Bartsch, S. and Schiesaro, A. (eds.), *The Cambridge Companion to Seneca* (Cambridge), 224–38.

Aßkamp, R., Brouwer, M., Christiansen, J., Kenzler, H., and Wamser, L. (2008) (eds.), *Luxus und Dekadenz. Römisches Leben am Golf von Neapel* (Meinz).

Asso, P. (2010), *A Commentary on Lucan*, De Bello Civili *IV* (Berlin/New York).

Astin, A. E. (1978), *Cato the Censor* (Oxford).

Aubreville, P. (2021), *Der Hass im antiken Rom. Studien zur Emotionalität in der späten Republik und frühen Kaiserzeit* (Stuttgart).

Audano, S. (2021), 'Nerone *exclusus amator* in Svetonio (*Otho* 3, 2)', *Pan* 10: 151–62.

Austin, R. C. (1948), *Ad M. Fabii Quintiliani institutionis oratoriae librum XII* (Oxford).

Austin, R. G. (1988) (ed.), *M. Tullius Cicero, Pro Caelio* (Oxford).

Avotins, I. (1977), 'Training Frugality in Epicurus and Seneca', *Phoenix* 31.3: 214–17.

Badel, C. (2012), 'Vomir le plaisir à Rome', in Karila-Cohen, K. and Quellier, F. (eds.), *Le corps du gourmand. D'Héraclès à Alexandre le Bienheureux* (Rennes/Tours), 179–89.

Baker, R. J. (1990) (ed.), *Propertius I* (Warminster).

Baldo, G. (2004) (ed.), *M. Tulli Ciceronis In C. Verrem Actionis Secundae Liber Quartus (De Signis)* (Firenze).

Baltrusch, E. (1989), Regimen morum. *Die Reglementierung des Privatslebens der Senatoren und Ritter in der römischen Republik und frühen Kaiserzeit* (München).

Baltrusch, E. (2009), 'Luxus II', *RAC* 182: 711–37.

Bannon, C. (2014), 'C. Sergius Orata and the Rhetoric of Fishponds', *CQ* 64.1, 166–82.

Baratta, G. (2023), 'El lujo en la mesa de los Romanos', in Pons Pujol, L., Pérez González, J. (eds.) De luxuria propagata romana aetate. *Roman luxury in its many forms* (Oxford) (forthcoming).

Baraz, Y. (2008), 'From Vice to Virtue: The Denigration and Rehabilitation of *Superbia* in Ancient Rome', in Sluiter, I. and Rosen, R. M. (eds.), Kakos. *Badness and Anti-Value in Classical Antiquity* (Leiden-Boston), 365–97.

Baraz, Y. (2020), *Reading Roman Pride* (Oxford/New York).

Barchiesi, A. (1992) (ed.), *P. Ovidii Nasonis Epistulae Heroidum 1–3* (Florence).

Barchiesi, A. (1994), *Il poeta e il principe. Ovidio e il discorso augusteo* (Rome/Bari).

Bardzell, J. (2009), *Speculative Grammar and Stoic Language Theory in Medieval Allegorical Narrative* (New York).

Barney, R./Brennan, T./Brittain, C. (2012) (eds.), *Plato and the Divided Soul* (Cambridge).

Barney, S. A./Lewis, W. J./Beach, J. A./Berghof, O. (2006) (eds.), *The Etymologies of Isidore of Seville* (Cambridge).

Barr, W. (1987) (ed.), *The Satires of Persius*, The Latin Text with a Verse Translation by G. Lee, Introduction and Commentary by W. Barr (Liverpool).

Barrett, A. (2016), *Introduction*, in Barrett, A., Fantham, E., and Yardley (eds.), *The Emperor Nero: A Guide to the Ancient Sources* (Princeton), xi–xxiii.

Barsby, J. (2001) (ed.), *Terence, Phormio; The Mother-in-law; The Brothers*, (Cambridge/London).

Barton, C. A. (1993), *The Sorrows of the Ancient Romans: The Gladiator and the Monster* (Princeton).

Bartsch, S. (1994), *Actors in the Audience. Theatricality and doublespeak from Nero to Hadrian* (London/Cambridge MA).

Bartsch, S. (2012), 'Persius, Juvenal, and Stoicism', in Bartsch, S. and Osgood, J. (eds.), *A Companion to Persius and Juvenal* (Chichester), 217–38.

Bartsch, S. (2015a), *Persius. A Study on Food, Philosophy, and the Figural* (Chicago).

Bartsch, S. (2015b), 'Senecan Selves', in Bartsch, S. and Schiesaro, A. (eds.), *The Cambridge Companion to Seneca* (Cambridge), 187–98.

Bartsch, S. (2017), 'Philosophers and the State under Nero', in Bartsch, S., Freudenberg, K., and Littelwood, C. (eds.), *The Cambridge Companion to the Age of Nero* (Cambridge), 151–63.

Bäumler, A. (2014), 'Zwischen Evergetismus und Ostentation: Konsum und Vergesellschaft bei Festen in der frühen Römischen Kaiserzeit', *Hermes* 42.3: 298–325.

Beagon, M. (1992), *Roman Nature. The Thought of Pliny the Elder* (Oxford).

Beagon, M. (2005) (ed.), *The Elder Pliny on Human Being. Natural History, Book 7* (Oxford).

Beekes, R. (2009), *Etymological Dictionary of Greek* (Leiden/Boston).

Bellincioni, M. (1978), *Educazione alla* sapientia *in Seneca* (Brescia).

Bellincioni, M. (1979) (ed.), *Seneca, Lettere a Lucilio. Libro XV: le lettere 94 e 95* (Brescia).

Berno, F. R. (2003), *Lo specchio, il vizio e la virtù. Studio sulle* Questioni naturali *di Seneca* (Bologna).

Berno, F. R. (2006) (ed.), *L. Anneo Seneca, Lettere a Lucilio, libro VI: Le lettere 53–57* (Bologna).

Berno, F. R. (2008), 'Seneca e la semantica della pienezza', *BStudLat* 38: 549–66.

Berno, F. R. (2011), 'Seneca, Catone e due citazioni virgiliane (Sen. *epist.* 95, 67–71 e 104, 31–32)', *SIFC* 104: 233–53.

Berno, F. R. (2013), 'Il compromesso impossibile: Marco Celio fra vizi e virtù', *Lexis* 31: 321–35.

Berno, F. R. (2014a), 'In Praise of Tubero's Pottery: A Note on Seneca, *Ep*. 95.72–3 and 98.13', in Colish, M. L. and Wildberger, J. (eds.), Seneca Philosophus (Berlin/Boston), 369–91.

Berno, F. R. (2014b), 'Seneca contro Baia, ovvero il vizio in villeggiatura. Lettura di Sen., *Ep*., 51', in Devillers, O. (ed.), Neronia *IX. La villégiature dans le monde romain de Tibère à Hadrien* (Bordeaux), 123–32.

Berno, F. R. (2014c), 'Il saggio destino di Didone. *Aen*. 4, 653 in Seneca (*vit. b*. 19,1; *benef*. 5, 17, 5; *ep*. 12, 9)', *Maia* 66: 123–36.

Berno, F. R. (2017a), 'Nurses' Prayers, Philosophical *otium*, and Fat Pigs. Seneca *epist*. 60 vs Horace *epist*. 1, 4', in Stöckinger, M., Winter, K., and Zanker, A. T. (eds.), *Horace and Seneca: Interactions, Intertexts, Interpretations* (Berlin), 53–71.

Berno, F. R. (2017b), '*Omnia peccata paria*. Intorno ad un paradosso stoico, fra Cicerone, Orazio e Petronio', *Hormos* 9: 499–517.

Berno, F. R. (2018) (ed.), *Seneca, De constantia sapientis—La fermezza del saggio* (Naples).

Berno, F. R. (2019), 'The *porticus Liviae* in Ovid's *Fasti* (6.637–648), part II: Words', in Loar, M. P., Murray, S. C., and Rebeggiani, S. (eds.), *Texts and Monuments in Augustan Rome* (Cambridge), 115–25.

Berno, F. R. (2021a), 'Ovidius sapiens. *The Learned Man in Ovid*', in Williams, G. D. and Volk, K. (eds.), Ovidius Philosophus. *Philosophy in Ovid, Ovid as a Philosopher* (Oxford), 23–45.

Berno, F. R. (2021b), 'Due letture dell'esordio della lettera 64 di Seneca, 2. Il banchetto che non c'è', *Lucius Annaeus Seneca* 1, 25–46.

Berno, F. R. (2022), 'I vizi, indimenticabili amanti. La lettera 69 di Seneca', *Lucius Annaeus Seneca* 2: 81–99.

Berno, F. R. (2024), 'La concessione dell'*otium*. Nerone e la lettera 73 di Seneca', *Scienze dell'Antichità* 30.1 (forthcoming).

Bernstein, N. W. (2009), 'Adoptees and Exposed Children in Roman Declamation: Commodification, Luxury, and the Threat of Violence', *CPh* 104.3: 331–53.

Berrendonner, C. (2001), 'La formation de la tradition sur M.' Curius Dentatus et C. Fabricius Luscinus: Un homme nouveau peutre-il être un grand homme?', in Coudry, M. and Späth, T. (eds.), *L'invention des grands hommes de la Rome antique—Die Konstruktion der großen Männer Altroms* (Paris), 97–116.

Berry, C. J. (1994), *The Idea of Luxury. A Conceptual and Historical Investigation* (Cambridge).

Berti, N. (1989), 'La decadenza morale di Roma e i *viri antiqui*: riflessioni su alcuni frammenti degli *Annali* di L. Calpurnio Pisone Frugi', *Prometheus* 15.1: 39–58.

Berti, E. (2000) (ed.), *M. Annaei Lucani Bellum Civile liber X* (Firenze).

Berti, E. (2007), Scholasticorum studia. *Seneca il Vecchio e la cultura retorica e letteraria della prima età imperiale* (Pisa).

Berti, E. (2018) (ed.), *Lo stile e l'uomo. Quattro epistole letterarie di Seneca (Sen.* epist. *114; 40; 100; 84)* (Pisa).

Bessone, F. (2018), 'Memorie del passato, memoria dei modelli: la traccia di Virgilio, *Eneide* 8 in Seneca, *epistola* 86', *RFIC* 146.2: 432–9.

Beste, H.-J. (2011), '*Domus Aurea*, il padiglione dell'Oppio', in Tomei, A. and Rea, R. (eds.), *Nerone* (Milano), 160–9.

Beste, H.-J./von Hesberg, H. (2013), 'Buildings of an Emperor—How Nero Transformed Rome', in Buckely, E. and Dinter, M. T. (eds.), *A Companion to the Neronian Age* (Malden MA/Oxford), 314–31.

Bianco, M. M. (2018), 'Prendere ad esempio: quando padri e figli sono innamorati (con una lettura di Sen. *contr.* II 6)', *Maia* 70.1: 50–72.

Billerbeck, M. (1979), *Der Kyniker Demetrius: ein Beitrag zur Geschichte der Fruhkeiserzeitlichen Popularphilosophie* (Leiden).

Billerbeck, M. (1982), 'La réception du Cynisme à Rome', *AntCl* 51: 151–73.

Bischop, D. (2008), 'Der zerbrechliche Luxus. Tafelluxus als Edelstein und Glas', in Aßkamp, R., Brouwer, M., Christiansen, J., Kenzler, H., and Wamser, L. (eds.), *Luxus und Dekadenz. Römisches Leben am Golf von Neapel* (Meinz), 163–77.

Blackburn, S. (2004), *Lust. The Seven Deadly Sins* (Oxford).

Blake, S. (2011), 'Martial's Natural History: The *Xenia* and *Apophoreta* and Pliny's Encyclopedia', *Arethusa* 44.3: 353–77.

Blänsdorf, J. (1996), 'L'*otium illiteratum* dans la littérature impériale', in André, J.-M., Dangel, J., Demont, P. (eds.), *Les loisirs et l'héritage de la culture classique* (Bruxelles), 268–78.

Blösel, W. (2000), 'Die Geschichte des Begriffes *mos maiorum* von den Anfängen bis zu Cicero', in Linke, B. and Stemmler, M. (eds.), Mos maiorum. *Untersuchungen zu den Formen der Identitätsstiftung und Stabilisierung in der römischen Republik* (Stuttgart), 25–97.

Bloomer, V. M. (1992), *Valerius Maximus and the Rhetoric of New Nobility* (Chapel Hill/London).

Bloomfield, M. W. (1952), *The Seven Deadly Sins. An Introduction to the History of a Religious Concept* (East Lansing MI).

Boehm, I./Ferrary, J.-L./Franchet d'Espèrey, S. (2016) (eds.), *L'Homme et ses passions* (Paris).

Boeri, M. D. (2020), 'Galen and the Stoic 'Double-Perversion' Theory', *Pege/Fons* 5: 135–49.

Bok, S. (2010), *Exploring Happiness. From Aristotle to Brain Science* (Yale).

Bömer, F. (1958) (ed.), *P. Ovidius Naso, Die Fasten, II. Kommentar* (Heidelberg).

Bond, R. P. (1987), 'The Characterization of the Interlocutors in Horace, *Satires* 2.3', *Prudentia* 19: 1–21.

Bond, R. P. (1998), 'Horace on Damasippus on Stertinius on…', *Scholia* 7.1: 82–108.

Bonner, S. F. (2012), *Education in Ancient Rome. From the Elder Cato to the Younger Pliny* (London/New York), 1977[1].

Borgo, A. (1991), '*Per luxum*. Uso e riuso di un nesso insolito', *BStudLat* 21: 306–12.

Borgo, A. (1998), *Lessico morale di Seneca* (Napoli).

Bosman, P. R. (2012), 'Lucian among the Cynics: the "Zeus Refuted" and Cynic Tradition', *CQ* 62.2: 785–95.

Bottiglieri, A. (2002), *La legislazione sul lusso in età repubblicana* (Napoli).

Bourgery, A. (1923) (ed.), *Sénèque, Dialogues, 2. De la vie heureuse, De la brevité de la vie* (Paris).

Boyle, A. J. (1987) (ed.), *Seneca's Phaedra* (Liverpool).

Boyle, A. J. (2017) (ed.), *Seneca, Thyestes*, Edited with Introduction, Translation and Commentary (Oxford).

Boyle, A. J./Woodward, R. D. (2000) (eds.), *Ovid, Fasti* (London).

Bradley, K. (2012), *Apuleius and Antonine Rome* (Toronto).

Bramble, J. C. (2009), 'Style and Expression in Persius' Fifth Satire', in Plaza, M. (ed.), *Persius and Juvenal* (Oxford), 57–71.

Braund, S. (2015), 'Seneca *Multiplex*: The Phases (and Phrases) of Seneca's Life and Works', in Bartsch, S. and Schiesaro, A. (eds.), *The Cambridge Companion to Seneca* (Cambridge), 15–28.

Braund, S./Gill, C. (1997) (eds.), *The Passions in Roman Thought and Literature* (Cambridge).

Braund, S./Most, G. W. (2004) (eds.), *Ancient Anger. Perspectives from Homer to Galen* (Cambridge).

Brennan, T. (2003), 'Stoic Moral Psychology', in Inwood, B. (ed.), *The Cambridge Companion to the Stoics* (Cambridge), 257–94.

Bringmann, K. (2015), 'The Roman Republic and Its Internal Politics between 232 and 167 BC', in Mineo, B. (ed.), *A Companion to Livy* (London), 394–406.

Briscoe, J. (1981), *A Commentary on Livy: Books 34–37* (Oxford).

Briscoe, J. (2008), *A Commentary on Livy: Books 38–40* (Oxford).

Brouwer, R. (2020), 'Why Human Beings Become Bad. The Early Stoic Doctrine of Double Perversion', *Pege/Fons* 5: 61–82.

Brown, P. (1988), *The Body and Society. Men, Women, and Sexual Renunciation in Early Christianity* (New York).

Bruno, L. (1966), '*Crimen regni* e *superbia* in Livio', *GIF* 19: 236–59.

Brunschwig, J., (1986) 'The Cradle Argument in Epicureanism and Stoicism', in Schofield, M., Striker, G. (eds.), *The Norms of Nature: Studies in Hellenistic Ethics* (Cambridge), 113–44.

Bruzzese, L. (2011), *Studi su Filemone comico* (Lecce).

Bütler, H.-P. (1970), *Die geistige Welt des jüngeren Plinius: Studien zur Thematik seiner Briefe* (Heidelberg).

Bureau, B. (2003), 'L'utilisation de la Bible dans la *Psychomachie* de Prudence', *Vita Latina* 168: 94–124.

Burgeon, C. (2017), 'La notion de *virtus* sous les Julio-Claudiens dans les *Annales* de Tacite', *Circé* 9: 1–13.

Busch, S. (1999), Versus balnearum. *Die antike Dichtung über Bäder und Baden im römischen Reich* (Stuttgart/Leipzig).

Byers, S. C. (2015), 'Augustine's Debt with Stoicism in the *Confessions*', in Sellars, J. (ed.), *The Routledge Handbook of the Stoic Tradition* (London), 56–69.

Byrne, S. N. (2007), 'Maecenas and Petronius' Trimalchio Maecenatianus', *Ancient Narrative* 6: 31–49.

Cairns, D. (2019), *A Cultural History of the Emotions in Antiquity* (London).

Calboli, G. (1993) (ed.), *Cornifici Rhetorica ad C. Herennium* (Bologna) (1969[1]).

Carey, S. (2003), *Pliny's Catalogue of Culture. Art and Empire in the Natural History* (Oxford).

Cary, E. (1925) (ed.), *Dio's Roman History, VIII: Books 61–70* (London/Cambridge MA).

Cary, E. (1955) (ed.), *Dio's Roman History, VII: Books 56–60* (London/Cambridge MA) (1924[1]).

Casagrande, C./Vecchio, S. (2000), *I sette vizi capitali. Storia dei peccati nel Medioevo* (Torino).

Casagrande, C./Vecchio, S. (2015), *Passioni dell'anima. Teorie e usi degli affetti nella cultura medioevale* (Firenze).

Casinos Mora, F. J. (2015), 'Pasión por el lujo y renovación moral en los inicios del principado', *EClás* 147: 55–70.

Casinos Mora, F. J. (2023), '*Indumenta vetita.* Sentido y alcance de las disposiciones restrictivas a la indumentaria suntuaria en la Roma imperial', in Pons Pujol, L., Pérez González, J. (eds.) De luxuria propagata romana aetate. *Roman luxury in its many forms* (Oxford) (forthcoming).

Castillo, C. (1971), 'Tópicos de la sátira romana', *CFC* 2: 147–63.

Caston, R. R. (2011), 'Lucan's Elegiac Moments', in Asso, P. (ed.), *Brill's Companion to Lucan* (Leiden/Boston), 133–52.

Chaplin, J. D. (2000), *Livy's Exemplary History* (Oxford).

Cipriani, G. (1990), 'Il galateo del comandante. Modelli comportamentali in Sallustio (*Cat.* 60–61) e Cesare (*civ.* 3, 94–96)', *Aufidus* 11–12: 101–25.

Citroni Marchetti, S. (1986), 'L'avvocato, il giudice, il *reus* (la psicologia della colpa e del vizio nelle opere retoriche e nelle prime orazioni di Cicerone)', *MD* 17: 93–124.

Citroni Marchetti, S. (1991), *Plinio il Vecchio e la tradizione del moralismo romano* (Pisa).

Citroni Marchetti, S. (2011), 'La rappresentazione del denaro', in Citroni Marchetti, S., *La scienza della natura per un intellettuale romano. Studi su Plinio il Vecchio* (Pisa), 172–92.

Cizek, E. (1977), *Structures et idéologie dans* Les vies des douze Césars *de Suétone* (Bucureşti/Paris).

Clemente, G. (1981), 'Le leggi sul lusso e la società romana tra III e II secolo a. C.', in Giardina, A. and Schiavone, A. (eds.), *Modelli etici, diritto e trasformazioni sociali* (Roma/Bari), 1–14.

Coffee, N. (2017), *Gift and Gain. How Money Transformed Ancient Rome* (Oxford).

Connors, C. (2000), 'Imperial Space and Time: The Literature of Leisure', in Taplin, O. (ed.), *Literature in the Greek and Roman Worlds. A New Perspective* (Oxford), 492–518.

Conradie, I. M. (2010) (ed.), *Seneca in His Cultural and Literary Context: Selected Moral Letters on the Body* (Utrecht).

Conte, S. (2005), '*Libido* e *luxuria* dal latino alle lingue romanze. Elementi per la ricostruzione di una evoluzione di significato (Orosio e l'*Histoire ancienne* in *IF* 5,55–57)', in Bianchini, S. (ed.), *Lessico, parole-chiave, strutture letterarie del Medioevo romanzo* (Roma), 399–451.

Cooper, J. M. (2004), *Knowledge, Nature, and the Good. Essays on Ancient Philosophy* (Princeton).

Cooper, J. M. (2006), 'Seneca on Moral Theory and Moral Improvement', in Volk, K. and Williams, G. D. (eds.), *Seeing Seneca Whole. Perspectives on Philosophy, Poetry and Politics* (Leiden/Boston), 43–55.

Corbeill, A. (2002), 'Ciceronian Invective', in May, J. M. (ed.), *Brill's Companion to Cicero: Oratory and Rhetoric* (Leiden), 197–218.

Cornell, T. J. (2013) (ed.), *The Fragments of the Roman Historians, 3. Commentary* (Oxford).

Correa, S. (2021), '*Est (…) virtuti etiam in lectulo locus*: una nueva forma de ejemplaridad en Sen., *Ep.* LXXVII y LXXVIII', *Auster* 26: 1–13.

Corsano, M. (2004), 'Sul secondo combattimento della *Psychomachia* di Prudenzio', in Taragna, A. M. (ed.), *La poesia tardoantica e medioevale* (Alessandria), 95–107.

Costa, S. (2013), Quod olim fuerat. *La rappresentazione del passato in Seneca prosatore* (Hildesheim/Zürich/New York).

Costa, S. (2014) (ed.), *Mecenate. Frammenti e testimonianze latine* (Milano).

Costantini, L. (2019), *Magic in Apuleius'* Apologia. *Understanding the Charges and Forensic Strategies in Apuleius' Speech* (Berlin/Boston).

Cotrozzi, A. (2004) (ed.), *Seneca, La* Consolatio ad Helviam matrem *con un'antologia di testi* (Rome).

Coudry, M. (1998), 'Conclusion générale', in David, J.-M. (ed.), *Valeurs et Mémoire à Rome: Valère Maxime ou la vertu recomposée* (Paris), 183–92.

Coudry, M. (2004), 'Loi et société: la singularité des lois sumptuaires de Rome', *Cahiers du centre Gustave Glotz* 15: 135–71.

Courcelle, P. (1975), *Connais-toi toi-même, de Socrate à Saint Bernard* (Paris).

Courtil, J.-C. (2014), 'Torture in Seneca's Philosophical Works: Between Justification and Condemnation', in in Colish, M. L. and Wildberger, J. (eds.), Seneca Philosophus (Berlin/Boston), 189–207.

Courtil, J.-C. (2018a), 'Le goût de la sagesse: Sénèque et les assaisonnements', *Pallas* 106: 119–35.

Courtil, J.-C. (2018b), '*Redeo inhumanior*. Cruauté et déshumanisation chez Sénèque: l'inhumain, l'animal et le monster', *Vita Latina* 197–198: 99–116.

Courtil, J.-C. (2021), 'Les origins de la médecine dans la lettre 95 de Sénèque: une construction morale de l'histoire médicale', *Pallas* 116: 141–59.

Courtney, E. (1991), *The Poems of Petronius* (Atlanta).

Courtney, E. (2013), *A Commentary on the Satires of Juvenal* (Berkeley).

Cozzoli, U. (1980), 'La *tryphe* nell'interpretazione delle crisi politiche', in *Tra Grecia e Roma. Temi antichi e metodologie moderne* (Roma), 133–45.

Cucchiarelli, A. (2020) (ed.), *Orazio, Epistole I. Introduzione, traduzione e commento* (Pisa) (2019[1]).

Cugusi, P. (2005), '*Strenui militis et boni imperatoris officia simul exequi*. Cenni sulla 'ideologia' del condottiero nella letteratura romana', in Bessone, F. and Malaspina, E. (eds.), *Politica e cultura in Roma antica. Atti dell'incontro di studio in ricordo di Italo Lana* (Bologna), 35–58.

Curran, L. C. (1975), 'Nature to Advantage Dressed: Propertius 1.2', *Ramus* 4.1: 1–16.

Dal Chiele, E. (2016) (ed.), *Apuleio, De Platone et eius dogmate* (Bologna).

Dalby, A. (2000), *Empire of Pleasures. Luxury and Indulgence in the Roman World* (London).

Dari-Mattiacci, G./Plisecka, A. E. (2010), 'Luxury in Ancient Rome: Scope, Timing and Enforcement of Sumptuary Laws', *Amsterdam Center for Law and Economics* 3: 1–26.

D'Arms, J. H. (1999), 'Performing Culture: Roman Spectacle and the Banquets of the Powerful', *Studies in the History of Arts* 56: 300–19.

D'Arms, J. H. (2003), *Romans on the Bay of Naples and Other Essays on Roman Campania*, Edited by F. Zevi, with a Preface by A. Tchernia (Bari) (1970[1]).

Davis, G. (2007), 'Wine and the Symposium', in Harrison, S. J. (ed.), *The Cambridge Companion to Horace* (Cambridge), 207–20.

Debru, A. (1988), 'Consomption et corruption: l'origin et le sens de *tabes*', in Sabbah, G. (ed.), *Études de médecine romaine* (Saint-Étienne), 19–31.

De Caro, A. (2009), '*Voluntas liceat*. Riconoscimento e riconoscenza nel *beneficium*', in Picone, G., Beltrami, L. and Ricottilli, L. (eds.), *Benefattori e beneficati. La relazione asimmetrica nel* De Beneficiis *di Seneca* (Palermo), 121–58.

Degl'Innocenti Pierini, R. (2001), 'Tra Lucrezia e Virginia: su un'eco liviana in un coro dell'*Octavia*, vv. 291ss. (e in Seneca tragico)', in *ΠΟΙΚΙΛΜΑ. Studi in onore di M. R. Cataudella* (La Spezia), 349–59.

Degl'Innocenti Pierini, R. (2004), 'Il cielo e il soffitto. Speculazione filosofica e realtà romana nell'epistola 90 di Seneca', in De Finis, L. (ed.), *Colloquio su Seneca* (Trento), 65–88.

Degl'Innocenti Pierini, R. (2013), 'Seneca, Mecenate e il 'ritratto in movimento' (a proposito dell'*epistola* 114', in Gasti, F. (ed.), *Seneca e la letteratura greca e latina. Per i settant'anni di Giancarlo Mazzoli* (Pavia), 45–65.

Degl'Innocenti Pierini, R. (2022), 'Seneca e il rispetto del paesaggio. Riflessioni a partire dall'epistola 89', *Quaderni Borromaici* 9: 35–61.

Delarue, F. (2014), 'L'eau et l'imaginaire. Les villas des *Silvae* des Stace', in Devillers, O. (ed.), Neronia *IX. La villégiature dans le monde romain de Tibère à Hadrien* (Bordeaux), 89–98.

Del Giovane, B. (2012), 'Seneca, Scipione, e l'ombra di Cicerone: a proposito dell'epistola 86', *Prometheus* 38: 155–74.

Del Giovane, B. (2014), 'Retorica, immaginazione e autopsia. Seneca e il caso della colpevole *luxuria* (*epist.* 110.14 e *benef.* 7.10.2)', *Athenaeum* 102.2: 490–508.

Del Giovane, B. (2015a), *Seneca, la diatriba e la ricerca di una morale austera. Caratteristiche, influenze, mediazioni di un rapporto complesso* (Firenze).

Del Giovane, B. (2015b), 'Attalus and the Others. Diatribic Morality, Cynicism and Rhetoric in Seneca's Teachers', *Maia* 67: 3–24.

Del Giovane, B. (2022), 'Da *iocosus* a *consularis scurra*. Rappresentazioni del Cicerone umorista', in Berno, F. R. and La Bua, G. (eds.), *Portraying Cicero in Literature, Culture, and Politics* (Berlin/Boston), 283–311.

Delpeyroux, M.-F. (2014), 'Architecture, luxe et thermalisme chez Sénèque le philosophe', in Devillers, O. (ed.), Neronia *IX. La villégiature dans le monde romain de Tibère à Hadrien* (Bordeaux), 67–77.

De Maria, S. (2021), 'Seneca e il *balneolum* di Scipione', in *Lucrezio, Seneca e noi. Studi per Ivano Dionigi* (Bologna), 309–19.

De Martinis, L. (2022), 'La nascita e lo sviluppo del nesso *tryphe*-decadenza nella storiografia ellenistica', *Erga-Logoi* 10.2: 121–56.

De Melo, W. (2013) (ed.), *Plautus, Stichus, Three-Dollar Day, Truculentus, The Tale of a Traveling Bag, Fragments*, (London/Cambridge MA).

De Mitri, C. (2001), 'Il concetto di ricchezza nelle tragedie di Seneca', *Latomus* 60: 182–3.

Dench, E. (1996), 'Images of Italian Austerity from Cato to Tacitus', in Cébeillac-Gervasoni, M. (ed.), *Les élites municipals de l'Italie péninsulaire des Gracques à Néron* (Rome/Naples), 247–54.

Desmond, W. (2008), *Cynics* (Swansea).

de Vaan, M. (2008), *Etymological Dictionary of Latin and the Other Italic Languages* (Leiden/Boston).

De Vivo, A. (1984), '*Luxuria* e *mos maiorum*: indirizzi programmatici della storiografia velleiana', *Vichiana* 13.3: 249–64.

Dietsche, U. (2014), *Strategie und Philosophie bei Seneca. Untersuchungen zur therapeutischen Technik in den* Epistulae morales (Berlin/Boston).

Di Paola, O. (2014), 'The Philosophical Thought of the School of the Sextii', *Epekeina* 4: 327–39.

Di Serio, C. (2018), '*Psychomachia*: le *virtutes* e la fondazione del *templum animae*', *Eruditio antiqua* 10: 45–58.

Dixon, S. (2001), *Reading Roman Women. Sources, Genres and Real Life* (London).

Dorati, M. (2003), 'La Lidia e la *tryphe*', *AevAnt* n.s. 3: 503–30.

Dover, K. J. (1980) (ed.), *Plato, Symposium* (Cambridge).

Dressler, A. (2016), *Personification and the Feminine in Roman Philosophy* (Cambridge).

Drogula, F. K. (2019), *Cato the Younger: Life and Death at the End of the Roman Republic* (Oxford).

Ducos, M. (2010), 'Rhétorique et politique chez Tite-Live: le débat sur la *Lex Oppia*', *AevAnt* n.s. 10: 267–77.

Duff, J. D. (1962) (ed.), *Lucan, The Civil War* (London/Cambridge MA) (1928[1]).

Dunkle, J. R. (1971), 'The Rhetorical Tyrant in Roman Historiography: Sallust, Livy, and Tacitus', *CW* 65.1: 12–20.

Du Prey, P. (1994), *The Villas of Pliny from Antiquity to Posterity* (Chicago).

D'Urso, V. (2022) (ed.), *Lucano, Pharsalia o La guerra civile*, saggio introduttivo di P. Esposito, trad. di N. Lanzarone, comm. di V. D'Urso (Santarcangelo di Romagna).

Dyck, A. R. (2013) (ed.), *M. Tullius Cicero, Pro Marco Caelio* (Cambridge).

Dyson, S. L. (1970), 'The Portrait of Seneca in Tacitus', *Arethusa* 3.1: 71–83.

Dyson, H. (2010), 'Pleasure and the *Sapiens*: Seneca *De vita beata* 11.1', *CPh* 105: 313–18.

Earl, D. C. (1966), *The Political Thought of Sallust* (Amsterdam).

Edwards, C. (1993), *The Politics of Immorality in Ancient Rome* (Cambridge).

Edwards, C. (2000) (ed.), *Suetonius, Lives of the Caesars* (Oxford).
Edwards, C. (2017), 'Saturnalian Exchanges: Seneca, Horace, and Satiric Advice', in Stöckinger, M., Winter, K., and Zanker, A. T. (eds.), *Horace and Seneca: Interactions, Intertexts, Interpretations* (Berlin), 73–89.
Edwards, C. (2019) (ed.), *Selected Letters of Seneca* (Cambridge).
Edwards, C. (2021), 'Looking for the Emperor in Seneca's Letters', in Geue, T. and Giusti, E. (eds.), *Unspoken Rome. Absence in Latin Literature and Its Reception* (Cambridge), 165–84.
Edwards, H. J. (1963) (ed.), *Caesar, The Gallic Wars* (London/Cambridge MA).
Eichholz, D. E. (1971) (ed.), *Pliny, Natural History* X: *Books XXXVI–XXXVII* (London/Cambridge MA) (1962[1]).
Eisenhut, W. (1973), Virtus Romana. *Ihre Stellung im römischen Wertsystem* (München).
Elsner, J. (1994), 'Constructing Decadence: The Representation of Nero as Imperial Builder', in Elsner, J. and Master, J. (eds.), *Reflexions of Nero. Culture, History, and Representation* (London), 112–27.
Esposito, P. (1993), '*Parsimonia* e *luxuria* edilizia: Seneca e alcuni eccessi neroniani', *Vichiana* 4: 211–21.
Evenepoel, W. (2014), 'The Stoic Seneca on *virtus*, *gaudium*, and *voluptas*', *AntClass* 83: 45–78.
Fairweather, J. (1981), *Seneca the Elder* (Cambridge).
Fantham, E. (1977a), 'Philemon's *Thesauros* as Dramatization of Peripatetic Ethics', *Hermes* 105: 406–21.
Fantham, E. (1997b), 'Images of the City in Propertius' New-Old Rome', in Habinek, T. and Schiesaro, A. (eds.), *The Roman Cultural Revolution* (Cambridge), 122–35.
Fantham, E. (2013) (ed.), *Cicero's Pro L. Murena oratio* (Oxford).
Fantham, E. (2014) (ed.), *Seneca, Hardship and Happiness*, Translations by E. Fantham, H. M. Hine, J. Ker, and G. D. Williams (Chicago/London).
Favez, C. (1918) (ed.), *L. Annaei Senecae ad Helviam matrem De consolatione* (Lausanne/Paris).
Fedeli, P. (1980) (ed.), *Sesto Properzio, Il primo libro delle Elegie* (Firenze).
Fedeli, P. (1985) (ed.), *Properzio, Il libro terzo delle Elegie* (Bari).
Fedeli, P. (1994) (ed.), *Quinto Orazio Flacco, le opere*, vol. 2.2: *Le Satire* (Roma).
Fedeli, P. (2021) (ed.), *Properzio, Elegie*, vol. I: *libri I–II* (Milano).
Fedeli, P. (2022) (ed.), *Properzio, Elegie*, vol. II: *libri III–IV* (Milano).
Fedriani, C. (2016), 'Ontological and Orientational Metaphors in Latin', in Short, W. M. (ed.), *Embodiment in Latin Semantics* (Amsterdam/Philadelphia), 115–39.
Feichtinger, B. (2015), 'Streiten über *luxuria*. Überlegungen zur *lex-Oppia* Episode bei Livius', *Latomus* 74.3: 671–88.
Feldherr, A. (1988), *Spectacle and Society in Livy's History* (Berkeley).
Fellmeth, U. (2001), *Brot und Politik. Ernährung, Tafelluxus und Hunger im antiken Rom* (Stuttgart/Weimar).
Felton, K./Lee, K. H. (1972), 'The Theme of Juvenal's Eleventh Satire', *Latomus* 31.4: 1041–6.
Ferri, R. (2003) (ed.), *Octavia. A Play Attributed to Seneca*, Edited with Introduction and Commentary (Cambridge).
Fiorini Ripert, L. (2020), 'Seneca, Baia e l'imperatore. Per una rilettura dell'*epistola* 51', *Maia* 72.3: 610–27.
Fischer, S. (1983), '*Avaritia*, *luxuria* und *ambitio* in der Satire II 3 des Horaz', *Philologus* 127.1: 72–9.
Fitzgerald, J. T. (2008) (ed.), *Passions and Moral Progress in Greco-Roman Thought* (London/New York).
Fitzgerald, W. (2016), *Variety. The Life of a Roman Concept* (Chicago).

Fletcher, R. (2014), *Apuleius' Platonism* (Cambridge).

Flory, M. B. (1988), 'Pearls for Venus', *Historia* 37: 498–504.

Forster Smith, C. (1935) (ed.), *Thucydides*, vol. I: *History of the Peloponnesian War, Books I and II* (London/Cambridge MA).

Foster, B. O. (1957) (ed.), *Livy, I: Books I and II* (London/Cambridge MA).

Fowler, H. N. (2005) (ed.), *Plato, Euthyphro, Apology, Crito, Phaedo, Phaedrus*, Introduction by W. R. M. Lamb (London/Cambridge MA) (1914[1]).

Fowler, R. C. (2016) (ed.), *Imperial Plato: Albinus, Maximus, Apuleius: text and translation, with an introduction and commentary* (Las Vegas).

Franchi, P. (2013), *La battaglia interiore. Prova di commento alla* Psychomachia *di Prudenzio*, Diss. (Wien).

Fratantuono, L. M./Smith, R. A. (2018) (eds.), *Virgil, Aeneid 8—Text, Translation, and Commentary* (Leiden/Boston).

Frazer, J. G. (1929) (ed.), *The* Fasti *of Ovid*, vol. IV: Commentary on Books V and VI (London).

Fredericks, S. C. (1976), 'Juvenal's Fifteenth Satire', *ICS* 1: 174–89.

Freudenberg, K. (1993), *The Walking Muse. Horace on the Theory of Satire* (Princeton).

Freudenberg, K. (2004), *Satires of Rome. Threatening poses from Lucilius to Juvenal* (Cambridge).

Freudenberg, K. (2017), 'Petronius, Realism, Nero', in Bartsch, S., Freudenberg, K., and Littlewood, C. A. J. (eds.), *The Cambridge Companion to the Age of Nero* (Cambridge), 107–20.

Frisch, M. (2020) (ed.), *Prudentius, Psychomachia: Einleitung, Text, Übersetzung und Kommentar* (Berlin/Boston).

Fucecchi, M. (2019), 'Seneca e la villa di Scipione a Literno: spunti per la (ri)costruzione di un personaggio carismatico', in Citroni, M., Labate, M., and Rosati, G. (eds.), *Luoghi dell'abitare, immaginazione letteraria e identità romana. Da Augusto ai Flavi* (Pisa), 247–64.

Fuchs, H. (1958), 'Friede als Gefahr—Zum Zweiten Einslieder Hirtengedichte', *HSCP* 63: 363–85.

Fusi, A. (2006) (ed.), *M. Valerii Martialis Epigrammaton liber tertius* (Hildesheim/Zürich/New York).

Gäth, S. (2010), *Die literarische Rezeption des Cato Uticensis* (Frankfurt am Main-Berlin).

Galtier, F. (2011), *L'image tragique de l'histoire chez Tacite. Étude des schèmes tragique dans les* Histoires *et les* Annales (Bruxelles).

Gardner, R. (1958) (ed.), *Cicero in Twenty-eight Volumes*, vol. 13: *Pro Caelio, De Provinciis Consularibus, Pro Balbo* (London/Cambridge MA).

Gascou, G. (1984), *Suétone historien* (Rome).

Gauly, B. M. (2004), *Senecas* Naturales Quaestiones. *Naturphilosophie für die römische Kaiserzeit* (München).

Gazzarri, T. (2014), 'Gender-Based Differential Morbidity and Moral Teaching in Seneca's *Epistulae Morales*', in Colish, M. L. and Wildberger, J. (eds.), Seneca Philosophus (Berlin/Boston), 209–27.

Gazzarri, T. (2020), *The Stylus and the Scalpel. Theory and Practice of Metaphors in Seneca's Prose* (Berlin/Boston).

Gazzarri, T. (2021), 'Due letture dell'esordio della lettera 64 di Seneca, 1. La simbologia del fumo', *Lucius Annaeus Seneca* 1: 3–24.

Giancotti, F. (1992), 'Le *sententiae* di Publilio Siro e Seneca', in Grimal, P. (ed.), *La langue latine langue de la philosophie* (Rome), 9–38.

Giazzi, E. (2011), 'La figura di Annibale nell'opera in prosa di Seneca', in *Studi su Seneca e Properzio offerti a Roberto Gazich da allievi e collaboratori* (Milano), 53–73.
Gibson, R. K. (2003), 'Pliny and the Art of (In-)Offensive Self-Praise', *Arethusa* 36.2: 235–54.
Gibson, R. K. (2006), 'Ovid, Augustus, and the Politics of Moderation in *Ars Amatoria* 3', in Gibson, R. K., Green, S., and Sharrock, A. (eds.), *The Art of Love. Bimillennial Essays on Ovid's* Ars amatorial *and* Remedia Amoris (Oxford), 121–42.
Gibson, R. K./Morello, R. (2012), *Reading the Letters of Pliny the Younger: An Introduction* (Cambridge).
Gildenhard, I. (2020), '*Frugalitas*, or: The Invention of a Roman Virtue', in Gildenhard, I. and Viglietti, C. (eds.), *Roman Frugality. Modes of Moderation from the Archaic Age to the Early Empire and Beyond* (Cambridge), 237–346.
Gildenhard, I./Viglietti, C. (2020), 'Introduction', in Gildenhard, I. and Viglietti, C. (eds.), *Roman Frugality. Modes of Moderation from the Archaic Age to the Early Empire and Beyond* (Cambridge), 1–126.
Giusti, E. (2017), 'The Metapoetics of Liberty. Horace's Bacchic Ship in Seneca's *De Tranquillitate animi*', in Stöckinger, M., Winter, K., and Zanker, A. T. (eds.), *Horace and Seneca: Interactions, Intertexts, Interpretations* (Berlin), 239–63.
Gleason, M. W. (1994), *Making Men: Sophists and Self-Presentation in Ancient Rome* (Princeton).
Goar, R. (1987), *The Legend of Cato from the I Century b. C. to the V Century a. C.* (Bruxelles).
Goddard, J. (1994), 'The Tyrant at Table', in Elsner, J. and Master, J. (eds.), *Reflexions of Nero. Culture, History, and Representation* (London), 67–82.
Goelzer, H. (1920) (ed.), *Oeuvres de Tacite* (Paris).
Gonzales, A. (2014), 'La *villa* plinienne expression de l'*humanitas*? Conditions de vie, statuts, santé et *obsequium*', in Devillers, O. (ed.), Neronia *IX. La villégiature dans le monde romain de Tibère à Hadrien* (Bordeaux), 105–14.
Goodyear, F. R. D. (1972) (ed.), *The Annals of Tacitus: Books 1–6* (Cambridge).
Gorman, R. J./Gorman, V. B. (2014), *Corrupting Luxury in Ancient Greek Literature* (Ann Arbor).
Goulet-Cazé, M.-O. (1990), 'Le Cynisme à l'époque impériale', *ANRW* II.36.4: 2720–833.
Gourévitch, D. (1974), 'Le menu de l'homme libre. Recherches sur l'alimentation et la digestion dans les oeuvres en prose de Sénèque', in Gros, P. and Morel, J.-P. (eds.), *Mélanges de philosophie, de littérature et d'histoire ancienne offerts à Pierre Boyancé* (Rome), 311–44.
Gowers, E. (1996), *The Loaded Table. Representations of Food in Roman Literature* (Oxford).
Gowing, A. M. (2013), 'Tully's Boat: Responses to Cicero in the Imperial Period', in Steel, C. (ed.), *The Cambridge Companion to Cicero* (Cambridge), 233–50.
Graver, M. (1998), 'The Manhandling of Maecenas: Senecan Abstractions of Masculinity', *AJPh* 119: 607–32.
Graver, M./Long, A. A. (2015) (eds.), *Lucius Annaeus Seneca, Letters on Ethics, Translated with an Introduction and Commentary* (Chicago/London).
Greenwood, L. H. G. (1959) (ed.), *Cicero, The Verrine Orations*, vol. I: *Against Cecilius; Against Verres, Part one; Part two, Books I and II* (London/Cambridge MA).
Greenwood, L. H. G. (1960) (ed.), *Cicero, The Verrine Orations*, vol. II: *Against Verres, Part two, Books III, IV and V* (London/Cambridge MA).
Grelle, F. (1980), 'La *correctio morum* nella legislazione flavia', *ANRW* II.13: 340–65.
Griffin, J. (1985a), 'Augustan Poets and the Life of Luxury', in Griffin, J., *Latin Poets and Roman Life* (London), 1–31.
Griffin, J. (1985b), 'The Pleasures of Water and Nakedness', in Griffin, J., *Latin Poets and Roman Life* (London), 88–111.

Griffin, M. (2007), 'The Younger Pliny's Debt to Moral Philosophy', *HSCPh* 103: 451–81.

Griffin, M. T. (1996), 'Cynicism and the Romans: Attraction and Repulsion', in Bracht Branham, R. and Goulet-Cazé, M.-O. (eds.), *The Cynics. The Cynic Movement in Antiquity and Its Legacy* (Berkeley/Los Angeles/London), 190–204.

Griffin, M. T. (2003), *Seneca: A Philosopher in Politics* (Oxford) (1976[1]).

Griffin, M. T./Inwood, B. (2011) (ed.), *Seneca, On Benefits* (Chicago/London).

Griffin, M. T. (2013), *Seneca on Society. A Guide to* De Beneficiis (Oxford).

Griffith, T. (2000) (trans.), *Plato, The Republic*, Edited by G. R. F. Ferrari (Cambridge).

Grillo, L. (2011), *The Art of Caesar's* Bellum Civile (Cambridge).

Grimal, P. (1969), *Les jardins romains* (Paris).

Guerrini, R. (1979), 'Moduli sallustiani in Valerio Massimo. Il capitolo *De luxuria et libidine* (IX, 1)', *RIL* 113: 152–66.

Guite, H. (1962), 'Cicero's Attitude to the Greeks', *G&R* 9: 142–59.

Gunderson, E. (2014), 'E. g. Augustus: *exemplum* in *Augustus* and *Tiberius*', in Power, T. and Gibson, R. K. (eds.), *Suetonius the Biographer* (Oxford), 130–45.

Gwyn, W. B. (1991), 'Nero: The Concept of the Tyrant and the Image of Nero in Western Political Thought', *History of Political Thought* 12.3: 421–55.

Habermehl, P. (2021) (ed.), *Petronius, Satyrica 79–141. Ein philologisch-literarischer Komment. Bd. 3: Bellum civile (Sat. 119–124)* (Berlin/Boston).

Habinek, T. N. (1988), *The Politics of Latin Literatur. Writing, Identity, and Empire in Ancient Rome* (Princeton).

Hadot, I. (2012), *Sénèque. Direction spirituelle et pratique de la philosophie* (Paris).

Haehling, R. von. (1991), 'Der obstessende Kaiser—Ein Paradigma für *Luxuria* in den Tyrannentopik der *Historia Augusta*', in Rosen, K. (ed.), *Bonner* Historia Augusta *Colloquium* (Bonn), 93–106.

Hannah, R. (1977), 'The Sources and the Art of Prudentius' *Psychomachia*', *CPh* 72.2: 108–15.

Hardie, P. (2013), 'Lucan's *Bellum Civile*', in Buckely, E. and Dinter, M. T. (eds.), *A Companion to the Neronian Age* (Malden MA/Oxford), 225–40.

Hardie, P. (2017), 'How Prudentian is the *Aeneid*?', *Dictynna* 14: 1–13.

Hardie, P. (2019), 'Augustan and Late Antique Intratextuality: Virgil's *Aeneid* and Prudentius' *Psychomachia*', in Harrison, S., Frangoulidis, S., and Papanghelis, T. D. (eds.), *Intratextuality and Latin Literature* (Berlin/Boston), 159–70.

Harmon, A. M. (1913) (ed.), *Lucian, I. Phalaris, Hippias or the Bath, Heracles, Amber of the Swans, The Fly, Nigrinus, Demonax, The Hall, My Native Land, Octogenarius, A True Story, Slander, The Consonants at Law, The Carousal (Symposium) of The Lapiths* (London/Cambridge MA).

Harris, W. V. (2001), *Restraining Rage: The Ideology of Anger Control in Classical Antiquity* (Cambridge/London).

Harrison, S. J. (2005), 'Decline and Nostalgia', in Harrison, S. J. (ed.), *A Companion to Latin Literature* (London), 287–99.

Harrison, S. J. (2007), 'Town and Country', in Harrison, S. J. (ed.), *The Cambridge Companion to Horace* (Cambridge), 235–47.

Harrison, S. J. (2013), *Framing the Ass. Literary Texture in Apuleius'* Metamorphoses (Oxford).

Harrison, S. J. (2017) (ed.), *Horace, Odes Book 2* (Cambridge).

Haskins, S. L. (2014), 'A Gendered Reading for the Character of Psyche in Apuleius' *Metamorphoses*', *Mnemosyne* 67.2: 247–60.

Haworth, K. R. (1980), *Deified Virtues, Demonic Vices and Descriptive Allegory in Prudentius'* Psychomachia (Amsterdam).

Hay, P. (2019), 'Saecular Discourse: Qualitative Periodization in First-Century-BCE Rome', in Morrell, K., Osgood, J., and Welsh, K. (eds.), *The Alternative Augustan Age* (Oxford), 216–30.

Heinz, K. (1948), *Das Bild der Kaiser Neros bei Seneca, Tacitus, Sueton und Cassius Dio* (Bern).
Henderson, J. (2002) (ed.), *Aristophanes, Frogs, Assemblywomen, Wealth* (London/Cambridge MA).
Henderson, J. (2004), *Morals and Villas in Seneca's Letters. Places to Dwell* (Cambridge).
Hermann, A. (1959), 'Edelsteine', *RAC* 4: 506–52.
Hermann, J. P. (1978), '*Psychomachia* 423–426 and *Aeneid* 5, 468–470', *CB* 54: 88–9.
Hertel, G. (1969), *Die Allegorie von Reichtum und Armut. Ein aristophanisches Motiv und seine Abwandlungen in der abendländischen Literatur* (Nürnberg).
Heseltine, M. (1969) (ed.), *Petronius Arbiter, Satyricon; Seneca, Apocolocyntosis*, Reviewed by E. H. Warmington and W. H. D. Rouse (London/Cambridge MA).
Heyworth, S. J./Morwood, J. H. W. (2011), *A Commentary on Propertius, Book 3* (Cambridge).
Hijmans, B. L. (1987), 'Apuleius, *Philosophus Platonicus*', *ANRW* II.36.1: 396–475.
Hine, H. M. (2010) (ed.), *Seneca, Natural Questions* (Chicago/London).
Hoffer, S. E. (1999), *The Anxieties of Pliny the Younger* (Atlanta GE).
Hollmann, E. (2016), *Die plautinischen Prologues und ihre Funktion. Zur Konstruktion von Spannung un Komik in den Komödien des Plautus* (Berlin/New York).
Hönscheid, C. (2004), Fomenta Campaniae. *Ein Kommentar su Senecas 51., 55. Und 56. Brief* (Munich-Leipzig).
Hopkins, K. (1999), *A World Full of Gods. Pagans, Jews, and Christians in the Roman Empire* (London).
Hooley, D. M. (1997), *The Knotted Thong. Structures of Mimesis in Persius* (Ann Arbor).
Hornblower, S. (2003), *A Commentary on Thucydides, I: Books I–III* (Oxford/New York) (1991[1]).
Horsfall, N. (1989) (ed.), *Cornelius Nepos. A Selection, Including the Lives of Cato and Atticus. Translated, with Introduction and Commentary* (Oxford).
Hunink, J. L. (2001a) (ed.), *Apuleius, Rhetorical Works*, Translated by S. J. Harrison, J. L. Hunink, and V. J. C. Hunink (Oxford).
Hunink, V. (2001b) (ed.), *Apuleius of Madauros, Florida* (Amsterdam).
Hunter, R. (1980), 'Philemon, Plautus and the *Trinummus*', *MusHelv*, 37: 216–30.
Hurley, D. W. (2014), 'Suetonius' Rubric Sandwich', in Power, T. and Gibson, R. K. (eds.), *Suetonius the Biographer* (Oxford), 21–37.
Imber, M. (2008), 'Live without Father: Declamation and the Construction of Paternity in the Roman Empire', in Bell, S. (ed.), *Role Models in the Roman World. Identity and Assimilation* (Ann Arbor), 161–9.
Inwood, B. (1985), *Ethics and Human Action in Early Stoicism* (Oxford).
Inwood, B. (2005a), 'Seneca and Psychological Dualism', in Inwood, B., *Reading Seneca. Stoic Philosophy at Rome* (Oxford), 23–64.
Inwood, B. (2005b), 'Getting to Goodness', in Inwood, B., *Reading Seneca. Stoic Philosophy at Rome* (Oxford), 271–301.
Inwood, B. (2010) (ed.), *Seneca. Selected Philosophical Letters* (Oxford) (2007[1]).
Inwood, B. (2014), 'Walking and Talking: Reflections on Divisions of the Soul in Stoicism', in Corcilius, K. and Perler, D. (eds.), *Partitioning the Soul: The Debates from Plato to Leibniz* (Berlin/Boston), 63–83.
Isager, J. (1993), 'The Hellenization of Rome. *Luxuria* or *liberalitas*?' in Guldager Bilde, P., Nielsen, I., and Nielsen, M. (eds.), *Aspects of Hellenism in Italy: Towards a Cultural Unity?* (Copenhagen), 257–73.
Isager, J. (1998), *Pliny the Elder on Art and Society. The Elder Pliny's Chapters on the History of Art* (Oxford).
Isetta, S. (1986) (ed.), *Tertulliano, L'eleganza delle donne—De cultu feminarum* (Bologna).

Jacquemin, A. (1998), 'Valère Maxime, lecteur et utilisateur de Salluste', in David, J.-M. (ed.), *Valeurs et Mémoire à Rome: Valère Maxime ou la vertu recomposée* (Paris), 97–110.

Janka, M. (1997), *Ovid, Ars Amatoria, Buch 2. Kommentar* (Heidelberg).

Johnson, M. P. (ed.) (2020), *The Holy Bible: World English Bible* (ebible.org).

Jones, M. (2014), 'Seneca's Letters to Lucilius: Hypocrisy as a Way of Life', in Colish, M. L. and Wildberger, J. (eds.), Seneca Philosophus (Berlin/Boston), 393–429.

Jones, W. H. S. (1951) (ed.), *Pliny, Natural History* VI: *Books XX–XXIII* (London/Cambridge MA).

Jones-Lewis, M. A. (2012), 'Poison: Nature's Argument for the Roman Empire in Pliny the Elder's *Naturalis Historia*', *CW* 106.1: 51–74.

Kalimtzis, K. (2012), *Taming Anger: The Hellenic Approach to the Limitations of Reason* (London/New Delhi/New York/Sydney).

Kapust, D. J. (2011), *Republicanism, Rhetoric, and Roman Political Thought. Sallust, Livy, and Tacitus* (Cambridge).

Kaster, R. A. (2005), *Emotion, Restraint and Community in Ancient Rome* (Oxford).

Kaster, R. A. (2010) (ed.), *Seneca, Anger, Mercy, Revenge, Translated by R. A. Kaster and M. C. Nussbaum* (Chicago/London).

Kaster, R. A. (2011) (ed.), *Macrobius, Saturnalia, Books 3–5* (London/Cambridge MA).

Keane, C. (2012), 'Historian and Satirist: Tacitus and Juvenal', in Pagán, V. E. (ed.), *A Companion to Tacitus* (Malden MA/Oxford), 403–27.

Keegan, P. (2021), *Livy's Women. Crisis, Revolution, and the Female in Rome's Foundation History* (London/New York).

Kennedy, G. (1963), *The Art of Persuasion in Greece* (Princeton).

Kenty, J. (2017), '*Altera Roma*: Livy's Variation on a Ciceronian Theme', *ICS* 42.1: 61–81.

Ker, J. (2004), 'Nocturnal Writers in Imperial Rome: The Culture of *lucubratio*', *CPh* 99.3: 209–42.

Ker, J. (2009), *The Deaths of Seneca* (Oxford).

Ker, J. (2010), 'Socrates speaks in Seneca, *De vita beata* 24–28', in Nightingale, A. and Sedley, D. (eds.), *Ancient Models of Mind. Studies in Human and Divine Rationality* (Cambridge), 180–95.

Ker, J. (2012), 'Seneca in Tacitus', in Pagán, V. E. (ed.), *A Companion to Tacitus* (London), 305–29.

Ker, J. (2014) (ed.), *Seneca, Hardship and Happiness*, Translations by Fantham, E., Hine, H. M., Ker, J., and Williams, G. D. (Chicago/London).

Ker, J. (2020), 'Diurnal Selves in Ancient Rome', in Miller, K. J. and Simmons, S. L. (eds.), *Down to the Hour: Short Time in Ancient Mediterranean and Near East* (Leiden/Boston), 184–213.

Kidd, I. G. (1971), 'Stoic Intermediates and the End for Man', in Long, A. A. (ed.), *Problems in Stoicism* (London), 150–72.

Kidd, I. G. (1988), *Posidonius, II: The Commentary, 2: Fragments 150–293* (Cambridge).

Kidd, I. G. (1999), *Posidonius, III: The Translation of the Fragments* (Cambridge).

Kindstrand, J. F. (1980), 'Demetrius the Cynic', *Philologus* 124.1: 83–98.

Kloft, H. (2008), '*Luxuria*. Begriff und Sache in der römischen Kaiserzeit', in Aßkamp, R., Brouwer, M., Christiansen, J., Kenzler, H., and Wamser, L. (eds.), *Luxus und Dekadenz. Römisches Leben am Golf von Neapel* (Meinz), 65–75.

Knorr, O. (2012), '*Morbus Campanus* in Horace, *Satire* 1.5.62', *Classical Quarterly* 62.2: 869–73.

Knuuttila, S. (2004), *Emotions in Ancient and Medioeval Philosophy* (Oxford).

Koestermann, E. (1971) (ed.), *C. Sallustius Crispus, Bellum Iugurthinum* (Heidelberg).

Koestermann, E. (1973), 'Römische Dekadenz bei Sallust und Tacitus', *ANRW* I.3: 781–810.

Konstan, D. (2006), *The Emotions of the Ancient Greeks* (Toronto).

Konstan, D. (2020), 'The Invention of Emotion?', in Candiotto, L. and Renaut, O. (eds.), *Emotions in Plato* (Leiden/Boston), 372–81.

Kragelund, P. (2000), 'Nero's *luxuria*, in Tacitus and in the *Octavia*', *CQ* 50.2: 494–515.

Kuen, G. (1994), *Die Philosophie als* dux vitae. *Die Verknüpfung von Geahlt, Intention und Darstellungsweise im philosophischen Werk Senecas am Beispiel des Dialogs* De vita beata. *Einleitung, Wortkommentar und systematische Darstellung* (Heidelberg).

La Bua, G. (2013), 'Horace's East: Ethics and Politics', *HSCPh* 107: 265–96.

Lana, I. (1973), '*Sextiorum nova et romani roboris secta*', in Lana, I., *Studi sul pensiero politico classico* (Napoli) 339–84.

Lana, I. (1992), 'La scuola dei Sestii', in Grimal, P. (ed.), *La langue latine langue de la philosophie*, (Rome), 109–24.

La Penna, A. (1989), 'La legittimazione del lusso privato da Ennio a Vitruvio', *Maia* 41: 3–34.

La Penna, A./Funari, R. (2015) (eds.), *C. Sallusti Crispi Historiae I. Fragmenta 1.1–146* (Berlin/Boston).

Lamb, W. R. M. (1967) (trans.), *Plato in Twelve Volumes*, vol. III (London/Cambridge MA).

Lamberti, F. (2021), 'Stereotipi familiari nelle *Declamazioni maggiori*', in Lovato, A., Stramaglia, A., and Traina, G. (eds.), *Le* Declamazioni maggiori *pseudoquintilianee nella Roma imperiale*' (Berlin/Boston), 173–84.

Lampe, K. (2008), 'Seneca's Nausea. "Existential" Experiences and Julio-Claudian Literature', *Helios* 35.1: 67–87.

Lanciotti, S. (1977), 'Silla e la tipologia del tiranno nella letteratura latina tardorepubblicana, I', *Quaderni di Storia* 3.6: 129–53.

Lanciotti, S. (1979), 'Silla e la tipologia del tiranno nella Roma tardorepubblicana, II', *Quaderni di Storia* 8: 191–225.

Landolfi, L. (1990), *Banchetto e società romana. Dalle origini al I sec. a. C.* (Roma).

Langlands, R. (2006), *Sexual Morality in Ancient Rome* (Cambridge).

Langlands, R. (2014), 'Exemplary Influences and Augustus' Pernicious Moral Legacy', in Power, T. and Gibson, R. K. (eds.), *Suetonius the Biographer* (Oxford), 111–29.

Langlands, R. (2018), *Exemplary Ethics in Ancient Rome* (Cambridge).

Lanzarone, N. (2021), 'La rappresentazione del palazzo di Cleopatra in Lucano, *Bellum civile* X', *Maia* 73.2: 318–35.

Lao, E. (2011), 'Luxury and the Creation of a Good Consumer', in Gibson, R. K. and Morello, R. (eds.), *Pliny the Elder: Themes and Contexts* (Leiden/Boston), 35–56.

La Rocca, E. (2017), 'Staging Nero: Public Imagery and the *Domus Aurea*', in Bartsch, S., Freudenberg, K., and Littlewood, C. A. J. (eds.), *The Cambridge Companion to the Age of Nero* (Cambridge), 195–212.

Laudizi, G. (2003) (ed.), *L. Anneo Seneca, Lettere a Lucilio, libro terzo (*epp. *XXII–XXIX)* (Napoli).

Laudizi, G. (2004), 'Seneca (*ep.* 114) e la corruzione dello stile', *BStudLat* 34: 38–56.

Lazzarini, C. (2018) (ed.), *Ovidio, Rimedi contro l'amore* (Venice) (1986^1).

Leach, E. W. (2003), '*Otium* as *luxuria*: Economy of *Status* in the Younger Pliny's Letters', *Arethusa* 36: 147–65.

Leary, T. J. (1996) (ed.), *Martial, Book XIV: The Apophoreta*, Text with Introduction and Commentary (London).

Leary, T. J. (2001) (ed.), *Martial, Book XIII: The Xenia*, Text with Introduction and Commentary (London).

Lee, G. (1994) (ed.), *Propertius, The Poems*, with an Introduction by O. Lyne (Oxford).

Lefebvre, L. (2017), *Le mythe Néron. La fabrique d'un monstre dans la littérature antique (Ier–Ve s.)* (Villeneuve d'Ascq).

Lefèvre, E. (1993), 'Politics and Society in Plautus' *Trinummus*', in Scodel, R. (ed.), *Theater and Society in the Classical World* (Ann Arbor), 177–90.

Lefèvre, E. (1995), *Plautus und Philemon* (Tübingen).

Lehmann, Y. (1998), 'Les revendications morales et politiques de Valère Maxime', in David, J.-M. (ed.), *Valeurs et Mémoire à Rome: Valère Maxime ou la vertu recomposée* (Paris), 19–26.

Letta, C. (1984), *L'Italia dei* mores romani *nelle* Origines *di Catone* (Como).

Levene, D. S. (2000), 'Sallust's Catiline and Cato the Censor', *CQ* 50.1: 170–91.

Levene, D. S. (2015), 'Allusions and Intertextuality in Livy's Third Decade', in Mineo, B. (ed.), *A Companion to Livy* (London), 205–16.

Levick, B. (1982), 'Morals, Politics, and the Fall of the Roman Republic', *G&R* 29.1: 53–62.

Limburg, F. J. G. (2007), Aliquid ad mores. *The Prefaces and Epilogues of Seneca's* Naturales Quaestiones (Diss. Leiden).

Limburg, F. J. G. (2008), 'The Representation and Role of Badness in Seneca's Moral Teaching: A Case from the *Naturales Quaestiones* (*NQ* 1.16)', in Sluiter, I. and Rosen R. M. (eds.), Kakos*: Badness and Anti-Value in Classical Antiquity* (Leiden/Boston), 433–50.

Lintott, A. W. (1972), 'Imperial Expansion and Moral Decline in the Roman Republic', *Historia* 21: 626–38.

Lista, M. (2008), '"Befreit von den sinnlosen Trinkgesetzen." Tafelluxus bei Gastmahl und Gelage', in Aßkamp, R., Brouwer, M., Christiansen, J., Kenzler, H., and Wamser, L. (eds.), *Luxus und Dekadenz. Römisches Leben am Golf von Neapel* (Meinz), 151–9.

Littlewood, R. J. (2006), *A Commentary on Ovid's* Fasti, *Book 6* (Oxford).

Lombardo, M. (1983), '*Habrosyne* e *habra* nel mondo Greco arcaico', in Nenci, G. (ed.), *Modes de contacts et processus de transformation dans les sociétés anciennes. Actes du colloque de Cortone, 24–30 mai 1981* (*Rome*), 1077–103.

Lonardi, A. (2007), 'Alimentazione e banchetto. Le leggi suntuarie di Silla e Cesare', in Bortolin, R. and Pistellato, A. (eds.), *Alimentazione e banchetto. Forme e valori della commensalità dalla preistoria alla tarda antichità* (Venezia), 71–88.

Lotito, G. (2001), Suum esse. *Forme dell'interiorità senecana* (Bologna).

Luce, T. (1977), *Livy: The Composition of his History* (Princeton).

Macdonald, C. (1977) (ed.), *Cicero, In Catilinam I–IV; Pro Murena; Pro Sulla; Pro Flacco* (London/Cambridge MA).

Machosky, B. (2003), 'The Face that is Not a Face: The Phenomenology of the Soul in the Allegory of *Psychomachia*', *Exemplaria* 15.1: 1–38.

MacKay, L. A. (1956), 'The Well-Disposed and Ill-Used Door (Propertius 1.16)', *Phoenix* 10.1: 13–19.

Magie, D. (1980) (ed.), *The* Scriptores Historiae Augustae *in Three Volumes*, vol. II (London/Cambridge MA) (1924[1]).

Maier, H. O. (2004), 'Kleidung II', *RAC* 162: 2–60.

Maiuro, M. (2019), 'Tacitus, *modus* and *mensura*, or the Right Place for Senatorial Riches', in Righi, L. and Vettori, G. (eds.), *Il lusso e la sua disciplina. Aspetti economici e sociali della legislazione suntuaria tra antichità e medioevo* (Trento), 85–110.

Malaspina, E. (2020), 'Sul significato di *cicrumlitio*: nota a Sen. *epist.* 86, 6, Plinio, *nat.* 35, 133, e Quint. 8, 5, 26', *BStudLat* 50.1: 156–78.

Malaspina, E. (2021), 'L'ossessione della tortura in Seneca: una falla nella resistenza del *sapiens*?' *GIF* 73: 147–64.

Mantovanelli, P. (1981), Profundus. *Studio di un campo semantico dal latino arcaico al latino cristiano* (Roma).

Mantovanelli, P. (1998), '*Libido victrix.* Forme dell'intertestualità in Sen. *Thy.* 40ss.', *Paideia* 53: 237–49.

Mantovanelli, P. (2008), '*Libido/luxuria* nella *Phaedra* di Seneca', in Castagna, L. and Riboldi, C. (eds.), Amicitiae templa serena. *Miscellanea di studi in onore di G. Aricò* (Milano), 969–85.

Manuwald, G. (2018) (ed.), *Cicero, Agrarian Speeches. Introduction, Text, Translation, and Commentary* (Oxford).

Marchesi, I. (2015), 'The Unbalanced Dinner between Martial and Pliny', in Deviller, O. (ed.), *Autour de Pline le Jeune. En hommage à Nicole Méthy* (Bordeaux), 117–29.

Mariotti, I. (2007) (ed.), *Gaio Sallustio Crispo, Coniuratio Catilinae* (Bologna).

Marshall, A. (2008), 'Law and Luxury in Augustan Rome (Tacitus, *Annals* 3.53–4)', *Journal of Ancient Civilization* 23: 97–115.

Martin, (1976) (ed.), *Terence, Adelphoe* (Cambridge).

Martinet, H. (1981) (ed.), *C. Suetonius Tranquillus, Divus Titus. Kommentar* (Königstein).

Martino, L. M. (2008), '*Optime Romae custos gentis... redi. Mos maiorum* e imagen de Augusto en las *Odas* de Horacio', *Praesentia* 9: 1–12.

Maruotti, A. (2015), 'Les lieux de l'*otium* comme expression des *mores*: Vatia et Scipion dans les *Lettres à Lucilius* de Sénèque', in Voisin, P. and de Béchillon, M. (eds.), *L'espace dans l'Antiquité* (Paris), 345–54.

Mastrangelo, M. (2008), *The Roman Self in Late Antiquity. Prudentius and the Poetics of the Soul* (Baltimore).

Mastrorosa, I. (2006), 'Speeches pro and contra women in Livy 34.1–7: Catonian Legalism and Gendered Debate', *Latomus* 65: 590–611.

Mastrorosa, I. (2007), 'Politica suntuaria ed economia imperiale in un intervento di Tiberio (Tacito, *Ann.* III 52–55)', in Giua, M. A. (ed.), *Ripensando Tacito (e Ronald Syme). Storia e storiografia* (Pisa), 181–99.

Mattiacci, S. (2014), '*Apuleius and* Africitas', in Todd Lee, B., Finkelpearl, E., and Graverini, L. (eds.), *Apuleius and Africa* (London/New York), 87–111.

Mayer i Olivé (2023), 'Ciceró i la *luxuria*', in Pons Pujol, L., Pérez González, J. (eds.) De luxuria propagata romana aetate. *Roman luxury in its many forms* (Oxford) (forthcoming).

Mayor, J. E. B. (2010), *Thirteen Satires of Juvenal with a Commentary* (Cambridge) (1872^1).

Mazzoli, G. (1991), 'Effetti di cornice nell'epistolario senecano', in Setaioli, A. (ed.), *Seneca e la cultura* (Perugia), 67–87.

Mazzoli, G. (2005), 'La Roma di Seneca', Bessone, F. and Malaspina, E. (eds.), *Politica e cultura in Roma antica. Atti dell'incontro di studio in ricordo di Italo Lana* (Bologna), 123–33.

Mazzoli, G. (2016), 'Natura vs uomo', in Mazzoli, G., *Il* chaos *e le sue architetture. Trenta studi su Seneca tragico* (Palermo), 85–97.

Mazzoli, G. (2017a), 'Semantica senecana del primitivo', in Rocchi, S. and Mussini, C. (eds.), Imagines antiquitatis. *Representations, Concepts, Reception of the Past in Roman Antiquity and the Early Italian Reinassance* (Berlin/Boston), 27–38.

Mazzoli, G. (2017b), 'Prudenzio e Draconzio travizi e virtù', *Il calamo della memoria* 7: 51–66.

Mazzoli, G. (2021), '*Se fugere*, da Lucrezio ad Agostino, passando per Seneca', in *Lucrezio, Seneca e noi. Studi per Ivano Dionigi* (Bologna), 363–70.

McClintock, A. (2022), *La ricchezza femminile e la* lex Voconia (Napoli).

McDonnell, M. (2006), *Roman Manliness.* Virtus *and the Roman Republic* (Cambridge).

McGushin, P. (2005) (ed.), *Sallust, The Histories, I. Books i–ii* (Oxford).

McKim, R. (1986), 'Philosophers and Cannibals in Juvenal's Fifteenth Satire', *Phoenix* 40.1: 58–71.

Meinel, P. (1972), *Seneca über seine Verbannung* (Bonn).

Merriam, C. U. (2006), *Love and Propaganda. Augustan Venus and the Latin Love Elegists* (Bruxelles).

Méthy, N. (2007), *Les Lettres de Pline le Jeune. Une representation de l'homme* (Paris).

Migliario, E. (1989), 'Luoghi retorici e realtà sociale nell'opera di Seneca il Vecchio', *Athenaeum* 77.3–4: 525–49.

Miles, G. B. (1995), *Reconstructing Early Rome* (Ithaca NY).

Mineo, B. (2015), 'Livy's Historical Philosophy', in Mineo, B. (ed.), *A Companion to Livy* (London), 139–52.

Mitchell, T. N. (1984), 'Cicero on the Moral Crisis of the Late Republic', *Hermathena* 136: 21–41.

Moles, J. (1983), '*Honestius quam ambitiosius*? An Exploration on the Cynics' Attitude to Moral Corruption in his Fellow Man', *JHS* 103: 103–23.

Moles, J. (2007a), 'The Cynics', in Rowe, C. and Schofield, M. (eds.), *The Cambridge History of Greek and Roman Political Thought* (Cambridge) (2000[1]), 415–34.

Moles, J. (2007b), 'Philosophy and Ethics', in Harrison, S. J. (ed.), *The Cambridge Companion to Horace* (Cambridge), 165–80.

Montiglio, S. (2006), 'Should the Aspiring Wise Man Travel? A Conflict in Seneca's Thought', *AJ1Ph* 127.4: 553–86.

Montone, F. (2010), 'Il *topos* della *Campania felix* nella poesia latina', *Salternum* 14.24–5: 47–58.

Moore, C. H. (1956) (ed.), *Tacitus, The Histories, The Annals*, vol. I: *Histories, I–III* (London/Cambridge MA).

Morcillo, M. G. (2010), 'Zwischen Kunst und *luxuria*: Die korinthischen Bronzen in Plinius' *Naturalis Historia*', *Hermes* 138: 442–54.

Moretti, G. (1994), *Gli antipodi. Avventure letterarie di un mito scientifico* (Parma).

Morford, M. P. O. (1968), 'The Distortion of the *Domus Aurea* Tradition', *Eranos* 66: 158–79.

Morgan, T. (2007), *Popular Morality in the Early Roman Empire* (Cambridge).

Morrell, K./Osgood, J./Welsh, K. (2019) (eds.), *The Alternative Augustan Age* (Oxford).

Mortensen, D. E. (2008), 'The *loci* of Cicero', *Rhetorica* 26: 31–56.

Morton Braund, S. (1996), 'The Solitary Feast: A Contradiction in Terms?', *BICS* 41: 37–52.

Morton Braund, S. (2004) (ed.), *Juvenal and Persius* (London/Cambridge MA).

Morwood, J. (2010), 'Cupid grows up', *G&R* 57.1: 107–16.

Most, G. W. (2006) (ed.), *Hesiod, Theogony, Works and Days, Testimonia* (London/Cambridge MA).

Motto, A. L. (1966), 'Seneca on Trial. The Case of the Opulent Stoic', *CJ* 61: 254–8.

Motto, A. L. and Clark, J. R. (1990), 'Seneca on Drunkenness', *RCCM* 32: 105–10.

Motto, A. L. and Clark, J. R. (1993), 'Seneca (a proposito del lusso)', *StudRom* 41: 310–16.

Mouroutsou, G. (2020), 'Moral Philosophy in Imperial Roman Stoa', in Arenson, K. (ed.), *The Routledge Handbook of Hellenistic Philosophy* (London), 319–31.

Mozley, J. H. (1979) (ed.), *Ovid, The Art of Love and Other Poems*, Revised by G. P. Goold (London/Cambridge MA) (1929[1]).

Müller, H.-F. (2002), *Roman Religion in Valerius Maximus* (London/New York).

Müller-Reineke, H. (2008), '*Rarae fidei atque singularis pudicitia femina*—The Figure of Plotina in Apuleius' Novel', *Mnemosyne* 61.4: 619–33.

Murray, O. (2017), 'Greek Luxuries. Rev. to R. J. Gorman, V. B. Gorman, *Corrupting Luxury in Ancient Greek Literature*, Ann Arbor, University of Michigan Press, 2014', *Histos* 11: civ–cx.

Mutschler, F.-H. (2014), '*De vita beata*', in Damschen, G. and Heil, A., (eds.), *Brill's Companion to Seneca. Philosopher and Dramatist* (Leiden/Boston), 141–6.

Myers, K. S. (2005), '*Docta Otia*: Garden Ownership and Configurations of Leisure in Statius and Pliny the Younger', *Arethusa* 38.1: 103–29.

Naas, V. (2002), *Le projet encyclopédique de Pline l'Ancien* (Paris).
Naas, V. (2011), 'Imperialism, *mirabilia* and Knowledge: Some Paradoxes in the *Naturalis Historia*', in Gibson, R. K. and Morello, R. (eds.), *Pliny the Elder: Themes and Contexts* (Leiden/Boston), 57–70.
Nadeau, Y. (2011), *A Commentary on the Sixth Satire of Juvenal* (Bruxelles).
Nagy, F. (1968), 'The Contrast Signs of an Antique Topos', *AAHung* 16: 275–7.
Naumann-Steckner, F. (2008), 'Luxus in Gold—Ein Verbrechen an der Menscheit?', in Aßkamp, R., Brouwer, M., Christiansen, J., Kenzler, H. and Wamser, L. (eds.), *Luxus und Dekadenz. Römisches Leben am Golf von Neapel* (Meinz), 139–49.
Nelson, H. (1950), 'Cato the Younger as a Stoic Orator', *CW* 44.5: 65–9.
Nenci, G. (1978), '*Graecia capta ferum victorem cepit* (Hor. *Epist.* 2, 1, 156)', *Annali della Scuola Normale Superiore di Pisa, Classe di Lettere e Filosofia* 8.3: 1007–23.
Nenci, G. (1983), '*Tryphe* e colonizzazione', in Nenci, G. (ed.), *Modes de contacts et processus de transformation dans les sociétés anciennes. Actes du colloque de Cortone, 24–30 mai 1981* (Rome), 1019–31.
Neri, V. (1999), 'Considerazioni sul tema della *luxuria* nella *Historia Augusta*', in Paschoud, F. (ed.), *Historiae Augustae. Colloquim Genevense. Atti dei convegni sulla* Historia Augusta, *VII* (Bari), 217–40.
Newhauser, R. (2007), 'Introduction: Cultural Construction and the Vices', in Newhauser, R. (ed.), *The Seven Deadly Sins. From Community to Individuals* (Leiden/Boston), 1–17.
Nisbet, R. G. M./Hubbard, M. (1978) (eds.), *A Commentary on Horace, Odes Book 2* (Oxford).
Novara, A. (1992), *Les idées romaines sur le progrès d'après les écrivaines de la Rèpublique (essai sur le sens latin du progrès)* (Paris).
Nugent, S. G. (1985), *Allegory and Poetics. The Structure and Imagery of Prudentius'* Psychomachia (Frankfurt am Main).
Nussbaum, M. (1994), *The Therapy of Desire* (Princeton).
O'Connor, J. F. (1990), 'Horace's *Cena Nasidieni* and Poetry's Feast', *CJ* 86.1: 23–34.
Oakley, S. P. (1998), *A Commentary on Livy: Books VI–X.* 2: *Books VII and VIII* (Oxford).
Ogilvie, R. M. (1965), *A Commentary on Livy: Books 1–5* (Oxford).
Oliensis, E. (1997), '*Ut arte emendaturus fortunam*: Horace, Nasidienus, and the Art of Satire', in Habinek, T. and Schiesaro, A. (eds.), *The Roman Cultural Revolution* (Cambridge), 90–103.
Olson, S. D. (2008) (ed.), *Athenaeus, The Learned Banqueters, Books VI–VII* (London/Cambridge MA).
Page, S. (2015), *Der ideale Aristokrat. Plinius der Jüngere und das Sozialprofil der Senatoren in der Kaiserzeit* (Heidelberg).
Panella, C. (2011), 'La *Domus Aurea* nella valle del Colosseo e sulle pendici della Velia e del Palatino', in Tomei, A. and Rea, R. (eds.), *Nerone* (Milano), 156–9.
Pani, M. (1992), 'Sviluppi della tematica dell'*otium* in Plinio il giovane', in Pani, M., *Potere e valori a Roma tra Augusto e Traiano* (Bari), 181–92.
Papini, M. (2021), '"Non ti posso scrivere nulla di preciso": Seneca e le ville', in Delvigo, M. L. (ed.), *Centro e periferia nella letteratura latina di Roma imperiale* (Udine), 97–134.
Parsons, W. (1981) (ed.), *The Fathers of the Church. Saint Augustine, Letters,* vol. V: *204–270*, Translated by W. Parsons (New York) (1956[1]).
Pasco-Pranger, M. (2015), 'Finding Examples at Home: Cato, Curius Dentatus, and the Origins of Roman Literary Exemplarity', *Classical Antiquity* 34.2: 296–321.
Passerini, A. (1934), 'La *tryphe* nella storiografia ellenistica', *SIFC* 11: 35–56.
Passet, L. (2010), 'Frugalité et banquet offert au peuple à l'occasion de funérailles: la vaisselle de terre et les peaux de bouc de Quintus Aelius Tubéron', *Ktèma* 35: 51–67.

Passet, L. (2020), 'Frugality as a Political Language in the Second Century BCE: The Strategies of Cato the Elder and Scipio Aemilianus', in Gildenhard, I. and Viglietti, C. (eds.), *Roman Frugality. Modes of Moderation from the Archaic Age to the Early Empire and Beyond* (Cambridge), 192–212.

Paul, G. M. (1984), *A Historical Commentary on Sallust's* Bellum Jugurthinum (Liverpool).

Pavlovskis, Z. (1973), *Man in an Artificial Landscape. The Marvels of Civilization in Imperial Roman Literature* (Leiden).

Paxton, J. J. (1994), *The Poetics of Personification* (Cambridge).

Pearcy, L. T. (1977), 'Horace's Architectural Imagery', *Latomus* 36: 772–81.

Pelttari, A. (2019) (ed.), *The* Psychomachia *of Prudentius. Text, Commentary, and Glossary* (Norman OK).

Pérez González, J. (2021), *Sumptuary Specialists and Consumer Elites in Rome's World Order* (Barcelona).

Perrin, B. (1926) (ed.), *Plutarch's Lives*, XI: *Aratus, Artaxerxes, Galba, Otho* (London/Cambridge MA).

Perrin, B. (1959) (ed.), *Plutarch's Lives*, VIII: *Sertorius and Eumenes, Phocion and Cato the Younger* (London/Cambridge MA) (1919[1]).

Peskett, A. G. (1961) (ed.), *Caesar, The Civil Wars*, (London/Cambridge MA).

Petrone, G. (1993a), 'Nuove prospettive sul teatro plautino. *Luxuria* e *Avaritia*: per una semantica delle passioni', in Amata, B. (ed.), *Cultura e lingue classiche, 3* (Rome), 259–70.

Petrone, G. (1993b), 'Il *Trinummus*, ovvero il valore dei soldi', in Scandola, M. (ed.), *Plauto, Le tre dracme* (Milan), 15–33.

Petrone, G. (2012), 'Personificazioni e insiemi allegorici nelle commedie di Plauto', in Moretti, G. and Bonandini, A. (eds.), Persona ficta. *La personificazione allegorica nella cultura antica fra letteratura, retorica e iconografia* (Trento), 123–38.

Philips, H. (1976), 'Zeitkritik bei Plinius dem Jüngeren: Interpretation von *Epist.* 2,6', *Anregung* 22: 363–70.

Pià Comella, J. (2019), 'Quand un milliardaire fait l'éloge de la pauvreté. Les cynismes de Sénèque dans les *Lettres à Lucilius*', *RThPh* 151: 393–420.

Pinotti, P. (1988) (ed.), *P. Ovidius Naso, Remedia Amoris* (Bologna).

Piwowarczyk, D. R. (2016), 'The Origins of the Latin *-ia/-ies* inflexion', *Historical Linguistics* 129: 108–23.

Plaza, M. (2006), *The Function of Humor in Roman Verse Satire. Laughing and Lying* (Oxford).

Pollitt, J. J. (1978), 'The Impact of Greek Art in Rome', *TAPhA* 108: 155–74.

Pontier, P. (2020), 'Remarques sur la mollesse (*malakia*) chez Platon et Xénophon', in Veillard, C., Renaut, O., and El Murr, D. (eds.), *Les philosophes face aux vices, de Socrate à Augustine* (Leiden/Boston), 35–55.

Puccini-Delbey, G. (2003), *Amour et désir dans les* Métamorphoses *d'Apulée* (Bruxelles).

Purcell, N. (1994), 'Women and Wine in Ancient Rome', in McDonald, M. (ed.), *Gender, Drinks, and Drugs* (London), 191–208.

Quain, E. A. (1959) (ed.), *The Fathers of the Church, 40. Tertullian, Disciplinary, Moral and Ascetical Works*, Translated by R. Arbesmann, E. J. Daly, E. A. Quain (New York).

Rackham, H. (1940) (ed.), *Pliny, Natural History* III: *Books VIII–XI* (London/Cambridge MA).

Rackham, H. (1961a) (ed.), *Pliny, Natural History* II: *Books III–VII* (London/Cambridge MA) (1942[1]).

Rackham, H. (1961b) (ed.), *Pliny, Natural History* V: *Books XVII–XIX* (London/Cambridge MA) (1950[1]).

Rackham, H. (1986) (ed.), *Pliny, Natural History* IV: *Books XII–XVI* (London/Cambridge MA) (1945[1]).

Raffaelli, R. (2009), *Esercizi plautini* (Urbino).

Ramsey, J. T. (2007) (ed.), *Sallust's Bellum Catilinae* (Oxford).

Re, A. (2021), 'Ville in Plinio il Giovane: orizzonte reale o spazio ideale?', in Delvigo, M. L. (ed.), *Centro e periferia nella letteratura latina di Roma imperiale* (Udine), 135–94.

Reckford, K. J. (2009), *Recognizing Persius* (Princeton/Oxford).

Reed, J. D. (2011), 'The *Bellum Civile* as a Roman Epic', in Asso, P. (ed.), *Brill's Companion to Lucan* (Leiden/Boston), 21–31.

Reid, J. S. (1925) (ed.), *M. Tulli Ciceronis* De finibus bonorum et malorum *libri I et II* (Cambridge).

Renaut, O. (2020), 'Une théorie des vices dans la *République* de Platon', in Veillard, C., Renaut, O., and El Murr, D. (eds.), *Les philosophes face aux vices, de Socrate aux Augustine* (Leiden/Boston), 72–94.

Reydams-Schils, G. (2005), *The Roman Stoics. Self, Responsibility, and Affection* (Chicago).

Ricchieri, T. (2020) (ed.), *Prima della Sicilia. Cicerone*, Verrine *2, 1 (*De praetura urbana*), 1–102* (Pisa).

Richardson-Hay, C. (2006), *First Lessons. Book 1 of Senecas'* Epistles (Bern/Berlin/New York).

Richardson-Hay, C. (2009), 'Dinner at Seneca's Table: The Philosophy of Food', *G&R* 56: 71–96.

Riggsby, A. M. (2003), 'Pliny in Space (and Time)', *Arethusa* 36.2: 167–86.

Righi, L./Vettori, G. (2019), 'Prefazione', in Righi, L. and Vettori, G. (eds.), *Il lusso e la sua disciplina. Aspetti economici e sociali della legislazione suntuaria tra antichità e medioevo* (Trento), 7–23.

Rimell, V. (2005a), 'The Poor man's Feast: Juvenal', in Freudenberg, K. (ed.), *The Cambridge Companion to Roman Satire* (Cambridge), 81–94.

Rimell, V. (2005b), 'The Satiric Maze: Petronius, Satire, and the Novel', in Freudenberg, K. (ed.), *The Cambridge Companion to Roman Satire* (Cambridge), 160–73.

Rimell, V. (2013), 'The Best a Man Can Get: Grooming Scipio in Seneca *Epistle* 86', *CPh* 108: 1–20.

Rimell, V. (2015a), 'Seneca and Neronian Rome: In the Mirror of Time', in Bartsch, S. and Schiesaro, A. (eds.), *The Cambridge Companion to Seneca* (Cambridge), 122–34.

Rimell, V. (2015b), *The Closure of Space in Roman Poetics. Empire's Inward Turn* (Cambridge).

Rimell, V. (2022) (ed.), *Ovidio. Rimedi contro l'amore*, a c. di V. Rimell, trad. di G. Paduano (Milano).

Ripoll, F. (1999), 'Aspects et fonction de Néron dans la propagande impériale flavienne', in Croisille, J.-M., Perrin, R., and Martin, Y. (eds.), *Neronia V. Néron: Histoire et Légende* (Bruxelles), 137–51.

Rives, G. B. (1999) (ed.), *Tacitus, Germania* (Oxford).

Roche, P. (2009) (ed.), *Lucan, De Bello Civili, Book I*, Edited with Introduction, Text and Commentary (Oxford).

Rolfe, J. C. (1960) (ed.), *The Attic Nights of Aulus Gellius* (London/New York) (1927[1]).

Rolfe, J. C. (2013) (ed.), *Sallust, The War with Catiline, The War with Jugurtha*, Revised by J. T. Ramsey (London/Cambridge MA).

Rolland, E. (1906), *De l'influence de Sénèque le Père et des rhéteurs sur Sénèque le jeune* (Gand).

Roller, M. (2001), *Constructing Autocracy: Aristocrats and Emperors in Julio-Claudian Rome* (Princeton).

Roller, M. (2013), 'On the Intersignification of Monuments in Augustan Rome', *AJPh* 134.1: 119–31.

Romano, A. (2003), '*Luxuria/luxuries*', *REC* 31: 13–23.
Romano, E. (1991–3), '*Publica magnificentia* e *privata luxuria*. Il dibattito sul lusso edilizio da Cicerone a Orazio', *Annali del liceo classico 'G. Garibaldi' di Palermo* 28–30: 219–29.
Romano, E. (1994), 'Dal *De Officiis a Vitruvio, da Vitruvio a Orazio: il dibattito sul lusso edilizio*', in *Le projet de Vitruve. Objet, destinataires et réception du* De Architectura (Rome), 63–73.
Romano, P. (2011), 'Il rapporto tra cultura pagana e cristiana nell'opera di Prudenzio', *RCCM* 53.2: 263–84.
Rosen, S. (1987), *Plato's* Symposium (New Haven/London) (1968[1]).
Rosenmeyer, T. G. (1989), *Senecan Drama and Stoic Cosmology* (Berkeley/Los Angeles).
Rosivach, V. J. (1995), 'Seneca on the fear of Poverty in the *Epistulae morales*', *AntCl* 64: 91–8.
Roskam, G. (2005), *On the Path to Virtue. The Stoic Doctrine of Moral Progress and Its Reception in (Middle-)Platonism* (Leuven).
Rossi, L. (1993), 'Il problema dell'endiadi in greco e le orazioni politiche di Demostene', *AION* 15: 121–44.
Rossi, A. (2000), 'The Camp of Pompey. Strategy of Representation in Caesar's *Bellum civile*', *CJ* 95: 239–56.
Röttig, S. (2022), *Affekt und Wille. Senecas Ethik und ihre handlungspsychologische Fundierung* Heidelberg).
Ruden, S. (2012) (ed.), *Apuleius, The Golden Ass*, Translated by S. Ruden (Yale).
Rushton Fairclough, H. (1961) (ed.), *Horace, Satires, Epistles and Ars Poetica* (London/Cambridge MA).
Russell, D. A. (2001) (ed.), *Quintilian, The Orator's Education, Books 3–5* (London/Cambridge MA).
Russo, M. (2022), 'Amore, vino e tirannide. Il banchetto di Antonio e Cleopatra nella lettera 83 di Seneca', *LAS* 2: 177–201.
Sansone, D. (1989) (ed.), *Plutarch, Lives of Aristeides and Cato* (Warminster).
Santorelli, B. (2012) (ed.), *Giovenale, Satira IV* (Berlin/Boston).
Sauron, G. (2005), 'Le Leitmotiv de la transgression dans les *Vitae* de Suétone', in Poli, F. and Vottéro, G. (eds.), *De Cyrène à Catherine: trois mille annes de Libyennes* (Nancy), 451–63.
Sblendorio, M. T./Cugusi, P. (2001) (eds.), *Marco Porcio Catone, Opere* (Torino).
Scappaticcio, M. C. (2020) (ed.), *Seneca the Elder and his rediscovered* Historiae ab initio bellorum civilium. *New Perspectives on Early Imperial Roman Historiography* (Berlin).
Scarpat, G. (1975) (ed.), *Seneca, Lettere a Lucilio, libro primo. Epp. I–XII* (Brescia).
Scheidle, K. (1993), Modus optumum. *Die Bedeutung des 'recthen Maßes' in der römischen Literatur (Republik—frühe Kaiserzeit). Untersucht an der Begriffen* Modus, Modestia, Moderatio, Temperantia (Frankfurt am Main/Berlin).
Schields, C. (2014), 'Plato's Divided Soul', in Corcilius, K./Perler, D. (eds.), *Partitioning the Soul: The Debates from Plato to Leibniz* (Berlin/Boston), 15–38.
Schiesaro, A. (2003), *The Passions in Play.* Thyestes *and the Dynamics of Senecan Drama* (Cambridge).
Schimmel, S. (1992), *The Seven Deadly Sins. Jewish, Christian, and Classical Reflections on Human Nature* (New York/Toronto).
Schmatz, J. (1905), *Baiae, Das erste Luxusbad der Römer* (Regensburg).
Schmauder, M. (2019), 'Schmuck', *RAC* 232: 978–1006.
Schmeling, G. L. (2011), *A Commentary the* Satyrica *of Petronius* (Oxford).
Schmeling, G. L. (2020) (ed.), *Petronius, Satyricon; Seneca, Apokolokyntosis* (London/Cambridge MA).
Schofield, M. (2015), 'Seneca on Monarchy and the Political Life: *De clementia, De tranquillitate animi, De otio*', in Bartsch, S. and Schiesaro, A. (eds.), *The Cambridge Companion to Seneca* (Cambridge), 68–81.

Schuckburg, E. S. (2002) (ed.), *The Histories of Polybius, Book Seven, Eight, and Nine* (Cambridge ON).
Schmidt, M. G. (1986), *Caesar und Cleopatra. Philologischer und historischer Kommentar zu Lucan 10.1–171* (Frankfurt am Main/Bern/New York).
Schultze, C. (2007), 'Making a Spectacle of Oneself: Pliny on Curio's Theatre', *BICS* 100: 127–45.
Schulz, V. (2019), *Deconstructing Imperial Representation: Tacitus, Cassius Dio, and Suetonius* (Leiden/Boston).
Schwameis, C. (2019) (ed.), *Cicero,* De praetura siciliensi *(*Verr. *2,2). Einleitung und Kommentar* (Berlin/New York).
Scott-Kilvert, I. (1979) (ed.), *Polybius, The Rise of the Roman Empire*, with an Introduction by F. W. Walbank (London/New York).
Seal, C. (2021), *Philosophy and Community in Seneca's Prose* (Oxford/New York).
Seewald, M. (2008), *Studien zum 9. Buch von Lucans* Bellum Civile (Berlin/New York).
Segal, C. (1974), 'The Purpose of the *Trinummus*: For J. Arthur Hanson', *AJPh*, 95: 252–64.
Seita, M. (1982), 'Un affare politico-giudiziario dell'antica Roma: l'attacco di Suillio a Seneca', *Latomus* 41.2: 312–28.
Sellars, J. (2014), 'Context: Seneca's Philosophical Predecessors and Contemporaries', in Damschen, G. and Heil, A. (eds.), *Brill's Companion to Seneca. Philosopher and Dramatist* (Leiden/Boston), 97–110.
Serbat, G. (1987), 'Il y a Grecs et Grecs! Quel sens donner au prétendu antihellénise de Pline?', *Helmantica* 38: 273–82.
Setaioli, A. (2011), *Petronius' Short Poems in the* Satyrica (Frankfurt am Main).
Setaioli, A. (2014a), 'Poems in Petronius' *Satyrica*', in Cueva, E. P. and Byrne, S. N. (eds.), *A Companion to the Ancient Novel* (Malden MA/Oxford), 371–82.
Setaioli, A. (2014b), 'Ethics I. Philosophy as Therapy, Self-Transformation, and "Lebensform"', in Damschen, G. and Heil, A. (eds.), *Brill's Companion to Seneca. Philosopher and Dramatist* (Leiden/Boston), 239–56.
Shackleton Bailey, D. R. (1993a) (ed.), *Martial, Epigrams*, vol. I (London/Cambridge MA).
Shackleton Bailey, D. R. (1993b) (ed.), *Martial, Epigrams*, vol. III (London/Cambridge MA).
Shackleton Bailey, D. R. (2000) (ed.), *Valerius Maximus, Memorable Doings and Sayings, Books 6–9* (London/Cambridge MA).
Shapiro, A. (2009) (ed.), *Euripides, Trojan Women*, with Introduction and Notes by P. Burian (Oxford).
Sharland, S. (2009), 'Soporific Satire: Horace, Damasippus and Professor Snore (Stertinius) in Satire 2.3', *AC* 52: 113–31.
Sharrock, A. (2014), 'Reading Plautus' *Trinumms*: Who'd Bother?', in Perysinakis, I. N. and Karakasis, E. (eds.), *Plautine Trends: Studies in Plautine Comedy and Its Reception. Festschrift in Honour of Prof. D. K. Raios* (Berlin/New York), 167–95.
Shaw, B. D. (1975), 'Debt in Sallust', *Latomus* 34.1: 187–96.
Shaw, E. (2022), *Sallust and the fall of the Republic: historiography and intellectual life at Rome* (Leiden/Boston).
Sherwin-White, A. N. (1966), *The Letters of Pliny. A Historical and Social Commentary* (Oxford).
Shipley, F. W. (1961) (ed.), *Velleius Paterculus, Compendium of Roman History* (London/Cambridge MA) (1924[1]).
Showerman, G. (1977) (ed.), *Ovid, Heroides and Amores*, Revised by G. P. Goold (London/Cambridge MA).
Simonetti, E. G. (2017), 'L'immagine del saggio nelle opere di Apuleio', *RhM* 160.3–4: 371–92.

Sjoblad, A. (2015), *Metaphorical Coherence. Studies in Seneca's* Epistulae morales (Diss. Lund).

Skidmore, C. (1996), *Practical Ethics for Roman Gentlemen. The Work of Valerius Maximus* (Exeter).

Skinner, M. B. (2012), '*Fortunata* and the Virtues of Freedwomen', in Futre Pinheiro, M. P., Skinner, M. B., and Zeitlin, F. I. (eds.), *Narrating Desire: Eros, Sex, and Gender in the Ancient Novel* (Berlin/Boston), 199–210.

Sklenář, R. (1998), 'La République du signes: Caesar, Cato, and the Language of Sallustian Morality', *TAPhA* 128: 205–20.

Smith, M. (1976), *Prudentius'* Psychomachia*: A Reexamination* (Princeton).

Soldevila, R. M./Castillo, A. M./Valverde, J. F. (2019), *A Prosopography to Martial's Epigrams* (Berlin/Boston).

Soldo, J. (2021) (ed.), *Seneca, Epistulae Morales Book 2. A Commentary with Text, Translation, and Introduction* (Oxford).

Sommerstein, A. H. (2001) (ed.), *Aristophanes, Wealth* (London).

Sorabji, R. (2000), *Emotion and Peace of Mind: From Stoic Agitation to Christian Temptation* (Oxford).

Stahl, J. (2015), 'Physically Deformed and Disabled People', in Peachin, M. (ed.), *The Oxford Handbook to Social Relations in the Roman World* (Oxford/New York), 715–33.

Star, C. (2012), *The Empire of the Self. Self-Command and Political Speech in Seneca and Petronius* (Baltimore).

Star, C. (2016), *Seneca* (London).

Star, C. (2021), *Apocalypse and Golden Age. The End of the World in Greek and Roman Thought* (Baltimore).

Stärk, E. (1995), *Kampanien als geistige Landschaft. Interpretationen zum antiken Bild des Golfs von Neapel* (Munich).

Stein-Hölkeskamp, E. (2001), 'Ciceronische *convivia*: Der Rastlose Republikaner und die Zügellosen Zecher', *Hermes* 129: 362–76.

Stein-Hölkeskamp, E. (2002a), 'Culinarische Codes: Das ideale Bankett bei Plinius d. Jüngeren und seinen Zeitgenossen', *Klio* 84.2: 465–90.

Stein-Hölkeskamp, E. (2002b), 'Tödliches Tafeln. *Convivia* in neronischer Zeit', in Castagna, L. and Vogt-Spira, G. (eds.), Pervertere*: Ästhetik der Verkehrung. Litertatur und Kultur neronischer Zeit und ihre Rezeption* (München-Leipzig), 3–28.

Stramaglia, A. (2008), *Giovenale, Satire 1, 7, 12, 16. Storia di un poeta* (Bologna).

Sullivan, J. P. (1968), *The* Satyricon *of Petronius: A Literary Study* (Bloomington/London).

Sullivan, J. P. (1985), *Literature and Politics in the Age of Nero* (Ithaca/London).

Sussman, L. A. (1971), 'The Artistic Unity of the Elder Seneca's First Preface and the *Controversiae* as a Whole', *AJPh* 92.2: 285–91.

Sussman, L. A. (1972), 'The Elder Seneca's Discussion on the Decline of Roman Eloquence', *CSCA* 5: 195–210.

Sussman, L. A. (1995), 'Sons and Fathers in the *Major Declamations* ascribed to Quintilian', *Rhetorica* 13.2: 179–92.

Syed, Y. (2005), 'Romans and Others', in Harrison, S. J. (ed.), *A Companion to Latin Literature* (London), 360–71.

Tabacco, R. (1984–5), 'Il tiranno nelle declamazioni di scuola in lingua latina', *Memorie dell'acc. delle scienze di Torino* 5.9: 1–139.

Tatum, W. J. (2014), 'Another Look at Suetonius' *Titus*', in Power, T. and Gibson, R. K. (eds.), *Suetonius the Biographer* (Oxford), 159–77.

Thomson, H. J. (1949) (ed.), *Prudentius*, vol. I (London/Cambridge MA).

Thurn, A. (2018), *Rufmord in der späten römischen Republik: Charakterbezogene Diffamierungstrategien in Ciceros Reden* (Berlin/Boston).

Tomassi, G. (2010), 'L'allegoria di Pluto in Luciano', *Aevum* 84.1: 251–68.
Toner, J. P. (1995), *Leisure and Ancient Rome* (Cambridge).
Toohey, P. (2004), *Melancholy, Love, and Time. Boundaries of the Self in Ancient Literature* (Ann Arbor).
Torre, C. (1997), 'Il banchetto di *luxuria* nell'opera in prosa di Seneca', *Paideia* 52: 377–96.
Torre, C. (2021), 'Affari di coscienza, tra Seneca e Cicerone: a proposito dell'*Epistola* 97 a Lucilio', *Lucius Annaeus Seneca* 1: 73–110.
Tracy, J. (2011), 'Internal Evidence for the Completeness of the *Bellum Civile*', in Asso, P. (ed.), *Brill's Companion to Lucan* (Leiden/Boston), 33–53.
Tracy, J. (2014), *Lucan's Egyptian Civil War* (Cambridge).
Ussani, V. (1984), '*Otium* y *pax* en Plinio el Joven', *Nova Tellus* 2: 7–26.
van den Berg, C. S. (2020), 'The Rhetoric of Decline and the Rhetoric for *Declamatio*', in Dinter, M. T. Guerín, C., and Martinho, M. (eds.), *Reading Roman Declamation: Seneca the Elder* (Oxford): 201–17.
van der Poel, M. (2009), 'The Use of *exempla* in Roman Declamation', *Rhetorica* 27.3: 332–53.
van der Veen, M. (2003), 'When Is Food a Luxury?' *World Archaeology* 34.3: 405–27.
van der Wal, R. L. (2007), '"What a Funny Consul We Have!" Cicero's Dealing with Cato Uticensis and Prominent Friends in Opposition', in Booth, J., Gildenhard, I., *et al.* (eds.), *Invective and Subversion in the Orations and Beyond* (Swansea), 183–205.
Vassiliades, G. (2013), 'Les sources et la fonction du *metus hostilis* chez Salluste', *BAGB* 1: 127–68.
Vassiliades, G. (2019), 'Le *Catilina* de Salluste: une histoire du progrès et de la décadence de Rome', *Vita Latina* 199: 108–31.
Vegetti, M. (1982), 'Zoologia e antropologia in Plinio', in Vegetti, M., *Plinio il vecchio sotto il profilo storico e letterario* (Como), 117–31.
Vegetti, M. (1983), 'Passioni e bagni caldi. Il problema del bambino cattivo nell'antropologia stoica', in Vegetti, M., *Tra Edipo ed Euclide. Forme del sapere antico* (Milan), 71–90.
Vegetti, M. (1999), *Guida alla lettura della* Repubblica *di Platone* (Rome/Bari).
Venini, P. (1977) (ed.), *C. Svetonio Tranquillo, Vite di Galba, Otone, Vitellio* (Torino).
Venturini, C. (1979), '*Luxus* e *avaritia* nell'opera di Sallustio. (Osservazioni e problemi)', *Athenaeum* 57.1–2: 277–92.
Vesley, M. E. (2003), 'Father-Son Relations in Roman Declamations', *Ancient History Bulletin* 17.3–4: 158–80.
Vettori, G. (2019), 'Il lusso che non si poteva concedere alle donne. Matrone e disciplina suntuaria nella Roma d'età repubblicana', in Righi, L. and Vettori, G. (eds.), *Il lusso e la sua disciplina. Aspetti economici e sociali della legislazione suntuaria tra antichità e medioevo* (Trento), 51–84.
Vigourt, A. (2001), 'M.' Curius Dentatus et M. Fabricius Luscinus: les grands hommes ne sont pas exceptionnels', Coudry, M. and Späth, T. (eds.), *L'invention des grands hommes de la Rome antique—Die Konstruktion der großen Männer Altroms* (Paris), 117–29.
Vimercati, E. (2004) (ed.), *Posidonio. Testimonianze e frammenti* (Milan).
Viscogliosi, A. (2011), 'La *Domus Aurea*', in Tomei, A. and Rea, R. (eds.), *Nerone* (Milano), 152–5.
Vogt-Spira, G. (2022), 'Der ältere Cato: ein Beispiel für Doppelmoral?', in Vogt-Spira, G., *Studien zur römischen Anthropologie* (Baden-Baden), 203–14.
Voisin, J.-L. (1987), '*Exoriente sole* (Suétone, *Ner.* 6). D'Alexandrie à la *domus aurea*', in Pietri, C. (ed.), *L'urbs. Espace urbain et histoire, I*er *siècle avant J.-C.—III*e *siècle après J.-C.* (Paris), 509–43.
Vössing, K. (2004), Mensa regia. *Das Bankett beim hellenistischen König und bei römischen Kaiser* (Berlin/New York).

Wagoner, R. (2014), 'Seneca on Moral Theory and Moral Improvement', *CPh* 109: 241–62.

Walbank, F. W. (1967) (ed.), *A Historical Commentary on Polybius* III. *Commentary on Books XIX–XL* (Oxford).

Walbank, F. W. (1979) (ed.), *A Historical Commentary on Polybius* II. *Commentary on Books VII–XVIII* (Oxford).

Walbank, F. W. (2002), *Polybius, Rome, and the Hellenistic World. Essays and Reflections* (Cambridge).

Wallace-Hadrill, A. (1983), *Suetonius. The Scholar and His Caesars* (London).

Wallace-Hadrill, A. (1990), 'Pliny the Elder and Man's Unnatural History', *G&R* 37.1: 80–96.

Wallace-Hadrill, A. (1997), '*Mutatio morum*: The Idea of a Cultural Revolution', in Habinek, T. and Schiesaro, A. (eds.), *The Roman Cultural Revolution* (Cambridge), 3–22.

Wallace-Hadrill, A. (2004), 'The Golden Age and Sin in Augustan Ideology', in Osborne, R. (ed.), *Studies in Ancient Greek and Roman Society. Past and Present* (Cambridge), 159–76.

Wallace-Hadrill, A. (2008), *Rome's Cultural Revolution* (Cambridge).

Walsh, P. G. (2000) (ed.), *Cicero, On Obligations (De Officiis)* (Oxford).

Walsh, P. G. (2009) (ed.), *Pliny the Younger, Complete Letters* (Oxford).

Watson, P. (2012), 'The Flight of *Pudicitia*: Juvenal's Vision of the Past and the Programmatic Function of the Prologue in the Sixth Satire', *Mnemosyne* 65: 62–79.

Webster, T. B. L. (1953), *Studies in Later Greek Comedy* (Manchester).

Weeber, K.-W. (2015), *Die Schwelgerei, das süße Gift... Luxus im alten Rom* (Darmstadt) (2003[1]).

Weiden Boyd, B. (1987), 'Virtus Effeminata *and Sallust's Sempronia*', *TAPhA* 117: 183–201.

Weinstock, S. (1971), *Divus Julius* (Oxford).

Wenzel, S. (1968), 'The Seven Deadly Sins: Some Problems of Research', *Speculum* 43.1: 1–22.

West, M. L. (1966) (ed.), *Hesiod, Theogony*, Edited with Prolegomena and Commentary (Oxford).

Wheeler, A. L. (1988) (ed.), *Ovid, Tristia, Ex Ponto*, Revised by G. P. Goold (London/Cambridge MA).

White, R. T. (2014), *Luxury at Rome:* avaritia, aemulatio *and the* mos maiorum, *Ex Historia* 6: 117–43.

Whitton, C. (2013) (ed.), *Pliny the Younger, Epistles Book II* (Cambridge).

Wick, C. (2004) (ed.), *Marcus Annaeus Lucanus, Bellum Civile, liber IX*, vol. II: *Kommentar* (München/Leipzig).

Wiegandt, D. (2016), '*Otium* als Mittel der literarischen Selbstinszenierung römischer Aristokraten in Republik und früher Kaiserzeit', in Eikhoff, F. C. (ed.), *Muße und Rekursivität in der antiken Briefliteratur* (Tübingen), 43–57.

Wilberding, J. (2012), 'Curbing One's Appetites in Plato's *Republic*', in Barney, R./Brennan, T./Brittain, C. (eds.), *Plato and the Divided Soul* (Cambridge), 128–49.

Wildberger, J. (2006), *Seneca und die Stoa: Der Platz des Menschen in der Welt* (Berlin/New York).

Wilkinson, L. P. (1975), *The Roman Experience* (London).

Williams, C. A. (2004) (ed.), *Martial, Epigrams, Book 2* (Oxford).

Williams, G. (1978), *Change and Decline. Roman Literature in the Early Empire* (Berkeley/Los Angeles).

Williams, G. D. (2012), *The Cosmic Viewpoint. A Study of Seneca's* Natural Questions (Oxford/New York).

Williams, G. D. (2014) (ed.), *Seneca, Hardship and Happiness*, Translations by E. Fantham, H. M. Hine, J. Ker, and G. D. Williams (Chicago).

Williams, G. D. (2017), 'Lucan's *Civil War* in Nero's Rome', in Bartsch, S., Freudenberg, K., and Littlewood, C. A. J. (eds.), *The Cambridge Companion to the Age of Nero* (Cambridge), 93–106.

Wilson, E. (2016), *Seneca. A Life* (London).

Winkler, J. J. (1990), *The Constraints of Desire. The Anthropology of Sex and Gender in Ancient Greece* (London).

Winterbottom, M. (1974) (ed.), *Seneca the Elder, Declamations*, vol. I (London/Cambridge MA).

Woodman, A. J. (1969), 'Sallustian Influence on Velleius Paterculus', in Bibauw, J. (ed.), *Hommages à Marcel Renard* (Bruxelles), 785–99.

Woodman, A. J. (2004) (ed.), *Tacitus, The Annals* (Indianapolis/Cambridge).

Woodman, A. J. (2012), '*Aliena Facundia.* Seneca in Tacitus', in Woodman, A. J., *From Poetry to History. Selected Papers* (Oxford/New York), 294–308.

Woodman, A. J. (2017) (ed.), *The Annals of Tacitus, Books 5 and 6* (Cambridge).

Woodman, A. J. (2018) (ed.), *Tacitus, Annals, Book 4* (Cambridge).

Woodman, A. J./Martin, R. H. (1996) (eds.), *The Annals of Tacitus, Book 3* (Cambridge).

Woolf, R. (2001) (trans.), *Cicero, On Moral Ends*, Edited by J. Annas (Cambridge).

Wyke, M. (2002), *The Roman Mistress. Ancient and Modern Representations* (Oxford).

Yardley, J. C. (2013) (ed.), *Livy, Rome's Italian Wars (Books 6–10)*, with an Introduction and Notes by D. Hoyos (Oxford).

Yardley, J. C. (2017) (ed.), *Livy, History of Rome, Books 31–34*, Introduction by D. Hoyos (London/Cambridge MA).

Yardley, J. C. (2018) (ed.), *Livy, History of Rome, Books 38–40* (London/Cambridge MA).

Yardley, J. C. (2020) (ed.), *Livy, History of Rome, Books 23–25* (London/Cambridge MA).

Yona, S. (2018), *Epicurean Ethics in Horace: The Psychology of Satire* (Oxford).

Zago, G. (2012), *Sapienza filosofica e cultura materiale. Posidonio e le altre fonti dell'*Epistola *90 di Seneca* (Bologna).

Zanda, E. (2011), *Fighting Hydra-Like Luxury. Sumptuary Regulation in the Roman Republic* (Bristol).

Zecchini, G. (1982), 'Cn. Manlio Vulsone e l'inizio della corruzione a Roma', in Sordi, M. (ed.), *Politica e religione nel primo scontro tra Roma e l'Oriente* (Milano): 159–78.

Zecchini, G. (2001), *Cesare e il* mos maiorum (Stuttgart).

Zecchini, G. (2002), 'Sylla selon Salluste', *Cahiers du Centre Gustave Glotz* 13: 45–55.

Zechel, H. (1966), *Lucius Annaeus Seneca Briefe 89. Textkritische Ausgabe mit Sachkommentar und sparchlich-stilistischen Erläuterungen* (Würzburg).

Zwierlein, O. (1974), 'Cäsar und Kleopatra bei Lucan und in späterer Dichtung', *A&A* 20: 54–73.

Index of Passages

For the benefit of digital users, indexed terms that span two pages (e.g., 52–53) may, on occasion, appear on only one of those pages.

General Index

For the benefit of digital users, indexed terms that span two pages (e.g., 52–53) may, on occasion, appear on only one of those pages.